Textual Mothers / Maternal Texts

Textual Mothers / Maternal Texts

Motherhood in Contemporary Women's Literatures

ELIZABETH PODNIEKS AND ANDREA O'REILLY, EDITORS

Wilfrid Laurier University Press

[WLU]

This book has been published with the help of a grant from the Canadian Federation for the Humanities and Social Sciences, through the Aid to Scholarly Publications Programme, using funds provided by the Social Sciences and Humanities Research Council of Canada. Wilfrid Laurier University Press acknowledges the financial support of the Government of Canada through the Book Publishing Industry Development Program for our publishing activities.

Library and Archives Canada Cataloguing in Publication

Textual mothers / maternal texts : motherhood in contemporary women's literatures / Elizabeth Podnieks and Andrea O'Reilly, editors.

Includes bibliographical references and index.
Also available in electronic formats.
ISBN 978-1-55458-180-1

1. Mothers in literature. 2. Motherhood in literature. 3. Mother and child in literature. 4. Canadian literature—Women authors—History and criticism. 5. American literature—Women authors—History and criticism. 6. Canadian literature—20th century—History and criticism. 7. American literature—20th century—History and criticism. I. Podnieks, Elizabeth II. O'Reilly, Andrea, 1961–

PS8089.5.W6T45 2010   820.9'35252   C2009-904029-8

Library and Archives Canada Cataloguing in Publication

Textual mothers / maternal texts [electronic resource] : motherhood in contemporary women's literatures / Elizabeth Podnieks and Andrea O'Reilly, editors.

Includes bibliographical references and index.
Electronic monograph available in PDF, XML, and ePub formats.
Also available in printed format.
ISBN 978-1-55458-209-9

1. Mothers in literature. 2. Motherhood in literature. 3. Mother and child in literature. 4. Canadian literature—Women authors—History and criticism. 5. American literature—Women authors—History and criticism. 6. Canadian literature—20th century—History and criticism. 7. American literature—20th century—History and criticism. I. Podnieks, Elizabeth II. O'Reilly, Andrea, 1961–

PS8089.5.W6T45 2010a   820.9'35252

Cover image: *Mother and Child*, a painting by F. G. Davis (fgdavis.co.uk).
Cover design by Blakely Words+Pictures. Text design by Martyn Schmoll

This book is printed on FSC recycled paper and is certified Ecologo. It is made from 100% post-consumer fibre, processed chlorine free, and manufactured using biogas energy.

Printed in Canada

Contents

Part 2: Maternal Ambivalence

Part 3: Maternal Agency

Acknowledgements

Textual Mothers/Maternal Texts is the product of many people whose efforts supporting and producing the collection we wish to acknowledge here. To the more than one hundred scholars who submitted proposals in response to our call for papers, and who thus underscored the vital timeliness of this work on motherhood and literatures, we express both our gratitude for their interest and our apologies that we could not include them all. To our twenty contributors, we extend our congratulations for their compelling scholarship and our appreciation for their eager and patient willingness to work with us and with our Laurier Press editors in bringing their chapters to final form.

We are indebted to Jacqueline Larson, who as acquisitions editor for the Press first put the proposed collection under contract, and to her successor, Lisa Quinn, for her continuing commitment to the project. Lisa's unfailing support and encouragement throughout the various stages has been invaluable. We recognize the enormous amount of time offered by the two readers for the Press, and thank them for their insights and suggestions, which were most helpful to us as we made our revisions. We value the efforts of Rob Kohlmeier, managing editor; Marcia Gallego, copy editor; and Leslie Macredie, website and marketing coordinator, who came aboard in the latter stages of production and who worked so efficiently and creatively. We are, as well, most grateful for the financial support provided by the Aid to Scholarly Publications Program (ASPP).

Podnieks would like to thank Ryerson University for its ongoing support of her research, specifically through two grants: a Ryerson SSHRC Institutional Grant and a Ryerson Faculty of Arts SRC Fund Research Grant, which afforded her the time and resources to research and write her chapter as well as to co-author the introduction and to co-edit the entire collection. Her work has been facilitated by conscientious and dedicated research assistants Christopher Richardson and Carolyn Winters. Podnieks owes everything to her family: her brother and sister-in-law Andrew and Mary-Jane Podnieks; her aunt, Mairi Macdonald; and her husband, Ian Smith, for being everywhere every step of the way. This collection would likely not have occurred to her had it not been for three folks: her own mother, Elizabeth Podnieks, who shows her every day what it means to mother; and her own two children, Zachary Smith and Emily Smith, who inspire all things maternal.

O'Reilly would like to thank the Social Science Research Council of Canada and its continued support of her research though various grants, most notably the Standard Research Grant and the International Opportunities Fund grant. Special thanks are due to my brilliant research assistants Sarah Trimble, Melissa Nurse, Ayla Lefkowich, and to my remarkable proofreader, Randy Chase. All scholars should be so blessed. Thank you to the members of the Association for Research on Mothering: my thinking on mothering, as always, was enriched and sustained by this splendid community of scholars. A particular word of thanks to my early mentors in women's literature: Elizabeth Sabiston, Eleanor Hine, Leslie Sanders, Rusty Shteir, and Barbara Godard: thank you for causing me to fall in love with women's literature and saving me from a degree in economics. Special thanks to Renée Knapp at ARM, who comforts and commiserates when I need these the most. And as always, my deepest gratitude to my family, in particular my mother, Jean O'Reilly; my sister Jennifer O'Reilly; my children, Jesse, Erin, and Casey O'Reilly-Conlin; and my partner, Terry Conlin. They continue to inspire and sustain my maternal story.

We would, in the end, like to thank each other. We conceived the project at one of the many conferences hosted by the Association for Research on Mothering, and developed it in due course over numerous meetings and phone calls, not to mention hundreds of emails between ourselves as well as our contributors from disparate global parts. In dialogue with a host of maternal scholars, we have gathered individual practices, theories, and experiences of diverse writers and mothers into this collection. As colleagues and as friends we have been stimulated, challenged, and rewarded throughout this whole process, just as we hope this book will do the same for our readers, in turn.

ELIZABETH PODNIEKS AND ANDREA O'REILLY

Introduction

Maternal Literatures in Text and Tradition: Daughter-Centric, Matrilineal, and Matrifocal Perspectives | BY ELIZABETH PODNIEKS AND ANDREA O'REILLY

> It is hard to speak precisely about mothering. Overwhelmed with greeting card sentiment, we have no realistic language in which to capture the ordinary/ extraordinary pleasures and pains of maternal work.
>
> —SARA RUDDICK, *Maternal Thinking*, 29

In her introduction to *The Mother/Daughter Plot: Narrative, Psychoanalysis, Feminism* (1989), Marianne Hirsch queries why, in Sophocles' *Oedipus Rex*, the voice of Jocasta, Oedipus's mother, is missing, and she connects this narrative silence to a larger literary lacunae: "in asking where the story of Jocasta is in the story of Oedipus, I am asking not only where the stories of women are in men's plots, but where the stories of mothers are in the plots of sons and daughters" (4). She concludes that in order "to know Jocasta's maternal story ... we would have to *begin* with the mother" (5). *Textual Mothers / Maternal Texts* begins with the mother, foregrounding how she is represented in diverse literary traditions. Our collection focuses on mother subjects and mother writers, on women who produce auto/biography, fiction, and poetry about mothering, motherhood, and being mothered, who thus engage in the process or act of textual mothering and who produce what we call, in the broadest terms, maternal texts. *Textual Mothers / Maternal Texts* examines how authors use textual spaces to accept, embrace, negotiate, reconcile, resist, and challenge traditional conceptions of mothering

1

and maternal roles, and how they offer alternative practices and visions for mothers in the present and future. In considering, further, the connections between a text and life itself, the collection examines how textual representations reflect and help to define or (re)shape the realities of women and families, and how mothering and being a mother are political, personal, and creative narratives unfolding within both the pages of a book and the spaces of a life. It illuminates how the authors and their respective protagonists "read" their own maternal identities as well as the maternal scripts of their families, cultures, and nations in their quest for self-knowledge, understanding, agency, and artistic expression.

The overarching goal of *Textual Mothers / Maternal Texts* is to map shifts from the daughter-centric stories (those which privilege the daughter's voice) that have, to be sure, dominated maternal traditions, to the matrilineal and matrifocal perspectives that have emerged over the last few decades as the mother's voice—in all its rhythms and ranges—has moved slowly, as Hirsch describes, from silence to speech (16). Chapters by and about subjects from English and French Canada, the United States, Central America, Britain, Europe, the Caribbean, Asia, and Australia underscore that the collection is a timely one, bringing together a wide range of maternal scholarship in order to show how both academic and popular literary conceptions of the maternal have developed; to showcase the present status of maternal aesthetics; and to comment on the future of motherhood studies as it intersects with literature, in terms of what work is being and still needs to be done regarding maternal subjectivity.

Drawing on Hirsch's assertion that to know the mother "we would have to *begin* with" her story (5), Brenda O. Daly and Maureen T. Reddy emphasize, in *Narrating Mothers: Theorizing Maternal Subjectivities* (1991), that even of the limited number of fictional or theoretical texts that do "*begin* with the mother in her own right, from her own perspective," few "seldom hold fast to a maternal perspective; further when texts do maintain this perspective, readers and critics tend to suppress the centrality of mothering" (2–3). Daly and Reddy coined the term "daughter-centricity" to describe the fact that "we learn less about what it is like to mother than about what it is like to be mothered, even when the author has had both experiences" (2). Within the last four decades, as motherhood studies has emerged as a distinct and established academic discipline, this daughter-centricity has been countered and corrected in both fiction and theory. Indeed, a central if not defining aim of motherhood studies has been to articulate and theorize "the voice of the mother":[1] to analyze, in other words, becoming and being a mother from the perspective and subjectivity of mothers themselves. However, this task requires that we first, as Susan Maushart urges, "unmask motherhood." To be masked in motherhood, Maushart explains, "is to deny and repress what we experience, to misrepresent it, even to ourselves" (1–2). More specifically, the mask of motherhood confers an idealized and hence unattainable image of motherhood that causes women to feel guilt and anxiety about their own (often messy and muddled) experiences of mothering. The mask of motherhood, as Maushart elaborates, "keeps women from speaking clearly what they know and from hearing truths too threatening to face" (7). The unmasking of motherhood thus necessitates what may be termed "an archaeology of maternity": an excavation of the truths of motherhood disguised and distorted beneath the mask.[2]

Adrienne Rich concludes her monumental work *Of Woman Born* (1976) by affirming that, "The words are being spoken now, are being written down, the taboos are being broken, the masks of motherhood are cracking through" (239). Whether such rebellions are conveyed by way of a sociological study of mothers or in a popular motherhood memoir, feminist writers and scholars alike endeavour to unmask motherhood by documenting the lived reality of mothering. In so doing, they counter the daughter-centricity described by Daly and Reddy above to create and compose what one of the authors of this introduction—O'Reilly—has identified elsewhere as a matrifocal narrative.[3] O'Reilly's use of the term is drawn from Miriam Johnson's discussion of matrifocality in *Strong Mothers, Weak Wives* (1989). Matrifocal societies, according to Johnson, "tend to have greater gender equality because of the power of a maternal paradigm. In these societies, regardless of the particular type of kinship system, women play roles of cultural and social significance and define themselves less as wives than as mothers." Johnson emphasizes that matrifocality "does not refer to domestic maternal dominance so much as it does to the relative cultural prestige of the image of the mother, a role that is culturally elaborated and valued" (226). A matrifocal narrative, then, borrowing from Johnson's terminology, is one in which a mother plays a role of cultural and social significance, and in which motherhood is thematically elaborated and valued, and structurally central to the plot. In other words—and to draw on Hirsch, Daly and Reddy quoted earlier—matrifocal narratives "*begin* with the mother in her own right, from her own perspective," and they "hold fast to a maternal perspective." Matrifocal readings, practised by our contributors here, attend to and accentuate the maternal thematic in any given text.

Mothers unmask themselves when they speak truthfully and authentically about their experiences of mothering. Writing on *Of Woman Born*,

Maushart comments: "Rich remained acutely aware of the riskiness of the enterprise she had undertaken. Unmasking motherhood, she grasped, was a greater challenge to the feminist imagination than all the other 'women's issues' put together" (239). Because no mother can live the idealized perfection of the mask of motherhood, to unmask oneself is to "out" oneself as a flawed, if not failed, mother. "Given the punishing rules—and the contemptuous labels for any mom who breaks them," Mary Kay Blakely remarks in her 1994 memoir of motherhood, "mothers are reluctant to admit even having bad days, let alone all the miserable details leading up to them" (11). Thirty-five years earlier, Rich wrote in her diary: "My children cause me the most exquisite suffering of which I have experienced. It is the suffering of ambivalence; the murderous alternation between bitter resentment and raw-edged nerves, and blissful gratification and tenderness" (21). Indeed, as Sara Ruddick reminds us, the "idealized figure of the Good Mother casts a long shadow on many actual mothers' lives" (31). This shadow looms in the construction of textual mothers, too, as writers draw on age-old dichotomies to position the mother who is seen to be selfless, sacrificial, and domestic as angel/Madonna ("good"), the mother who is judged to be selfish for seeking autonomy beyond her children as whore/Magdalene ("bad").

Sociological studies of motherhood confirm that ambivalence and anger are typical and expected dimensions of motherhood, but it nonetheless takes candour, courage, and community for mothers to "out" themselves in public, never mind in print. And while the rise of the motherhood memoir over the last decade has opened up some space for maternal outlawdom,[4] the "new momism" ideology that (in)forms much of this genre often results in a censorship of these truths of motherhood.[5] As Blakely urges, unmasked and outlaw mothers must turn to one another for support and validation: "After I discovered the real life of mothers bore little resemblance to the plot outlined in most of the books I'd read, I started relying on the expert advice of other mothers.... This great body of knowledge is essentially an oral history, because anyone engaged in motherhood on a daily basis had no time to write an advice book about it" (9). As our collection testifies, however, unmasked motherhood may also be found in women's writings, or more specifically in matrifocal narratives discussed above.

In a similar sense, Myrl Coulter, referring to *Of Woman Born*, asserts that the "twentieth century's much needed critical investigation into the institution of motherhood was launched by a pen" (37)—that is, by Rich's pen. While we agree, we would add that a plethora of creative texts have contributed to reconceptualizing motherhood. Maternal writing, Emily Jeremiah has noted, "entails a publicizing of maternal experience, and it subverts the traditional notion of mother as an instinctual, purely corporeal being" (231). "It is thus," she continues, "to be understood as a key tool in the redefinition of maternity in which feminists are engaged" (231). Patrice DiQuinzio argues that "It is impossible for feminist theory to avoid the issue of motherhood, and it is impossible for feminist theory to resolve it" (xx). We contend that matrifocal narratives, in unmasking motherhood and redefining maternity, allow for such encounters and explorations. Perhaps, to paraphrase the words of Coulter, if feminist theory is not the means to a resolution, matrifocal narratives may well be.

Textual Mothers / Maternal Texts proposes some of the ways that contemporary novelists, poets, and auto/biographers use matrifocal narratives to unmask and redefine maternal roles and subjectivities. Within the last few decades of the twentieth and the first decade of the twenty-first century, authors have been writing about maternal themes, identities, and experiences to a perhaps unprecedented degree, a focus supported and enriched by motherhood studies, which, as noted earlier, has come into its own since the 1990s as a distinct and established academic discipline. These agendas are part of larger, ongoing feminist projects that have for the past few decades been revising the Western literary canon in a plethora of ways:[6] to account for and include women's contributions to male-centred literary histories; to argue for specifically female-centred traditions; to theorize decidedly female and feminine forms of writing; and to foreground the ways that not only gender but also race, class, religion, and sexuality of both authors and protagonists must be considered when assessing the aesthetic and cultural value of texts. It is not surprising that a body of scholarship focused on literary mothering has been produced out of and alongside broader revisionist mandates given that women have historically been—and often still are—defined and represented (by both themselves and societies at large) within literature according to their roles as wives and mothers.

The fact that so much attention of late has been so fully directed at locating literary mothers underscores the obvious: they have been missing. The theme of the mother lost in and to history, and the ensuing quest to locate her, underpins maternal research. Critics and theorists are not only documenting and anthologizing expanding traditions of maternal literatures but also have been recovering and retracing the very origins and developments of such traditions. While it is not our aim here to review several rich decades of such scholarship, we want to draw attention to some of the most influential studies that serve as both context and inspiration for our work and that of our contributors. Indeed, our collection is a response to as well as a dialogue with the ongoing scholarship that charts and theorizes maternal traditions in diverse and intersecting ways such as the following: by genre; throughout history and across generations; according to race, class, and nationhood; and in thematic terms such as birthing, sex, and the maternal body.

Looking at genre, for instance, we turn to Susan C. Greenfield, who highlights a symbiotic relationship between the novel and mothering in *Mothering Daughters: Novels and the Politics of Family Romance: Frances Burney to Jane Austen* (2002). Providing a historical overview of the eighteenth century, during which the nuclear family was entrenched, she concludes that "regardless of whether maternal practice or feeling radically changed in the 1700s, motherhood was idealized with exceptional fervor by the century's end and commonly represented as a full-time occupation" (14). Consequently, "women were defined by their maternity, and maternity was supposed to occupy a woman's perpetual interest" (14–15). The novel was developing as a genre at this same historical moment, early on becoming associated with women authors and largely domestic and feminine characters and stories, such that "women's novels helped construct modern maternity, generating a literary tradition with politically complex and psychologically enduring effects" (13). Many chapters in our collection, such as those by Myrl Coulter, Nancy Peled, and Denys T. Landry, signal continuities as well as disruptions of patriarchally driven and sanctioned ideologies and plots within fiction.

Poetry, too, is a site of compliance and resistance for the maternal subject. For example, in "Claiming Our Birth-Write: The Poetry of American Mothers" (2000), Susan MacCallum-Whitcomb examines a tradition of "maternity poetry" which dates back to seventeenth-century English American writer Anne Bradstreet, "America's first poet," who was, "it should be remembered ... a literary mother" and for whom motherhood "was a defining experience" (39). MacCallum-Whitcomb draws attention to how the form of a poem itself makes possible and yet problematizes women's creative potential: a poem can be written in fits and starts, composed between childcare and domestic responsibilities. Identifying a tradition from the seventeenth to the twentieth centuries, she finds that "issues of occupation and interruption continue to jeopardize the literary production of mothers," with these themes being "so common ... that they comprise a whole sub-genre in American maternity poetry" (39–40). At the same time, she uncovers themes in which mothers are empowered by being imaged as "providers or protectors" (46), or celebrated for their reproductive (literal and metaphoric) capacities (46–51), testifying to models of poetry grounded in maternal experience which "not only allowed for the possibility of motherhood, but recognized it as asset rather than an artistic liability" (45). Poetic models like these inform the chapters by our contributors Elizabeth Beaulieu, Rita M. Jones, and Susan Driver.

Life-writing genres have also "helped construct modern maternity," to quote Greenfield, as revealed in the recent proliferation of the scholarship on and anthologizing of women's auto/biographies, such as the following: *Between Women: Biographers, Novelists, Critics, Teachers and Artists Write about Their Work on Women* (1984), edited by Carol Ascher, Louise DeSalvo, and Sara Ruddick; *Telling Women's Lives: The New Biography* (1994), by Linda Wagner-Martin; *Women's Life-Writing: Finding Voice/Building Community* (1997), edited by Linda Coleman; *Representing Lives: Women and Auto/Biography* (2000), edited by Alison Donnell and Pauline Polkey; and *The Voice of the Mother: Embedded Maternal Narratives in Twentieth-Century Women's Autobiographies* (2000), by Jo Malin.[7] These studies foreground women's lives, subjectivities, and creativities in terms of, among other things, mothering and motherhood. Autobiography (including the diary and memoir) is an especially valuable arena in which we can register and understand the ways that women inscribe an "I" or series of "I's" in the authoring of their own maternal selves, accounting for and expressing awareness of factors such as the body, sexuality, gender, race, class, and nationhood. Autobiographers tell their own stories through matrifocal speech, seeking agency as they shape and control both their lived realities and the textual representations of those realities. Moreover, while we recognize that life writings comprise their own literary traditions, we also work on the premise—one that informs literary and life-writing theory—that developments in Western fiction were simultaneous to those in auto/biography, allowing for an appreciation of how autobiographers often use novelistic techniques to tell their stories, just as fiction writers draw on life material for theirs.[8] We agree with Daly and Reddy, who posit that "in the process of redefining mothering it is also necessary to redefine genres and their conventions," so that genre fluidity reflects a political as well as aesthetic agenda (12), as evidenced in chapters in this collection by Kate Douglas, Joanne Frye, Andrea O'Reilly, Kim Hensley Owens, and Elizabeth Podnieks.

Many studies trace maternal traditions to and through specific historical as well as national/geographic locations, and are often inseparable from considerations of race and class, such as *The Lost Tradition: Mothers and Daughters in Literature* (1980), edited by Cathy N. Davidson and E. M. Broner; the aforementioned *The Mother Daughter Plot* (1989), by Marianne Hirsch; *Wild Mother Dancing: Maternal Narrative in Canadian Literature* (1993), by Di Brandt; *Women's Fiction Between the Wars: Mothers, Daughters and*

Writing (1998) and the accompanying *Mothers and Daughters in the Twentieth Century: A Literary Anthology* (1999), by Heather Ingman; and *Writing Mothers and Daughters: Renegotiating the Mother in Western European Narratives by Women* (2002), edited by Adalgisa Giorgio.

The Lost Tradition, for instance, is perhaps the earliest full-scale attempt to find the "missing" mother, and details a staggering "forty centuries of a literature of mothers and daughters" in Near Eastern, British, and North American literatures, and in forms such as novels, short stories, poems, diaries, autobiographies, tales, myths, and songs (xi–xii). Introducing us to or reacquainting us with figures ranging from mythic and biblical times, like Demeter and Persephone, Clytemnestra and Iphigenia, and Ruth and Naomi, to mothers and daughters inhabiting twentieth-century texts by authors like Sylvia Plath, Alice Munro, and Nikki Giovanni, contributors to Davidson and Broner's collection demonstrate that mothers and daughters were depicted in close and empowered relations in ancient literatures, but were increasingly driven apart as patriarchal forces from the first Christian centuries through to the early Renaissance sought to silence and or devalue the roles of women in society, including that of mothering. The period of the High Renaissance through to the Victorian times saw the re-emergence of the mother as occupying a respected place within society, but her status was not translated into British and American literatures, where she was more often than not an absence or an impediment to the daughter's individuation. It is only in the beginnings of the late twentieth century that the rebellious daughter finds a way back to the mother, reclaiming her through an acceptance of and celebration of generational—or matrilineal—bonds registered especially in the literatures of minority women who, participating in the oral traditions of their communities, give voice to their often silenced mothers: hence "the lost mother is found" (254). However, this search for the mother has been daughter-centric in that she is positioned almost entirely in terms of her relations with, and as perceived by, the daughter.

This pattern of loss, rebellion, and recovery on the part of the daughter shapes the work of Hirsch and Ingman. Echoing and expanding on *The Lost Tradition*, Hirsch reads from what she calls maternal perspectives that the mother and daughter have been "submerged in traditional plot structures" in nineteenth- and twentieth-century Western European and North American fictions (3). While the Freudian triangular structure of the father, mother, and son effectively negates the mother and daughter in the family romance, Hirsch conceives an alternative model of mother, father, and daughter, in which the female characters are privileged. Conceiving "both motherhood and daughterhood as *story*—as narrative representation of social and subjective reality and of literary convention," she asserts that the novel is "the optimal genre in which to study the interplay between hegemonic and dissenting voices," and a site on which ideologies are both inscribed and queried (9). She questions the ideology of gender, specifically of mothering, as rendered in the literary conventions of realism, modernism, and postmodernism.

Like the contributors to *The Lost Tradition*, Hirsch finds that in late-nineteenth-century realist plots by writers like Jane Austen, the Brontës, and George Sand, the mother is silent, absent, and/or dismissed by the daughter, who disidentifies with her as the only possible route to autonomous and independent selfhood (10). However, in early-twentieth-century modernist plots by authors such as Virginia Woolf, Colette, and Edith Wharton, there is female agency, as factors such as emancipation and scientific advancements made birth control possible and motherhood a choice. The mother's voice is thus reinscribed by the daughter heroine, who, filled with ambitions for (artistic) success, turns not just to male but also to female models in her formation of selfhood (15).

The modernist years from the end of the First World War to the start of the Second World War are the focus for Ingman, who links mothering, politics, and public discourse as she analyzes maternal relationships authored in the prose by women of middle- or upper-middle-class status in Britain. During and after the First World War, although women gained unprecedented access to the workplace, they were conversely urged to direct their income and new free time (created by inventions such as the vacuum cleaner) to their families, especially children. Novelists Rose Macaulay, Elizabeth Bowen, Ivy Compton-Burnett, and Jean Rhys used their fictional sites, as Ingman reveals, to interrogate these contradictions and expectations, and to give greater attention to the mother, albeit in largely daughter-centric ways.

As the twentieth century progressed, scholars document vital shifts in the representation of maternal subjectivity, with matrifocal narratives coming into their own. In postmodernist plots of the 1970s and 1980s by, among others, Margaret Atwood, Marguerite Duras, and Christa Wolf, Hirsch finds the daughter heroine engaged in complex, "multiple relational identities" (10), and mothers are significantly prominent, displacing "fathers, brothers, husbands, and male lovers" (15). Here, she measures the "points at which feminist discourse situates itself at a distance from the maternal and points at which a maternal discourse emerges" (15), paying attention to when and how the daughter speaks for the mother, and the mother speaks for herself. Similarly, in her anthology *Mothers and Daughters in the Twentieth*

Century, Ingman shows that by the 1970s, literatures reflect the impact of feminism that on the one hand promoted sisterhood over mother/daughterhood, while on the other offered a more positive consideration of the mother and an acknowledged "debt to the mother" (25). Much writing from the 1970s on, rather than being "done in spite of and against the mother," involves, according to Ingman, the mother in the creative process (25–26).

Scholars point to the fact that some of the most sustained and challenging matrifocal narratives are found in traditions involving writers and subjects from minority or marginalized communities and relationships. Dialogues are opened up between daughter-centric and matrifocal perspectives, creating matrilineal thinking and writing that extends across generations, and which we will take up more fully in this introduction, in our section on communication. Like Davidson and Broner, Hirsch suggests that the successful recovery of the mother by the daughter is embedded in the literatures of American women of colour like Toni Morrison and Alice Walker, "writers who clearly identify themselves as a new feminist generation in relation to the maternal tradition of the past" and "who are in a more distant relation to cultural and literary hegemony" (16). Ingman, writing about Walker and Maya Angelou, shows they have traced their creative spirits and functions back through a maternal heritage, and in naming and remembering the mothers of history are more empowered to name themselves and their experiences as mothers today (*Mothers* 27–28). The intersections of maternity and race are especially crucial here, for while white women may have experienced a need to sever themselves from their mothers—to disidentify with them, in Hirsch's terms—Black women in discriminatory societies necessarily "struggle to affirm the value of their lives: race, class and gender oppression intensify their need to uncover a strong matrilineal heritage" (*Mothers* 28).

Further, Ingman highlights how Asian Canadian and American authors as well as those from the Caribbean, for example, write stories in which motherhood and nationhood may be conflated, and which foreground the importance of tracing and celebrating maternal as well as geographic and cultural identities (Ingman, *Mothers* 33–35). Aldalgisa Giorgio similarly maps a vital Western European tradition of contemporary mother–daughter narratives by numerous authors from Spain, Ireland, Italy, and France, specifically according to internal (local, regional) and transnational interests and perspectives. Relatedly, in her work on contemporary Canadian narratives by figures such as Margaret Laurence, Daphne Marlatt, and Jovette Marchessault, Di Brandt contends that some of the most exciting developments in maternal literatures are produced by those who have "escaped colonization, and thus write on the very margins of Western discourse" (18). Topics include mothering as a lesbian, an immigrant, or a member of Indigenous or religious communities, for example. The possibility for revised maternal narratives emerging out of the experiences and literatures of women who are outside the mainstream of white, Western, heterosexual communities are reflected in chapters in our book by Brandt herself as well as Sheila Hassell Hughes, Eden Robinson, Gill Rye, Nicole Willey, Tanja Stampfl, and Rita Bode.

In addition to race and nationhood, the relationship between the body and maternal subjectivity is a theme constituting its own literary traditions, as illuminated by Tess Cosslett in *Women Writing Childbirth: Modern Discourses of Motherhood* (1994). Just as the broader experiences of mothering have been largely absent until the twentieth century, so Cosslett shows that childbirth "has long been marginalised as a subject for public representation," especially as narrated from the perspective of the woman giving birth (1). Her research reveals that while earlier examples may have referenced childbirth from the point of view of the father, or (medical) attendant, it was not until the 1938 publication of Enid Bagnold's novel *The Squire* that the taboo against talking about the maternal body was broken and the pregnant and birthing woman's subjectivity made the focus of a text. *The Squire* helped to launch a tradition manifested in the work by British, American, and Commonwealth authors such as Doris Lessing, Toni Morrison, Margaret Atwood, Toi Derricote, and Sharon Doubiago. Julie Tharp and Susan MacCallum-Whitcomb, along with the contributors to their collection *This Giving Birth: Pregnancy and Childbirth in American Women's Writing* (2000), further examine the maternal body and the impact of childbirth on women's personal and artistic selfhoods. They posit that Sharon Olds's 1980 poem "The Language of the Brag" broke ground with its attention to "the corporeal reality of pregnancy and childbirth, shying away from no bodily function, and it did so in a way that was unsentimental, unembarrassed, and, most importantly, wholly unapologetic" (1). Her poem, Tharp and MacCallum-Whitcomb contend, is so crucial because it "forcefully confirms that pregnancy and childbirth are legitimate subjects for literature" (2). A tradition of maternal body narratives is evidenced in collections such as Laura Chester's *Cradle and All: Women Writers on Pregnancy and Birth* (1989) and Charlotte Otten's *The Book of Birth Poetry* (1995) (3), and registered in the chapters in our collection by Rita Jones, Susan Driver, Denys Landry, and Ruth Panofsky, for example, which examine the mother in physical terms and as a sexual being, and mothering as a potentially erotic desire and act.

Textual Mothers / Maternal Texts identifies and extends traditions such as those reviewed above. In emphasizing matrifocal narratives, it unearths maternal themes, perspectives, and texts, and thereby contributes to the archaeology of maternity mentioned earlier. The collection seeks to excavate the matrifocal perspective that is denied and distorted by both a daughter-centric perspective and the larger mask of motherhood. However, daughter-centric narratives can inscribe the matrifocal as well, and therefore the collection also considers the ways in which mothers are the objects of their children's narratives but assume at various points in the stories a subject position. In organizing these diverse approaches, we have divided the collection into four sections, absence, ambivalence, agency, and communication, themes that most significantly reflect for us the trajectory from daughter-centric to matrilineal and matrifocal narratives. While the chapters foreground the themes of their respective categories, most of the chapters placed in one section could equally be placed in other sections. Greenfield has noted that, "Dispelling the possibility of a politically unified maternity, the novels studied here indicate the ambiguity and flexibility of the institution [of motherhood] itself" (14). Though she refers to eighteenth- and nineteenth-century fiction, her description has relevance to our study, which showcases the complexities surrounding theoretical, critical, and creative approaches to maternity that persist today. The multiple identities mothers take on, exhibit, and live through, as registered in the plethora of chapters that in themselves can be read as an interconnected network of maternal possibilities, underscore how our collection participates in the creation of and acknowledgment of what Yi-Lin Yu calls "a female-dominated world founded on women's mothering activities and experiences" (66).

Absence

The first section begins by considering the issue of maternal absence, a theme that launched the recovery of maternal literary traditions, as previously discussed. Not only has the mother been lost to the broader traditions of literary history that have privileged narratives by and about male figures, but also she has been lost within the daughter-centric literatures that do depict the mother: she is absent to her children (almost always daughters) and to her self in that her own voice is silent, her subjectivity lacking or erased.

A mother's absence can take many forms and can affect both mother and child in a variety of ways. Greenfield suggests that the mother's absence from eighteenth- and early-nineteenth-century fiction serves only to reinforce her status: "in many of the novels the absence also becomes the point around which maternal ideals are articulated and reinforced. As the family and social order collapse without the mother, the novels prove her fundamental importance" (18). Assessing maternal absence in daughter-centric literatures produced over 150 years later, editor Mickey Pearlman, in *Mother Puzzles: Daughters and Mothers in Contemporary American Literature* (1989), discovers that mothers are, puzzlingly, in some sense (still) lost. As she observes, "'missing' mothers (what psychiatrists call 'custodial' mothers who are physically present but emotionally absent)" dominate stories by Sue Miller, Candace Flynt, and Mona Simpson, among others; the mothers are "infantilized," "dependent and confused," or "repressed, depressed, or obsessed" (2), signalling that we continue to witness an ambivalent response by the daughter to her mother, and an ongoing struggle by the daughter to define herself in opposition to, or by separation from, the mother.

Elaine Tuttle Hansen takes up these issues from the point of view of the mother. In *Mother without Child: Contemporary Fiction and the Crisis of Motherhood* (1997), she defines the literary theme of absence, or "mother without child," to be an expansive term encompassing "nontraditional mothers and 'bad' mothers" such as "lesbians and slave mothers; women who have abortions and miscarriages; women who refuse to bear children, or whose children are stolen from them; and mothers who are ... sometimes criminals, murderers, prisoners, suicides, time travelers, tricksters, or ghosts" (11). Echoing Pearlman in querying why there are so many stories, even today, in which mother and child are separated from each other, Hansen suggests that second-wave feminism may be in part responsible, for in its contention that motherhood leads to women's oppression, it seemed "to threaten to take women away from the children they bear, or ought to bear" (19). In a different sense, she posits that stories in which the mother is severed—either voluntarily or involuntarily—from child force us to "reconsider our assumptions about what motherhood is 'really' like," and to question whether "'the' maternal voice or an autonomous maternal subject can or should be sought" (19). The chapters in this section reflect these various approaches and responses to maternal absence, considering the topic in terms of how women negotiate patriarchal imperatives to be a "good" mother with their own desires for autonomy and self-realization, which too often leads to their being judged "bad."

Myrl Coulter (ch. 1) shows us, for instance, that in Jane Urquhart's fiction, including *The Whirlpool* (1986) and *Changing Heaven* (1990), the mothers are "usually dead, missing, relegated to the background, alienated from society or suffering severe psychological distress." Women who deviate from conventional expectations as to how "present" a mother should be and or how she should fulfill her maternal duties are ultimately categorized (by men as well as other women) as "bad" or inappropriate role models. Urquhart reveals "motherhood in crisis" as she depicts the disparity between the persistence of the late-nineteenth and early-twentieth-century ideological conceptions and lived realities of mothering, conflicts that persist in our supposedly "postfeminist" era today.

The next two chapters treat absence in terms of abuse, from daughter-centric perspectives that emerge into matrifocal ones as the authors/narrators become mothers themselves. Nancy Peled (ch. 2), like Coulter, expands our understanding of Canadian literature in her feminist psychoanalytical readings of three novels by Margaret Atwwood: *Cat's Eye* (1989), *The Robber Bride* (1994), and *The Blind Assassin* (2001). Peled finds that Atwood's absent mothers, in being associated with the classic stereotypes of wicked witch or stepmother, are "both culpable yet blameless enactors of their daughters' suffering." The daughters who grow up to be women have survived the traumas of their childhoods in part through gaining even a little insight into their mothers' lives under the law of the father; in turn these women learn that in order to be "safe" and to be available to their own daughters and granddaughters they must resign themselves to assimilation within and maintenance of the traditional social order. Kate Douglas (ch. 3) goes on to examine one of the most provocative and courageous strains to emerge in life writing today: narratives by women exposing their childhood physical, sexual, and psychological abuses at the hands of their mothers and stepmothers. She focuses on the autobiography *Ugly* (2006) by Constance Briscoe, who survived a tortuous childhood to become one of the United Kingdom's first Black female judges; and *Shadow Child: A Memoir of the Stolen Generation* (1998) by Rosalie Fraser, an Indigenous Australian who endured physical and sexual abuse by her white foster mother in the 1960s and 1970s. Douglas probes the tension created by the need to write out and through experiences of trauma, and the ethical concerns and responsibilities that come with revelations of the intimate actions and lives of others.

The last two chapters here consider the absent mother who is outcast in many senses of the term: from her children, from her maternal self, and from her community, be it one of nationhood, race, religion, or family. Sheila Hassell Hughes (ch. 4) examines the work of French Ojibwe and German American author Louise Erdrich and discovers that the list of "motherless characters is stunning in its weight and variety." Hassell Hughes offers a close reading of "Red Mother," a section of *The Last Report on the*

Miracles at Little No Horse (2001), which features the figure of Marie Kash-paw searching for knowledge of her birth mother in order to (re)claim her own identity, one that will allow her eventually to become a mother herself. Hassell Hughes contends that the missing mother embodies the "literal and spiritual displacement, homelessness, and motherlessness" of Indigenous peoples as a consequence of colonialism and Christianity, and she pushes for an approach to Erdrich that is politically charged as well as spiritually transformative. And Ruth Panofsky (ch. 5) asseses representations of Jew-ish prostitutes who "dare to become mothers" in the fiction of Adele Wise-man (*Crackpot*, 1974) and Lilian Nattel (*The Singing Fire*, 2004). Panofksy draws connections between real and fictional experiences of Jewish mater-nal prostitutes, especially in terms of how their behaviours and emotions debunk traditional assumptions that the prostitute has no maternal sen-sibilities. Both novels feature protagonists who were early on denied pro-tection by their own absent mothers and who subsequently, as prostitutes, become absent to their own children. Panofsky demonstrates that the pros-titute/mother figure remains an outcast from society, doomed to suffer for her past and ultimately condemned to be absent from maternal discourse.

Ambivalence

The collection's second section addresses the theme of maternal ambiva-lence, a term defined by Rozsiska Parker in "The Production and Purposes of Maternal Ambivalence" as constituting "not an anodyne condition of mixed feelings, but a complex and contradictory state of mind, shared by all mothers, in which loving and hating feelings for children exist side by side" (18). The concept of maternal ambivalence, as Parker notes, is well estab-lished within psychoanalytical theory. However, because cultural expecta-tions and assumptions presume and demand that a mother love her child unconditionally and selflessly, the mother who exhibits or admits to ma-ternal ambivalence is judged harshly and rendered the object of shame and disbelief by society, by other mothers, and by the mother herself. Parker cites a double standard informing approaches to ambivalence: for the de-veloping child, the ability to feel both love and hate toward the mother is a sign of healthy individuation; for the mother, the same feelings are deemed unnatural in the mother and detrimental to the child (17).

Over the last decade, maternal ambivalence has emerged as a central theme in women's writings, but as Parker qualifies, more often than not such ambivalence is sanitized and domesticated through the device of hu-mour, for it is only in this context that these taboo feelings and responses can be articulated "safely": "In novels, women's magazines, and national newspapers, column after column is devoted to comic accounts of maternal ambivalence. Safely cloaking their 'confessions' in laughter, mothers admit to being forever enraged, entranced, embattled, wounded and delighted by their children" (17). However, in women's literatures, and in particular within matrifocal narratives in their attention to unmasking motherhood, we find, as evidenced in the fiction and poetry studied in the chapters below, a more multifaceted, nuanced, and authentic representation of maternal ambivalence—one that is seldom recuperated through humour. Moreover, as these narratives grapple with the thorny and messy reality of maternal ambivalence with unflinching clarity and candour, they also position motherhood itself as an ambivalent concept and identity.

The section opens with two chapters that view maternal ambivalence from the standpoint of Canadian daughters. Nathalie Foy (ch. 6) looks at how First Nations author Eden Robinson crafts a story that "both mocks the perfectibility of motherhood and mourns its impossibility." Narrated by the daughter and chronicling her journey from childhood to late adolescence, the story introduces us to the many mothers and families of Lisa: her biological mother, who is incarcerated for murder when Lisa is a child and with whom Lisa lives while on the run when her mother escapes from prison; her Aunt Gena; her foster parents; and finally her adoptive parents. In "Dogs in Winter," the saintly and demonic extremes represented by Lisa's biological and surrogate mothers signify and enact the larger inherent ambiguity and ambivalence of motherhood, an ambivalence the daughter seeks to negotiate and resolve throughout the narrative. Then, Kathleen Kellett-Betsos (ch. 7) explores the secularization of Quebecois society, the ensuing changes in ideals of womanhood, and the impact of these on the ambivalent representation of mothers and motherhood in Gabrielle Poulin's six novels. The daughters in Poulin's fiction reject the ideal of the *mater dolorosa* of pre–Quiet Revolution Catholic Quebec as well as the societal role of the patriarchal mother. While largely daughter-centric, Poulin's fiction, in its use of the archetypal narrative of Demeter and Persephone, moves from matraphobia to a reconciliation of daughters and mothers, both biological and surrogate. This reunion, Kellett-Betsos suggests, is made possible in the recognition and acceptance of the inevitable ambivalent nature of the mother–daughter relationship.

Elizabeth Beaulieu (ch. 8) next examines selected poems by African American Rita Dove—*Thomas and Beulah* (1986), *Grace Notes* (1989), and *Mother Love* (1995)—focusing on how maternal ambivalence in Dove's poetry functions, in Beaulieu's words, as "a transformative power" that may be a source of creative agency for mothers and the necessary foundation for a healthy mother–daughter relationship. Beaulieu suggests that Dove's poetry reveals the necessity of acknowledging and dealing with maternal ambivalence—"the terrible beauty of motherhood"—so that women, especially Black women, can embrace motherhood in all its complexities.

The final two chapters consider mothers in ambivalent relationships with their sons. Denys Landry (ch. 9) assumes a matrifocal perspective to argue that in Doris Lessing's *The Fifth Child*, protagonist Harriet Lovatt, who at times appears to hate her fifth child, suffers from postpartum depression. Landry argues that while the novel is a gothic narrative and Harriet invents herself as a modern female gothic persona, the true monstrosity of the text is the societal denial of her postpartum depression and the ensuing demonization of maternal ambivalence. Emily Jeremiah (ch. 10) dissects a mother's varying contempt for her murderous son in Lionel Shriver's *We Need to Talk about Kevin*, and in so doing shows how Shriver's text questions whether women are naturally or necessarily able parents, and that femininity is neither a desirable nor a stable gender identity. In challenging traditional assumptions that women are, or should be, both feminine and maternal, the novel aligns itself with queer theory, which posits that gender and sexuality are not fixed givens. The novel, in Jeremiah's words, "overturns or 'queers' dominant ideas about gender, [thus] paving the way for new conceptions of sex and of parenting," suggesting, ultimately, that the concept of maternity itself is ambivalent.

Agency

Maternal agency is the focus of section three. "We do not think," Adrienne Rich writes in *Of Woman Born*, "of the power stolen from us and the power withheld from us in the name of the institution of motherhood" (275). The aim of empowered mothering is to reclaim that power for mothers, to imagine and implement a mode of mothering that mitigates the many ways that patriarchal motherhood, both discursively and materially, regulates and restrains mothers and their mothering. Much has been published on patriarchal motherhood since Rich's inaugural text, which documents why and how patriarchal motherhood is harmful, indeed unnatural, to mothers and children alike. However, only in the last few years has a theory of empowered mothering begun to develop in feminist scholarship. While empowered mothering eludes a precise definition, this mode of mothering, in the first instance, functions as an oppositional discourse of motherhood, one that seeks to challenge the dominant ideology of motherhood and change the various ways that the lived experience of patriarchal motherhood is limiting or oppressive to women. Whether it be termed feminist (Glickman, Gordon, Green, O'Reilly), outlaw (Rich), radical (Cooper), rebellious (Douglas and Michaels), or hip (Gore and Lavender), the central aim of empowered mothering is to confer to mothers the agency, authority, authenticity, and autonomy denied to them in patriarchal motherhood (O'Reilly; see "Rocking" and "Feminist Mothering"). More specifically, as Green observes from her study of feminist mothers, "empowered mothers seek to live Rich's emancipatory vision of motherhood" (130).

Agency, explains Bronwyn Davies, involves the ability to recognize discursive constitutions of self and "to resist, subvert, and change the discourses through which one is being constituted. It is the freedom to recognize multiple readings such that no discursive practice ... can capture and control one's identity" (51). Agency in mothering enables, nay empowers mothers, as Amy Middleton notes, to "face and resist the pressure of other people's policing of their mothering, and, in fact, gain confidence in doing so" (74). Agency means, to use Rich's words, "to refuse to be a victim and then go on from there" (246). In patriarchal culture, however, we find few models, in literature or in life, of maternal agency in empowered mothering. That is why the emergence of the genre and tradition of matrifocal narratives is crucial: matrifocal narratives, in unmasking motherhood and redefining maternity, impart such empowering depictions of maternal agency.

The first two chapters in this section consider how the contemporary motherhood memoir allows for a critique of patriarchal motherhood to construct alternative meanings of motherhood based on maternal agency. Joanne Frye (ch. 11) opens with the question she asked 11 years ago at the Association for Research on Mothering's first conference: "What does it mean to write as a mother?" and here she seeks to answer this question by way of an analysis of three memoirs, or momoirs: Carole Maso's *The Room Lit by Roses* (2000), Rachel Cusk's *A Life's Work* (2001), and Anne Enright's *Making Babies* (2004). Despite the tendency of momoirs to essentialize gender, Frye is convinced that through the maternal voices of these texts, "we might not only find ways to move beyond the hazards of essentialism, beyond the paradox of representing maternal subjectivity; we might also develop a dynamic way of rethinking what is means to be a 'self' at all." And in this, the motherhood memoir can be read as both modelling and mentoring the desired maternal agency. This conclusion is challenged by Andrea O'Reilly (ch. 12), who considers explanations given for the rise of the motherhood memoir at the turn of the twenty-first century: feminism, purchasing power of women, and changing demographics. O'Reilly suggests another reason, arguing that the emergence of this literary genre may be linked to the development of a new ideology of motherhood, what Sharon Hays has termed "intensive mothering" and Susan Douglas and Meredith Michaels call the "new momism." The chapter examines the momoir's compliance and complicity with these philosophies to argue that real maternal agency becomes possible only when this genre confronts and counters this discourse of motherhood and its naturalization and reification of gender difference.

The following three chapters examine maternal agency in the context of female sexuality. Chapters by Susan Driver (ch. 13) and Gill Rye (ch. 14) look at lesbian mothering in particular. Driver considers how for poet Minnie Bruce Pratt, the erotic dimensions of subjectivity become a resistance against the repudiation of her right to mother as a lesbian. Reading Pratt's *Crimes Against Nature* (1990), Driver examines how the poet, in articulating her lesbian desire as that which unsettles her reader's presumptions of what constitutes a maternal self, plays up the ambiguities that challenge the oxymoronic status of lesbian motherhood. The point, as Driver writes, "is not to resolve the tensions between desire and identity but to turn the problem onto those troubled by ambiguity." For it is precisely this ambiguity that allows for Pratt's erotic-maternal to be a site of agency. Rye then explores how two French novels, Éliane Girard's *Mais qui va garder le chat?* and Myriam Blanc's *Et elles eurent beaucoup d'enfants ... : Histoire d'une famille homoparentale* (both published in 2005) respectively portray lesbian mothers as "normal," "ordinary," "just like other mothers" and represent them as forging new terrain, experimenting with social forms, reinventing the family. Rye focuses on the issue of visibility, the question of the father, and the figure of the second mother, suggesting that same-sex parenting may offer a model for the (French/European) family of the future. Rita Jones (ch. 15) next analyzes poems by Sharon Olds from three collections—*The Dead and the Living* (1983), *The Wellspring* (1985), and *Blood, Tin, Straw* (1999)—showing that they refute contemporary American constructions of proper womanhood and mothering by offering a woman who is a loving as well as sexually satisfied mother. The mothers of Olds's poetry construct maternal sexuality and sexual maternity as a site of agency for mothers.

Considering sexuality as well as other issues, Di Brandt (ch. 16) offers a provocative new reading of Margaret Laurence's *The Diviners*, "arguably the most important, most unusual, and most prescient Canadian novel of the twentieth century," one which breaks ground for its focus on the moment when writer and protagonist Morag Gunn enters menopause. Contextualized within a (post)colonial Canada of the 1950s and 1960s, the novel,

Brandt argues, is a revolutionary text—an "ecofeminist manifesto"—in which the staving off of an environmental, apocalyptic doom can be seen as coming from the recuperation of agency and power (in sexual, creative, spiritual terms) for and by mothers and grandmothers.

Communication

We close the collection with our section on communication because it bridges, and is a response to, the other sections on absence, ambivalence, and agency, and it signals a matrilineal tradition formed in dialogue between children (especially daughter-centric) and mothers (matrifocal). Mothers may be lost in countless forms, even in definitional terms, but scholarship also points to the ways that mothers find, are reunited with, and or are reconciled with their children. Mothers find *themselves* as mothers, as well, engaging in dialogue with multiple facets of their own identities as they may or may not come to terms with their maternal roles, desires, and needs.

The theme of communication has informed maternal thinking, to use Ruddick's phrase, as well as maternal writing. Virginia Woolf posited that we "think back through our mothers if we are women" in order to communicate and commune with a maternal past and a maternal community (26). In *Mother, She Wrote: Matrilineal Narratives in Contemporary Women's Writing* (2005), Yi-Lin Yu focuses on the promise of communication across the generational spectrum that sees daughters become mothers, and mothers become grandmothers. She expands the concept of the maternal narrative from a mother–daughter dyad to a "grandmother–mother–daughter triad" (a phrase coined by Audre Lorde)[9] which has, within the last 30 years, become recognized as a distinctly "matrilineal" narrative, the definition of which is taken from Cosslett: "one which either tells the stories of several generations of women at once, or which shows how the identity of a central character is crucially formed by her female ancestors" ("Feminism," quoted in Yu 2). Yu also notes how this definition intersects with Jo Malin's conception of twentieth-century women's autobiography as a genre in which the mother's narrative/biography is embedded in that told by the daughter, to create a "dialogic relationship between mothers and daughters" (quoted in Yu 2). The matrilineal narrative, Yu expands from our earlier discussion, is a particularly crucial site on which "nonwhite and nonmainstream" authors inscribe in their narratives (about both biological and nonbiological mothering), "the lifeline and the family line that sustain and safeguard the continuation of marginalized, endangered cultures or subcultures" (3). She refers to Alice Walker, who, in *In Search of Our Mothers' Gardens* (1983), locates and reclaims her matrilineage; and Trinh T. Minh-ha, who, in *Women, Native, Other: Writing Postcoloniality and Feminism* (1989), similarly exemplifies how African women have been, and continue to be, "keepers and tramsmitters" of female traditions and histories through oral storytelling (20)—as are Asian and Asian Canadian women through their tradition of "talk story," examined in this section.

Drawing on Hirsch (who we have earlier seen reshaping Freud's family romance to a feminist family romance) and on Lorde's triad, Yu proposes the term "new feminist family romances" to describe matrilineal narratives in which the role of the father is diminished and actually replaced by the maternal figure of the grandmother. Her expansion of the matrilineal narrative to focus on three generations of women allows for "multiple female voices and identities" such that protagonists may be daughters, mothers, and or grandmothers (66). Yu's conception of the new feminist family romance as a matrilineal narrative is further informed by Naomi Ruth Lowinsky's *Stories from the Motherline: Reclaiming the Mother–Daughter Bond, Finding Our Feminine Souls* (1992). Yu foregrounds that for Lowinsky, the motherline is akin to "the weaving of a tapestry whose threads are tied to different generations and as the spinning goes on, a more complicated network of relationships is thus developed" (68). Moreover, Yu explains how, for Lowinsky, the process of "looping" unites the stories, quoting her thus: "Looping ties together life stages, roles, and generations. It disregards linear time. It involves a cyclical view of life, it finds meaning in patterns that repeat. We measure our lives in our mother's terms, and in our daughter's terms.... You re-experience your past in your children and anticipate your future in your parents, while at the same time your children constellate the future and your parents the past" (quoted in Yu 68). The chapters in this section show how mothers (try to) communicate with children within specific periods and across time, and from one generation to the next. In texts that weave, link, or loop, contributors reveal how mothering is as much a lived action as it is a narrated dialogue.

In the first chapter, Nicole Willey (ch. 17) argues that in Jamaica Kincaid's novel *Annie John*, Annie's relationship with the mother is fraught with anger and antagonism because it cannot be separated from colonial discourse. Willey's reading of the 1985 novel shows that when women are kept from self-definition due to the oppression of race and class, it can become difficult or even impossible to pass on positive definitions of womanhood and motherhood to daughters. However, the healing possibilities (literal and figurative) of an African feminist tradition, as embodied in Annie's grandmother Ma Chess, empower Annie and potentially other daughters

to define and construct a female identity outside of and against both colonial and patriarchal constructs of womanhood, and through the matrilineal
line and women's communities. In a similar spirit, Rita Bode (ch. 18) turns
to two novels by Mexican American Sandra Cisneros—*The House on Mango
Street* (1984) and *Caramelo* (2002)—to illuminate the author's depiction
of mothers and daughters within the Latino community. Bode argues that
while fictional mothers seem permanently trapped in their roles as guardians of home and hearth, they do, in disparate ways, voice a "muted feminism that leads them to recognize and nurture, consciously as well as instinctively, the possibilities for independence and self-fulfillment in their
daughters." Cisneros's fiction celebrates how daughters move from listening to their mothers' stories to communicating their own stories as narrators of these novels, giving voice to the past while articulating the promises
of the future.

Tanja Stampfl (ch. 19) then reads Bapsi Sidhwa's novel *Cracking India*
(1991) "as a critique of the concept of Mother India (*Bharat Mata*) and an
investigation of female nation building." The novel is set in August 1947,
with India on the eve of gaining independence from Great Britain. Sidhwa
underscores that even after the British have gone, Mother India does not
fulfill her allegorical role of nurturing the nation and instead perpetu-
ates the oppression of the imperialists, "especially toward her daughters."
Stampfl generalizes that while the novel presents biological mother–
daughter bonds in failed terms, it celebrates women who perform maternal
functions on a communal level, surrogate mothers who nurture bonds that
dissolve religious and ethnic differences. The women who mother as and
through a community are, Stampfl suggests, communicating tolerance and
compassion as they give birth not only to new generations of empowered
daughters but to new nations as well.

Anne-Marie Lee-Loy (ch. 20) further considers the theme of communication between mothers and daughters within two Japanese Canadian
novels, Joy Kogawa's *Obasan* (1983) and Hiromi Goto's *Chorus of Mushrooms*
(1994). Lee-Loy connects a mother-driven language to the "talk stories"
described by Wendy Ho in her study of Asian American fiction, stories laden
with cultural and ethnic knowledge that mothers tell their daughters in order that they can survive, and challenge, mainstream society. As Lee-Loy
finds, however, talk story is noticeably absent in Kogawa's and Goto's texts,
suggesting that the failures of the daughters to forge autonomous selfhoods,
or to make meaningful connections within their families and communities
at large, only reifies the importance of talk story.

Looking at a different kind of talk story, Elizabeth Podnieks (ch. 21) describes the life writings produced by three generations of women as "a tapestry of maternal and matrilineal design." She considers *Save Me the Waltz* (1932), the autobiographical novel by American modernist Zelda Sayre Fitzgerald, alongside *Scottie, the Daughter Of...: The Life of Frances Scott Fitzgerald Lanahan Smith* (1995) by Eleanor Lanahan, the biography of Zelda's mother, Scottie, that also inscribes a memoir by Scottie as well as the autobiography of Scottie's daughter Eleanor. Though themes of maternal ambivalence are registered in the narratives of each woman, Podnieks reads the trajectory of life writings as a conversation between mother, daughter, and granddaughter, in which strains of empathy, forgiveness, and ultimately love echo through and across the texts.

Finally, we close with a chapter that announces how the Internet affords some of the most innovative communication today by and among mothers who form an online community. Kim Hensley Owens (ch. 22) turns to the explosion of electronic maternal narratives, navigating how online writing reconciles childbirth expectations with experiences, and how these stories are a remediation or reformulation not only of birth itself but of more traditionally narrated birth narratives. Classifying these stories as a new genre— "part memoir, part political tract, part testimonial"—she underscores that these "rich rhetorical documents" are used by mothers to change, challenge, and communicate how childbirth is represented and interpreted throughout both cyberspace and the world.

...

Of Woman Born opens with Rich's oft-cited quote, "We know more about the air we breathe, the seas we travel, than about the nature and meaning of motherhood" (11). Later, in the chapter "Motherhood and Daughterhood," Rich writes, "The cathexis between mother and daughter—essential, distorted, misused—is the great unwritten story" (235). In the 30-plus years since Rich lamented the absences and silences of the maternal and identified "the loss of the daughter to the mother, and the mother to the daughter as the essential female tragedy" (337), hundreds of matrifocal and matrilineal narratives have been unearthed and written. Indeed, the majority of narratives examined in this collection were written after 1976. It is our hope that this collection, in its consideration of many and diverse maternal texts and textual mothers, delivers, to paraphrase Rich's concluding words, new meanings of motherhood to transform maternal thinking itself. This transformation, as Rich reminds us, "is where we have to begin" (286), and where this present collection takes us.

Notes to Introduction

1 See Malin's *The Voice of the Mother*.
2 See O'Reilly (*Mother Matters*, 12) for a discussion of this concept of an archaeology of maternity.
3 O'Reilly and Caporale-Bizzini, "Introduction."
4 In *Of Woman Born*, Adrienne Rich, when discussing a vacation with her children one summer while her husband remained in the city, writes: "We were conspirators, outlaws from the institution of motherhood. I felt enormously in charge of my life" (195). Since then, the terms "mother outlaw" and "maternal outlawdom" refer to mothers who resist and refuse patriarchal motherhood. Please see Blakely, and O'Reilly (*Mother Outlaws, Rocking the Cradle*) for further discussion on this.
5 Please see chapter 14 of this volume for a discussion of the "new momism" and the motherhood memoir.
6 See, for example, Blain et al., Ezell, Gilbert and Gubar, Kime Scott, Showalter.
7 In using the term "auto/biography" we signal first-person texts (including the diary, memoir, and formal autobiography) as well as third-person biographical narratives.
8 Timothy Dow Adams contends, for instance, not that life stories are necessarily fabrications but that they are "composed of the author's metaphors of self that attempt to reconcile the individual events of a lifetime by using a combination of memory and imagination" (3). For more on the relationship between fact and fiction, and fact and "truth," see, for example, Eakin, Podnieks, Zinsser.
9 Yu quotes from Lorde's *Zami: A New Spelling of My Name*: "I have felt the age-old triangle of mother father and child, with the 'I' at its eternal core, elongate and flatten out into the elegantly strong triad of grandmother mother daughter, with the 'I' moving back and forth flowing in either or both directions as needed" (Yu 65).

Works Cited

Ascher, Carol, Louise DeSalvo, and Sara Ruddick, eds. *Between Women: Biographers, Novelists, Critics, Teachers and Artists Write about Their Work on Women*. Boston: Beacon Press, 1984.

Blain, Virginia, Isobel Grundy, and Patricia Clements. *The Feminist Companion to Literature in English*. New Haven: Yale University Press, 1990.

Blakely, Mary Kay. *American Mom: Motherhood, Politics, and Humble Pie*. Chapel Hill: Alonguin Books of Chapel Hill, 1994.

Brandt, Di. *Wild Mother Dancing: Maternal Narrative in Canadian Literature*. Manitoba: University of Manitoba Press, 1993.

Coleman, Linda S., ed. *Women's Life-Writing: Finding Voice/Building Community*. Bowling Green, OH: Bowling Green State University Popular Press, 1997.

Cooper, Baba. "The Radical Potential in Lesbian Mothering of Daughters." *Politics of the Heart: A Lesbian Parenting Anthology*. Ed. Sandra Pollack and Jeanne Vaughn. Ithaca, NY: Firebrand Books, 1987. 233–40.

Cosslett, Tess. "Feminism, Matrilinealism, and the 'House of Women' in Contemporary Women's Fiction." *Journal of Gender Studies* 5.1 (1996): 7.

——. *Women Writing Childbirth: Modern Discourses of Motherhood*. Manchester: Manchester University Press, 1994.

Coulter, Myrl. "Feminism and Motherhood, Jane Urquhart, Carol Shields, Margaret Laurence and Me." Diss. Women and Gender Studies, University of Regina, 2007.

Daly, Brenda O., and Maureen T. Reddy, eds. *Narrating Mothers: Theorizing Maternal Subjectivities*. Knoxville: University of Tennessee Press, 1991.

Davidson, Cathy N., and E. M. Broner, eds. *The Lost Tradition: Mothers and Daughters in Literature*. New York: Frederick Ungar, 1980.

Davies, Bronwyn. "The Concept of Agency: A Feminist Poststructuralist Analysis." *Social Analysis* 30 (1991): 42–53.

DiQuinzio, Patrice. *The Impossibility of Motherhood: Feminism, Individualism, and the Problem of Mothering*. New York: Routledge, 1999.

Donnell, Alison, and Pauline Polkey. *Representing Lives: Women and Auto/Biography*. New York: St. Martin's Press, 2000.

Douglas, Susan J., and Meredith Michaels. *The Mommy Myth: The Idealization of Motherhood and How It Has Undermined Women*. New York: New York: Free Press, 2004.

Dow Adams, Timothy. *Telling Lies in Modern American Autobiography*. Chapel Hill: University of North Carolina Press, 1990.

Eakin, Paul John. *Fictions in Autobiography: Studies in the Art of Self-Invention*. Princeton: Princeton University Press, 1985.

Ezell, Margaret J. M. *Writing Women's Literary History*. Baltimore: Johns Hopkins University Press, 1993.

Gilbert, Sandra M., and Susan Gubar. *The Norton Anthology of Literature by Women*. New York: W. W. Norton & Co., 1985.

Giorgio, Adalgisa, ed. *Writing Mothers and Daughters: Renegotiating the Mother in Western European Narratives by Women*. New York: Berghahn Books, 2002.

Glickman, Rose. *Daughters of Feminists: Young Women with Feminist Mothers Talk about Their Lives*. New York: St. Martin's Press, 1993.

Gordon, Tuula. *Feminist Mothers*. New York: New York University Press, 1990.

Gore, Ariel, and Bee Lavender. *Breeder: Real Life Stories from the New Generation of Mothers*. Seattle: Seal Press, 2001.

Green, Fiona. "Feminist Mothers: Successfully Negotiating the Tensions Between Motherhood and Mothering." *Mother Outlaws: Theories and Practices of Empowered Mothering*. Ed. Andrea O'Reilly. Toronto: Women's Press, 2004. 31–42.

Greenfield, Susan C. *Mothering Daughters: Novels and the Politics of Family Romance: Frances Burney to Jane Austen*. Detroit: Wayne State University Press, 2002.

Hansen, Elaine Tuttle. *Mother without Child: Contemporary Fiction and the Crisis of Motherhood*. Berkeley: University of California Press, 1997.

Hirsch, Marianne. *The Mother/Daughter Plot: Narrative, Psychoanalysis, Feminism*. Bloomington: Indiana University Press, 1989.

Ingman, Heather, ed. *Mothers and Daughters in the Twentieth Century: A Literary Anthology*. Edinburgh: Edinburgh University Press, 1999.

——. *Women's Fiction Between the Wars: Mothers, Daughters and Writing*. New York: St. Martin's Press, 1998.

Jeremiah, Emily. "Troublesome Practices: Mothering, Literature, and Ethics." *Mother Matters: Motherhood as Discourse and Practice*. Ed. Andrea O'Reilly. Toronto: ARM Press, 2004. 231–41.

Johnson, Miriam, *Strong Mothers, Weak Wives: The Search for Gender Equality*. Berkeley: University of California Press, 1989.

Lowinsky, Naomi Ruth. *Stories from the Motherline: Reclaiming the Mother–Daughter Bond, Finding Our Feminine Souls*. Los Angeles: Jeremy P. Tarcher, 1992.

MacCallum-Whitcomb, Susan. "Claiming Our Birth-Write: The Poetry of American Mothers." *This Giving Birth: Pregnancy and Childbirth in American Women's Writing*. Ed. Julie Tharp and Susan MacCallum-Whitcomb. Bowling Green: Bowling Green State University Popular Press, 2000. 39–54.

Malin, Jo. *The Voice of the Mother: Embedded Maternal Narratives in Twentieth-Century Women's Autobiographies*. Carbondale: Southern Illinois University Press, 2000.

Maushart, Susan. *The Mask of Motherhood: How Becoming a Mother Changes Our Lives and Why We Never Talk about It*. New York: Penguin Books, 1999.

Middleton, Amy. "Mothering Under Duress: Examining the Inclusiveness of Feminist Mothering Theory." *Journal of the Association for Research on Mothering* 8.1&2 (Summer/Winter 2006): 72–81.

Minh-ha, Trinh T. *Women, Native, Other: Writing Postcoloniality and Feminism*. Bloomington: Indiana University Press, 1989.

O'Reilly, Andrea. "Between the Baby and the Bathwater: Towards a Mother-Centred Theory and Practice of Empowered Mothering." *Journal of the Association for Research on Mothering* 8.1&2 (Summer/Winter 2006): 72–81.

——. "Feminist Mothering." *Maternal Theory: Essential Readings*. Ed. O'Reilly. Albany: Demeter Press, 2007. 792–821.

——, ed. *From Motherhood to Mothering: The Legacy of Adrienne Rich's* Of Woman Born. Albany: SUNY Press, 2004.

——, ed. *Mother Matters: Motherhood as Discourse and Practice*. Albany: ARM Press, 2004.

——, ed. *Mother Outlaws: Theories and Practices of Empowered Mothering*. Toronto: Women's Press, 2004.

——. *Rocking the Cradle: Thoughts on Motherhood, Feminism, and the Possibility of Empowered Mothering*. Albany: Demeter Press, 2006.

O'Reilly, Andrea, and Silvia Caporale-Bizzini, eds. Introduction. *From the Personal to the Political: Toward a New Theory of Maternal Narrative*. Selinsgrove, PA: Susquehanna University Press, 2009.

O'Reilly, Andrea, Marie Porter, and Patricia Short, eds. *Motherhood: Power and Oppression*. Toronto: Women's Press, 2005.

Parker, Rozsiska. "The Production and Purposes of Maternal Ambivalence." *Mothering and Ambivalence*. Ed. Wendy Hollway and Brid Feathersone. London: Routledge, 1997. 17–36.

Pearlman, Mickey, ed. *Mother Puzzles: Daughters and Mothers in Contemporary American Literature*. New York: Greenwood Press, 1989.

Podnieks, Elizabeth. *Daily Modernism: The Literary Diaries of Virginia Woolf, Antonia White, Elizabeth Smart, and Anaïs Nin*. Montreal and Kingston: McGill-Queen's University Press, 2000.

Rich, Adrienne. *Of Woman Born: Motherhood as Experience and Institution*. New York: W. W. Norton, 1986.

Ruddick, Sara. *Maternal Thinking: Toward a Politics of Peace*. 1989. Boston: Beacon Press, 2002.

Scott, Bonnie Kime, ed. *Gender in Modernism: New Geographies, Complex Intersections*. Urbana: University of Illinois Press, 2007.

Showalter, Elaine. *A Literature of Their Own: British Women Novelists from Brontë to Lessing*. Princeton: University Press, 1999.

Tharp, Julie, and Susan MacCallum-Whitcomb, eds. *This Giving Birth: Pregnancy and Childbirth in American Women's Writing*. Bowling Green, OH: Bowling Green University Popular Press, 2000.

Wagner-Martin, Linda. *Telling Women's Lives: The New Biography*. New Brunswick, NJ: Rutgers University Press, 1994.

Walker, Alice. *In Search of Our Mothers' Gardens*. London: Women's Press, 1984.

Woolf, Virginia. *A Room of One's Own*. London: HarperCollins, 1977.

Yu, Yi-Lin. *Mother, She Wrote: Matrilineal Narratives in Contemporary Women's Writing*. New York: Peter Lang, 2005.

Zinsser, William, ed. *Inventing the Truth: The Art and Craft of Memoir*. Boston: Houghton Mifflin, 1998.

Part 1: Maternal Absence

Aberrant, Absent, Alienated: Reading the Maternal in Jane Urquhart's First Two Novels, *The Whirlpool* and *Changing Heaven* | BY MYRL COULTER

Reading Jane Urquhart's early novels for their maternal representations reveals their critical commentary about the continuing impact of patriarchally determined views of motherhood and mothering on women's lives. Western society's concept of motherhood is still too much that of a "natural" human condition, an immanent, cohesive continuum infused with a reified, normative immutability that gives it deified status seemingly above contemplation or examination. Urquhart's novels reflect that continuum by presenting a decidedly pessimistic view of motherhood. Although written in the late twentieth and early twenty-first centuries, Urquhart's novels include no portrayals of "feminist mothering" or "mothering, freed from the institution of motherhood … [and] experienced as a site of empowerment, a location of social change" (O'Reilly, Introduction 2).

In her first novel, *The Whirlpool* (1986), Urquhart features two female protagonists: Maud Grady, a widowed mother of a young autistic son, and Fleda McDougal, a married woman with no children who spends the summer of 1889 living in a tent pitched above a turbulent whirlpool in the Niagara River. Moving into the twentieth century while continuing her exploration of nineteenth-century ideals in her second novel, *Changing Heaven* (1990), Urquhart pairs the narrative of a dead balloonist, Arianna Ether, who encounters Emily Brontë's ghost, with a contemporary story about an English literature scholar, Ann Frear, who is living and loving badly in

Toronto. With these two novels, Urquhart sets an almost relentlessly bleak pattern for her portrayals of traditional motherhood that continues throughout the four subsequent novels she has published at this point in her career. Her last published work, *A Map of Glass* (2005), features several contrasting mother portrayals, from the strikingly abject to the dutifully invisible, thus continuing an eloquent, yet gloomy, novelistic meditation on maternal situations.

With their consistent inclusion of various mother figures, Urquhart's narratives highlight the impact of the traditional and the historical on the current state of Western motherhood. Adrienne Rich forcefully takes issue with Western notions of motherhood in her milestone work, *Of Woman Born: Motherhood as Experience and Institution*, when she writes that "the patriarchal institution of motherhood is not the 'human condition' any more than rape, prostitution, and slavery are" (33). When it was first published in 1976, Rich's controversial work drew much attention to the rigid, normative status of mothers by situating "mothering" as the way in which individual women approach their responsibilities as mothers, and "motherhood" as an ideological creation with specific social functions, a creation formed not by women but by Western civilization's male-dominant society. More than a quarter of a century later, virtually all investigations into mothering and motherhood gesture to *Of Woman Born* because of its status as, in Andrea O'Reilly's words, "the first and arguably still the best feminist book on mothering and motherhood" (*From Motherhood to Mothering*).[1] This esteemed status not only points to the significance of Rich's text, but also illustrates that motherhood, an ideal determined by patriarchal traditions and its inherited history, is automatically linked by gender issues to the twentieth-century waves of feminism and their mandates to challenge patriarchal structures that limit and exploit opportunities for women. An institutional cornerstone for the organization of patriarchal societies, motherhood is, by its very intimacy in everyone's lives, often an uncomfortable target for feminists. Such foundational connections stipulate that feminism and motherhood continue to co-exist in a congenital relationship that is both intimate and conflicted.

Just as with the wide-ranging debates about the state of feminism in the twenty-first century, current discussions about motherhood and mothering are urgent, intense, and at times confusing. The increase in options made possible by the women's movements of the twentieth century has resulted in critical debates scrutinizing every aspect of maternal situations. In *The Impossibility of Motherhood: Feminism, Individualism, and the Problem of Mothering*, Patrice DiQuinzio recognizes that the tensions between feminism and mothering must be resolved: while "the issue of mothering often functions as a sort of lightning rod in feminist theory ... neither feminism nor feminist theory can afford to ignore the issue of mothering" (xi). For DiQuinzio, both feminism and mothering are dynamic processes that could work together toward a focused future based on diversity and inclusiveness that will result in cultural reform.

Feminist mothering is one such dynamic process. An approach to the maternal situation characterized by plurality and diversity, feminist mothering is "a counter narrative," one that is "determined more by what it is not (i.e., patriarchal motherhood) than by what it is" (O'Reilly, *Rocking the Cradle* 16). Working toward cultural change in both individual families and the wider social sphere, feminist mothering takes on this monumental task that must derail the overwhelming historical and traditional conditioning that weighs on continuing prevalent perceptions of motherhood. Because artistic literary production has always been at the forefront of all social and political movements, the production of literature by mothers is "a key tool in the redefinition of maternity in which feminists are engaged" (Jeremiah 7). Thus, interrogation of the literature produced in specific cultural moments and locations for its representations of women's lives, whether feminine, feminist, maternal, and nonmaternal, is key to further understanding of the intricate dance mothers must perform to live their lives.

Although her novels do not "redefine" the maternal, Urquhart's works are rich resources, well worth exploring for their representations of how powerful the past is and how deeply embedded it remains in contemporary cultural conventions. Except for *The Whirlpool*'s Maud, mothers in Urquhart's novels are usually dead, missing, relegated to the background, alienated from society, or suffering severe psychological distress. Despite this noticeable aspect of Urquhart's oeuvre, the subject of motherhood rarely appears in critical analysis of her work; indeed, very little critical analysis of Urquhart's work is even feminist in perspective. In their introduction to *Narrating Mothers: Theorizing Maternal Subjectivities*, Brenda O. Daly and Maureen T. Reddy refer to this type of critical gap as "feminist avoidance of the maternal," observing that "few fictional or theoretical works *begin* with the mother in her own right ... and those that do seldom hold fast to a maternal perspective" (2–3).

While some feminist critics may avoid Urquhart's work because its content is so overtly white and middle class, *The Whirlpool* especially merits feminist consideration because it features Maud Grady, a mother "in her own right," and sustains that focus throughout. While it can hardly be deemed a feminist representation, Maud's story offers an important perspective to take to all of Urquhart's work: in her novels, the female characters are vivid depictions of aberrant, absent, and/or alienated motherhood. One of the most important ways in which Western society classifies adult women is by whether or not they are mothers. Moreover, mothers themselves are categorized in the broadly terrifying groups as "good" or "bad" mothers. These groups determine where a mother fits in relation to motherhood: "in patriarchal culture, women who mother in the institution of motherhood are regarded as 'good' mothers, while women who mother outside or against the institution of motherhood are 'bad' mothers" (O'Reilly, Introduction 2). For Urquhart's female characters, mothering means motherhood, and not becoming a mother, or failing in executing that experience according to the parameters of patriarchal motherhood, means trouble is on its way.

In all her novels, Urquhart depicts those characters who are not appropriate mothers as sidelined or exiled from active life, trapped in servile positions, or simply not present. One character significantly defies this pattern: *The Whirlpool*'s Fleda McDougal simply vanishes from her life, exiting without an explanatory word or indication of where she will go, suggesting that women who choose not to become mothers must go into social exile. However, those women who do become mothers, according to Urquhart's novels, must be prepared for isolation and angst no matter how they engage with motherhood and conduct themselves as mothers. Deviations from expected maternal behaviour are punished, again by exile or death, and even those characters who engage in what outwardly appears as acceptable motherhood struggle with the constraints this idealized role places on them: for example, Maud Grady struggles in her relationship with her young autistic son, a strained bond plagued by disrupted connections. More intriguingly, those mothers who conform to motherhood's stipulations, such as Ann Frear's mother in *Changing Heaven*, become grotesque, unsympathetic characters who simply fade away, having left indelible damages on their offspring. Also in *Changing Heaven*, the ghostly Arianna Ether refers to her mother as "the absent flower" (71) who disappeared into an enchanted land far from the dreary reality of Arianna's colourless childhood in late Victorian London.

Mourning and motherhood go together from the outset in Urquhart's work. At the beginning of *The Whirlpool*, widow Maud Grady is wrapped in the required nineteenth-century categorical form for women who have lost their husbands to death. The novel's opening exposition explains why Maud spends two years contained by the stiff black crepe of her mourning attire. Maud's mourning wear is so restrictive that it limits her movements and leads her to develop a "fear of weather" (22) because even the smallest amount of precipitation bleeds black stains onto her skin. Moreover, this requisite uniform contains Maud in other ways: the "weepers" or black ribbons hanging from the "oppressive bonnet" restrict her movements, both physically and psychically, and the heavy veil dangerously impairs her vision, almost causing her to step unknowingly into the path of oncoming streetcars or carriages (28). As a widow, however, Maud does not succumb to fear or panic, but, with trepidation at first, takes over the funeral business. Showing surprising enterprise and grit despite her lack of experience, Maud manages to keep the funeral home staff in her employ by convincing them that "she intended to survive and that ... the business should continue as usual" (27). Soon she is comfortable handling the corporate challenges, managing the accounts, and holding "the pen as easily as a teaspoon in her hand" (28).

Maud does, however, suffer moments of alienation from the women of the area who make their feelings known through the loudly murmured comments that reach Maud's ears: "'Looking for business,' the town matrons would whisper as they had the first, and last, time [Maud] attempted to visit an ailing friend" (114). With the inclusion of intricate, seemingly secondary, details such as these, Urquhart demonstrates how women are not only monitored by the men in their lives, but are also policed by socially adherent women in their communities who punish through exclusion when they determine that one of their own has strayed from conventional notions of female behaviour. Despite her community's disapproval, Maud's inherited business becomes an avenue to autonomy for her, and her determined endeavour to survive on her own reveals the subtle workings of the social conflicts that surface when women of this time enter a predominantly male realm—business—even when that business is death.

The business of death is a family enterprise for Maud in enlightening ways. Both serving and observing family rituals in her capacity as undertaker offers Maud moments of thought-provoking pause. Sam, the funeral home's embalmer, tells Maud the story of delivering a casket for a young tuberculosis victim, a young woman who had been engaged to be married. According to Sam, the girl's mother insisted that her dying daughter be married before her death, so the ceremony was performed at the girl's bedside with the wedding dress lying on top of the rapidly weakening bride (148). Death comes almost immediately, and the girl is buried, not only with her wedding dress on top of her, but also with her entire trousseau wardrobe, stuffed into the casket by her grieving mother. The vision of the young girl resting eternally under the weight of her wedding wardrobe is too much for Maud, who is distressed by the story and cannot stop thinking about it:

> Maud carried Sam's story around with her for the rest of the day, thinking about costumes. Lord, she thought, they are always dressing you up as something and then you are not yourself anymore. This young girl, the frozen, immobilized bride, coerced into it and then dead and unable ever to grow beyond it. No one now would even remember her name. Anecdotally, she would always be the bride, the one who was married and buried in the same breath. (149)

This troubling incident adds to Maud's determination to maintain an independent life. She recognizes that the deaths of her husband and his parents have allowed her to escape the limbo-like existence that was her married life: from Maud's new perspective she sees that marriage is itself a form of burial.

In addition, Maud realizes that she must also escape another kind of internment, the mourning wardrobe that names her as widow: "Bride, wife, widow. She would not stop now" (149). The "frozen," "immobilized" bride is "encased in [a] form" not of her making, and the "real Courtauld crape" (22) Maud is forced to wear as designated widow stains her skin until she looks gangrenous. These visions are connected to each other by the notion of containment within patriarchal institutions, a confinement that is both literal and ideological. Faced with her situation as a widowed mother in the restrictive late nineteenth century, Maud despairs of the distinctly unmaternal feelings she has for her child:

> He was like an invisible wall she ran into daily, bruising herself with each contact, until the very knowledge of its existence brought her only a memory of pain. And anger in the presence of pain. Suddenly this anger spilled out of Maud's heart and into her body, adrenalin rushing like fire through her veins. Turning around with one whirling gesture, she grabbed the child by the hair. Now they were facing directly into the sun and Maud became blinded, both by its strength and the strength of her own emotion. (66)

For Maud, the child disrupts her unexamined understanding of what motherhood is and dispels the notion that her presence alone in his life should cure his ills, should spur him to normal communication. Also, Maud discovers that her status as a mother does not render her immune to feelings of anger and frustration, feelings that are not consistent with patriarchal ideals of good mothering.

Maud's child remains nameless throughout the entire novel, referred to only as "he" or "the child," as if he is representative of either that long lost state of childhood every human being once occupied and cannot recapture or a seer-like mystical figure whose purpose is to disrupt the indisputable. For Maud, her child is, at this point, an "it" that brings her to the point of painful anger and causes her frustrations to vent in an almost-violent act of grabbing and shaking. In doing so, she forces the child, and herself, toward a life-giving sun, in the hopes that maybe, just maybe, some form of communication will result. And it does. Maud shouts the word "sun" into her little boy's ear with same violence as she grabs his hair. Finally, with a shudder that racks his small body, the boy's inner barriers collapse and he groans out a response, a pain-racked, almost inhuman vocalization of "sun": "s-a-a-a-w-n," repeated by the little boy several times (67). Only then does Maud return to the gentle, expected form of mothering and release her child from the sun's blinding glare. Thus, Urquhart demonstrates that mothering is filled with hotspots that invoke unpredictable reactions and results and that are inconsistent with conventional notions of what makes a good mother. In my capacity as a first-year university English teacher, I have included *The Whirlpool* on my syllabus several times. Inevitably, my students react to Maud as a neglectful "bad" mother, someone they cannot reconcile with their views of how a "good" mother would handle a difficult child.

While Maud struggles with her business and her child, *The Whirlpool*'s other female protagonist, Fleda McDougal, resists her husband David's desire that she participate in his Laura Secord fetish[1] one moment and be the epitome of angelic wifehood the next. However, Fleda's conflict is not only with David, but also with her would-be neighbours. The local mavens who criticize Maud for visiting the sick out of business rather than charitable motives do not neglect to consider Fleda's strange behaviour. As they do with Maud's unusual entrepreneurial situation, the town's matrons cannot let Fleda's unwifely behaviour go unnoticed, primly commenting to their mates that "[Fleda] should be having babies and minding the house" (71), instead of camping out in the woods.

Although *The Whirlpool*'s narrative is set totally in the year 1889, Urquhart's subsequent novels follow a pattern in which a contemporary story is intertwined with or runs parallel to a narrative from the past. In this way, Urquhart brings the past and all its buried influences into the present, exposing the roots of contemporary institutions such as marriage, motherhood, and heterosexuality as socially established and dispelling the normative myths that surround them. In *Changing Heaven*'s contemporary narrative, Ann Frear's mother is a present, and highly unlikeable, figure, but in the parallel Victorian story, absent mothers are prominent, missing in their person yet very present in their daughters' memories. Emily Brontë's ghost comments that

> Mama died ... and Papa never mentioned her. Someone ... told me that he cut the arms off her best silk dress. I imagined her armless then. A woman without arms: one who could not sew or draw or write or cook or hold me. I imagined that she died from severed arms. (129)

In other words, in death, Emily Brontë's mother is no longer capable of doing the basic things that mothers are supposed to do and thus, having no other purpose, is erased from her father's vocabulary and not spoken of again. Obviously, however, the memory of a mother who once had arms lingers much longer than forbidden conversations would indicate, lingers even as the unheld child grows from child to woman to ghost. Urquhart's choice of *Wuthering Heights*' creator as a narrative character is somewhat ironic in that Emily Brontë, who never became a mother in her life, is often used as an example of a woman who chose between her creativity and the more travelled path of domesticity.

The memory of a mother is similar, yet different for Emily Brontë's ghostly companion, Arianna, who refers to her mother as "the absent flower" (71): "Mama died ... coughing in the morning.... They carried her away. Papa returned with a bottle" (129). This elegiac memory of an absent mother carried away by death and a present father disappearing into an alcoholic stupor stays with the young Polly White as she changes identities to become the doomed balloonist Arianna Ether. In a publicity-motivated transformation engineered by her lover, Jeremy Jacobs, Arianna's image is promoted as the "apotheosis" (26) of the "very spirit of British womanhood" (25). Jeremy's version of British womanhood is a rendition of Coventry Patmore's famous nineteenth-century narrative poem "The Angel in the House":

> Who are these women who help us, after all, if not angels? Should they not be given the power to fly like other angels? And if this is impossible for all, should not there be one who can represent the rest?
>
> Arianna Ether has chosen to perform this task, to ascend like an angel to heaven and then, with the aid of this wonder of modern invention, the parachute, to float, sylph-like, back to earth again in order to demonstrate the absolute purity, the *lightness* of the cleansed female soul. (25–26)

Urquhart's ironic tone is unmistakable here, as she creates the opposite of an apotheosis. Unbeknownst to Arianna, Jeremy has disabled her parachute and she will not "float, sylph-like, back to earth" from her balloon, but instead plummet to her death on the very moors that Emily Brontë and her unforgettable creation, Catherine Earnshaw, wandered. These two passages show how Urquhart represents both motherhood and womanhood as esteemed patriarchal institutions stripped of agency and elevated through contrived sentiments. Their apotheosis is a living death for those who must live within the confines of those institutions.

In the contemporary narrative that runs parallel to the Emily Brontë/Arianna Ether ghost story in *Changing Heaven*, Urquhart depicts the impact of Victorian womanhood/motherhood on contemporary Canadian mothers and daughters. Ann Frear's mother raises her daughter with a fear-based, dismissive kind of mothering that is distinctly aware of the future her maternal training will bring for her daughter. In her youth, Ann Frear is caught between an absent father and a stoic mother, a resigned figure of resentment who forces her daughter to go to a dance because she has "to start this nonsense sooner or later" (69). Wearing this resigned resentment like a proper Sunday dress, Ann's mother is a murky maternal character who uneasily sentences her daughter to continue the traditional social cycle: mothers train daughters to perpetuate a system that works against their best interests.

As a child, Ann rides in her mother's car, asking questions about the world she sees around her. Travelling the overpasses and highways of southern Ontario, Ann spies what she sees as a colourful brass band: "Mummy, we have to stop and watch it!" she says. Ann's mother will have nothing to do with her daughter's enthusiasm and replies, "This isn't the kind of road you can ever stop on" (46). That suggestion of fear continues to mould Ann's transition from childhood to womanhood. Off to a church dance for the first time, Ann fears that she will not be asked to dance; her mother, however, has other fears for her daughter and thrusts a "pepper pot" into Ann's hand, telling her to stash it in her purse and use it if one of "them" tries "something" (68). This scene re-enacts images of anxious mid-twentieth-century mothers who nervously warned their daughters against vague dangers from the opposite sex without actually saying what those dangers were or how to recognize them. Urquhart captures the very ambiguity of disillusioned motherhood: mothers who must conspire to induce their female offspring to accept a social order that has already betrayed them and requires them to betray their daughters for its continuance. Urquhart makes her ambiguous references last and work beyond the moment. After that evening, Ann, who did not dance but also never had need to use the pepper pot, asks her mother if she ever used it: "'No,' replies her mother, 'unfortunately'" (69). In that terse response, Urquhart shows that with betrayal comes bitterness and resentment.

These two novels set the tone for maternal commentary in Urquhart's oeuvre thus far: because mothers in her novels are usually absent or in severe distress, they stand in stark contrast to the rhapsodic odes that govern popular assumptions associated with the modern maternal icon. Motherhood in crisis is a recursive theme in Urquhart's novels; thus, they form a collective reflection of the disparity between heralded ideals of mothering and the lived conflicts those ideals inflame when individual lives do not conform to the unexamined assumptions that dominate mainstream values. Potent recurring themes and intriguing secondary characters speak to the diversity of the lived Canadian experience, and demonstrate how Canadian social complexities and experience have been and continue to be influenced by European roots and connections. Yet, even with the thematic diversity present in her writing, women's issues find prominence in all the novels. A sadness pervades her entire body of work, and much of that sadness comes from portrayals, or rather nonportrayals, of mothers and motherhood: very few characters in her novels have living mothers, and very few characters in her novels become mothers. Interviews with Urquhart reveal no particular biographical source for this sadness, and to date, she has produced no memoir or other designated autobiographical text. Still, its presence is unmistakable. Those characters who do become mothers in these novels often have very difficult, traumatic experiences with motherhood. The result is that each one of Urquhart's fictional mothers brings a unique sensibility of experience, one that depicts the Canadian social order as a disorder where plurality of perspective must replace repressive notions of assigned identity categories and impossible universality.

When the childless Fleda McDougal of *The Whirlpool* simply walks out of her own story, Urquhart strongly implies that women who choose not to become mothers must leave the conventional social arena: "Departure. She could no longer live the closeted life of the recent past. And she could not live, forever, in the dream house of this grey, obsessive landscape" (218). For Fleda, the option of staying, of continuing to fulfill the role expected of her, is not viable. She becomes the absent nonmother who did not wait for absence through death, choosing instead an invisible life of self-determined direction. Thus, Urquhart's first two novels illustrate how social conventions punish aberrations from expected maternal behaviour by exile or death; those characters who do become mothers must be prepared for isolation and angst no matter how they engage with their status as beings absorbed into the institution of motherhood.

Urquhart's sixth and most recent work, *A Map of Glass*, depicts several strikingly different versions of motherhood that are connected by intricate imbrications of history, place, and marriage. *A Map of Glass* features contrasting mother portrayals and also a female character who is not a mother, but whose presence allows for productive comparison. Jerome McNaughton is a Toronto artist who remembers his mother as frozen in an abusive relationship. Memories of the emotional violence of his parents' marriage haunt him in his adult life. His memory includes camping trips in which his father would find the intrusions of civilization into the wilderness environment personally insulting, and take that insult out on his mother, "berat[ing] [her] about the food she had brought, her recent haircut, and the way she looked in a swimsuit" (15). For Jerome, the image of "his mother standing quietly by the water with her imperfect flesh exposed" (15) colours his childhood memories as "tawdry, embarrassing, something to be quickly discarded and forgotten" (15–16). Despite continuing memories of his childhood home, such as his parents' bedroom, with "the decorative lampshades and doilies that were his mother's sad attempt to bring some intimacy and joy into this corner of her life" (64), Jerome protects himself with a veneer of indifference, one that gives him an impenetrability both as lover and artist. He develops a strange relationship with 53-year-old Sylvia Bradley, the disaffected woman who leaves the safety of her husband's home to find out more about her lover's death from Jerome, the person who discovered Andrew Woodman's body floating on an ice floe in the St. Lawrence River.

Sylvia has a mysterious social disability that Urquhart does not clarify, much like Maud's child's vague affliction in *The Whirlpool*. Taken to doctors in the big city as a child, she refuses the doctor's doll play treatment, and "develop[s] ways to shut out the doctor, her mother, the dollhouse" (40). Her resolute closure to treatment and silence in the doctor's presence earn Sylvia her mother's disapproval: "she knew her punishment would be her mother's anger, her mother's refusal to look at her all the way home on the train" (41). The punishment continues after she is put to bed that night, as she "hear[s] the adult argument begin, her own name tossed back and forth between her mother and father long into the night" (41).

In a telling description of patriarchal motherhood, Sylvia reflects on the physical contact between her mother and herself, and knows that "her mother's few attempts at embraces had been meant to restrain her, to cause her to stop doing something, or to move her in a direction other than the one she had wanted to take" (70). Urquhart depicts Sylvia's mother as not only acquiescing to her husband's control over her and her daughter, but also surreptitiously contributing to Sylvia's lack of life possibilities in a role that implies hidden motives of jealousy or resentment. When Malcolm, the young doctor who will become Sylvia's husband, comes to dinner at her parents' home, he suggests that Sylvia could perhaps work part time in his office:

> Her father seemed pleased; her mother had looked irritated, doubtful. "Sylvia will never be able to maintain a job," she said. Malcolm had bristled. "She could most certainly maintain a part-time job," he said, "even after she is married."
>
> "Good lord," her mother had replied briskly, "who could ever have the patience for that?" She was not referring to the job. (84)

Sylvia's mother is an irritating character, steeped in resentment and self-interest, somewhat reminiscent of Ann Frear's mother in *Changing Heaven*. Her ideas of her daughter's future are determined by what she thinks her daughter will not be able to do, including becoming what her mother is supposed to produce, another wife and mother.

Sylvia's mother harbours the same sexual repressiveness that Ann Frear's mother instilled in her daughter. When talk turns to marriage between Sylvia and Malcolm, talk welcomed and even brokered by her father, Sylvia's mother turns on her daughter one night in the kitchen:

> She had spun around angrily from her place at the sink, suds and water dripping from her hands. "You'll have to let him touch you," she had hissed in the direction of her daughter. "You'll have to let him touch you in ways you can't even imagine. And you have never, never let me, your father, or anyone else touch you. You won't be able to do it, and he'll leave, and we'll all be worse off than before." (86)

Thus, for her mother, Sylvia is a social liability; for Sylvia, her mother is a "dark and pulsing presence" (91) who instills fears in her daughter instead of examining the fears in herself. The story is a puzzling one, however, in that Sylvia does not have to deal with unwanted touching from Malcolm. He is the epitome of a tolerant husband, who promises his wife that he will never touch her until she wants him to. Sylvia decides early on that she will never want him to, and that determines the tenor of their marriage: contented, but platonic. Urquhart's narrator does not clearly state what induces Sylvia to enter into a love affair with Andrew Woodman, but the suggestion is that, under the layers of undiagnosed mysterious ailments she suffers from, Sylvia is a woman of agency with physical desires and a need for intimacy that could be deemed completely "normal."

In the parallel nineteenth-century story that Sylvia brings to Jerome by way of Andrew's diary, the history of the Woodman family and their ship-building industry comes to light. This diary forms the second part of the novel, and it shifts the perspective of the story from Sylvia to Andrew. In true genealogy fashion, he begins as far back in his family tree as he can go: his great-great-grandfather. The entries are serial family events: births, marriages, pregnancies, and deaths, not necessarily in that order, but including an interesting spinster, Annabelle Woodman. Early on in the genealogy, the Woodman family hires an orphan girl, Marie, when Annabelle and her brother, Branwell,[2] are still children. Marie ultimately rises from servant status to wife with an unexpected pregnancy and a forced separation from Branwell. Eventually, with Annabelle's help, Branwell and Marie are married and raise their son together. From the beginning, Annabelle finds herself drawn to Marie and sets out to befriend her. Years later, Annabelle will view her childhood friend and, ultimately, sister-in-law, Marie, as "her other, her more beautiful self," feeling that "their two bodies would overlap and become three-dimensional like the twinned images on the photo cards she slipped into the stereoscope on Sunday afternoons" (178). Although Marie never seems to fit into her new life location, remains definitively interclass, and slides into the narrative background as a static, flat character, Annabelle's sense of Marie as the other half of her inner self continues as they grow into womanhood.

Annabelle takes on the spinster role of caring for her widower father in his declining years, and Marie takes the traditional route of becoming a wife and mother. Years later, on Marie's death, Annabelle feels utter grief and shame at not being available as her "better, more beautiful self, lay trembling on the edge of death" (276). But Marie's death had been a while in coming, her existence slowly being buried under the sand that inundated her home as a result of the faulty agricultural practices of her son and other farmers who grow nothing but the profitable barley crop on their fields, never rotating them, depleting the soil and its nutrients. After her death, Branwell feels his wife's loss most deeply when standing in her kitchen, the heart of her world:

> Her beautiful cook stove, The Kitchen Queen, stood unlit in the kitchen, its decorative features and its copper boiler cold and unpolished.... The last time he had opened one of the ovens, he had been appalled by the sight of the tiny dunes that had formed inside it, and the excess sand that descended like a pale brown curtain to the floor. (281)

While Branwell misses his wife's domestic presence, the narrative suggests that it is Annabelle who reads more deeply into the filling of Marie's stove with sand. Annabelle is the one who survives, the classic spinster figure: not wife, not mother, but resourceful, dutiful daughter. Somehow Annabelle stands as the most contented character of all at the end of the story.

From Marie and Sylvia to Ann and Arianna to Maud and Fleda, Urquhart creates female characters who demonstrate the lived impacts of their maternal situations. For readers of Urquhart's novels, the maternal characters they depict refute still popular idealized visions of motherhood consistent with obvious, indisputable "inherent goodness or justness."[3] The sadness that pervades Urquhart's entire body of work finds its source largely in the maternal portrayals it offers. Because motherhood in crisis is a recursive theme in her work, it constitutes a collective reflection of the disparity between heralded ideals of mothering and the lived conflicts those ideals inflame when individual lives do not conform to the unexamined assumptions that attempt to dominate mainstream values. Together, Urquhart's novels form a complex reflection about issues associated with mothering today. Western society's version of the maternal figure wraps her in idealized, inherited assumptions. Jane Urquhart's novels show that, while the twenty-first-century conditions of women's lives in the Western world may feel "post-feminist," these improved conditions are relatively recent, highly tenuous, and still in conflict with deeply embedded institutional conventions such as those attached to the words "mother" and "motherhood."

Notes to Chapter 1

1   Fleda's husband is Major David McDougal, an army historian who is an expert in the War of 1812's Battle of Lundy Lane. He is also obsessed with Laura Secord and at one point admits that he married Fleda because she looks like the Laura Secord he dreams about.

2   Not insignificantly given Urquhart's previously demonstrated interest in and admiration for Emily Bronte, Branwell's name comes from Bronte's beloved troubled brother, although Urquhart's narrative specifically denies that the family's ambitious original patriarch, Joseph Woodman, "would commemorate the dissolute brother of the by then famous Bronte sisters as he had never, to anyone's knowledge, read a work of fiction" (156).

3   This phrase is found in the 2004 edition of the *Canadian Oxford Dictionary* as part of its definition of "motherhood."

Works Cited

Daly, Brenda O., and Maureen T. Reddy, eds. Introduction. *Narrating Mothers: Theorizing Maternal Subjectivities*. Knoxville: University of Tennessee Press, 1991. 1–18.

DiQuinzio, Patrice. *The Impossibility of Motherhood: Feminism, Individualism, and the Problem of Mothering*. New York: Routledge, 1999.

Jeremiah, Emily. "Troublesome Practices: Mothering, Literature, and Ethics." *Mothering and Literature: Journal of the Association for Research on Mothering* 4.2 (Fall/Winter 2002): 7–16.

"Motherhood." *The Canadian Oxford Dictionary*. 2nd ed. Ed. Katherine Barber. Toronto: Oxford University Press, 2004. 1011.

O'Reilly, Andrea. *From Motherhood to Mothering: The Legacy of Adrienne Rich's* Of Woman Born. Albany: State University of New York Press, 2004.

——. Introduction. *Mother Outlaws: Theories and Practices of Empowered Mothering*. Ed. Andrea O'Reilly. Toronto: Women's Press, 2004. 1–28.

——. *Rocking the Cradle: Thoughts on Motherhood, Feminism and the Possibility of Empowered Mothering*. Toronto: Demeter Press, 2006.

Rich, Adrienne. *Of Woman Born: Motherhood as Experience and Institution*. 1976. New York: W. W. Norton & Company, 1986.

Urquhart, Jane. *Changing Heaven*. Toronto: McClelland & Stewart, 1990.

——. *A Map of Glass*. Toronto: McClelland & Stewart, 2005.

——. *The Whirlpool*. Toronto: McClelland & Stewart, 1986.

2

Motherless Daughters: The Absent Mothers in Margaret Atwood | BY NANCY PELED

The world of women is a place where you are unsafe, but girls cannot turn to their mothers for comfort because "between us and them is a gulf, an abyss that goes down and down. It is filled with wordlessness." (*Cat's Eye* 98)

Margaret Atwood's writing concerns itself with the female identity and how that identity is subjected to social expectations. These may confuse, restrain, and anger many of the protagonists in her novels. Again and again, she deals with the pain of becoming and being a woman. Atwood's novels are often narratives told in the classic fairy-tale tradition, as defined by Lutz Rohrich in the introduction to *Fairy Tales and Society*: they mirror "a world view" that "reflect[s] the society in which it is told ... [and contain] astonishing relics and role constraints in connection with gender from the patriarchal realm.... Negative female stereotypes reveal themselves particularly in the female antagonistic roles of wicked stepmother or witch" (3–6). Some of the more blatant witch characters people *Cat's Eye* (1989), *The Robber Bride* (1994), and *The Blind Assassin* (2001). In these novels, Atwood's protagonists suffer so relentlessly at the hands of such antagonistic females that reading their stories is painful. Using a psychoanalytical/feminist approach, I examine how the absent mothers of Elaine, Cordelia, and Carol (*Cat's Eye*); Tony, Roz, and Charis (*The Robber Bride*); and Iris and Laura (*The*

Blind Assassin), manifest a classic fairy-tale motif and thus are culpable yet blameless enactors of their daughters' suffering.

Elaine Risley, the protagonist of *Cat's Eye*, is a successful painter who has returned to Toronto, the city of her youth, for a retrospective exhibition of her work. This event is the catalyst for Elaine to begin a retrospective of her own life, in an attempt to define who she has become. The journey eight-year-old Elaine embarks on toward womanhood, led and shared by her "friends" Cordelia, Grace, and Carol, is devastating. However, she is entirely dependent on Cordelia, Grace, and Carol to help her navigate this new world, for her own mother cannot help her; she is "different" from the other mothers, and unavailable to her. Thus Elaine enters into the milieu of destructive female relationships, one from which her mother cannot, or will not, protect her. *The Robber Bride* relates the story of three middle-aged women who have become friends through their shared devastating experiences at the hands of the malicious Zenia. The attempts of Tony, Roz, and Charis in *Robber Bride* to deal with the machinations and ramifications of Zenia in their lives distress us. And because, as Atwood tells us in *Cat's Eye*, "you don't look back along time but down through it, like water. Sometimes this comes to the surface, sometimes that.... Nothing goes away" (3), each woman's childhood experiences illuminate how the lack of mothering in their early years shaped the women who became vulnerable to the predatory Zenia. And reading Iris's narrative of how she and Laura are manipulated and abused in *Blind Assassin* generates an anxiety that equals the characters'.

The frame narrative of this multifaceted chronicle has the 82-year-old protagonist, Iris Chase Griffen, recording her memories for her initially unidentified audience, as a "re-envisioned" version of the past. The novel begins with Laura's death, so that in telling their story, Iris is resurrecting Laura. Given that Iris begins with Laura's death, she first goes back in their personal history, and thus explicates how their mother's death positions Iris as Laura's mother, assigning Iris the role of both victim and agent of "bad" mothering. In these novels we are taken into the characters' pasts, through a seamless "weaving" narrative technique that Atwood has perfected, with the past playing a smoothly integral role in the present story, much as it does in life. All these female characters suffer from some form of lack of mothering. Whether the mother is truly, physically absent—she has died, she has left, she has been institutionalized—or metaphorically so—she has no awareness of, or influence on, her daughter's life—her absence has a ruinous effect on her daughter, which is then compounded or refracted, or re-created in the daughter's relations with others as portrayed in the events of the novel, not least of which is with her own daughter if she becomes a mother herself. The fairy-tale allusions in these Atwood novels reverberate strongly, for a constant motif of these ubiquitous texts is the death of the princess's mother when the tale begins, leaving the young female vulnerable to manipulation by the usurping stepmother and/or witch. In fairy tales, happiness is promised when the princess marries the prince. In Atwood's novels, finding the prince—or having him find the princess/protagonist—is not the happy ending. That comes when the central character finds *herself*. Atwood's mothers are both accountable and helpless when happiness eludes these princesses.

The silence between mother and daughter that Elaine is referring to in the quotation from *Cat's Eye* above essentially manifests the "absent mother" of Lacanian-influenced psychological feminist theory. The source of identity is positioned in the loss of the pre-Oedipal mother (in Freudian terms), the "imaginary" state that Lacan defined as prelinguistic. In the introduction to their book *The [M]other Tongue*, editors Garner, Kahane, and Sprengnether explain that "Lacanians translate maternal loss into the more general concept of originary loss, of a lack in the subject [i.e., identity] displaced and veiled by language but persisting as unconscious desire" (21). Atwood's protagonists yearn for their mothers' comforting presence, explanations, and support. But in Atwood's novels women are often the principle enforcers of the "law of the father" both in the literal and the Lacanian sense:

> [In] Lacan's complex narrative ... the child desires to be what the mother desires. But both mother and child are themselves already located within the symbolic order of language and culture, in which the mother's desire is governed by the "law of the Father" ... [which] enjoins the subject to line up according to an opposition, man/woman, to assume its place as "he" or "she" in a preexisting order of language and culture. (21)[1]

What Hélène Cixous refers to as man's "greatest crime against women,... [leading] them to hate women" (248), is essential to the horror inherent in *The Handmaid's Tale* (1985), and to the protagonist's experiences in *Alias Grace* (1996). In the three novels I discuss, the mother, or mother substitute, is invested in propagating the "law of the father" and functions as an enforcer of social norms that denigrate women, to the detriment of her daughter. Mothers may intend to love and protect but in fact fall short as a result of their own powerlessness in the social dynamic of the family. Or, conversely, mothers may withhold their protection out of the belief that this is for their daughters' own good, having internalized the viewpoint that *"true woman* signifies submission" (Ostriker 6).

In *Cat's Eye*, Elaine, as narrator, expresses a yearning desire on behalf of the four young friends to understand what being a woman will mean, to have their fears abated, explained away with a mother's comforting words. But "lacking a language that can articulate their experience, women are left mute or mimics" (Garner, Kahane, and Sprengnether 23). The "abyss" Elaine refers to reflects that lack; their mothers' powerlessness is manifested in the things they do *not* say. Their place has been predetermined in the cultural order, and because the mothers in *Cat's Eye* cannot change that preexisting order, they are dedicated to being its guardians.

Elaine meets Cordelia, her childhood nemesis, at a particularly vulnerable time in her life. She has come to live in Toronto, after spending her first eight years roaming the woods in northern Ontario with her entomologist father, because of whom the whole family led a nomadic, half-wild existence. It is a lifestyle Elaine describes as "irregular and slightly festive" (*Cat's Eye* 30), and, essentially, Elaine has grown up in another culture, one that has not prepared her for the suburban life of postwar Toronto. In this social and gender-defined environment, Elaine is an alien, one who has no knowledge of the accepted local customs and modes of behaviour. "I see there's a whole world of girls and their doings that has been unknown to me," she confides to her readers early in the tale (*Cat's Eye* 57).

Initially, her guides into this strange, new world are Carol Campbell and Grace Smeath; Cordelia moves into their neighbourhood during the first summer after Elaine's family moves to Toronto. With Cordelia's entrance into the girls' lives, circumstances subtly, quickly, and irrevocably begin to change. These changes occur in what popular psychology terms the "latent period," ages eight to eleven, the time of transition of the mother-dependent child into peer-influenced preteen, ensuring that Elaine's experience will shape the development of her mature identity.

Cordelia is quickly established as a leader and a transgressor. She enacts what Howells calls an "unconscious resistance to her social destiny" (16) and is unable to comply with the expectations her family place upon her, which mimic society's expectations of women in general. When the girls are young and first meet Cordelia's sisters, Cordelia tells them that her sisters are gifted. "I ask Cordelia if she is gifted, but she puts her tongue in the corner of her mouth and turns away" (*Cat's Eye* 77), the first indication that there is something disappointing about Cordelia. Unlike her sisters she is less able to do what she likes without "disappointing Mummie.... This is what Mummie says when she's angry: 'I'm disappointed in you.' If she gets very disappointed, Cordelia's father will be called into it, and that is serious. None of the girls [in Cordelia's family] jokes or drawls when mentioning him" (*Cat's Eye* 77). When the girls are older, Cordelia fails a grade. It is her older sister who rebukes her: "Pull up your socks Cordelia, or you'll flunk your year again. You know what Daddy said last time" (*Cat's Eye* 224). For Cordelia, as for all women, "disappointing" the Father is a dangerous position to be in.

Through Cordelia's experiences and behaviour we recognize the responsibility that women bear for perpetuating female subordination when they themselves enforce the patriarchal status quo. Cordelia's "bad behaviour" is her response to the social pressures she faces daily at home and at school to live up to expectations that are contrary to her desires. In her environment, as in most women's experience, the majority of these "patriarchal enforcers" are mother, sisters, and female teachers, and as such are responsible for the outcome: unhappy little girls whose feelings of abjection are acted out against a weaker target than themselves. In *Cat's Eye*, this is Elaine. Cordelia later confesses to Elaine, "I used to think that if I kept very still and out of the way and didn't say anything, I would be safe.... I used to get into trouble a lot, with Daddy. When he would lose his temper. You never knew when he was going to do it. 'Wipe that smirk off your face,' he would say. I used to stand up to him" (*Cat's Eye* 271).

"Outside," Cordelia takes control where she can to compensate for her powerlessness within her own home. She becomes the one who decides not only what the girls will do, but how and when. In other words, she executes the patriarchal code among her friends. She dictates the rules of behaviour, the dress codes, and the acceptable activities for the little group. The "voice of Cordelia" tells Elaine when she may or may not join the group (*Cat's Eye* 125). The voice of Cordelia mimics the voice of the Father, awarding or denying social acceptance, which is, in essence, love. Although it is Elaine who will become the focus of Cordelia's scorn, and the victim of her manipulative power, Grace and Carol's complicity in an "educational program" for Elaine reflects their own powerlessness to protest in the face of Cordelia's enactment of what is patriarchally sanctioned. "Every time I do something wrong, a stack of plates comes crashing down. I can see these plates. Cordelia can see them too, because she's the one who says *Crash!*... 'Wipe that smirk off your face,' says Cordelia. I say nothing" (*Cat's Eye* 183). In using her father's identical words to rebuke Elaine, Cordelia guards and enforces the very norms she herself fails to meet, allowing us to recognize them as societal rules for all proper female deportment. And the girls' mothers are nowhere to be seen.

Every one of the girls undergoes similar inculcation. When Carol (aged 11) is caught wearing lipstick her mother is appalled, and "right in front of us she scrubs Carol's face with the dirty dishcloth. 'Don't let me catch you doing such a cheap thing again! ... Just wait till your father comes home!' her mother says in a cold, furious voice. 'Making a spectacle of yourself,' as if there's something wrong in the mere act of being looked at" (175–76). Carol's mother cannot allow Carol to discover that making herself attractive will give her power over men; her job is to ensure Carol understands her place as a woman in a man's world. All the girls' mothers, except perhaps Elaine's, and Cordelia's sisters have internalized and accepted their place in this society, and this frightens the young protagonists:

> Whatever has happened to them, bulging them, softening them, causing them to walk rather than run, as if there's some invisible leash around their necks, holding them back—whatever it is may happen to us too. We look surreptitiously at the breasts of women on the street, of our teachers; though not of our mothers, that would be too close for comfort. We examine our legs and underarms for sprouting hairs, our chests for swellings. But nothing is happening; so far we are *safe*. (97; emphasis added)

For J. Brooks Bouson, a "bad mother" in an Atwood novel is one who "acts as a guardian and enforcer of the patriarchal codes that confine and injure women [and] acts as [a] dangerous and destructive force in the life of the heroine.... The fact that the good mother is dead or absent points to the potency of the bad mother in Atwood's fictional world" (11–12). The mothers in *Cat's Eye* do not have an identity other than as "the object of the infant's desire or the matrix from which he or she develops an infant subjectivity. The mother herself as speaking subject ... is missing" (Bouson 25).

Even when the mothers are physically present, the girls are intimidated into silence: "We can't ask our mothers. It's hard to ... think of them as having bodies at all, under their dresses. There's a great deal they don't say.... The world is dirty no matter how much they clean and we know they will not welcome our grubby little questions" (*Cat's Eye* 98). Thus their mothers are as good as absent, and this missing mother is a prerequisite for the appearance of the surrogate mother, who, in fairy-tale tradition, is always evil. Cordelia steps into the void left by Elaine's "absent" mother—indeed, Bouson points out that her mother's physical body is all but erased from the text (171)—as an extension of her own "bad mothers" (for Cordelia's sisters also function as mothers for Cordelia), and in this role of surrogate mother she terrorizes Elaine. This terror is redolent of more than just the fears of a child being bullied and threatened; it is representative, as Bouson explains, of the "cultural terrors implicit in fulfilling the prescribed roles of dutiful daughter or passive wife or ... sexual object or female victim" (11). These fears obtain in most of Atwood's texts, and as we shall see, they are integral in *The Robber Bride* and *The Blind Assassin*. Of course, many feminist psychoanalytic theorists resent the implicit marginalization of women in Lacan's theories, which privilege the phallus. Both Hélène Cixous and Julia Kristeva propone the theory that female sexuality is directly connected to poetic creativity. For Kristeva, the semiotic discourse closely parallels pre-Oedipal "language" (actually nonlanguage, or "babble"). Language retains traces of the semiotic, and the female artist is especially sensitive to recovering these traces in their work. This is expressed here in Atwood's description of the relationship between the girls and their mothers as "filled with wordlessness." Cixous' "écriture feminine" is meant to be represented in literary writing by women—women who "write their bodies." That Elaine's mother is so conspicuously physically absent is one example in *Cat's Eye* that points to the need for this celebration of the female body.

Elaine's adult memories of this horrific time in her childhood are interspersed with almost unconscious reflections on her mother, whose silence was tantamount to Elaine's own, and while Elaine never shares with her mother what she is experiencing, she secretly longs for her mother to rescue her: "What would I have done if I had been my mother? She must have realized what was happening to me, or that something was.... If it were happening now, to a child of my own, I would know what to do. But then? There were fewer choices and *a great deal less was said*" (*Cat's Eye* 160; emphasis added). And yet later in the novel when Elaine remembers her mother communicating, albeit indirectly, that she sees Elaine is suffering, Elaine is afraid that her mother will do something and it will be the wrong something, thus making things worse for Elaine. She does not take advantage of the moment to involve her mother. Finally her mother hugs her, saying, "I wish I knew what to do." For Elaine this only validates her own silence: "Now I know what I've been suspecting: as far as this thing is concerned, she is powerless" (168). This is a devastating indictment of her mother.

In the end, Elaine seems unable to forgive her mother because she is "held back" (420), and in describing this moment she uses the same term ("held back") she used when describing the girls' fears of what having breasts would do to them (97) . Wordlessness itself prevents her from being truly close to her mother, even as her mother is dying from an *unnamed* disease (414), as if wordlessness itself is a female affliction to be feared. This silence manifests for Elaine her mother's inability to support her. Her absence from Elaine's childhood motivates Elaine to treat her own girls "sensibly"—they have sensible names, and Elaine knows they have made sensible choices "so different from many of my own" (15). In creating a normal childhood for her own daughters, Elaine finally expiates her mother's inadvertent sins, and her presence in her daughters' lives compensates for her mother's absence in her own.

The Robber Bride relates the story of Tony, Charis, and Roz, who have become friends because Zenia manipulated them, won their sympathies and trust, and then betrayed them, "stealing" their men. Each of their stories is related to us in a memory-ordered chronology from present to past to present, and each narrative not only covers a specific period of time in which the character interacts with Zenia, but also includes a journey back into a dark childhood, where, like Elaine, each woman must face the abuse she suffered. Tony, Charis, and Roz are similar to other Atwoodian heroines, having grown up with a "missing" mother whose absence has made the character vulnerable to the manipulations of a predator like Zenia. This "recurring trauma" (Bouson 11) is part of Atwood's narrative strategy of investigating "the effects on women of not having legitimised power. The lack can turn them into victims or manipulators" (Howells 17). *The Robber Bride* is populated with both. Furthermore, in Bouson's view, "Atwood's fiction is governed by the compulsion to repeat because it deals with the basic fears and persisting conflicts that plague women in a male-dominant culture" (12). Indeed these fears pervade most Atwood texts, and dominantly so in the three novels under discussion. Thus Atwood is able to demonstrate that although women have achieved many advancements in Western society at the end of the twentieth century (both Tony and Roz are successful professionals: Tony as an academic and Roz as a businesswoman), the traumas of the past continue to influence a woman's psychic environment. In keeping with psychological realism, Atwood expresses the distress that accompanies a modern woman's ambition to "have it all" through the function of that modern woman's mother, who is still confined by the dictates of earlier patriarchal codes. And the experiences of each daughter as a young girl shape, often fatefully, their adult lives. Atwood's characters in *The Robber Bride* are not free from the identity confusion that afflicts women who were raised in one cultural climate, yet aspire to belong to the present, more enfranchised environment in which they are living. As mothers themselves they must navigate ever more complex waters in order to raise their daughters to be stronger women than they have become.

The absent mother for whom each protagonist yearns is foregrounded by Atwood in her use of multiple names, as if one is for the mother and one for the daughter:[2] Tony / Antonia Fremont / Tnomerf Ynot; Roz Andrews / Rosalind Greenwood / Roz Grunwald; Charis/Karen.[3] As Howells points out, each character has been split, reflecting what Alison Light, writing about Daphne Du Maurier's *Rebecca*, says "demarcates a feminine subjectivity which is hopelessly split within bourgeois gendered relations ... [where the definitions of femininity] are never sufficient and are always reminders of what is missing" (177). Tony is not only ambidextrous—a meritorious adjective for today's multitasking woman—but since childhood has spoken and written backwards: "It's her seam, it's where she's sewn together; it's where she could split apart" (*Robber Bride* 19). Charis appears when Karen is raped by her uncle; she was "split in two" (263). And when Roz's father returned from the Second World War, her life "was cut in two" (332) when she discovered he was Jewish. "What is missing" in each woman's identity occupies the metaphorical gap where they have "split," and it is here that Zenia operates, "on this edge of desire and lack" (Howells 83). She can do this because each protagonist has been irrevocably scarred by her mother's absence, and the moment of abandonment remains an integral and vulnerable part of each woman's identity. Thus an element of Zenia's power over the women lies in her "ability to create and inspire powerful self-narratives ... [functioning] like a therapist or the mother during infancy ... to create ... a place of safety where it is possible to move freely between fantasy and reality" (Perrakis 156). Like the innocent young protagonists of the classical fairy tale who are duped by the wicked witch into entering her realm, or allowing her into theirs,[4] Tony, Charis, and Roz hold on to their fantasy image of Zenia because she is what "they most desire and dread to be" (Howells 81), until they are forced to recognize the truth of her malicious intent. In this psychological realm of experience, there can be no forearming against what is essentially oneself, a legacy from the mother whose initial abandonment destroyed that "place of safety" mothers are meant to provide their children.

Thus all three women are adults with fragmented identities who need to integrate the various pieces of their "selves" in order to "move beyond otherness and difference toward likeness" (Howells 168). In this, for the first time in an Atwood novel, the female protagonists are not alone, but help and support one another in a narrative that reflects both the nurturing and the injurious aspects of female–female relationships, and in part they replace the absent mothers of their childhood.

Each one of them fantasizes about killing Zenia and comes very close to accomplishing this. The magically realistic narrative style Atwood employs to describe Charis's final encounter with Zenia intentionally misleads the reader into believing that Charis has, indeed, killed her (*Robber Bride* 429). In those moments of rage that lead Tony, Charis, and Roz to contemplate murdering Zenia, they are symbolically rebelling against the cultural oppression, exploitation, and manipulation facilitated by their mothers and effected by men. These negative cultural influences controlled their earlier lives, and Zenia embodies them. At the same time, Zenia, like Cordelia, simultaneously manifests the role of rebel and transgressor. By defeating Zenia, Tony, Charis, and Roz free themselves from those confining codes, but they also take on some of the very attributes they abhorred in her because, although transgressive, those attributes are powerful. That power is needed in order for women to navigate the idea of "self" in the treacherous waters of the culturally defined maternal identity. Atwood's characters often describe with great anxiety the ways their mothers are "different" from other mothers; this difference culminates with the real or metaphorical abandonment that leaves the child in crisis. Roz's mother lies to her about who her father is and speaks to her only in clichés, Karen's mother has an emotional breakdown and is institutionalized, and Tony's mother runs away with another man, leaving Tony, feeling guilty, with her broken father. The particularity of these absences embodies the intellectual, emotional, and physical, thus representing the absence of the mother who is meant to be an all-powerful guarantor of her daughter's security but disappears before she can assure the daughter of who she is or is meant to be. Zenia's dark power over each of the three protagonists encompasses these elements as well: intellectually and emotionally, Zenia relates stories about herself that gain their sympathy, a different one for each woman, manipulating the emotional vulnerability rooted in their motherless childhoods. Once she has gained their trust, she "attacks"—in each case by having sexual relationships with the men in their lives—causing the women to be abandoned yet again. Zenia's betrayal of each woman re-enacts the mother's betrayal of her daughter when she abandons her. The repetition of the plot structure highlights its universality. As Tony, Charis, and Roz's stories unfold, they reveal the conflict each character has when she reaches a level of understanding (if not forgiveness) regarding her own mother's behaviour. That their mothers were unhappy in their marriages, and exploited in the male-dominated circumstances in which they raised their daughters, is conveyed marginally through the narrative of each protagonist, but as readers we have the power of a "double" consciousness to appreciate that the mother who so brutally abandoned her daughter was herself a victim of the "law of the father"—dominated culture in which she lived.

In *The Blind Assassin*, Iris and Laura Chase are abandoned repeatedly, first by their mother and then by subsequent surrogate mothers. Their mother dies after a miscarriage—by no coincidence is this maternal image of blood and death a recurrent motif in Atwood's texts—and Reenie, the housekeeper, is the first pseudo-mother for the girls. Her nonstatus in the social hierarchy of the novel predetermines her inadequacy in this role. The girls' father has a girlfriend, Callie, but she is a political rather than a maternal role model and in fact represents the antithetic approach to one their mother would have endorsed, had she lived. After Iris marries, she is meant to mother Laura, but she is only a child herself, and Winifred Griffin, Iris's sister-in-law, steps into the breach. She is the quintessential fairy-tale wicked stepmother whose behaviour is grounded in resentment and hate, and she controls and manipulates the beautiful, helpless princess[es]. Susan Suleiman reminds us that the "traditional psychoanalytic view of motherhood is indissociable from the more general theory of normal female development" (353), quoting Nancy Chodorow that "women are prepared psychologically for mothering through the developmental situation in which they grow, and in which woman have mothered them" (354). Thus their mother's death early in their lives disrupts the "normal development" of the Chase sisters and leaves them psychologically unprepared to develop any kind of feminine identity, let alone that of "mother." Iris, nine years old, resents her mother for dying: "I felt that in some way she was betraying me—that she was shirking her duties, that she'd abdicated" (*Blind Assassin* 115). This literal death enacts Iris's extant feelings, for indeed her mother has abdicated by succumbing to her husband's desires even though she had been advised not have any more children after Laura's birth nearly killed her. We assume that her husband was cognizant of this situation, and while we are not privy to this part of their story, it is reasonable to believe that Iris's father wanted a son. In performing her so-called wifely duties, she pays with her life.

Iris's mother's legacy to her daughter is what Luce Irigaray calls "nonexistence ... your obliviousness of yourself" (65). For Iris, her mother's obliviousness encompasses her own sense of self, because her mother dies, leaving Iris trapped by "her idea of me; with her idea of my goodness pinned onto me like a badge, and no chance to throw it back at her (as would have been the normal course of affairs with a mother and a daughter—if she'd lived, as I'd grown older)" (*Blind Assassin* 117). Iris's words are a textual re-enactment of Irigaray's daughter desire: "And what I wanted from you,

Mother, was this: that in giving me life you still remain alive" (67). Laura too falls prey to this desire, and a few months after her mother's death, throws herself into the river in attempt to exchange her own life for her mother's. The image of Laura "in the icy black water ... her hair spread out like smoke in a swirling wind ... her wet face ... gleam[ing] silvery" (*Blind Assassin* 184) simultaneously evokes death by drowning and the prenatal state in the womb, incarnating the desire for the return of the absent mother. The impossibility of bringing their mother back to life infuses the rest of Laura and Iris's story with her absence, and her loss is re-enacted throughout the text. Richard Griffin, Iris's husband, sexually abuses Laura and then forces her to have an abortion against her will. She is committed to an asylum, the baby is aborted, and all of this is managed by Winifred. Winifred and Richard lie to Iris about what is happening to Laura, but in any event Iris is too involved in her own suffering and duplicities to understand what is truly going on. Her absence betrays Laura and leaves her vulnerable to manipulation much in the same way that their mother's death betrayed Iris and left Iris vulnerable to manipulation. In Iris's case, her father literally sells her in marriage to Richard (who is much older) in order to save his business. Later, Iris loses custody of her daughter, Aimee, to Winifred, as punishment for daring to leave Richard.

These events are redolent with fairy-tale motifs: the motherless daughters who are a staple of most fairy tales, here Iris and Laura; wicked stepmothers who attempt to destroy the hapless, helpless younger heroine, here enacted by Winifred; and stolen children, as manifested both in Laura's forced abortion and in Winifred's winning custody of Aimee, Iris's daughter, and later her granddaughter, Sabrina. Thus Winifred functions as the wicked surrogate mother, or witch, of fairy-tale mode. The appearance and function of the fairy-tale witch depend on the absence of the real mother. In fairy tales, evil behaviour is always punished, yet the power the stepmother wields over her innocent victims (almost always female) is a reflection of how society views women as bad when they *act* in order to get what they want. Indeed they *are* bad; otherwise they would never have been able to accomplish what they desire. The protagonist's desire to regain her child/ husband/position is jumpstarted by her suffering at the hands of a wicked woman, a cruel or inadequate or simply small-minded mother figure who is invested in preserving the patriarchal status quo, however detrimental it may be to her personally, to the protagonist, or to women in general. In *The Blind Assassin*, Laura and Iris consistently struggle against Winifred in this role. However, distinct from the classic fairy-tale paradigm, this wicked witch does not die as punishment for her evil deeds. Winifred dies an old lady long after Laura and Aimee have died. It is only at the novel's end, when Iris confesses that she is writing for Sabrina, her granddaughter, who is "no relation at all to Winifred and none to Richard. There's not a speck of Griffin in [her] at all: [her] hands are clean on that score," that hope is offered Sabrina for her future: "Your real grandfather was Alex Thomas.... Your legacy from him is the realm of infinite speculation. You're free to invent yourself at will" (*Blind Assassin* 627).

Thus, at the novel's end, Iris the narrator offers her granddaughter the opportunity to "invent herself" as a woman and potential mother with all the infinite possibility that opportunity implies, despite the absence of her own mother (Aimee was an addict who died when Sabrina was very young). As in the other two novels discussed here, the female protagonists confront the failures of their mothers to live up to their own images and thus are able to realize a more successful personal socialization. This stronger identity is carried forward, creating better mothering of their daughters and granddaughters. When remembering her mother's death, Iris writes: "What fabrications they are, mothers. Scarecrows, wax dolls for us to stick pins into, crude diagrams. We deny them an existence of their own, we make them up to suit ourselves—our own hungers, our own wishes, our own deficiencies. Now that I've been one myself, I know" (116). In *The Blind Assassin*, Iris affirms her mother's existence by writing her diaries as a legacy for Sabrina.

In their introduction to *Determined Women*, editors Jennifer Birkett and Elizabeth Harvey explain that "fundamental to the perpetuation of patriarchy is the way it is inscribed in the consciousness of women and in their perceptions of themselves from earliest childhood" (2). Margaret Atwood has concerned herself with this method of "perpetuating patriarchy" not only in *Cat's Eye*, *The Robber Bride*, and *The Blind Assassin*, but in most of her oeuvre.[5] Elaine and Cordelia; Tony, Charis, and Roz; and Laura and Iris are all victims of absent mothers and childhood abuse. They have endured patriarchal expectations that are alien to their own experiences of a female sense of "self." That this abuse is often received at the hands of other women foregrounds the encounter with the absent mother each character must undergo in her quest for the imperative production of a whole "self." When she fails to confront her mother or mother substitutes, as Cordelia and Laura fail, she self-destructs. These mothers subjugated their daughters not by choice, but as a result of the lack of their own power within the framework of their lives. This powerlessness was expressed in their silence, their passivity, and, most devastating of all, their absence when their daughters most needed them. Finally, however, the female protagonists who do survive are able to reach a modicum of understanding about the lives their mothers had to live obeying the "law of the father."

The conflict between writing and motherhood haunts many female-authored texts, and perhaps one way in which Atwood deals with this conflict is to absent the mother from her female protagonist's text/life. Indeed, there are artist/writers in each of the novels discussed in this paper (Elaine is a painter, Tony is an historian, and Iris is an author). In Atwood's novels, the mother's absence may break the child, but as adult women, Atwood's characters are assimilated, however resignedly, into the maintenance of conventional social order. This role, finally, keeps them safe and allows for their own daughters (or granddaughters) to forge identities not in the reflection of absence, but in emulation of the presence of their mothers and grandmothers who have saved themselves from potential destruction within the patriarchal world.

Notes to Chapter 2

1   Robert Clark comments that "for Lacan, developing from Freud's theory of the importance of castration, the symbolic order is always structured around the Name-of-the-Father (or the phallus which is its emblem) and the patriarchal injunction, to which Lacan refers by the punning phrase *le nom du père* (which is phonetically almost indistinguishable in French from *le non du père*, the father's no.)" The subjugated place of women in relation to men in Atwood's novels is foregrounded every time fathers dictate their wives' and daughters' behaviour, echoing this Lacanian "no."

2   Multiple names operate on several other levels, but the restrictions of this article prevent pursuing those functions here.

3   Atwood's real-life experience supports my theory; she recounts in *Negotiating with the Dead*, "Due to the romanticism of my father, I was named after my mother; but then there were two of us, so I had to be called something else" (36).

4   This motif appears particularly obviously in "Hansel and Gretel" and "Snow White," as well as in "The Robber Bridegroom."

5   Other than her most recent novel, *Oryx and Crake*, Atwood's fiction has focused on female protagonists suffering from a crisis of identity, the roots of which can be traced to their childhood, narrated as a crisis of feminine identity in various forms.

Works Cited

Atwood, Margaret. *The Blind Assassin*. London: Virago Press, 2001.

——. *Cat's Eye*. New York: Doubleday, 1989.

——. *Negotiating with the Dead: A Writer on Writing*. Cambridge, UK: Cambridge University Press, 2002.

——. *The Robber Bride*. London: Virago Press, 1994.

Birkett, Jennifer, and Elizabeth Harvey, eds. *Determined Women: Studies in the Construction of the Female Subject, 1900–90*. Savage, MD: Barnes & Noble Books, 1991.

Bouson, J. Brooks. *Brutal Choreographies: Oppositional Strategies and Narrative Design in the Novels of Margaret Atwood*. Amherst: University of Massachusetts Press, 1993.

Cixous, Hélène. "The Laugh of the Medusa." Trans. Keith Cohen and Paula Cohen. New French Feminism. Ed. Elaine Marks and Isabelle de Courtivron. Brighton: Harvester, 1980. 243–67.

Clark, Robert. "The Symbolic Order." *The Literary Encyclopedia*. 7 March 2004. The Literary Dictionary Company. 26 April 2007. 24 June 2009, http://www.litencyc.com/php/stopics.php?rec=true&UID=1082.

Garner, Shirley Nelson, Claire Kahane, and Madelon Sprengnether, eds. *The [M]other Tongue: Essays in Feminist Psychoanalytic Interpretation*. Ithaca, NY: Cornell University Press, 1985.

Howells, Coral Ann. *Margaret Atwood*. Macmillan Modern Novelists Series. London: Macmillan Press, 1996.

Irigaray, Luce. "And the One Doesn't Stir without the Other." Trans. Helene Vivienne Wenzel. *Signs* 7.1 (1981): 60–67.

Kristeva, Julia. *Powers of Horror: An Essay on Abjection*. Trans. Leon S. Roudiez. New York: Columbia University Press, 1982.

Light, Alison. *Forever England: Femininity, Literature, and Conservatism between the Wars*. London: Routledge, 1991.

Ostriker, Alicia Suskin. *Stealing the Language: The Emergence of Women's Poetry in America*. Boston: Beacon Press, 1986.

Perrakis, Phyllis Sternberg. "Atwood's *The Robber Bride*: The Vampire as Intersubjective Catalyst." *Mosaic: A Journal for the Interdisciplinary Study of Literature* 30:3 (September 1997): 151–68.

Rohrich, Lutz. Introduction. *Fairy Tales and Society: Illusion, Allusion and Paradigm*. Ed. Ruth B. Bottigheimer. Philadelphia: University of Pennsylvania Press, 1986.

Suleiman, Susan Rubin. "Writing and Motherhood." *The [M]other Tongue: Essays in Feminist Psychoanalytic Interpretation*. Ed. Shirley Nelson Garner, Claire Kahane, and Madelon Sprengnether. Ithaca, NY: Cornell University Press, 1985. 352–77.

3

Writing about Abusive Mothers: Ethics and Auto/biography | BY KATE DOUGLAS

Introduction

In the prologue to her autobiography of childhood, *Ugly: The True Story of a Loveless Childhood*, Constance Briscoe describes a visit she made to Social Services when she was 11 years old. She asks the woman at the reception desk if she can book herself into a children's home. The woman replies, "You cannot refer yourself to a children's home, luvvie. You need to get your parents' consent first. Why don't you go home and think about it?... I can't book you in just because you feel like leaving home. Do you want us to contact your mother?" Constance replies, "No thanks ... I'll handle it myself" (1). Afraid that she will receive another beating from her mother, Constance goes home and drinks a glass of diluted bleach. She writes, "I chose Domestos because Domestos kills all known germs and my mother had for so long told me that I was a germ. I felt very sick, happy and sad. I was happy because tonight, if the bleach worked, I would die" (2). Briscoe survived to write her autobiography. She went on to become a barrister and one of the first black women to sit as a judge in the United Kingdom (Meeke n.p.).

Briscoe's autobiography describes the physical and emotional abuse she endured from her mother during her childhood. *Ugly* is one of countless autobiographies recounting childhood abuse to have been published during the late 1990s and early 2000s. Significantly, a number of recent autobiographies have tackled the matter of abusive and/or neglectful mothers or stepmothers. This is a difficult subject, particularly in relation to sexual abuse by women, which remains a taboo topic. It has long been established that the majority of child abuse is perpetrated by men, and as a consequence, the issue of female perpetrators of abuse has been largely unexamined. Obviously, feminist issues are at stake here. Labelling women as abusive redraws the boundaries of gender and power, and may take the attention away from long-fought battles to place gender and male power at the centre of analysis of abuse.

These issues considered, then, how are abusive mothers represented in contemporary autobiographies of childhood by women? In this paper I primarily look at two examples of autobiographies of childhood abuse: Constance Briscoe's *Ugly* (2006) and Rosalie Fraser's *Shadow Child: A Memoir of the Stolen Generation* (1998). These autobiographies are necessarily relational; they become "auto/biographies" conveying the life narratives of both the authors and their mothers. They are also what G. Thomas Couser refers to as "intimate life writing—that done within families or couples" (xii). Couser writes, "the closer the relationship between writer and subject ... the higher the ethical stakes" (xii). Whom is the auto/biographer responsible to in constructing life narratives, or, as Couser asks, "What are the author's responsibilities to those whose lives are used as 'material'" (34)? And do the stakes shift if the author is writing about abuse? I compare and contrast these two auto/biographical depictions of abusive mothers and suggest the different ideological concerns and ethical dilemmas that underlie these different auto/biographical projects. I argue that in these auto/biographies we can see the tension between the weight of traumatic life writing, or the need to write, and the ethical and cultural responsibilities that relational auto/biography summons.

Auto/biographies of Child Abuse

As previously suggested, countless examples of autobiographies of child abuse are currently in circulation. A cursory search of the ubiquitous Amazon.com reveals a plethora of these types of autobiographies dating back to the mid 1990s, and the trend has continued with many notable autobiographies of abuse being published in the early 2000s. Like Briscoe's aforementioned autobiography, U.K. author Donna Ford's *The Step Child: A True Story* (published in 2006) and U.K. author Sandra Crossley's *Friday's Child: What Has She Done That Is So Terrible?* (2004) each recount experiences of emotional, physical, and sexual abuse at the hands of a stepmother. Jenny

Tomlin's *Behind Closed Doors* (published in 2005) recounts Tomlin's experiences of abuse by her father and neglect by her mother growing up in London. Sara Davis's *Running from the Devil* (2006) and Toni Maguire's *Don't Tell Mummy: A True Story of the Ultimate Betrayal* (2006) tell a similar story of an abusive father and a mother who was unable to offer any escape.

Why is there such an interest in these autobiographies? Much has been written about the cultural significance of the autobiographical "boom" that has occurred in the past ten years.[1] And many of the most prominent and popular autobiographies have been traumatic autobiographies.[2] Autobiographies of child abuse reflect and respond to broader cultural agendas for witnessing and acting upon child abuse. These autobiographies of child abuse circulate within a range of discourses concerned with the rights of the child and in representing and addressing child abuse. In the new millennium, autobiographical narratives of child abuse can be found in a range of literature, from poetry and plays to self-help books. Amazon.com lists hundreds of traumatic autobiographies under the categories of "recovery," "family and relationships," "abuse," "incest," "psychic trauma," "child abuse," and "adult child-abuse victims." Traumatic narratives are also a constant presence on television talk shows and current affairs bulletins. Indeed, mainstream cultural domains—particularly film, television, and documentary—have recently played an increasingly important role in representing and defining child abuse.

However, autobiographical interventions into child abuse have been met with a great deal of skepticism, even condemnation. Accusations of sensationalism and distrust over the veracity of autobiographies of childhood abuse have pervaded the media.[3] As Paul John Eakin argues:

> Life writers are criticized not only for not telling the truth ... but also for telling too much truth.... The public airing of private hurt ... was not universally welcomed; many of these narratives not only featured abuse as a primary content but also were perceived by some reviewers to *be* abusive in their candour. (3)

For example, American author Kathryn Harrison's controversial autobiography, *The Kiss*, was the catalyst for a literary backlash against traumatic autobiography, or what Laura Frost terms "memoirs of extremity."[4] It is a common assumption that popular autobiography, like television talk shows, is becoming too sensationalized in its depictions of people in distress.

My long-term research in the field of traumatic autobiographies of childhood has revealed that there are also many autobiographies that offer sophisticated, sensitive, and complex accounts of childhood trauma. Where some autobiographies of abusive childhoods have offered condemnatory and unapologetic representations of "bad parents," others have offered more forgiving accounts. For example, Andrea Ashworth's *Once in a House on Fire* offers a very sympathetic representation of her mother. Despite her mother's neglect and her inability to protect Ashworth and her sister from abusive stepfathers, Ashworth recounts her mother's affectionate love for her and her sisters. For instance, she writes of her mother tenderly waking her: "Her face lowered to the pillow, close to mine. My heart always speeded up at the scent of her face cream" (34). Ashworth represents her mother as a victim. Her mother suffers from a mental illness and is violently abused by her husband. She has very little agency, and Ashworth never blames her mother for the abuse Ashworth herself suffered. In her autobiography, Ashworth is much more interested in contextualizing their histories within the social history of the time—for instance, Ashworth has more cultural opportunities available to her (she ultimately attends Oxford) compared to her mother, who is emotionally and financially dependent on her husbands.

Other autobiographies of childhood have offered complicated, fragmented accounts of abuse that refuse to label the abuse or condemn the perpetrators. An example is Jenny Diski's *Skating to Antarctica*. Diski explores the complications and tensions inherent within representing her parents, particularly her mother. These complications lie not in the ethics of representing parents autobiographically, but in the ambiguities of experience and the fragility of memory on the part of the autobiographer. In her autobiography, Diski grapples with the label "abuse" when she describes the "games" her parents played with her as a child:

> What flashed into my mind ... were those nights, many of them, when my naked mother ... would enter my room ... shake me awake telling me I had to go and sleep with my father because she wasn't going to sleep in the same bed as him.... I adored being held in his arms and feeling his big hands stroking me. Stroking me where? Everywhere, I think. I took in his physical affection like draughts of delicious drinks. I don't ever recall feeling anything but safe and loved in this private midnight comforting.... There was a game both my parents used to play when I was small on the occasions when they were in accord. Usually after an evening bath, I would dry myself in the living room and then run naked between them as each, on opposite sides of the room reached out for my vagina and tried to tickle it. When they caught me, their fingers at my vulva, I would squeal and shriek and wriggle with the equivocal agony tickling engenders, and the game would go on until I was exhausted and they were weak with laughter. (115)

Diski's narrator does not label her parents' actions as abuse, nor does she discuss it at length within the text. This increases the impact of the depiction because it may unsettle readers' expectations and make particular demands on them to recognize and interpret events the narrator is unable or unwilling to. This representation of abuse serves to demonstrate the difference between a child's and an adult's perceptions or consciousness of abuse.

In reviewing a range of texts published in the past ten or so years, a number of paradigms have emerged for representing abusive or neglectful mothers: the abusive stepmother or foster mother emerges again and again, perhaps aligning with the "wicked stepmother" trope in fairy tales. Autobiographies depicting abuse by the father and neglect by the mother (where the mother is aware of the abuse being perpetrated upon her child but chooses not to act, or is unable to act because she is suffering from some form of abuse herself) also dominate the genre. Such texts are enabled by feminist ideologies that require the reader to contextualize the child's abuse within the mother's. A less common (though seemingly growing) form of autobiography is that of depicting abuse by biological mothers. Briscoe's *Ugly* is one such autobiography.

Mothers as "Vulnerable Subjects": Ethics and Auto/biography

In *Ugly*, Briscoe recounts how her mother subjected her to constant abuse throughout her childhood, from calling her names to punching and kicking her, spitting at her, and depriving her of food. Briscoe writes:

> By the time I was seven, my beatings were as regular as ever. The [bed wetting] alarm failed to wake me, yet my mother always heard it. She would dash into my room when she heard it ring and drag me out of bed. Sometimes when she came into my room, she would remove the wet bedclothes and give me a mighty slap on the bare backside, then leave me naked and shivering. My humiliation was complete. Not only was I unable to prevent myself wetting the bed, the mere presence of my mother and/or a bedtime beating made me so nervous that I sometimes emptied my bladder in front of her. (11–12)

According to the auto/biography, in Briscoe's late adolescence, her mother tried to disrupt her efforts to go to university. And Deirdre Fernand states, "In 1999 [Briscoe's mother] tried to sabotage Briscoe's career, writing to the Bar Council to allege that her daughter had hired a hitman to kill her. The council dismissed the claim as unsubstantiated" (Fernand n.p.).

Briscoe's mother is now reportedly suing Briscoe for defamation because of the contents of *Ugly* (Saunders n.p.).'

This is clearly not a happy story, and the writing of it has deepened the conflict. The auto/biographer faces a range of ethical dilemmas when writing about a parent, as John D. Barbour contends:

> One of the most significant ethical dimensions of life writing is the writer's evaluation of his or her parents.... A central theme in many autobiographies is judging one's parents, as the author sorts out what parental virtues he affirms and which things he denies, at least as normative for his own life. (73)

An adult auto/biographer who retrospectively writes about his or her parent necessarily contextualizes the parent's life within his or her own adult life—within the writer's own values and morals. Barbour goes on to argue:

> There are several reasons why we should be careful about judging others.... To the degree that a writer focuses on her relationship to a parent, she must explore the parent's life, explaining how the parent came to have specific values and a certain moral character.... Intergenerational autobiography is a matter of both judging and "not judging." Moral judgment is not negated but made more complex by causal interpretations of behaviour, by forgiveness, and by scruples about the appearance or reality of self-righteousness. (73–74)

There is a much-spoken-of unspoken rule within contemporary auto/biography that writers must not appear too bitter in their depiction of their childhood or too condemnatory of their parents. Bitterness appears as uncontrolled emotion. And as I have argued elsewhere, "forgiveness" is a highly valued commodity in autobiography ("Blurbing Biographical," 819). For example, in her review of another auto/biography of childhood abuse, Rosalie Fraser's *Shadow Child: A Memoir of the Stolen Generations*, Jan Mayman applauds the forgiveness that Fraser's autobiography displays. Mayman writes, "Fraser was four years old when her foster mother raped her with a knitting needle during one bout of drunken madness; yet she has forgiven this monstrous woman: [she quotes Fraser] 'I realise how sick she was.... I still put flowers on her grave'" (n.p.).

So, what are we to do with auto/biographers who do not forgive their abusive mothers and write their auto/biography from this position? In her auto/biography, *Ugly*, Briscoe goes against all the standards set down by Barbour regarding the ethical responsibilities of representing parents. Briscoe is judgmental and unforgiving of her abusive mother, and never seeks to explore or explain the reasons behind her mother's abuse. For instance, though the auto/biography makes references to the domestic violence her mother suffered, there is little detail or discussion about it. Briscoe's mother is clearly abused and oppressed by the various male partners she has. Bella Brodzki argues that auto/biographies by daughters "often present themselves first and foremost as having been "sinned" against—by their mothers and ... by the patriarchal structures that have made her mother an unknowing collaborator with male authority" (159). Briscoe does not delve into this feminist territory. Of her mother, Briscoe writes, "I never knew why my mother wanted children. Not once did I think that she liked me or my sisters and brothers. Why she had so many of us is a mystery" (24). In an interview Briscoe is asked if she "made an effort" to try to understand her mother's actions. Briscoe replies:

> I have never thought about her motivation. I took the view that she didn't like me and I caused her problems by wetting the bed and so on. Why did it happen? Because I was a problem child. Do I understand her? Now that I have my own children, I do not understand it for one moment. I hope that my mother will, one day before she goes to her grave, realise that I was not a bad kid. It would please me if she knew me as her daughter. (Meeke n.p.)

Is Briscoe's mother a "vulnerable subject" (to use Couser's term)? She has little right of reply to Briscoe's charges against her. However, Briscoe is writing about a traumatic event, and her writing reflects particular needs—to speak out against the previously unspeakable. Linda Martin Alcoff and Laura Gray-Rosendale explain:

> At various times and in different locations [child abuse] has been absolutely prohibited, categorized as mad or untrue, or rendered inconceivable: presuming objects (such as a rapist father) that were not statable and therefore could not exist within the dominant discourses. The speech of incest survivors has been especially restricted on the grounds that it is too disgusting and disturbing to the listeners' constructed sensibilities.... Incest survivors have also been constructed as mad: "hysterical" women who are unable to distinguish reality from their own imaginations. (203)

Traumatic autobiographies are offered to the public as testimony of their narrators' endurance of trauma. For many autobiographers who represent their shamed childhood selves, the autobiographical act becomes a means, to quote Rosamund Dalziell, "for the mature self to become visible in a deliberate way in order to confront shame and re-evaluate self-worth" (7). Traumatic childhoods commonly emphasize that it is only through the adult voice, and the particular contemporary cultural environment they find themselves in, that they are able to recite their narratives. This also seems to be an axiom of therapeutic discourse for, as Sonia C. Apgar suggests, "writing provides the survivor with a psychological distance that allows her [or him] the possibility of analyzing her [or his] past" (48). Leigh Gilmore discusses the paradox that trauma is largely considered "unrepresentable," yet at the same time language, such as writing or speaking, is authorized as one of the primary modes for healing trauma (6). They are a means via which the previously disempowered person (in this instance, the child) can "write back" (as an adult) after the fact, to offer a revised version of events.

Briscoe's auto/biography is angry and triumphant. Briscoe writes from a position of power: she is part of a conventionally happy family; she is a mother and a wife. She has a very successful career. To paraphrase Sidonie Smith and Julia Watson, Briscoe has "got a life" (*Getting a Life*). But this "self" is an autobiographical construct, a performance. Part of Briscoe's project is to set herself up against her mother and to set her adult self up against her child self—to offer a comparison between the different selves and the different mothers—and to thus authenticate her experience and herself.

Briscoe's auto/biography is not burdened by sympathy because she has none for her mother. Briscoe represents her mother as not having one redeeming quality. Briscoe's auto/biography is not an act of forgiveness; Briscoe writes, "My mother's behaviour was a combination of temperament and circumstances. But now that I am a mother, I think even more that her treatment was completely incomprehensible and unacceptable. I do not forgive her" (Fernand n.p.). In writing this auto/biography, Briscoe's responsibilities appear to be to Briscoe and her immediate family only.

So, ethically, what do we do with the conflict between Briscoe's right to tell her story, to expound her trauma, and Briscoe's mother's right to be represented in a more complex manner? Does Briscoe have a responsibility to her mother to try to understand her as part of her autobiographical project? Or is she exempted because of the trauma she suffered? Other auto/biographers have approached similar subject matter very differently. Rosalie Fraser's *Shadow Child* relates her experiences living with a (non-Indigenous) foster family in the 1960s and 1970s after being removed from her parents' care as a child.[5] Like Briscoe, Fraser endures horrific physical and sexual abuse from her foster mother; she is racially vilified and denigrated. Fraser describes this abuse in shocking detail in the early chapters of her autobiography. One particular incident of sexual assault leads her to be hospitalized for over a week.

The first time she speaks of the abuse is when she is in an institution and she tells a psychiatrist. Fraser writes:

> I told her how we were tied to a chair and put under cold showers, how we were dunked in the copper head first and held under the water until we could no longer struggle, and how we had to run around naked. I told her about the thrashings with the iron cord, and showed her the scars on my heels from having them caught in the door. I could not bring myself to tell her of some of the other things, as they were far too personal, and I was trying to forget them. I had pushed the worst atrocities that our foster mother committed into the back of my mind—but I used to have bad dreams.... I assume she [the psychiatrist] told [these stories] to the Welfare. But, you know, I do not think the Welfare believed me. As far as I know, they took no action over any of the horrors I related. (62)

Fraser names her foster mother—Mrs. Kelly—as the perpetrator of intense physical, sexual, and emotional abuse. Her foster mother's actions are plainly represented, and, like Briscoe, Fraser gives only a little space to interpreting her foster mother's actions. She writes, "I could never understand my foster mother: she would have these uncontrollable rages and then regret her actions. And always afterwards she would try to patch up the damage she had inflicted upon us" (38).

Fraser describes having very mixed feelings about her foster mother (whom she called "Mum"); for instance, she writes, "Strange as it may seem they [these moments of cooking meals together] have left me with some lifelong, loving memories of my foster mother" (51). It is perhaps because of this, then, that Fraser does not direct all the blame for the abuse she suffered upon her foster mother. Instead, Fraser links the direct forms of abuse that she suffered to the cultural abuse and neglect levelled at her and her siblings by the welfare institutions that were responsible for them. It was the government welfare state that separated Fraser from her family in the first instance, and every time Fraser sought help from "the Welfare" (as she calls them), they failed to help her. For instance, the narrator reflects on the ease with which Mrs. Kelly was able to fool "the Welfare" into believing that she was providing a good foster home for her foster children:

> The only time we had a nice room and our own bed was when the Welfare came to see us. So nice, in fact that great lengths were taken to make sure another bed was

borrowed for the day, and dolls that belonged to my foster mother's own daughters were placed on our so-called beds for the grand occasion. How dumb those officers were, not to see through the façade. (27)

Shadow Child seeks to expose the official version of her life, imposed upon her by welfare institutions and her foster mother, as false. The narrator reveals how as a child she was forced to lie about the abuse being perpetrated upon her. *Shadow Child* functions as a silence-breaker: the writing of this autobiography works to replace official histories with personal testimony and to vehemently assert this counter history as "truth." This deconstruction of official sources of knowledge, along with the assertion of autobiography as authentic knowledge, suggests that this autobiography of childhood cannot be any less reliable than these other "official" sources. It is an empowering revelation for the narrator when she and her sister can construct their childhood narrative:

> Bev and I decided that no one—not the Welfare, not the hospital, nor our foster parents, nor the others associated with our pain and the crimes done to us—should be allowed to get away with what happened to us as children. As far as we could see, no one had ever cared about us. They just left us to rot. Especially the Welfare, whose so-called caring hands were safely in their pockets. (23)

Carolyn Steedman explains how writing about childhood involves interpreting the past through the agency of social information; this interpretation can be made only when people gain a sense of the social world and their place in it ("Stories" 243). *Shadow Child* cannot be an auto/biography solely about childhood, because Fraser's experiences of childhood invaded her adult life. Writing about childhood creates a frame for the narrator to write about her adult insecurities about parenting and her alcoholism, but also allows her to contextualize her adult experience in terms of removal. The narrator uses the text as an opportunity to publicly inscribe the blame for her removal on welfare institutions, not her parents (or her foster mother, for that matter):

> The Welfare. I blamed them for a lot. They could have helped Mum and Dad on their feet; they could have supplied bedding and clothing as they did while we were in foster care; they could have helped Dad out with his bills.... No, Dad, I do not blame you, but I left my thoughts in this book, so people could see the struggles I have had in my mind, due to my childhood. (228)

Conclusion: Autobiography, Mothers, and Anger

Smith and Watson contend that "what counts as experience changes over time with broader cultural transformations of collective history" (*Reading Autobiography* 26). In *Ugly* and *Shadow Child* we have two quite different representations of abusive mothers, and thus these auto/biographies reveal something of the diverse available spaces for writing about abusive mothers within auto/biography—what it is possible to say or not to say about an abusive mother, and what cultural scripts are available. In both auto/biographies, the writer uses the auto/biographical form to exercise agency denied to her as a child—to purge trauma and to direct anger toward the perpetrators of her abuse. Both auto/biographies are angry in tone and represent attacks against child abuse and its perpetrators. However, where Fraser chooses to forgive her foster mother and direct her anger toward social institutions, Briscoe levels her anger squarely at her mother. These auto/biographies demonstrate the conflict that exists within many traumatic auto/biographies—between the author's need to articulate his or her trauma in particular ways for him- or herself, and the ethical responsibilities (to others) that come with writing an auto/biography.

The success of an auto/biography such as Briscoe's, which firmly juxtaposes Briscoe's mother and the successful adult Briscoe to condemn her mother's abuse, suggests the continuing influence of conservative rhetoric demanding clear-cut heroes and villains within auto/biographical writing. In its representation of her abusive mother, Briscoe's auto/biography could be termed a postfeminist auto/biography, but the particular style and tone employed by Briscoe is likely also a consequence of the traumatic mode of life writing. Briscoe's ethical responsibilities become unbound by trauma. The traumatic form asserts that Briscoe's needs supersede those of her mother. This conflict between trauma and ethics is obviously a problematic tension. Many auto/biographers, such a Rosalie Fraser, are able to address this tension through a complex representation of abuse, motherhood, and social institutions; so, arguably, this is the difference between those auto/biographers who can resolve the tension and those who cannot.

For Couser, "readers are likely to be more receptive to writers who face up to the ethical challenges inherent in their projects" (201), but do the ethical stakes shift when an auto/biographer is writing about abuse? The diverse representations of abusive mothers within contemporary auto/biography suggest that this is an auto/biographical theme very much under negotiation. These are writers who have experienced trauma and are looking at ways to authenticate themselves and their stories. In writing their relational auto/biographies, various scripts are available in relation to where or how they will position their abusive mother within the texts. The ethics too are up for negotiation. As Michael Lambek and Paul Antze argue, "the right to establish authoritative versions never rests with the individual telling the story alone. It shifts from communal institutions and collective memory to the domain of experts and beyond—to market forces and the power of the state" (xvii). The auto/biographies that are published (and their ethics) are authorized by the cultures within which they emerge. Thus, these auto/biographies relating the experiences of having abusive mothers reflect shifts in the cultural representation of motherhood: it is possible to say more about an abusive mother than it once was. As more auto/biographies about abusive mothers are published, particular narratives will be enabled and written into the cultural memory of child abuse and motherhood.

Acknowledgements

Thanks to Tom Couser for his helpful feedback on this paper (as a conference paper and in written form).

Notes to Chapter 3

1 See Gilmore and Douglas for general discussions of the "autobiography boom."
2 Autobiography has become a significant cultural site for the representation and articulation of trauma. Indeed, trauma has been central to contemporary self-representation (Gilmore 3). Autobiography has become one of the most prominent cultural spaces for the articulation of traumas such as child abuse.
3 For examples of such criticism see Hughes "I Have Seen" and "Remembering Imagination"; Jones; Treneman; and Wolcott.
4 Frost summarizes this literary event: "Kathryn Harrison's memoir *The Kiss* appeared in 1997 at the peak of a publishing trend that has been called alternatively 'the memoir craze' and 'the memoir plague.' *The Kiss* followed, and in some ways was the culmination of, [U.S.] memoirs of extremity such as Susanna Kaysen's *Girl, Interrupted*, Lucy Grealy's *Diary of a Face*, Michael Ryan's *Secret Life* and James Ellroy's *My Dark Places*. But Harrison's subject matter—the author's four-year affair with her father, beginning when she was twenty—seemed to surpass them all" (51).
5 Gillian Whitlock writes, "In the winter of 1997 Australians were immersed in an ocean of testimony. It came in the form of the Report of the National Inquiry into the separation from their families and communities of Aboriginal and Torres Strait Islander children. This Report from the Australian Human Rights and

Equal Opportunity Commission (HREOC) is called Bringing Them Home. It records that 'between one in three and one in ten Indigenous children were forcibly removed from their families and communities' from 1910 to 1970 (Wilson 37). The Commission listened to 535 personal stories of forcible removal, and had access to another thousand or so in written form. The Commissioners travelled throughout the country gathering testimonies, listening and reading. In writing the Report they retained as far as possible the actual words as they heard them, and so first-person testimonies are placed alongside third-person reporting and analysis throughout" (198). The report is the best-selling government publication ever, and the Human Rights and Equal Opportunity Commission (HREOC) website "has facilitated the transit of these stories across a wide international readership" (Whitlock 198). These children were raised in institutions or white foster homes. The Australian government's policy of assimilation led to the cultural genocide of Indigenous Australians.

Works Cited

Apgar, Sonia. C. "Fighting Back on Paper and in Real Life: Sexual Abuse Narratives and the Creation of Safe Space." *Creating Safe Space: Violence and Women's Writing.* Ed. Tomoko Kuribayashi and Julie Tharp. New York: State University of New York Press, 1998. 47–58.

Ashworth, Andrea. *Once in a House on Fire.* London: Picador, 1999.

Barbour, John D. "Judging and Not Judging Parents." *The Ethics of Life Writing.* Ed. Paul John Eakin. Ithaca, NY: Cornell University Press, 2004.

Briscoe, Constance. *Ugly: The True Story of a Loveless Childhood.* London: Hodder & Stoughton, 2006.

Brodzki, Bella. "Mothers, Displacement and Language." *Women, Autobiography, Theory: A Reader.* Ed. Sidonie Smith and Julia Watson. Madison: University of Wisconsin Press, 1998.

Couser, G. Thomas. *Vulnerable Subjects: Ethics and Life Writing.* Ithaca, NY: Cornell University Press, 2004.

Crossley, Sandra. *Friday's Child: What Has She Done That Is So Terrible?* London: Mandarin Press, 2004.

Dalziell, Rosamund. *Shameful Autobiographies: Shame in Contemporary Australian Autobiographies and Culture.* Melbourne: Melbourne University Press, 1999.

Davis, Sara. *Running from the Devil.* London: John Blake, 2006.

Diski, Jenny. *Skating to Antarctica.* London: Granta Books, 1998.

Douglas, Kate. "Blurbing Biographical: Authorship and Autobiography." *Biography: An Interdisciplinary Quarterly.* 24.4 (2001): 806–26.

Eakin, Paul John. "Introduction: Mapping the Ethics of Life Writing." *The Ethics of Life Writing*. Ed. Paul John Eakin. Ithaca, NY: Cornell University Press, 2004.

Fernand, Deirdre. Interview with Constance Briscoe. *The Sunday Times* 15 Jan. 2006. 27 May 2006, http://www.timesonline.co.uk/article/0,,2092-1985687,00.html.

Ford, Donna. *The Step Child: A True Story*. London: Vermilion, 2006.

Fraser, Rosalie. *Shadow Child: A Memoir of the Stolen Generation*. Sydney: Hale & Iremonger, 1998.

Frost, Laura. "After Lot's Daughters: Kathryn Harrison and the Making of Memory." *A/B: Auto/Biographical Studies* 14.1 (1999): 51–70.

Gilmore, Leigh. *The Limits of Autobiography: Trauma and Testimony*. Ithaca, NY: Cornell University Press, 2001.

Harrison, Kathryn. *The Kiss*. London: Fourth Estate, 1997.

Hughes, Kathryn. "I Have Seen the Past and It Works." *Guardian Unlimited* 11 July 1999. Nov. 1999, http://www.guardian.co.uk/Archive/Article/0,4273,3882243,00.html.

———."Remembering Imagination: Have We Had Enough of Memoir?" *The Observer* 19 Aug. 2001. 17 Nov. 2001, http://www.observer.co.uk/review/story/0,6903,5389 44,00.html.

Jones, Malcolm. "It's Better to Tell All Than to Tell It Well." *Newsweek* 27 July 1998: 59.

Lambek, Michael, and Paul Antze. "Introduction: Forecasting Memory." *Tense Past: Cultural Essays in Trauma and Memory*. Ed. Paul Antze and Michael Lambek. New York: Routledge, 1996. xi–xxxviii.

Maguire, Toni. *Don't Tell Mummy: A True Story of the Ultimate Betrayal*. London: Harper Element, 2006.

Martin Alcoff, Linda, and Laura Gray-Rosendale. "Survivor Discourse: Transgression or Recuperation?" *Getting a Life: Everyday Uses of Autobiography*. Ed. Sidonie Smith and Julia Watson. Minneapolis: University of Minnesota Press, 1996. 198–225.

Mayman, Jan. "Stepping Out of a Childhood Shadow." Rev. of *Shadow Child*, by Rosalie Fraser. *The Age* 30 Oct. 1998. 1 Sept. 2001, http://theage.com.au/daily/981030/news/news20.html.

Meeke, Kieran. Interview with Constance Briscoe. *Metro.co.uk* 30 Jan 2006. 27 May 2006, http://www.metro.co.uk/fame/interviews/article.html?in_article_id=496 &in_page_id=11.

Saunders, Kate. "Their Winning Ways." Rev. of *Ugly*, by Constance Briscoe. *TimesOn-line* 29 Jan. 2006. 27 April 2006, http://www.timesonline.co.uk/article/0,,23113 -2008077,00.html.

Smith, Sidonie, and Julia Watson, eds. *Getting a Life: Everyday Uses of Autobiography*. Minneapolis: University of Minnesota Press, 1996.

——. *Reading Autobiography: A Guide for Interpreting Life Narratives*. Minneapolis: University of Minnesota Press, 2001.

Steedman, Carolyn. "Stories." *Women, Autobiography, Theory: A Reader*. Ed. Sidonie Smith and Julia Watson. Madison: University of Wisconsin Press, 1998. 243–54.

Tomlin, Jenny. *Behind Closed Doors*. London: Hodder and Stoughton, 2005.

Treneman, Ann. "When Did You Last See Your Panda?" *Independent* 8 Feb. 1998. 12 Dec. 1999, http://www.independent.co.uk/life-style/when-did-you-last-see-your-panda-1143531.html.

Whitlock, Gillian. "In the Second Person: Narrative Transactions in Stolen Generations Testimony." *Biography* 24.1 (Winter 2001): 197–214.

Wolcott, James. Rev. of *The Kiss*, by Kathryn Harrison. *New Republic* 31 Mar. 1997: 32–37.

4

"Red Mother":The Missing Mother Plot as Double Mystery in Louise Erdrich's Fiction

BY SHEILA HASSELL HUGHES

Louise Erdrich's first novel, *Love Medicine* (1984), opens with the death of June Kashpaw, a motherless American Indian woman who abandons her own child and later returns to haunt him and others throughout this book and the later novel *The Bingo Palace* (1994). June's is just the first of many such abandonments. Fleur Pillager; Lulu Lamartine; Lipsha Morrissey; Marie Kashpaw; Pauline Puyat; Karl, Mary, and Jude Adare; Augustus Roy I and II; Matilda Roy; Celestine James; Russell Kashpaw; and more: the list of Erdrich's motherless characters is stunning in its weight and variety. Children somehow severed from their mothers have, in fact, played important roles in every one of the ten adult novels the prolific and much acclaimed "mixed-blood" (French-Ojibwe and German-American) writer has produced since 1984. In many cases, the mother's loss is somewhat abated by one or more surrogates, but in every instance the original mother's absence remains as powerful as any physical or spiritual presence, haunting her children and readers alike. The story of the missing mother is also always a mystery. Indeed, this essay takes up the missing mother as the primary, endlessly repeated plot mystery of Erdrich's fiction and asserts that it carries other sorts of meaning, constituting, in effect, a religious mystery as well. In demonstrating the intertwining pattern of these two forms of maternal mystery in the trope of the "red mother," I will also argue that this multivalent figure requires multiple modes of reading and response, including not only cognitive *comprehension*, achieved through the employ-ment of multiple disciplinary and cultural frameworks, but also a more thoroughly transformative response—through both a religious sort of *appre-hension* that "rearranges" the reader, and through a resulting commitment to *political engagement* in the ongoing struggles of Indigenous women and their communities.

The implications of this pattern of double-mystery, I will demonstrate, are not only cultural, socio-political, and psychic, but also religious. The missing mother is in some sense an embodiment of colonial processes that have left generations of Indigenous people in varying degrees of literal and spiritual displacement, homelessness, and motherlessness. Again and again Erdrich embeds these larger processes and effects in the lives and psyches of her characters through maternal relations, and so it is through the prob-lem posed by the absent, failed, or forsaken mother that we find our way to religious mystery. But while Erdrich treats motherhood itself as something sacred and mysterious, it never appears in her fiction as something simply "natural" in the way the biological relationship is often romanticized. Ma-ternity has a radical power to shape identities and transform lives, but it is always open for disintegration, contestation, remaking. And while the con-crete facts of the mother's actions may eventually be established (though even these are likely to shift from one narrative account to the next), the meanings they hold for her, for her children, and for others remain open—like a wound, or like a sacred text—an enfolded secret that pulls us back into it again and again.

To apprehend the meaning of the missing mother's mystery, I contend, characters and readers alike must be able to respond in a way we might call "religious," recognizing her irreducible otherness, suspending final judg-ment in favour of fearful or awe-full recognition, and also looking within ourselves and allowing this present-absence to speak to us and to reframe our own roles in the grand scheme of social, political, and spiritual rela-tions. The notion of "religious reading" proposed by scholars in the field of literature and theology, such as Greg Salyer and Robert Detweiler, re-quires engaging the text dialogically, applying not only critical-interpretive but also imaginative and reflective faculties, allowing literary texts to chal-lenge and potentially to transform our own assumptions and beliefs. Such a practice is particularly difficult, but also especially important, for cultur-ally privileged scholars approaching works of nondominant traditions—traditions such as Erdrich's Anishinaabe culture, which offers a religious worldview that has been eroded and marginalized but nonetheless persists and continues to mend itself. I see the practice of religious reading as one strategy for attempting what Native critic Devon Mihesuah calls for from feminist scholars engaged in social-scientific research with Native women: "they must abandon any posturing about being an expert on what counts as knowledge about Native women," she asserts, and "engage in reciprocal, practical dialogue with their informants" so that "Native voices, too, will become a part of feminist discourse" (8). For literary scholars, I would argue, such dialogue involves an openness to the text working not only in service of one's argument but also upon it, and upon oneself.

Despite the rich array of maternal relationships to consider in Erdrich's fiction, this essay focuses on just one mother–daughter dyad: the infamous Pauline Puyat, a.k.a. Sister Leopolda, and her offspring, Marie Kashpaw, characters who make their most spectacular appearances in *Love Medicine*, *Tracks* (1988), and *Last Report on the Miracles at Little No Horse* (2001). They make an especially interesting pair because, between them, they embody what is arguably the worst example of the anti-mother, in Pauline, and one of the greatest redemptive maternal figures, in Marie, that Erdrich's oeuvre has to offer. Tracing the detailed history and developments of even this one relationship is still beyond the scope of what I can accomplish here, however, and so I will narrow my focus yet more, offering a careful analysis of one short narrative in the novel *Last Report*—a section titled "Red Mother"—in which the young Marie discovers the truth of her missing mother's identity. It is here, I will show, that we see articulated most clearly the religious weight carried by the missing mother trope.

Feminist literary critics have noted the pattern of missing mothers in Erdrich's fiction and traced its meaning in a number of helpful ways. Hertha Wong's study, one of the first to explore the meanings and challenges of maternity in Erdrich's work, does so in the context of Ojibwe cultural practices. Taking issue with the feminist psychology of Nancy Chodorow, Wong points out that from a Native American perspective, an identity that is shaped "in relation to others" is not an effect of "ambivalence and confusion over ego boundaries" but rather a realistic reflection of the nature of relations among all creation (Chodorow, qtd. in Wong 175). Because older generations of women are often the transmitters of such cultural views, Ojibwe mothers and grandmothers can provide important links to tribal heritage and identity (190). For this reason, broken bonds between mother and child have served in Native American literature as markers for a larger cultural alienation, insofar as "mother" stands for what Paula Gunn Allen elaborates as "an entire generation of women" who orient the Native child.

"But naming your own mother (or her equivalent)," Allen emphasizes, "enables people to place you precisely within the universal web of your life, in each of its dimensions: cultural, spiritual, personal, and historical" (208).

The possibility of an "equivalent" is important to note here. As Wong and others point out, mothering has always been something of a communal practice in Native communities. The mother who "throw[s] away" her child and breaks the link may be acting out the suffering and "cultural alienation" inflicted upon her by colonization (Wong 174, 189), but her action is often also partly redeemed, and the connection potentially mended, by others who continue to operate more traditionally, within a cultural system of extended and constructed familial responsibility.

Jeanne Smith's analysis of "transpersonal self-hood" also employs something of a psychological approach, but she emphasizes the connection of identity, body, and culture to landscape. Alienation is prompted by colonization, a process marked and measurable geographically, but it is primarily felt, she argues, in a loss of connection both to the mother and to one's own body and personal identity. Because boundaries are necessary to both identity and connection, threats to personal and communal boundaries can undermine both individual survival and cultural continuance. "By linking the boundaries of identity with shrinking reservation borders," Smith explains, "Erdrich affirms the inseparability of identity from land, and equates western encroachment on native American lands with an equally devastating threat to self-concept" (19). Mothers provide an especially important link to land because, like the earth itself, their very bodies are the source and sustenance of life. Smith quotes Erdrich:

> In our own beginnings, we are formed out of the body's interior landscape. For a short while, our mothers' bodies are the boundaries and personal geography which are all that we know of the world. Once we emerge we have no natural limit ... and yet we cannot abandon our need for reference, identity, our pull to landscapes that mirror our most intense feelings.[1]

For Native peoples who understand the Earth as co-creator, sustainer, and mother, and whose histories are carried by stories of emergence from and interaction with particular lands, the extended metaphor of the mother as embodied and psychic landscape is an especially powerful one. As Andrea Smith points out in *Conquest: Sexual Violence and American Indian Genocide*, however, "the connection between the colonization of Native people's bodies—particularly Native women's bodies—and Native lands is not simply metaphorical ... [since] [t]he colonial/patriarchal mind that seeks to control the sexuality of women and indigenous peoples also seeks to control nature" (55).

In her study of the adoption policies and practices represented in Erdrich's fiction, Jill Deans takes a "more new historicist" approach than Wong or J. Smith (Deans 239). Tracing the pattern of children abandoned or given over to adoptive care, Deans concludes that biological and adoptive relations are "not quite the same," but, drawing from Erdrich's memoir of maternity, *The Blue Jay's Dance* (1995), she concludes that "motherhood requires both biological and adoptive impulses" (235). Highlighting the role that "construction," as well as "conception," plays in the formation of personal identity, she concludes that in Erdrich's work identities, "like plants, *take* roots rather than *have* roots" (237). Dean's lengthy analysis of the role of maternity and adoption in Erdrich's own life with late husband Michael Dorris adds a strongly biographical component to her analysis, suggesting, however, that ideas as well as identities have sources beyond our own making.

Elaine Tuttle Hansen's discussion of Erdrich in her book *Mother Without Child: Contemporary Fiction and the Crisis of Motherhood* takes a postmodern view of the missing mother figure. After tracing the history of mothers without children in modern Native American literature, Hansen turns to a number of novels identified as the collaborative efforts of Erdrich and her late husband, Michael Dorris. She begins with socio-historical forces, noting that thanks to "disease, boarding school, and ... adoption ... the figure of the missing mother is more likely to represent the norm rather than the exception" in Native communities (118), but Hansen then moves into a more epistemological analysis of the trope, arguing that the figure "exceeds, though it by no means ignores, the demands of a realistic picture of either cultural alienation or the resources of collective childcare" (121). She articulates my own sense that the missing mother is a "haunting" figure, a "centripetal force," an insistent goad to storytelling, and a key to reading" Erdrich's oeuvre (121). Hansen portrays the mother who abandons or sacrifices her child as a woman who may eventually be understood to some degree, even forgiven, by her child, but who also remains beyond the scope of full recovery *as* mother (123). And even when a child seems to have come to "know" the answers, such truths are never final or infallible. Whether a "mystery" like Adelaide Adare (140) or a "ghost" like June Kasphaw (152), such mothers remain as "other," inaccessible, and lost to their offspring (and to readers) as most of what has been taken, collectively, from Native peoples.

In their discussions of mothers as emblems of connection to tribal lands and traditions and/or of tragic loss and alienation, Wong, J. Smith, Deans, and Hansen are cautious of the temptation to romanticize Native women either as uncorrupted "earth mother[s]" (Wong 174) or as tragic victims. While this is clearly a danger for non-Native scholars writing about American Indian women, in general, my own sense is that the variation among and within Erdrich's maternal characters significantly inhibits such a critical move. There is too much irony and humour, variety, idiosyncrasy, bizarre coincidence, and sheer human complexity in these characters and their plots to enable such reduction.

My goal here is thus not to reduce the missing mother figure to a single semantic trajectory, but rather to add another important layer of meaning to the pattern at large. I will do so by first laying out more carefully the religious issues I see as most relevant and then offering a careful reading of one passage of Erdrich's work that manifests these issues in relation to one mother-daughter pair. In part because other feminist critics have done such a fine job establishing the breadth of the missing-mother trope, I feel freer to narrow my study to one example, highlighting the religious implications that have been neglected by others.

As indicated above, the missing mother functions as a central mystery in every one of Erdrich's novels. But what kind of mystery does she represent? Clearly, the absence of a biological mother is not a mystery in the sense of being an historical anomaly in Native communities. Rather, on the most obvious level, she appears as a plot mystery. Indeed, Hansen classifies Erdrich's mother-without-child tales as mystery fiction (148). Such mysteries—the definitive form being the detective novel—are meant to be solved. But, as Navajo police detective Joe Leaphorn concludes at the close of a television adaptation of Tony Hillerman's crime novel *Coyote Waits*, "Sometimes I think we don't solve anything; we just rearrange the mystery." Finding out who did what to whom, with what weapon, and where—this is only part of the story, and if it is what drives Erdrich's characters in many instances, it is not what most interests the author or her readers.

What disturbs Hillerman's otherwise generic murder plot and, on a much grander scale, pervades Erdrich's fiction is the kind of mystery that is primarily to be experienced, wondered at, grappled with, and ultimately reverenced, honoured, or perhaps denied. The first kind of mystery—that of the literary genre—generally depends upon some material absence: a dead person, a missing body, a stolen treasure. Tied to an unfolding plot, it is inherently temporal. Particular places serve such mysteries primarily as variables of the central, always already past, action, and they require participants to uncover clues and provide a solution.

The second kind of mystery, by contrast, hinges not on an absence but on a spiritual presence: a force that might become noticeable only when it stirs up or "rearrange[s]" the structure of the material realities we have come to expect. Such presences—whether understood as forces of nature, divine intervention, spirits, or ghosts—are also deeply enmeshed in a Native understanding of religious mystery. Indeed, Indigenous terms such as the Anishinaabe *manitou*, often translated singly as "spirit" by Christian missionaries, can also be rendered in English as "mystery."[2] Hansen points in this direction when she identifies the multiple appearances of June Kashpaw's spirit in *The Beet Queen* (1986) as pushing the novel from mystery into the "ghost story" genre, while acknowledging that there is no question that "the ghost is real" (152).

In contrast to the temporal orientation of the simple plot mystery, American Indian spiritual mystery is bound up in a people's shared sense of place. Spatiality, according to Clara Sue Kidwell, Homer Noley, and George Tinker's *Native American Theology*, is the "foundational metaphor ... in Indian cultures." The authors elaborate: "Each nation has some understanding that they were placed into a relationship with a particular territory by spiritual forces outside of themselves and thus have an enduring responsibility for that territory just as the earth, especially the earth in that particular place, has a filial responsibility toward the people who live there." Because of this "kinship tie" to particular lands, "conquest and removal" of tribes from their historical homelands constitutes a form of cultural and religious genocide (45). This spiritual relationship to the earth sustains a religious sense of "mystery" because it is also a profoundly reciprocal relation. Kidwell, Noley, and Tinker explain: "The American Indian notion of reciprocity is fundamental to all human participation in world-balancing and maintaining harmony. Reciprocity involves first of all an understanding of the cosmos as sacred and alive, and the place of humans in the processes of the cosmic whole" (41). The epistemological implications of such a reciprocal vision—in which human and nonhuman spiritual beings relate and mutually depend upon each other—is dramatically different from Western approaches that emphasize separation and distinction between the knowing human subject and a natural world that exists in fixed and static space, waiting to be known, named, and dominated (39).[3] The fabric of reciprocity and mutual dependency is clearly torn by maternal abandonment (and these theologians are quick to point out themselves that "Two-Leggeds" are the only creatures who ever "forget" to care for their relations, both human and nonhuman, 38–39). But this spiritual perspective also suggests that the mysterious mother—even if literally or practically dead to her child—remains a spiritual relation to be reckoned with.

Finally, whereas plot mysteries invite solutions, sacred mysteries ask of human witnesses that they turn inward and then offer an appropriate response. As Abenaki scholar Joseph Bruchac explains, "When one begins to understand the Great Mystery, to know (in a way which transcends conventional knowing) that our human spirits are part of a great circle of spirit, then that understanding must also translate into action. We begin with thanks" (104). Kidwell, Noley, and Tinker add to the range of appropriate responses in the face of religious mystery: "It is [the] emotional experience of anxiety, fear, and wonder in the face of the power of the environment that best characterize[s] the religious experience of many Indian people.... [H]uman beings realize their humanity in relationship to beings in nature—trees, rocks, water, winds, animals—anything that has the capacity to move and change" (88). From a Native perspective, then, the metaphysical sort of mystery is tied to the sacredness and reciprocity of all creation, and to a sense of one's place in an active and never-ending set of relations.

Bruchac's explanation of a religious response to the "Great Mystery," as quoted above, also highlights for us the difference between two kinds of knowing: understanding based on reason and logical *comprehension*, by which the active subject masters and penetrates the depth of some passive object, on the one hand, and, on the other, a spiritual and relational *apprehension*—a recognition of oneself as one part of a cosmic whole, and a perception of that whole as entirely inspirited and inter-subjective. While this distinction bears some similarity to the "separated" and "connected" ways of knowing outlined in Belenky et al.'s study of female development, and also to common distinctions drawn between modern and postmodern epistemologies, the mindset identified by Bruchac is not simply nor primarily a feminist or postmodern one. It is an ancient way of being that is tied to particular cultural and religious practices and modes of perception. In any case, the apprehensive mode is not the kind of knowing that "solve[s] anything" in Detective Leaphorn's terms. It can, however, contribute to personal and communal healing. Acknowledging and entering fully into one's own place in the sacred scheme of relations can, in some sense, "rearrange" the mystery. It certainly implies a rearrangement and realignment of one's own life. In the analysis of "Red Mother" that follows, then, I suggest that these two kinds of mystery and two attendant ways of knowing intersect in the missing mother narrative in important ways, and that a religious reading of the text offers some hope of apprehension of the spiritual mystery at play in her work.

"Red Mother" is a subtitled section of about eight pages from Marie Kashpaw's interview with Father Jude Miller in the 2001 novel *Last Report on the Miracles at Little No Horse*. As the "confession" of the abandoned child of an unidentified mother, "Red Mother" both answers the question of Marie's origins and explores her own knowledge of that relation.

First, then, the facts—the mystery to be *solved*. The young Marie, rejected at birth, abandoned to the care of Bernadette Morrissey, and later raised by Bernadette's daughter, Sophie Morrissey Lazarre, knows little of her origins. She has been led to believe that Ignatius Lazarre is her father (*Love Medicine* 85–87), but neither this fact nor the revelation of its falsehood is of much interest to her here. At the time recounted in "Red Mother," what obsesses Marie is her missing mother. What she knows about her is only that she is, like the Morrisseys and Lazarrés, mixed-blood, but also worse: a despised Puyat (*Last Report* 321). The history of the Puyats, and especially of the "killing hatred" between mothers and daughters, is laid out for us earlier in *Last Report*. Erdrich identifies the historical root of familial violence—an enmity that was "passed down and did not die" (157)—in the relationship between Pauline's mother and grandmother (157). Caught in the grip of a mutual marital betrayal, her grandfather's dying words to his daughter were a command to kill her mother. Erdrich compares this mutual, intergenerational destruction to the "crazy ... grief" of the buffalo who, when "they saw the end of things" trampled their own calves, no longer "car[ing] to live" (158). Whether Marie knows the full story or not, it is clear that her suffering is in part the fruit of that cycle of abuse, a cycle of internalized destruction prompted by physical and cultural genocide.

In her adolescent encounter with a drunken and desperate Sophie Morrissey, as related toward the end of "Red Mother," Marie uses the promise of whisky to draw Sophie's story out and thus learns the fuller truth of her parentage. What she learns is that her parents are both closer and farther away than she might imagine. Her father, the murdered Napolean, was brother to Bernadette and uncle to Sophie (but now is dead), and Leopolda, the nun who clamours after Marie's devotion so violently in *Love Medicine*, is, in fact, the woman who gave birth to Marie, in her former life as Pauline Puyat. Marie's response to the news of her father is minimal; she is primarily intrigued because it suggests there is more to know of her mother. When she then learns of Leopolda, she is so shocked (and perhaps so overcome by a whole set of reverberating recognitions within) that all she can do is laugh hysterically at the news (*Last Report* 321, 324).

These identity questions are thus answered for Marie, and so the mystery of origins is *solved* to some degree. But faithful readers of Erdrich's Little No Horse saga have known all of this since first reading the much earlier novel *Tracks*. So the plot mystery is clearly not what drives us on here. Rather, it is the impact of the relational trauma that is so compelling. Whether and when the young Marie might be "ready for the truth of [her] beginnings" is the more profound question probed by her story than the facts themselves (*Last Report* 319). And this question, explored more directly in the earlier parts of this narrative, is presented as a *spiritual* mystery.

Marie is a baptized Christian—indeed, the experience related here comes immediately after her descent from a stint with Sr. Leopolda in the convent on the hill—and so Christian notions of religious mystery come into play. Centred among "The Passions" composing Part 4 of the novel, the emotional and epistemological suffering of the "Red Mother['s]" forsaken child is marked as Christ-like. "I went to the woods. I aimed to live by myself," she explains, and her ensuing sojourn reflects both Christ's temptation in the wilderness, which followed immediately upon his baptism and preceded his public ministry, and also his suffering in the Garden of Gethsemane just prior to his arrest and crucifixion (*Last Report* 318; Matt. 4 and 26). Like Christ, Marie senses that "the end of all things [is] drawing near" (*Last Report* 319). And she, too, then faces a powerful spiritual temptation, which she describes to Father Jude in these heart-wrenching terms:

> Before me, as the dark was all of a piece, then, I saw my real mother rearing up. Even booze has a spirit. Yes, I said, it is the liquor who cares for me now. Alcohol is my red mother. She was fire, she was stupidity, she was light. She was all I needed. Her heart was a golden catchall of sorrows and pains. She told me that if I chose her, she'd stay by me and she used the word forever, which with her I could believe. (320)

Unlike Christ, Marie succumbs to temptation and then spends some time as an alcoholic bootlegger, feeding the self-destructive fire of others, like the Morrisseys, as well. But what her metaphor of "red mother" makes clear is that she turns to booze (or "spirits") as a surrogate for her own missing mother. So, like Christ, she feels parentally abandoned in her hour of need. That she never voices the biblical question "Why have you forsaken me?" only heightens its power, I think, for her whole story poses it dramatically.

But to read the mystery of Marie's suffering primarily through a Christian lens is problematic. After all, the loss mourned here is one that was in large part wreaked upon Native peoples by the Church itself. This dispossession is figured directly in Marie's biological mother—Pauline Puyat—whose rebirth as the nun Sister Leopolda has been contingent upon the denial of her own maternity, and so of her offspring, Marie (and, in fact, also the invention of an ethnically "immaculate" conception in which she imagines herself no longer "Red" but instead "wholly white" [*Tracks* 137]). On a larger scale, the physical absence of the literal mother, here as elsewhere in Erdrich's fiction, is representative of the loss of cultural and spiritual origins—a loss advanced by historical practices of missionization and colonization. Just as the mother Pauline denies her offspring in order to enter the Church, so Native peoples were expected to turn away from the "Red Mother" of tribal tradition—from both women-centred practices and reverence for the earth—in order to convert to a Christianity that promoted domination of women and dominion over the earth. In discussing the environmental racism perpetrated against Native peoples, White Earth Anishinaabe activist and scholar Winona LaDuke clarifies the reciprocal relationship between these twin forms of domination:

> What befalls our Mother Earth befalls her daughters—the women who are the mothers of our nations. Simply stated, if we can no longer nurse our children, if we can no longer bear children, and if our bodies are wracked with poisons, we will have accomplished little in the way of determining our destiny or improving our condition. These problems, reflected in our health and well-being, are the result of historical processes and are inherently resulting in a decline of the status of women. ("Mothers" 216)

If, as LaDuke states, "women, all females, are the manifestation of Mother Earth in human form. We are her daughters, and ... are to care for her" ("Mothers" 211), then the severed relationship between Marie and her mother is a personal re-enactment of the grand narrative of contact—a process that uprooted and undermined not only individual families but also spiritual and cultural traditions. The mystery of maternal origins that forms such a prominent pattern in Erdrich's fiction is thus a grand murder plot in which colonialism and Christianity are the culprits.

Re-reading Pauline's time in the woods through this lens, we can see it quite differently. It is a time fraught with isolation and alienation, not because she is in an inhospitable wilderness or a seductive garden, but because she fails to relate to the spirits of the place, ultimately turning, instead, to the demon of alcohol. But the narrative begins more innocently and poignantly with a set of images embodying Marie's childhood quest for a "Red Mother":

> When you don't have a mother, as I never did, you have to make one. Get yourself a piece of clay and shape in your fingers and the shape you always make will be a mother. Or press her together of mud and sticks. Sometimes a tree would

do, gnarled around me. Bundles of reeds.... Sometimes just grass, grass was all I
needed. The warmth of it in the sun was her golden green smell and the soft brush
of it her fingers, stroking my face.

You don't have a mother, you make one up. That's how I made mine and still
she is standing where I made her, dark and red in the heavy woods. (*Last Report*
317–19)

As a dark figure fashioned out of clay by imagination instead of memory,
this red mother suggests how the work of art can forge spiritual connections
and play a part in the reconstitution of Indigenous cultures. The figure is an
artistic rendering and reconstruction that relies on natural substance—the
red earth—and an understanding of one's relation to it as a "Red" person.

But the natural and crafted surrogates described here are not enough
for Marie, in part because as a child she is also denied the other forms of
relation that might sustain her sense of connection to and care for and by
the earth. Her connection to the earth is thus played out in absolute isolation, and her art is pure invention without the necessary and sustaining conversation of tradition. She finds no human resources to clarify her
place on Mother Earth, for she is a mere "dog" to the Lazarres; she is told
by the Morrisseys that a Puyat is "a thing not of this earth [but] [d]own below it"; and the only love she senses—from the vicious nun Leopolda—she
feels "like a blow" (*Last Report* 321, 318). So when she flees both the convent
and the Lazarres and retreats to the woods, she is not able to find a place
and healing there. There are ducks, turtles, muskrats, and plenty to eat, but
instead of forging a life of mutual sustainability, she "support[s]" herself
selling whisky diluted with slough water to desperate alcoholics (*Last Report*
318). She cannot simply live with the land, but instead lives off other people.
She has yet to learn to relate in nonexploitative ways.

Marie is thus "not ready for the truth of [her] beginnings" when Sophie
discloses it. It is only, perhaps, through her subsequent marriage and in-
corporation into the Kashpaw family that she begins to grasp the positive
power of maternal presence (*Last Report* 319). While she resists Margaret
Kashpaw in many ways (claiming in this story that she held on to Nector "in
spite of his mother" [324]), when Margaret and Fleur Pillager help Marie
through the dangerous birth of her youngest child, Eugene, their relationship changes, and, as Peter Beidler and Gay Barton point out, she "at last
finds in Margaret the mother she never had" (154). Marie eventually learns,
then, how to be a mother herself, emerging as one of the grand maternal
dames of Erdrich's saga, bearing and raising many of her own children and
also taking in the motherless June—the series' original missing mother—
and, later, her rootless son, Lipsha.

Through her pursuit of a maternal mystery of the literal-temporal kind, Marie learns the truth of her origins. Through her struggle to know her place in the natural, social, and spiritual world of extended relations around her, she bumps up against maternal mysteries of the religious kind. The family and community relationships she weaves in years to come bring a degree of healing, I think, but whether she ever achieves a full sense of the Great Mystery—a spiritual and relational apprehension, a recognition that she is part of a cosmic whole that includes her Mother, Earth, and that all Creation is inspirited and inter-subjective—is perhaps more than we can say. But her story here and others like it folded again and again into Erdrich's novels point to that Mystery for readers. It is up to us, then, not only to read, study, and teach such stories as plots to be resolved, but also to allow them to "re-arrange" us—and the social order—in response.

Acknowledgements

I am grateful for the feedback I received on earlier drafts of this work from participants at the 2004 Native American Literature Symposium, in Mystic Lake, Minnesota, and from the University of Dayton's 2005–06 Colloquium for Research on Women and Gender. I am also indebted to the University of Dayton Research Council, which supported my work on this project with a summer research grant.

Notes to Chapter 4

1   Louise Erdrich, "Where I Ought to Be: A Writer's Sense of Place." *New York Times* 28 July 1985, sec. 7: 24. Quoted in J. Smith 14.

2   Frederic Baraga's 1853 *Dictionary of the Ojibway Language*, for example, translates *manito* as "spirit" or "ghost." It offers no entry for *Kitchi Manito*. In contrast, the work of Anishinaabe scholar Basil Johnston offers a range of context-dependent meanings for *manitou* and explains that *Kitchi Manitou* refers to "the Great Mystery of the supernatural order, one beyond human grasp, beyond words, neither male nor female, not of the flesh." Inaccessible and indescribable in "human corporeal terms," the great creator spirit is known only through the manifestations of creation. *Kitchi Manitou* does not interact intimately with creatures, but rather has given them all they need "to continue the work put into motion by the Creator" and so has "abdicat[ed]" the world, inviting all creatures to imitate their Creator's work and generosity (2–4).

3   In *Recovering the Sacred*, Winona LaDuke provides compelling analyses of the cultural traditions that give rise to these different epistemologies in relation to the sacred and to the land of the Americas.

Works Cited

Allen, Paula Gunn. *The Sacred Hoop: Recovering the Feminine in American Indian Traditions*. Boston: Beacon, 1986.

Baraga, Frederic. *A Dictionary of the Ojibway Language*. 1853. St. Paul, MN: Minnesota Historical Society Press, 1992.

Beidler, Peter G., and Gay Barton. *A Reader's Guide to the Novels of Louise Erdrich*. Columbia: University of Missouri Press, 1999.

Belenky, Mary, Blythe Clinchy, Nancy Goldberger, and Jill Tarule. *Women's Ways of Knowing: The Development of Self, Voice, and Mind*. New York: Basic, 1986.

Bruchac, Joseph. "Understanding the Great Mystery." *The Soul of Nature: Celebrating the Spirit of the Earth*. Ed. Michael Tobias and Georgianne Cowan. New York: Penguin, 1996. 99–104.

Coyote Waits. By Tony Hillerman. Adapt. Lucky Gold. Dir. Jan Egleson. Perf. Wes Studi and Adam Beach. American Mystery Series. PBS. 16 Nov. 2003.

Deans, Jill R. "'File It Under "L" for Love Child': Adoptive Policies and Practices in the Erdrich Tetralogy." *Imagining Adoption: Essays on Literature and Culture*. Ed. Marianne Novy. Ann Arbor: University of Michigan Press, 2001. 231–49.

Detweiler, Robert. *Breaking the Fall: Religious Readings of Contemporary Fiction*. Westminster: John Knox, 1995.

Erdrich, Louise. *The Beet Queen*. New York: Harper, 1986.

——. *The Bingo Palace*. New York: Harper, 1994.

——. *The Blue Jay's Dance*. New York: Harper, 1995.

——. *The Last Report on the Miracles at Little No Horse*. New York: Harper, 2001.

——. *Love Medicine*. 1984. New York: Harper, 1993.

——. *Tracks*. New York: Harper, 1988.

Hansen, Elaine Tuttle. *Mother Without Child: Contemporary Fiction and the Crisis of Motherhood*. Berkeley: University of California Press, 1997.

Johnston, Basil. *The Manitous*. St. Paul: Minnesota Historical Society, 2001.

Kidwell, Clara Sue, Homer Noley, and George E. "Tink" Tinker. *A Native American Theology*. Maryknoll, NY: Orbis, 2001.

LaDuke, Winona. "Mothers of Our Nations: Indigenous Women Address the World." *The Winona LaDuke Reader*. Stillwater, MN: Voyageur, 2002. 211–17.

——. *Recovering the Sacred: The Power of Naming and Claiming*. Boston: South End, 2005.

Mihesuah, Devon Abbott. *Indigenous American Women: Decolonization, Empowerment, Activism*. Lincoln: University of Nebraska Press, 2003.

Salyer, Greg, and Robert Detweiler, eds. *Literature and Theology at Century's End*. Atlanta: Scholars, 1995.

Smith, Andrea. *Conquest: Sexual Violence and American Indian Genocide*. Cambridge, MA: South End, 2005.

Smith, Jeanne. "Transpersonal Selfhood: The Boundaries of Identity in Louise Erdrich's *Love Medicine*." *SAIL* 3.4 (1991): 13–26.

Wong, Hertha D. "Adoptive Mothers and Thrown-Away Children in the Novels of Louise Erdrich." *Narrating Mothers: Theorizing Maternal Subjectivities*. Ed. Brenda O. Daly and Maureen T. Reddy. Knoxville: University of Tennessee Press, 1991. 174–92.

5

"This was her punishment": Jew, Whore, Mother in the Fiction of Adele Wiseman and Lilian Nattel

BY RUTH PANOFSKY

Miriam Waddington's 1942 poem "The Bond" characterizes a "Jewish whore" as "twice outcast" (9), "twice isolate" (10). As "Jewess" (10) and as whore, the woman who forms the locus of Waddington's poem is positioned at the margins of Canadian society. Ostracized for being a Jew—she experiences anti-Semitism on Toronto's Jarvis Street, where she works during the 1940s—she is condemned to further isolation for her crime of prostitution and suffers alienation. In fact, as historian of medicine Lara Marks confirms, the Jewish prostitute faced "a triple oppression—as a woman, as a Jew and as a member of the Jewish working-class" ("Jewish Women" 7)—and she "symbolized the tenuous position and vulnerability of Jewish women as a whole" (10). A rare enough figure in Canadian literature, the Jewish prostitute reappears in the fiction of Adele Wiseman and Lilian Nattel, with an important difference: she is also a mother. Through a study of two novels, Wiseman's *Crackpot* (1974) and Nattel's *The Singing Fire* (2004), this essay considers the punishing cost to Jewish prostitutes who dare to become mothers. In charting the course of maternal suffering in novels by Adele Wiseman and Lilian Nattel, this essay shows the Jewish whore/mother as a figure thrice outcast, thrice isolate.

In Wiseman's comic novel, the protagonist, Hoda, is an obese Jewish prostitute who services the boys and men of her North Winnipeg community. When she becomes pregnant, Hoda labours alone, delivers her son in the isolation of her bedroom, and severs the umbilical cord that joins mother and baby. She soon realizes, however, that caring for a newborn will prevent her from earning a living to support herself and her blind father. Against her will, Hoda leaves her infant son in the care of the local orphanage, only to re-encounter him years later when, as an adolescent, he presents himself as a client. When Nehama Korzen arrives from Plotsk, Poland, in 1875, Nattel's protagonist immediately is trapped within the corrupt and fetid streets of London's East End and forced into a life of prostitution. Following a brutal beating by her pimp, she suffers a miscarriage and is close to death. For her illicit behaviour, Nehama is punished with infertility and is unable to bear a child in marriage. Although she yearns for a child of her own, she must be satisfied as an adoptive mother to a daughter who, as a teenager, is also lured to prostitution.

In configuring their protagonists as mothers, Wiseman and Nattel may appear to be subverting the conventional view of the prostitute as amoral and antisocial, as well as the traditional notion of the Jewish mother as proper upholder "of the family's morality and respectability" (Marks, "Jewish Women" 9) and as guardian of the community. Neither novel, however, sanctions the Jewish prostitute/mother. Denied maternal protection, neither Hoda nor Nehama enters prostitution knowingly, for example. Further, each woman is made into an aberrant mother of a child who is tainted at birth. Finally, that neither Hoda nor Nehama remains a prostitute suggests that prostitution and mothering are irreconcilable; in fact, the Jewish prostitute must be made to suffer in extraordinary ways for her trespass into motherhood.

Despite the persistent and widespread belief that prostitution within the Jewish community "was always insignificant" (Marks, "Jewish Women" 6), historical and literary evidence suggest otherwise. Scholarly studies, government documents, and archival records confirm the presence of Jewish prostitutes in urban centres such as Warsaw, London, Buenos Aires, New York, and Montreal.[1] Maimie Pinzer (1885–?), who worked as a prostitute in Philadelphia in the early years of the twentieth century, left a remarkable record of her life in voluminous letters written between 1910 and 1922 to her benefactor, Fanny Quincy Howe (1870–1933), a wealthy Bostonian. At the request of Philadelphia social worker Herbert Welsh, who sought to prevent Pinzer's return to prostitution after she had lost her left eye, "possibly to syphilitic infection" (Rosen xiv), Howe initiated a correspondence that would foster a deep friendship between herself and Pinzer, women of vastly dissimilar backgrounds. In a correspondence housed at the Schlesinger Library of the Radcliffe Institute, and published as a selected edition in 1997, Pinzer articulates the vulnerable and pitiable position of the contemporary prostitute in a society that regarded her as foul and dispensable.

More pertinent to the focus of this essay, however, are the maternal experiences and feelings Pinzer describes throughout her correspondence. Repeatedly, Pinzer shows herself to be as much nurturer as former prostitute. She claims, for example, that she "really can do almost any work that a child's nurse does, for I have helped so often with them" (20), and her letters show this to be the case. She is "in the room" (49) when her sister-in-law Caroline gives birth in 1911, and she helps care for her infant niece Sarah, even as she writes to Howe—"I have the baby on my lap and she seems quiet, [content] just to watch the pen bob about, since it is a red pen-holder and attracts her eye" (99). She attends to the baby's daily needs, often sleeps with her, and regularly brings her gifts. When she has to assist in her brother's grocery store, Pinzer cannot bear leaving her charge: "I love her so much that it is hard to be away from her all day. She's so heavy now that it leaves me all worn out to frolic with her, and yet I can't resist her" (113). Later, when a rift with her brother prevents Pinzer from seeing Sarah, she feels "forced to drive the baby out of my thoughts and heart; otherwise, I should be very miserable when I think of her" (135).

In 1918, Pinzer successfully nursed her niece through an influenza pandemic that swept the United States. When her sister-in-law succumbed to the disease, she adopted Sarah and younger brother David, and raised them with her husband, Ira Benjamin, whom she had known since adolescence and married in January 1917. Pinzer herself likely suffered a miscarriage in 1917, a loss she must have felt keenly, for she understood the depth of maternal love. When her sister-in-law died, she wrote openly to Howe:

> When I lost my baby last year, Caroline, who wrote to me secretly (for [my brother] James had forbidden it), said she felt so badly for me, that if she were able, she'd send Sarah to me to stay for awhile to comfort me. I can recall now that I thought that I'd rather have Potsy [Sarah] than even my own baby. And now I have her, and I love her, but how it hurts me; for she loved her mother, and it is so sad for her. (413–14)

The portrait of Maimie Pinzer that emerges from her letters, acclaimed for their historical and literary value, serves to counter the general perception of prostitutes as hardened individuals, incapable of love, and especially ill fitted to become mothers. Her honesty, emotional intensity, and maternal desire echo through the fictional lives of Hoda and Nehama. Along with Pinzer, who nurtured two adopted children but would neither bear nor raise her own child, they, too, suffer in motherhood.

Like Pinzer, Hoda and Nehama "fall" into prostitution. Following the murder of her father when she was 13, Pinzer was forced to leave high school and seek employment as a department store clerk. Her small earnings helped support her family, including her verbally abusive mother and sexually abusive uncle. Unable, however, to abide the pain of living at home and the restrictions imposed by her mother, Pinzer began to date boys. She was arrested upon a complaint made by her mother and uncle, imprisoned, and then sent for a year to Magdalen Home for wayward girls. When she was released in 1899, Pinzer and her lover Frank Sloan fled to Boston. For four years, between the ages of 14 and 18, Pinzer lived and worked in Boston as an actor at Columbia Theatre, a "nude model for art classes," and a prostitute (Rosen xxii).

As Marks explains, "exclusion from both the host society and the Jewish community [often] left women with little alternative but to turn to prostitution to support themselves" ("Jewish Women" 9). Hoda, like Pinzer, begins her life as a prostitute following the early death of a parent. When her humpbacked mother dies—Rahel's domestic work provided the family's sole income—Hoda is bereft of maternal guidance and family support. Her great-uncle Nate, who had sponsored Hoda and her parents and had paid for their voyage from Russia to North America, suggests that Hoda be sent to the Jewish Children's Orphanage and her father, Danile, to the Jewish Old People's Home. Unwilling to accept her uncle's selfish plans, the adolescent Hoda is left alone to care for her blind father. That she succeeds in doing so shows her youthful determination and resourcefulness as a prostitute in the face of ostracism.

The comic mode of Wiseman's novel, particularly its humorous scenes and affirming close, may leaven one's reading of *Crackpot*, but it does not soften Hoda's humiliating entry into prostitution and the exploitation she experiences. A childhood game of "Doctors and Nurses" (30) leads Hoda to seek out the "bad company" (93) of boys and men. Soon, she is masturbating Yankl the butcher in exchange for "meat scraps" (80) necessary for dinner. While cleaning the Pankess home, her late mother's customer, she receives a dime from Mr. Pankess when he fondles her buttocks. Hoda communes with boys, enjoys their rough language and play, but she quickly becomes a sexual target for adolescent males. After she gives in to her own sexual desire and that of her schoolmate Morgan, who wins the right to seduce Hoda in a betting match, she feels "let down," "uncomfortable," and "unclean," although she cannot remember the "reasons why she felt awful, and she didn't even know how far it was her own fault" (109). Hoda is ambivalent: she feels guilty for having sex but concedes that Morgan had made "her feel so good" (110).

Faced, however, with the pressing need to sustain herself and her father, Hoda is less moral than practical and reasons that "the money Morgan had given her [from his winnings] ... was another good thing. She and Daddy could use that all right" (109). When she learns that sex can be profitable, Hoda sheds her innocence among boys, but not her amiability, and determines "to work up a source of steadier income, so as not to have to rely on one person's whims for hers and her daddy's well-being" (121). She easily convinces her innocent father that she is helping students with their school work, sets up shop in her bedroom, and is soon servicing the boys of her vicinity. With her livelihood ensured, Hoda quickly abandons any lingering sense of guilt. As a moral being for whom the child—parent bond is paramount, however, she regrets having to deceive her father.

Despite her sexual precociousness, Hoda remains emotionally innocent, for she does not venture beyond the familiar boundaries of her home and her neighbourhood. The one time she travels downtown with her friend Seraphina to work at a dance hall, she is nearly raped by a hostile client. Hoda prefers the regular work available locally, at weddings, for example, where middle-aged men pay the "poor orphan, at times with an unexpected generosity born of schnapps and gratitude and the rare surprise of it all" (129), for their furtive sexual encounters in alleys, boiler rooms, against trees or walls. Hoda's presence at communal events is soon expected, in fact, and her role within the Jewish community accepted. Marks cites "many examples of Jewish prostitutes being accepted as part of a 'natural' way of life. While the middle-class, older, established Jews bitterly criticized it, the newcomers, who were mostly working-class and facing poverty, had much more sympathy with it and could understand the reasons women went into [prostitution]" ("Jewish Women" 9–10). The fictional community that embraced Hoda—although it is unnamed, it resembles the North End of Winnipeg of the 1930s and 1940s, where Wiseman was raised—was composed largely of immigrants concerned more with day-to-day survival than the moral issues surrounding prostitution. Eventually, Hoda becomes "something of a legend in the district, as the girl who had broken in just about every mother's son of them" (144).

Although she is less ostracized in fiction than Maimie Pinzer was in life, Hoda feels isolated, without "a real friend" (140). She is physically intimate with boys and men, but Hoda remains outside the community of women.

She lacks girlfriends, and her mother died before she could "answer the [pressing] questions" (140) Hoda increasingly ponders. She assumes she is "pretty safe the way she operated because when you went out with a lot of guys it was more like scrambling the parts of a whole bunch of jig-saw puzzles" (141), but Hoda is not confident that she knows all that is necessary to avoid becoming pregnant, for example. Like Pinzer, who was rejected by her mother, Hoda lacks maternal affection and protection. As women alone, Pinzer and Hoda are especially vulnerable to misinformation, illness, and violence. As prostitutes, they are seen as deserving of suffering, however.

Hoda's suffering is extreme when she becomes a mother. Although her aberrant work as a prostitute is condoned by the community, when she gives birth to a son, she commits an unsanctioned moral trespass, albeit unknowingly. The prostitute is tolerated as long as she serves the sexual needs of men. When she dares to become a mother and thereby an agent who must act independently, in the interests of herself and her child, she defies communal standards for sex workers. Hoda pays dearly for that defiance—she must give up her child and suffer emotional trauma—for neither fiction nor life will accommodate the prostitute/mother.

Hoda's ignorance and her obesity mask her pregnancy. Thus, when she goes into labour she thinks "the sudden, atrocious pain" (153) is a severe stomach cramp and realizes that she has delivered an infant only when the slimy lump on her bed squirms and squawks. Having given birth in the middle of the night, while her father sleeps in the next room, Hoda grows frantic with anxiety. Terrified that Danile will waken to the baby's cries and discover the truth about his daughter, Hoda takes decisive action. After she washes and swaddles her newborn, she deposits him on the steps of the Jewish orphanage, where he is found and subsequently raised to adolescence under the particular care of the director's wife. The boy is doubly tainted by his illegitimate birth and a protruding navel, a disfigurement that results from his mother's clumsy severing and double knotting of the umbilical cord. In fact, the moment of birth remains indelibly imprinted on both son and mother, whose private burden of "memory of her black night" (170) and irreconcilable guilt is felt as regular assaults of "almost superstitious fear" and "acute panic" (188).

At the moment of delivery Hoda understands that to keep her son would have a devastating impact on the child, herself, and her father. First, as the illegitimate child of a prostitute, the boy would lack any status in the community. Further, Hoda's status as mother would negatively affect her ability to work freely as a prostitute to support herself and her family. Moreover, she might risk rejection by her beloved father. In fact, many unmarried mothers, a large number of whom were prostitutes, "found it difficult [if not impossible] to keep their infants.... Unmarried mothers were not encouraged to take on the role of 'caring mother.' Rather, motherhood was promoted as a responsibility which would remind unmarried mothers not to fall again" (Marks, "Luckless Waifs" 130–31). Indeed, Hoda learns from experience and becomes a responsible sex worker. Following the birth of her son, she acquires the knowledge she previously lacked and learns "how babies are made." She begins to use birth control and is examined regularly for sexually transmitted diseases. Over time, she even comes "to accept the idea, particularly in relation to herself, that there were some things that she might not ever be able to make good" (221).

But to atone for her unnatural crime of becoming a mother, the prostitute must be made to suffer in extraordinary ways. Remorse and reform do not prevent the extreme pain that is finally meted out to Hoda in punishment for her "enormous, inerasable debt" (252). When her adolescent son presents himself as a client, Hoda, who recognizes him by his navel, must accept him. For her trespass into motherhood, she must become the incestuous prostitute/mother who initiates her son into sex. Here, incest becomes an unusually moral act that Hoda undertakes to protect her son; it is an act of atonement for the prostitute's crime of bearing a child; it is also an act that leads Hoda to "the outermost boundary of aloneness that can be reached by a human being" (256).

During the brief interval that her son becomes a regular client, Hoda never reveals her true identity as his mother. Rather, as a prostitute she comforts him, converses with him, and eases his difficult entry into adulthood. Hoda's extended sexual relationship with her son serves to prolong her private suffering, but it also affords the reconciliation of "all the aching fragments" (258) of her life. In fiction, as in life, the moral impropriety of the prostitute who becomes a mother, willingly or not, appears to justify her extreme punishment. That the prostitute/mother must be redeemed through excessive anguish attests to the heinousness of her crime and corroborates Adrienne Rich's assertion that women, who "have always been outside the (manmade) law,... have been much more stringently punished than men for breaking the law, as in the case of prostitution" (270).

Gradually, Hoda is released from suffering, but only after she ceases to work as a prostitute. When she accepts the job of hostess at a delicatessen, owned by a former client, she is able to relinquish sex work as a means of economic support. Still at the centre of her community as the doyenne of Limpy Letz's eating and gambling establishment, Hoda acquires a respectability she never knew as the local whore. She also acquires a suitor who seeks her hand in marriage. Through Lazar, a Holocaust survivor who literally crawled out of an open grave and over the corpses of his wife and children to claim his own life, Hoda is offered final redemption. By the close of *Crackpot*, in fact, both Hoda and Lazar are given new opportunities: she through her work in the delicatessen, he as a survivor who is determined to make a new life for himself in North America. But it is Hoda who is truly made anew. No longer a prostitute, she is a restaurant hostess. No longer alone, she will soon become Lazar's wife. Most significant, however, is Hoda's closing dream in which she is *"Almost a real mother!"* (304). Newly virginal as fiancée to Lazar, the promise of "true" motherhood is finally held out to the former prostitute who, the novel implies, may still bear a child in marriage.

Fresh opportunities and the offer of renewed life may be read as hard-won rewards for Hoda's suffering as a prostitute. They also suggest the absolute incompatibility of prostitution and mothering, however, for Hoda must relinquish her prior life as a prostitute—the triumphs and trials of her past, and especially the connection with her son—before she may enter marriage with its prospect of "real" motherhood. That she must do so confirms that legitimate motherhood is not available to the prostitute, who will always remain alone, marginalized by the very community she serves.

In *The Singing Fire*, Nehama Korzen arrives in London from Plotsk in the late nineteenth century, a time when Jewish women, who settled in the crowded and impoverished East End of the city, where the sex trade was firmly established, "were being cursed for prostitution ... [and] the Jewish prostitute symbolized the social evils which were undermining the strength of the family and the empire" (Marks, *Model Mothers* 3). Seeking to avoid an arranged marriage and a traditional life as Jewish wife and mother, the 17-year-old Nehama plans her escape. From her older sisters she steals a pair of earrings, a silk kerchief, and a blouse, sells the valuable items, and defies her parents by purchasing a ticket for London and fleeing her *shtetl* in Poland. When she lands on foreign soil, Nehama, like Maimie Pinzer and Hoda, lacks the parental protection, worldly knowledge, and experience that could prevent her "fall" into prostitution. Rather, as she sits alone in the fog of St. Katherine's dock, Nehama "pray[s] to God, Help me please, because that is what a person does when there is no one else" (7). When her prayers are answered in Yiddish by Mr. Blink, a portly, congenial man who claims to be a fellow Jew, she cannot know that he would soon deliver her to a brutal pimp.

Unlike Pinzer and Hoda, however, Nehama's entry into prostitution is not gradual. As a young woman travelling alone in 1875, Nehama is taken for a whore. Upon her arrival in London, she falls prey to Blink, a pimp's scout. The next morning, Blink bribes a constable to escort Nehama to the London Hospital, where she undergoes an internal examination for venereal infection. Under the Contagious Diseases Acts of 1864, 1866, and 1869, "designed to eliminate venereal disease" (Marks "Jewish Women" 6), British police were permitted by law to detain and examine any woman they suspected of prostitution. That the virginal Nehama feels defiled by the physical examination is precisely the result Blink seeks as he intones, "So you're no longer a good girl" (20). Her defences already weakened, she is unprepared for her sadistic deflowering with a broom handle that is subsequently orchestrated by the Squire, the pimp who intends to ready her for work as a prostitute. Hence, within two days of her arrival, having been beaten into submission by physical brutality and private shame, Nehama yields to the will of her pimp and enters "the trade" (40).

A naive adolescent, Nehama accepts that she must work to repay the Squire's initial outlay of a ten-pound "entrance fee" (41) that admitted her to Britain. Increasingly dehumanized by the bleak circumstances of her life as an East End prostitute, Nehama grows convinced that "God ... [had] abandoned her to the evil inclination" (34). When she learns that she has been deceived, however, and that she is pregnant, she acts with the same agency that drove her flight from Poland and decides to escape to save herself and her baby. Like Pinzer and Hoda, Nehama is as much nurturer as whore. She sends loving letters to her family in Poland, for example, written to convince them that she is well and happy. She is protective of Sally, a much younger prostitute who is ill, even after Sally betrays Nehama's trust. Moreover, Nehama imagines a redemptive birth—she hopes to give birth "by the sea" to a baby with "fair hair" (45)—that will assuage her pain and heal her soul. She yearns for "her old life" (49) of hope, but Nehama's rescue will come at a tremendous cost.

Although she works among women, Nehama cannot rely on their friendship. When another woman reports her escape, Nehama's fate is sealed. Ironically, a niece's loyalty to her pimp uncle—the perverse result of extreme victimization—leads to Nehama's final release from prostitution, but not before she sustains permanent trauma. Following a brutal beating and knifing by the Squire, Nehama suffers a miscarriage. Close to death, she recognizes that she lives within "a block" (49) of Jewish shops, and that if she were to "die in a Jewish street, maybe someone would say the prayer for the dead" (50). Drained and bleeding, Nehama drags herself to salvation in London's teeming Frying Pan Alley, the heart of the Jewish district.

Like Hoda, Nehama must flee the whorehouse before she is offered suc-
cour and companionship. Rescued from the street by Minnie, a kind pass-
erby who intuits her plight, Nehama is afforded refuge when she is most vulnerable. As she recuperates in Minnie's home, where she mourns the loss
of a child conceived out of the hardship of the recent past, she rediscovers
her community, as well as her considerable talent as a seamstress. Having
rejected the aberrant life of the prostitute, Nehama is proffered gentleness,
but privately she remains "in exile," dreaming nightly "of a baby in a white
cap trimmed with lace" (62). Although her life as a prostitute was foreshortened by a miscarriage, the pain Nehama endures as a result of her brief trespass into motherhood is no less extreme than the suffering of either Pinzer
or Hoda. For her illicit behaviour, she, too, is denied the nurturing balm of
motherhood that might salve her emotional and physical wounds.

Through Minnie and her husband, Lazar, Nehama meets the man who
becomes her husband. Nathan's love for Nehama is purifying; when they
make love on Sabbath afternoons, "he trace[s] the scar on her thigh as if it
didn't ruin the smoothness of her leg" (86), and when she becomes pregnant with Nathan's child, she once again envisages redemption: "The first
one she miscarried didn't count. That was in another life. This baby was her
husband's, her beloved's ... and she awaited their child, her heart heavy
with joy" (88). In her late twenties, after she has long ceased to be a prostitute, Nehama enters marriage and anticipates legitimate motherhood. But
as a former prostitute who dared to become pregnant, she bears an indelible
stain that will bar her from bearing a child. When Nehama feels "a familiar
pain in her belly," she understands that she is miscarrying for a second time
and accepts "her punishment" (20): she "wasn't made right" and "there
won't be any more" (89) babies. That Nathan's "child had run away from
her womb" (90) is evidence of the taint that marks the prostitute/mother.
Although she is granted safe haven with Nathan, Nehama must be made to
suffer inconsolably within her marriage.

The trauma of losing a second baby leads Nehama back to St. Katha-
rine's dock. There she rescues a solitary traveller—Emilia Rosenberg reminds Nehama of her younger self—from a pimp "who called out in a familiar language, his face full of concern" (93). Having been seduced and later
abandoned by a young suitor, Emilia has forsaken her village in Poland for
London. As Marks notes, "unmarried mothers were known to leave home in
order to conceal their pregnancy; [and] some of them came from ... Eastern Europe to England to bear their child" ("Luckless Waifs" 123). Unlike
prostitutes, however, unmarried mothers were "[s]een as redeemable ...
[and] occupied a higher position in the hierarchy of fallen women" (127).

When she offers Emilia a place to stay and learns that the young woman is pregnant, Nehama becomes her protector. Bound to Emilia as Minnie was once bound to her, Nehama recognizes a unique opportunity to redress the pain of her own past by assisting Emilia through her pregnancy and caring for her newborn daughter. Ironically, it is Emilia, rather than Nathan, who gives Nehama what she most desires: the chance to be a mother.

When Emilia gives birth, she feels no connection to her daughter and abandons the one-week-old infant, leaving behind the cryptic note "Nehama, please take her" (133). Rather than deliver the baby to the Jews' Orphan Asylum, Nehama decides to keep her. Marks confirms that "neighbours ... who had some understanding of the desperate plight faced by an unmarried mother sometimes adopted ... illegitimate children" ("Luckless Waifs" 122). In fact, Nehama's neighbourly act benefits herself and Nathan, as well as Emilia and her abandoned daughter. Moreover, by accepting Emilia's baby as her own, Nehama initiates a healing process that would prove long and difficult, as she herself intuits: "Everything had worked out; she had a husband, she had a child, she had a means to earn a living. So why couldn't she sleep at night?" (139).

As an adoptive mother who is determined "to make a life" (227) for her daughter, Nehama faces extraordinary challenges that eventually lead to her redemption. When Nathan's right hand is severed in a cart accident and he can no longer work as a tailor, she rallies, helps dispel his depression, and encourages him to become a coffee vendor. Following a burglary in the family tailoring shop, Nehama manages to re-establish her business. It is her daughter, however, who tests Nehama's determination and will to survive.

An adolescent fantasy that her birth mother "was no good and somehow Gittel would make up for it" (318) lures the girl to Dorset Street, the haunt of pimps and whores, where Nehama must face her own past to save her daughter's future. Like Hoda, who is forced to confront the past when her son presents himself as a client, Nehama must follow her daughter's lead and return to the pub where the Squire still presides over his whores. There, she and Nathan find Gittel entertaining the elderly pimp by singing atop a table. When Nathan intervenes between Nehama and the Squire, who recognizes her as one of his former prostitutes, Gittel is saved.

Through the dramatic rescue of Gittel, each family member is healed. First, in the pub, where he finally discerns that his wife was once a prostitute, Nathan asserts, "Never mind. Just remember, where you go, I go" (308). Nathan's generous spirit and understanding bring new intimacy and trust to the bond he shares with his wife. Second, when she is reassured that her birth mother was not a prostitute for having borne an illegitimate child, Gittel feels newly bound to Nehama and "[holds] on to Mama's hand" (317). Absolved of guilt, which she is too young to fully comprehend, Gittel is returned safely to the protection of family. Finally, Nehama's fear of the Squire, which has terrorized her for years, is dispelled through the brave encounter with her past. In returning to Dorset Street, she effectively reclaims her past and rescues her daughter's future. Moreover, Nehama's daring fosters a new honesty between herself and Nathan, and between herself and Gittel. Having freed her daughter from the tantalizing grip of the same pimp who once commanded Nehama's life, she finally feels herself to be Gittel's "true" mother. As she proclaims, "You think I wouldn't come to find you, my Gittel-Sarah? If someone tried to hurt you, I would kill him. I would lie down in the gutter and let anyone walk on my back to keep you safe, my daughter. Even from the next world, you can't lose me. I promise you" (316).

But in the end, despite her strength of character, Nehama does not warrant the same grace accorded Emilia, her former charge. As an unmarried mother, Emilia enjoys full redemption: having rejected her past, she succeeds in establishing a new life for herself, marries well, and is pregnant with her husband's child. In fiction and in life, the unmarried mother may be rehabilitated to new status within her community. As former prostitutes who trespassed into motherhood, Nehama, Hoda, and Maimie Pinzer, however, can never relinquish the hold of the past. As I have shown, neither fiction nor life will accommodate the prostitute/mother whose redemption is tempered by excessive suffering. Moreover, the right to legitimate motherhood will elude the Jewish prostitute who remains thrice outcast, thrice isolate from the community of Jews, women, and mothers.

Acknowledgements

I am grateful to Danielle Deveau for invaluable research assistance and Annette Zilversmit for referring me to *The Maimie Papers*.

Note to Chapter 5

See, for example, Edward J. Bristow, *Prostitution and Prejudice: The Jewish Fight Against White Slavery, 1870–1939* (Oxford: Clarendon Press, 1982); L. P. Gartner, "Anglo-Jewry and the Jewish International Traffic in Prostitution, 1885–1914," *American Jewish Studies Review* 7–8 (1982–83): 129–78; and Isabel Vincent, *Bodies and Souls: The Tragic Plight of Three Jewish Women Forced into Prostitution in the Americas* (Toronto: Random House, 2005).

Works Cited

Marks, Lara. "Jewish Women and Jewish Prostitution in the East End of London." *Jewish Quarterly* 34.2 (1987): 6–10.

——. "'The Luckless Waifs and Strays of Humanity': Irish and Jewish Immigrant Unwed Mothers in London, 1870–1939." *Twentieth Century British History* 3.2 (1992): 113–37.

——. *Model Mothers: Jewish Mothers and Maternity Provision in East London, 1870–1939*. Oxford: Clarendon Press, 1994.

Nattel, Lilian. *The Singing Fire*. Toronto: Alfred A. Knopf, 2004.

Pinzer, Maimie. *The Maimie Papers: Letters from an Ex-Prostitute*. New York: Feminist Press, 1997.

Rich, Adrienne. *Of Woman Born: Motherhood as Experience and Institution*. 1976. New York: W. W. Norton, 1995.

Rosen, Ruth. Introduction. *The Maimie Papers: Letters from an Ex-Prostitute*. By Maimie Pinzer. New York: Feminist Press, 1997. xiii–xliv.

Waddington, Miriam. "The Bond." *Collected Poems*. By Waddington. Toronto: Oxford University Press, 1986. 9–10.

Wiseman, Adele. *Crackpot*. Toronto: McClelland & Stewart, 1974.

Part 2: Maternal Ambivalence

6

Eden Robinson's "Dogs in Winter": Parodic Extremes of Mothering | BY NATHALIE FOY

Even in the midst of the cacophony otherwise known as the "mommy wars," a romanticized vision of perfectible motherhood continues to be a normative aspect of mainstream North American culture. In spite of, and as Judith Warner argues, precisely because of the political and economic gains made by women, we continue to construct motherhood as sacrificial, requiring the devotion of mothers' entire physical, emotional, and intellectual beings. Susan Douglas and Meredith Michaels likewise examine trends in print and televised media that promote a definition of motherhood in which the standards of perfection are impossible to meet, and the influence of that media is almost impossible to escape. The "mommy myth" is ubiquitous; mothers are either sanctified or demonized, and this polarization serves not only to police women's maternal activity, but to measure that activity against extremes.

As a site for the articulation of the anxieties attending the cultural pressure to celebrate all things maternal, literature reveals the fault lines in how we construct motherhood, and Eden Robinson's "Dogs in Winter" is a wonderfully parodic response to the sanctification and demonization of mothers. "Dogs in Winter" appears in the collection *Traplines*, published in 1996 to critical acclaim, and Robinson has expanded two of the four short stories into novels: *Monkey Beach* (2000) and *Blood Sports* (2006). "Dogs in Winter," set in modern-day Vancouver, deftly juggles comedy and horror in a structurally fractured tale of a girl's attempt to negotiate the legacy of her mother's murderous past. Narrated by its protagonist, Lisa Rutford, the story is an achronological patchwork of comical and disturbing episodes from her childhood to late adolescence. The violent ruptures in chronology mirror the violent ruptures in Lisa's life as she is moved from one home to another, from one maternal figure to another. With this story, Robinson represents the sanctification and demonization of mothers from a child's point of view. Abandoned by her mother at a young age, Lisa is discovered alone at home by a police officer, who also finds the remains of several of her mother's victims. While her mother is in prison, Lisa is cared for by her Aunt Genna, who gives her a loving home. Mama subsequently escapes from prison and comes to reclaim Lisa, and they live together on the run. When Lisa is 12, she turns her mother in to the police, and she lives in foster care when her mother is reincarcerated. At 13, Lisa is taken into the permanent care of her foster parents, Paul and Janet, whom she idolizes, but in spite of the love and stability they offer her, they cannot protect her from her fear that her mother will escape and reappear again, this time to kill her. The sanitized normalcy of her adoptive home contrasts starkly with the gritty life Lisa leads with her peers, and she engages in self-mutilation and makes several suicide attempts. Notwithstanding the many gruesome episodes in the text and the palpable loneliness of the narrator, the tone is often comic. Witness this description of Lisa's three-page suicide note:

> At the time it seemed epic and moving, but now I squirm when I think about it. I'm glad I didn't die. What a horrible piece of writing to be remembered by. It was something out of a soap opera: "My Darling Parents, I must leave / I know you will, but you must not grieve" sort of thing. I guess it wouldn't have been so bad if I hadn't made everything rhyme. (51)

Lisa may be suicidal, but she narrates her story into existence; despair and nihilism are leavened by humour and creation. Lisa is a wonderfully wry narrator, and she consciously navigates the saintly and demonic extremes represented by her biological and surrogate mothers. Her attempts at individuation, however, are constantly thwarted by the weight of her mother's criminal legacy and by the unrealistic model of her idealized maternal surrogates.

In this story, Robinson creates extreme examples of good and bad mothers, and the first stage of my argument will be to examine the parodic ends of this hyperbole. Robinson's story, however, is not simply a straightforward satirization. Lisa's anxiety about her mother and her mother's replacements is profound, and she becomes trapped between the extremes of good and bad. The comic effect of Lisa's wry tone and the humour of hyperbole are offset by the pathos of her struggle. The reader, too, struggles with several interpretive impasses. The story blends comedy, horror, and tragedy, and it is difficult to reconcile the laughter, disgust, and pathos that the text elicits. Like the women Douglas and Michaels describe, who pride themselves on seeing through the impossible ideals of the "mommy myth" but nevertheless feel the threat of failing to meet the admittedly impossible standards of perfection, this story enacts a kind of ambivalence. It is at once dismissive of the idealization of motherhood and mournful about the very impossibility of maternal perfection.

Ambiguity is one of the hallmarks of Robinson's style, and discussions of her work often grapple with the question of race and its indeterminacy. Robinson is a First Nations writer whose father is Haisla and whose mother is Heiltsuk, and her novels deal explicitly with race, but in two of the four short stories that compose *Traplines*, the race of the protagonists is difficult to determine. In her discussion of the racial indeterminacy of "Dogs in Winter," Cynthia Sugars argues that Robinson is both "appropriating and reformulating the discourse of savagery" (79). Sugars observes that Robinson

> invokes the often negative imagery conventionally associated with Native peoples (hunting, cannibalism, savagery, primitivism, the windigo/sasquatch) [but] frustrates the reader's desire to interpret her characters on the basis of their ethno-cultural identity.... This strategic ambiguity enables Robinson to launch a radical "post-Indian" response to racist stereotypes by complicating the very origins of "savagery" and "primitivism" and by defying the reader to make a definitive identification of the characters (and their author) as either "white" or "Native." (78–80)

The negative stereotypes are ubiquitous, but without a definitive identification, they cannot obtain. With respect to Robinson's novel *Monkey Beach*, Rob Appleford examines the opposite challenge: the expectation that Aboriginal writers will portray exemplary characters: "All too frequently, Aboriginal artists are viewed (by Aboriginals and non-Aboriginals alike) as impersonal explicators of truths about their culture" (85). He argues that "Robinson recognises ... that a hermetic, authentic Aboriginal subjecthood is unattainable," and the novel's strategically ambiguous deployment of the figure of the Sasquatch "allows Robinson to embed Haisla cultural material in a contemporary context that resists normative images of Aboriginality"

(96, 99). For Appleford, racial indeterminacy means that Robinson escapes the expectation of authenticity. Helen Hoy also engages with the indeterminacy of race, but her struggle is with the very terms used to describe the characters and author:

> I find myself resisting the term "serial killer," used by Robinson's agent, her publisher, interviewers, and reviewers for the narrator's mother.... Despite its functional economy in describing the perpetrator of at least eight murders, most of them involving strangers killed without explanation and apparently for the pleasure of killing, the term seems to substitute the reductive reassurance of a familiar designation for what in the story remains a series of barely glimpsed and possibly inexplicable acts. Mama is a haunting figure in the story precisely because she eludes understanding. Terms such as "Native writer" and "non-Native subject matter" contain the same danger, functioning as empty signifiers purporting to convey or specify meaning when that meaning is, in fact, what is under negotiation. (178)

Hoy's observation about the deceptive "functional economy" of the terms "serial killer," "Native writer," and "non-Native subject matter" applies equally well to "mother." The meaning of motherhood is also under negotiation in this story, and these critics' observations about stereotypical and normative images, about the epistemological hollowness of the very terms we use to describe the characters, apply equally to the representation of mothers. Robinson creates maternal saints and demons only to confound our ability to make such absolute and static categorical demarcations. She undermines the "functional economy" of the terms "good mother" and "bad mother" by making good and bad so extreme that they become meaningless beyond their parodic function.

Critics necessarily equivocate about the race of the characters in this story, but if race is indeterminate, motherhood is overly determined. Moreen Rutford is named for her maternal role—Mama—a name that makes her murderous past more aberrant and abhorrent. In Mama, Robinson has created a hyperbolically evil mother, and Mama's crimes are many. Afraid that she will soon be arrested for the murder of six people, whose remains she has butchered and put in her basement, Mama kills her husband and abandons her daughter:

> "I'm going to have to leave you alone for a bit, honey. Can you take care of yourself? Just for a little while?... Don't let anyone in," she said. "Don't go out. You just watch TV and Mama will be back before you know it. I got you some comics."

"Yay!" I said.

And I never saw her again until she came to get me at Aunt Genna's. (70)

It is unclear from this scene whether Mama does, in fact, intend to return for Lisa. Leaving her in front of the overused substitute for parental care, the television, Mama drives away, "smiling and happy and lethal" (70). A police officer soon arrives to investigate complaints of a foul smell from the corpses, and Mama is arrested three days later (67, 69).

"Dogs in Winter" is replete with sound and image rhymes and with scenes that mirror each other, a technique that helps to offset the fragmentation of the achronological episodes. In a scene that mirrors her being left alone in front of the television, Lisa describes an encounter with her mother that takes place years later when, once again, she is alone in front of the television. This time, her mother is on the other side of the screen, on a sensationalist talk show. This venue exaggerates her depravity, and Mama is unrepentant about the murders she has committed:

> She was hooked in from her cell via satellite. Another woman, one who had murdered her mother and her grandmother, sat in front of the studio audience, handcuffed to the chair. Next to her was a girl who had drowned her baby in a toilet, thinking that it had been sent to her by the devil....
>
> The talk-show host gave the microphone to a man from the audience who asked, "When was the first time you killed?"
>
> For a long time Mama said nothing. She stared straight into the camera, as if she could see the audience.
>
> "I lost my virginity when I was twenty-seven," Mama said.
>
> "That wasn't the question," the talk-show host said impatiently.
>
> Mama smiled, as if they hadn't got the punch line. "I know what the question was."
>
> I shut the TV off. (45–46)

In this instance, Lisa's rejection of her mother is absolute. Her mother's juxtaposition with women guilty of matricide and infanticide, the sleazy talk-show venue, the puerile curiosity of the studio audience, all combine to make Mama appear even more depraved, and it is in this scene that Robinson's characterization is most exaggerated. These are all unnatural women, women who contravene laws of nature, and, this scene suggests, they must be locked away, but visibly so and available to a gawking public who will define them only by their crimes. Mama is publicly marked as wilfully and irredeemably bad.

In stark contrast, both of Lisa's surrogate mother figures, Genna and Janet, are idealized, and the similarity in their names highlights the way in which Lisa romanticizes each of the women who care for her in her mother's absence. Lisa spends the first years her mother is in prison with her Aunt Genna, and her first surrogate mother is a lovable eccentric. Genna's love and care are uncomplicated and unconditional, and Lisa recounts nothing but positive memories of her time with her aunt. Even her memory of Genna's fabricating a story about her parents' whereabouts has a nostalgic wistfulness:

> "They are in Africa.... They are both doctors and great explorers. They wanted so very much to take you with them, but there are too many snakes and tigers in Africa. They were afraid you'd be eaten.... My Lady Lisa, they didn't want to leave you. Your mother cried and cried when they took you out of her arms. Oh, how she cried. She was very sad.... But I will always be here for you," she said, patting my back. "I will always be here, my Lady Lisa."
>
> Aunt Genna told me other things. She told me there were monsters and bogeymen in the world, but all you had to do was be a good girl and they wouldn't get you. I always believed Aunt Genna until Mama killed her. (43–44)

The abrupt revelation of Genna's murder highlights the many levels on which Lisa's innocence is shattered by her mother's return. Not only is she robbed of a loving aunt, she is robbed of the comforting fiction of her mother's regret and her aunt's power to protect her. The bitterness in Lisa's tone when she declares that she "always believed Aunt Genna until Mama killed her" is directed not at the woman who lied to her about her history, but at the mother who robbed her of the innocence that the lies helped to preserve.

Lisa may have been robbed of a fiction about her past, but her idealism about her maternal surrogates survives. The child's world of tea parties gives way to an adolescent cynicism, and even though she is now wary of her impressions, she continues to idealize her maternal surrogates: "Janet and Paul are the parents I've always wanted. Sometimes I feel like I've stepped into a storybook or into a TV set" (41). When she first meets them, she immediately romanticizes them: "Paul and Janet looked like a couple out of a Disney movie. I couldn't believe my luck. I didn't trust it.... I couldn't get over how perfect they looked, how normal they seemed. I didn't want to say anything to them about Mama. If I did, they might send me back like a defective toaster" (42). At this point, it seems that Lisa's reticence about discussing her mother's crimes is purely self-protective. Afraid of being tainted by association, she keeps silent about her mother so that she can preserve the "perfect" and "normal" new family unit. However, we later learn that she takes on the burden of protecting her foster parents from her past and its continuing influence. When her mother sends emissaries to ask Lisa to visit her in prison, Lisa keeps the reason for their visit secret from Janet (50). When they find her crying in front of the television after an aborted suicide attempt, we witness another example of Lisa's need to protect Paul and Janet:

> Paul and Janet said they wanted to know everything about me, but there were things that made them cringe. What would they do if I said, "I'm afraid Mama will find me and kill me"?
>
> "I'm such a marshmallow. I even cry at B.C. telephone commercials," is what I said.
>
> Paul leaned over and smoothed my hair away from my face. "You know we love you, don't you, Pumpkin?"
>
> He smelled of Old Spice and I felt like I was in a commercial. Everything would be perfect, I thought, if only Canada had the death penalty. (57)

Unable simply to enunciate her fear, and unable to trust that their love can protect her, Lisa hopes in vain for the most extreme solution possible: her mother's execution. Her vulnerability is palpable, and so is her fear that their life is the stuff of televised fiction. In the case of Paul and Janet, television serves as a kind of emotional prophylactic. Their similarity to Disney characters and to life in a commercial, and their quotidian perfection, render Paul and Janet desirable but unreal. Even as she lives her life with them, she feels separated from them. With respect to her mother, however, the television makes her all too real, her crimes all too sordid, her existence all too threatening.

With television as an aid to characterization, Robinson seems, then, to have created positive and negative models of maternity that Lisa should be able respectively to embrace and reject, but she cannot. In part, this inability has to do with the parodic function of these characters. Genna and Janet are, quite literally, too good to be true, and Robinson demonstrates that the kind of maternal perfection and protection that they represent is the fictional stuff of television and children's stories. Their ability to protect her from a murderous mother has already proven feeble, and their perfection is incommensurate with the "real" and violent life that Lisa leads with her peers. Similarly, Mama is so random and prolific a murderer that she is reduced to a caricature of "savage," fodder for bad television. "Dogs in Winter" undermines normative images of beatific motherhood and racialized images of bad motherhood by making the mother figures so hyperbolic that they exit the realm of the real. To this extent, then, characterization is parodic and meaning is playfully suspended. With poles this extreme, "good" and "bad" become epistemologically empty, and we laugh at the absurdity of how far the poles by which we judge mothers have been pushed.

We can laugh at and dismiss these poles as parodic, but Lisa cannot; she is ambivalent about her mother(s) and cannot effectively embrace the good or reject the bad. As Rozsika Parker notes, ambivalence is a "concept developed by psychoanalysis according to which quite contradictory impulses and emotions towards the same person co-exist. The positive and negative components sit side by side and remain in opposition" (*Torn in Two* 5–6). In children, the co-existence of love and hate for the mother facilitates a positive stage of individuation. In "Dogs in Winter," however, Lisa struggles to achieve individuation. Robinson does not depict Genna's or Janet's doubts about their roles, and, ironically, Mama never doubts her ability to mother, to love and protect her child. Only Lisa is suspicious about the love her murdering mother could feel, especially considering that Lisa has betrayed her. Lisa's suspension between the multiple poles of attraction and repulsion—love and hate for Mama, wistfulness and cynicism about Genna and Janet, betrayal of Mama and loyalty to Genna and Janet—traps her. Lisa cannot adequately separate herself from all of these mothers, and her only outlet for action becomes self-destructive.

Lisa's inability to benefit from the models of maternity in this text is also due to a generational reversal: she unnaturally supersedes and is wiser than the women who mother her. Lisa has survived abandonment, abduction, disillusionment, and multiple suicide attempts, experiences that make her older than her years. Lisa's response to her vulnerability is to reverse the roles of protector and protected. Genna, with her tea parties and imaginary world of English ladies, is, in retrospect, hopelessly naive and vulnerable to Mama's revenge, and Lisa learns to fear her mother's return in case she meets with the same fate as Genna. Having lost her own innocence, Lisa feels that she must preserve it for Paul and Janet. Their "storybook" world, Janet's Peter Pan collars, and her work as an elementary school teacher suggest that Janet is trapped in a world of permanent childhood (41, 42). Genna and Janet are both untenable maternal figures for Lisa because Lisa feels older and wiser than them. In her postcolonial reading of the story, Cynthia Sugars notes a similar kind of generational reversal in Lisa's relationship to her mother. Sugars reads Mama's relationship to Lisa in terms of psychological abjection: "The abject is that which haunts the self by continuously bringing it into crisis—generally in the form of some cast-off part or product of the body (e.g., corpse, animal, flesh, excrement). In the colonial context, the abject becomes metaphorized as the subordinate colonial object that constantly brings the imperial self into question" (81). In her reading, Mama is that "subordinate," the Native Savage writ large, and the daughter feels superior to the murderous mother, who "produces the ultimate abject entity in the form of a corpse or cadaver which propels the 'I' (and by extension the civilized social world) into the vortex of abjection" (81). Her mother, having murdered Lisa's father and aunt and having failed in both her moral and maternal duties, leaves Lisa to bear the weight of the responsibility for civilized social behaviour. Wishing her dead at the hands of a penal system is a way to shift responsibility back to "the civilized social world." Lisa—disgusted, ashamed, and frightened—wants to sever her connection to her mother, to remove herself from the dysfunctional unfolding of generational sequence and cast off her subordinate mother.

One obstacle to this thorough rejection is that Robinson complicates and enriches the portrayal of Mama by adding a nurturing dimension. In her memory of their life on the run, Lisa idealizes their time alone and portrays Mama as both nurturing and child-like: "We camped by a turquoise lake. Mama made bacon and eggs and pancakes over a small fire. Everything tasted delicious.... Mama was happy.... Her cheeks were apple-red and dimpled up when she smiled" (61–62). Lisa's memory of the first time she saw Mama kill also softens her image. Mama saves her from an attacking pit bull, and Lisa's memory of the event is of Mama and the dog running toward each other "like lovers bounding across a sunlit field" (48). The incongruous image highlights the irony that Mama's first murder—that which makes her so deviant in the eyes of the talk-show public and so abhorrent to her daughter—was provoked by maternal protectiveness. The story's jumbled chronology also undercuts Lisa's rejection of her mother. Its structure does not depict Lisa's unfolding maturation with a linear chronology, and scenes from childhood lie alongside and often intrude on scenes from adolescence and young adulthood. We sense that Lisa has never outgrown her innocent childhood need and love for her mother because the story does not arrive and settle at her moment of rejection. Her ambivalence is not part of a healthy progress toward individuation; it is an aspect of her inability to leave her past behind.

The story's structural upsetting of chronological sequence mirrors the upsetting of generational sequence and the process of maturation. Lisa's experience of childhood is foreshortened by her mother's crimes, her aunt's murder, and her perceived need to protect her foster parents. Both the narrative and the biological and surrogate families on which Lisa depends for a sense of self are fractured, and Lisa lacks both matrilineal and narrative continuity. Lisa is adrift in her attempts to form an identity, a psychological impasse mirrored by the story's lack of closure. She clearly continues to be afraid of her mother's reappearance, and she admits to three suicide attempts, but it is unclear whether she will continue to attempt suicide as a response to the threat of her mother's return. The story's structure mirrors this ambiguity and turmoil with its lack of a teleological goal. The final scene of the story takes place when Lisa is a child and her mother first leaves her: "She kissed me all over my face and gave me a big hug before she left.... I watched her bounce down the walkway to the car, wave once, and drive away, smiling and happy and lethal" (70). Neither Lisa's life nor her story can move forward (as her mother's do here), and her future is uncertain as long as she waits in fear for her mother's return.

The idyllic interlude of their time alone after Mama takes Lisa from Aunt Genna ends when Lisa discovers Mama's scrapbook of newspaper clippings about her crimes, a discovery that triggers traumatic memories: "That night I dreamed of Aunt Genna showering in blood. Mama held me until I stopped trembling" (62). Even here there is an ambivalence; Mama is at once the cause of and the balm for the distress. The hymn she sings to comfort Lisa is telling: "Rock of ages, cleft for me.... Let me hide myself in thee" (62). Lisa is afraid not only that Mama lurks somewhere out there, waiting to kill her for her betrayal and for her ingratitude, but that her mother's evil is also hidden within her own genes.

The continuity represented by matrilineage is not only physically and psychologically threatening to Lisa; her mother's return constitutes a genetic threat as well. Throughout most of the story, the disjointedness of the achronological scenes is visually marked on the page by extra spaces between the episodes. However, in the most structurally jumbled scene of the story—the dinner at her friend Amanda's—Lisa does not discriminate between past and present. The venison that is served for dinner reminds Lisa of her mother's hunting—animal and human (the carcasses of her victims resemble "deer or calves") (69). The venison also reminds Lisa of a bloody rite her mother performed, smearing the blood of a butchered moose on Lisa's cheeks in honour of her menarche. Her rejection of her own matrilineage is so powerful that she cannot contain it, and, uncontrollably nauseated by the associations, she stains the symbol of Amanda's own orderly and genteel maternal inheritance:

> The maid brought in a large white ceramic tureen. As she lifted the lid, the sweet, familiar smell of venison filled the room. I stared at my plate after she placed it in front of me.

"Use the fork on the outside, dear," Amanda's mother said helpfully.

But I was down by the lake. Mama was so proud of me. "Now you're a woman," she said. She handed me the heart after she wiped the blood onto my cheeks with her knife. I held it, not knowing what to do. It was warm as a kitten.

"I think you'd better eat something," Amanda said.

"Maybe we should take that glass, dear."

The water in the lake was cool and dark and flat as glass. The bones sank to the bottom after we'd sucked the marrow. Mama's wet hair was flattened to her skull. She pried a tooth from the moose and gave it to me. I used to wear it around my neck.

"I'm afraid," I said. "She has a pattern, even if no one else can see it."

"Your stew is getting cold," Amanda's mother said.

The coppery taste of raw blood filled my mouth. "I will not be her," I said. "I will break the pattern."

Then I sprayed sour red wine across the crisp handwoven tablecloth that had been handed down to Amanda's mother from her mother and her mother before that. (60–61)

The non sequiturs in the dialogue mirror how her past has made Lisa an uncomfortable fit for every community that tries to welcome her, but she is uncomfortable in her own skin as well. As Sugars observes, Lisa "not only fears for her own life but, more significantly, also suspects that the same impulses may be germinating within her, thus echoing the early colonizers' notion that savagery was 'in the blood'" (82–83). What is literally and metaphorically "in the blood" gets spat out and rejected, but still constitutes a threat. Lisa's failure to separate disparate events here as she has elsewhere attests to the intractability of this blood connection. The confusing intrusion of the past into the present illustrates the degree to which Mama is physically, psychically, and genetically obtrusive.

Lisa eventually faces and conquers her fear that she may be capable of murder when she defends herself against a potential attacker. She points a gun at him but is unable to shoot: "Mama would never have hesitated. She'd have enjoyed killing him. I had waited too long.... I can't kill, I decided then. That is the difference. I can betray, but I can't kill. Mama would say that betrayal is worse" (66–67). Lisa is unambiguous about her rejection of murder as a solution to the threat she faces, but her tone is ambivalent. She seems to berate herself for having betrayed her mother, both in her failure to pull the trigger and in turning her in. Lisa can turn her mother off, she can spit her out, but these instances of dramatic rejection belie the intractable desire for her mother.

All the stories in *Traplines* are powerful examples of fiction that both activates a yearning for the ideal family and radically undercuts that yearning by highlighting its untenability. They also force us to examine what is at stake for children in the appeal of the perfect family. "Dogs in Winter" both mocks the perfectibility of motherhood and mourns its impossibility. In spite of the numerous ways in which the text challenges the reader— the epistemological impasse attending race and polarized models of maternity, the structural impasse regarding teleology, Lisa's psychological impasse with respect to her mother(s)—the reader benefits from an honesty and frankness that Lisa does not or cannot have with others. We know more about Lisa than any character internal to the diegesis, and that knowledge carries with it an interpretive and discursive responsibility. When Hoy hesitates to call Mama a serial killer, she is attune to that responsibility, and she calls attention to the way in which Robinson subverts stereotypical representations of bad mothers. If the text is haunted by the threat of maternal aggression being unleashed on the child, we as readers can be cautious about our own discursive aggression in our willingness to demonize Moreen. We will never know why Moreen kills, but I think that Robinson uses such extreme characterization for the same reason that she deploys strategically ambiguous Native savagery: to confound, not compound stereotypes. Lisa is not suicidal simply because her mother is a killer; she is convinced about her own inability ever to match the perfection of her idealized maternal surrogates. Robinson confounds the idealization of mothers by illustrating its disadvantages. Paul and Janet's perfection means that the only outlet for Lisa's dark and disturbing emotions is self-destructive. Robinson portrays, from a child's point of view, the very real threat of maternal saints and demons, and the reader can help to transform ambivalence, experienced by Lisa as a paralyzing and self-destructive state, into a productive interrogation of motherhood, in all of its guises.

Works Cited

Appleford, Rob. "'Close, very close, a b'gwus howls': The Contingency of Execution in Eden Robinson's *Monkey Beach*." *Canadian Literature* 184 (2005): 85–101.

Douglas, Susan, and Meredith Michaels. *The Mommy Myth: The Idealization of Motherhood and How It Has Undermined Women*. New York: Free Press, 2004.

Hoy, Helen. *How Should I Read These? Native Women Writers in Canada*. Toronto: University of Toronto Press, 2001.

Parker, Rozsika. *Torn in Two: The Experience of Maternal Ambivalence*. London: Virago, 1995.

Robinson, Eden. "Dogs in Winter." *Traplines*. Toronto: Vintage, 1996.

Sugars, Cynthia. "Strategic Abjection: Windigo Psychosos and the 'Postindian' Subject in Eden Robinson's 'Dogs in Winter.'" *Canadian Literature* 181 (2004): 78–91.

Warner, Judith. *Perfect Madness: Motherhood in the Age of Anxiety*. New York: Penguin, 2005.

7

Subverting the Saintly Mother: The Novels of Gabrielle Poulin | BY KATHLEEN KELLETT-BETSOS

Novelist, poet, and critic Gabrielle Poulin describes her initial impulse to write partly as a response to a frustrated maternal desire: "I felt the stirring of a nostalgia and regret that I had believed long gone: I had no child, I would never have one, except in my dreams. But, within me, a louder voice objected: Nothing is impossible for one who writes!" Her characters would be "the children of desire and promise."[1] Born in Saint-Prosper, Quebec, in 1929, Gabrielle Poulin had renounced maternity upon taking her vows as one of the Soeurs des Saints-Noms-de-Jésus-et-de-Marie in Outremont in 1950, working within the order as a teacher while pursuing studies first at the Institut de Spiritualité de Nicolet and later at the University of Montreal. Upon leaving religious orders in 1968, she continued her career as a teacher but also began to write poetry, literary criticism, and fiction. Although Poulin has lived in Ottawa since 1971, she considers her childhood home of Saint-Prosper to be an important source of inspiration (VE 18).

In 1979, Poulin published her first novel, *Cogne la Caboche*, an autofictional account of a young woman's life as a nun, ending with her departure from the convent in the wake of Quebec's Quiet Revolution, a tumultuous period of social change in the 1960s which saw a diminishing role for

This is a significantly revised version of a paper entitled "Images of Maternity in Novels by Gabrielle Poulin," given at the annual conference of the American Council for Quebec Studies in October 2000 in Montreal, Quebec. All translations are mine unless otherwise indicated.

religious orders and a correspondingly increased role for the modern state in health, education, and other institutions. As historian Micheline Dumont points out, from 1900 to 1961, the number of women entering religious orders in Quebec increased steadily, partly because the religious vocation offered young women in Quebec one of the few means of pursuing their aspirations for security and a socially valued career as an alternative to domestic service or marriage, for example (282–85). Outside the Church, maternity was considered a woman's destiny; Lori Saint-Martin, in her study *Le nom de la mère*, notes: "Religious discourse, broadly circulated in Quebec until the 1960s and even beyond, shows [the mother] as asexual, smiling despite her pain, and altruistic" (13). Such an image, although perhaps noble, can hardly be thought to inspire anything but an ambivalent maternal desire. At the same time, as Dumont indicates, religious orders promised women the exalted possibility of "spiritual maternity"; the nun was to be "a bride of Christ, a mother of souls" (285). As Quebec social institutions became more secular, new career paths opened to women and the religious vocation went into serious decline. The ideal of the selfless *mater dolorosa*, whether she be "mother of souls" or the mother of numerous offspring, long persisted in Quebec culture like the lingering odour of incense. The six novels written by Poulin present the lives of women touched by the increasing secularization of their society and by changing ideals of womanhood.

In Poulin's fiction, narrative and maternity are inextricably linked. As mothers, surrogate mothers, and daughters tell their life stories orally or in writing, the joys and, especially, the frustrations of the mother–child relationship constitute a recurrent theme. It is particularly useful then to consider Poulin's representations of the maternal in the context of Marianne Hirsch's study *The Mother/Daughter Plot*, which examines the ways in which women writers contest restrictive literary conventions created within a "sex-gender system which ... identifies writing as masculine and insists on the incompatibility of creativity and procreativity." Hirsch insists: "Female plots, as many feminist critics have demonstrated, act out frustrations engendered by these limited possibilities and attempt to subvert the constraint of dominant strategies by means of various 'emancipatory strategies'—the revision of endings, beginnings, patterns of progression" (8).[2] In examining the maternal role, Poulin reconstructs archetypal narratives, notably that of Demeter and Persephone, but situates them in the context of a society in transition.

Saint-Martin associates the theme of hostility toward the mother with Quebec women's writing beginning in the 1970s, when authors such as Nicole Brossard celebrated the "symbolic putting to death of the 'patriarchal mother'" (48).[3] Poulin's early novels follow this trend in their representation of matrophobia, if one recalls here Adrienne Rich's well-known remark that matrophobia is not fear of the mother but fear of becoming one's mother (Saint-Martin 25).[4] The main character of Poulin's 1983 novel *Les Mensonges d'Isabelle*[5] is a young university student who is part of a research team studying the representation of the family in Quebec literature. Although she has yearned for her own birth mother, Isabelle scorns her colleagues for their fascination with the mother figure: "Let the others deal with the dark phantoms of mothers, prisoners of words and conventions from the past" (*MI* 71–72).[6] Like Rachel Delisle in *Cogne la caboche* and Françoise Martin in *Un cri trop grand* (1980), Isabelle frees herself only by refusing the mother's most cherished norms. As Saint-Martin observes, it is not until the 1980s that Quebec women writers begin to focus on the mother as subject (48), a tendency that is evident in Poulin's novels *La Couronne d'oubli* (1990) and *Le Livre de déraison* (1994). These more recent novels explore the previously taboo theme of maternal anger, recognizing that the fossilized image of maternal saintliness denies the fundamental humanity of the mother. Finally, in Poulin's latest novel, *Qu'est-ce qui passe ici si tard?* (1998), the main female protagonist speaks as daughter, potential mother, and lover in counterpoint to the discourse of a desired and desiring male narrator heavily invested in the nostalgic yearning for pre-Oedipal fusion with the Mother. Caught between matrophobia and the desire for maternal love, between the ideal of the saintly mother and the very real burdens of childrearing, Poulin's female protagonists manifest a painful ambivalence toward maternity.

The role of the patriarchal mother in Quebec literature is to teach her daughters to conform to socially prescribed norms of femininity. Poulin's novels often represent the daughter rebelling against the mother's rigid views of womanhood. In *Cogne la caboche*, Rachel Delisle originally follows her filial destiny by entering religious orders, thus accomplishing what her mother, Anna, for reasons of ill health, could not. The convent assigns Rachel the name Soeur Marie-Anna-des-Anges, when in fact Anna was her third choice after Marie-Paule, the name of her dead sister, and Charles, her father's name. Anna herself considers that Rachel has taken her mother's place in the convent (11).[7] The critic Grahame Jones underlines Anna's role as enforcer of social conventions:

> Anna, Rachel's mother, applies to the moral complexities of life the philosophy of a seamstress: "It's like in dressmaking: myself, I always needed a good pattern, but I know there are some that can make all their clothes without one" [*AWH* 8]. Patterns govern the imagination of mothers especially determined to preserve the established order. (268)[8]

Rachel gradually learns to free herself from the pattern imposed on her by the rigid constraints of her religious order. Because Anna idealizes convent life, she has difficulty understanding Rachel's motivation for leaving the convent at the age of 35, but realizing that each must construct her own life with or without a pattern, she accepts her daughter's decision.

In *Un cri trop grand*,[9] the patriarchal mother is a more sinister character than the gentle Anna of *Cogne la caboche*. The protagonist, Françoise, is the oldest of the four girls that Fleurange Martin bore before finally producing the desired male child. One of the maids assures Françoise that the mother would give up all of her daughters in order to save her son (*CTG* 118). The mother tries to repress in Françoise both maternal and erotic desire. When Françoise plays with her baby brother, her mother descends upon her and snatches him away. As her brother, François, grows older and the mother less vigilant, Françoise tells him Bible stories, such as the story of Moses and the Pharaoh's daughter, but as her brother falls asleep, she imagines the Pharaoh's daughter frozen in the water as the baby in the basket drifts away (*CTG* 132). The mother pays attention only to Françoise's transgressions. Upon discovering Françoise admiring her own body in a mirror, the mother slaps her and accuses her of perversion (*CTG* 147). When Françoise's hunger for affection leads to her being raped, Fleurange Martin ensures that the rape, the subsequent pregnancy, and the adoption are well hidden from society. Only her father comes to visit in Quebec City to give support to his eldest daughter. Françoise will never be able to have other children, although as a teacher and an aunt, she will be a surrogate mother to many.

In *Les Mensonges d'Isabelle*, the adoptive mother, Suzanne, a child of the Quiet Revolution, feels that Isabelle should rejoice that her generation is free of the taboos and religious restrictions imposed on the previous one. At the same time, she tries to promote very rigid norms of feminine behaviour, reproaching her daughter for her unfeminine taste in colours, clothes, and activities; even contemporary nuns enjoy life more than Isabelle, according to the mother (*MI* 28). Isabelle resents her adoptive mother for having obliterated the name given her by her biological mother, imagining Suzanne choosing the name "Isabelle" ("belle") with her usual obsession with girlish prettiness (*MI* 12). Suzanne seeks emotional closeness with her daughter but is thwarted by Isabelle's nonconformist attitudes. When she violates Isabelle's privacy by reading the diary that she had given her for her birthday, she is disappointed to find no special place for herself as mother, not even the mention of her name. Isabelle resorts to writing two sets of diaries: the blue notebooks intended for her mother's eyes and the black notebooks in which she can present her private thoughts, hidden from the patriarchal mother. Only at the end of the novel, as Isabelle is about to embark on her own mother–daughter relationship with her divorced lover's daughter, Sophie, does she finally begin to accept her adoptive mother.

Turning away from the mother, the matrophobic daughter seeks a substitute worthy of emulation. The classic Electra complex defined by Freud would have the daughter turn to the father in reaction to her discovery that both mother and daughter are castrated and thus incomplete. Whether one attributes the daughter's attraction to the father as part of the development from the pre-Oedipal stage to the Oedipal stage or simply to the daughter's awareness that society accords more power to males, it is evident that mothers and daughters are often rivals for male affection. Certainly, in Poulin's novels, daughters tend to idolize the father. In *Cogne la caboche*, Rachel attributes life-giving properties to the father rather than the mother:

> The little girl in her father's hands, while attached to her mother's body, still had a link with death. It was he, the father, who cut the cord, freed the infant's throat from its anguish and allowed its cry to be heard. As long as the father lived, as long as he held her like a trophy in his outstretched arms, the little girl was immortal. Let him go, and the silence would gnaw its way into her very core. (*AWH* 136)

In *Un cri trop grand*, Françoise and her brother adore their father, David, associating him with the biblical King David (*CTG* 131). The comparison is in fact ironic, given the father's relative powerlessness within his own family. In *Les Mensonges d'Isabelle*, Isabelle addresses her father in her private journal, admitting that she loves to have him and her brother defend her against the mother's criticisms, since she and her mother have always had a certain rivalry (*MI* 20). In his study of Poulin's early novels, Grahame Jones affirms that the daughters turn to the father in reaction to the mother's repressed sexuality: "The dominant figure in the world of sexuality is the father. Just as the mother represents repression, so the father transmits freedom, the loss of inhibition" (275).[10] However, although the father may be a benevolent figure in Poulin's fiction, he offers no key to understanding the daughter's often sensual yearning for maternity. For example, Rachel, rebelling against the restrictions of convent life, loses herself in a highly erotic discourse, imagining herself as a free woman, with a "[…] living, naked, provocative woman's body, washed clean from sweat and tears, purified from the smells of incense, rancid oil and stagnant holy water […]" (*AWH* 94): "Women long to be like her; children seek the comfort of her arms; and infants, the warmth of her breasts, bursting with new milk…. And the earth takes back her daughter, and restores her primal vesture" (*AWH* 94). This passage presents an image of fertility and abundance, drawing on the myth of the Great Mother, of Demeter and Persephone reunited, Rachel's life as a Bride of Christ being equivalent to a sojourn in Hades. Hirsch points out that the Demeter myth, in which the daughter and mother are separated by male intervention, supplies the necessary break from the plenitude of the pre-Oedipal bond, thus stimulating the creative impulse: "narrative demands some form of breech, some space of anxiety and desire into which to inscribe itself" (35).

Despite the rivalry between mothers and daughters for male affection, psychoanalytic theory has insisted that the daughter, even more than the son, remains emotionally attached to the mother, having less reason to assert difference in order to break the pre-Oedipal bond.[11] In fact, in Poulin's novels, the father is not the primary substitute for the mother's affection. Frequently, in the context of Quebec society, Poulin's heroines seek the mother in the more highly revered figure of the nun. Remembering her time spent at convent school, Rachel recalls comparing the refinement of the nuns with her mother's humble manner:

> How she had longed, as a young girl, to be able to choose among these beautiful and distinguished women, a mother who would love her alone, who would come to her cubicle in the evening, to whom she would tell her joys and sorrows, her troubles and her dreams, who might have explained to her all the mysterious things that were happening in her body and her heart! (*AWH* 132)

After her years as a nun forbidden all physical contact with her students, Rachel is aware of the aridity of convent life and realizes the value of her mother's love: "All those mothers with their dried-up wombs had lost their haloes. Anna had been restored to her rightful place" (*AWH* 133). Isabelle also remembers favouring the nuns at the expense of her mother: "The nuns, on the other hand, seemed to me to be angels of perfection. They hardly ate, didn't drink, wore coarse fabric, moved silently, without the tapping of heels, never went into stores or banks, didn't have people over for tea and didn't play bridge" (*MI* 146).[12] The rejection of the idealized mother figure represented by the nun is essential to reconciliation with the mother.

In *Un cri trop grand*, Françoise finds a mother surrogate closer to home: her aunt Marie-Hélène. The aunt's early death from tuberculosis ends their relationship, but Françoise, forced to abandon her illegitimate child, in turn assumes the maternal role for her own niece Marie-Françoise, the two of them drawn together especially when Marie-Françoise loses her unborn son and her husband as a result of a car accident. In the novel's epilogue,

Marie-Françoise encounters a new student named Marie-Hélène, whose mysterious manner suggests that she is perhaps the phantom of the great-aunt. Thus, the cycle of maternal surrogacy, from aunt to niece, allows for the successful quest for the good mother.

In these novels, the mother quest inclines the narrative to a circular form, as events reunite mother and daughter. *Cogne la caboche* begins and ends with the perspective of Rachel's mother, Anna, contemplating her daughter's entry and departure from the convent. In the opening chapter, Anna recalls her own abandoned vocation, and her years as wife and mother. She ponders a dream image of Rachel bitten by a serpent that had escaped from beneath the foot of a statue of the Virgin Mary. In the dream Rachel goes on to free the crucified Jesus along with the two thieves executed with him at Golgotha. Christ smiles upon her and leaves with the body of Rachel's sister Marie-Paule, who died in childhood. As Anna is vaguely aware of Rachel's unhappiness at the convent, Christ's smile suggests approval of Rachel's desire for freedom and acknowledgment of an end to the need to expiate her sister's death. Anna's prayer at the end of this chapter also suggests that she liberates her daughter from fulfilling her own failed vocation: "Before she went to sleep again, she murmured almost in a whisper, perhaps to exorcize the dreams that might come, 'Oh God, Your will be done,' and shyly she added, 'in Rachel'" (*AWH* 12). In the penultimate chapter, upon walking away from the convent where she has lived for 15 years, Rachel wonders, "Must she tell all this, as one tells a story?" (*AWH* 200), at which point she repeats the opening words of the novel. She thus rejoins her mother and re-creates their story. The final chapter of *Cogne la caboche* presents Anna preparing herself for Rachel's visit. Rereading the letter in which Rachel announces that she has left religious orders, Anna remembers that she was sitting in that very chair when she had the first contractions announcing Rachel's birth. Again, she feels something like birth pangs:

> She felt no pain, but a slight tremor warned her that something was quickening within her. It was not a child, it was not a dream, nor was it the past. It was patient, persistent, like the seeds that had begun to germinate in the soil of the garden, like the stalks that were growing longer and already putting forth above the graves, over there, their colours and scents.... The door opened, and that was the signal to begin. (*AWH* 205–06)

The images of death associated with convent life throughout the novel reinforce the reading of *Cogne la caboche* as a retelling of the myth of Demeter and Persephone. Mother and daughter are reunited after the daughter's descent into the underworld: the seemingly refined but cold world of the convent is abandoned for the mother's more organic world. However, the tale evoked by Rachel herself is rather that of Sleeping Beauty, the story she tells her young charges at the convent; she prays: "O God, give me back my youth, waken me from my long sleep. I am only 35, but I have slept for a hundred years. Bring me out of this tomb before my skin is faded and wrinkled, my bones out of joint, my heart cold and hard" (*AWH* 22). Although Rachel is romantically inclined toward Father Jean, who has already left religious orders, her awakening does not depend on the arrival of a prince; her personal journey for fulfillment emerges from growing dissatisfaction with the spiritual emptiness of her life as a nun. The protagonist's name also suggests the biblical Rachel, who was originally barren but later gave birth to two sons; similarly, in Poulin's novel, Rachel suffers through a barren existence in the convent before giving birth to the narrative of her journey.

The link between narrative and maternal heritage is also evident in *Un Cri trop grand*, where Françoise feels free to tell the story of her illegitimate child only when Marie-Françoise, having lost her own child, asks her why her aunt has always called her simply "Marie." Her aunt confesses that in doing so, she may have hoped that her niece would one day feel compelled to ask about the story that her aunt had kept secret for so long (*CG* 75). Françoise had given this name to her own child, whom she was obliged to give up for adoption, and so the feminine genealogy suggested by the chapter title "Héritage" extends from Françoise to Marie-Françoise, as it could not extend to the lost illegitimate child. In *Les Mensonges d'Isabelle*, Isabelle's conformist adoptive mother provides the initial stimulus for her writing, first giving her daughter a diary and then, by violating her daughter's privacy, prompting Isabelle to have recourse to the black notebooks that present her own vision of the world. Isabelle refers to the writing in the black notebooks as "une écriture bâtarde," that is, a style of writing of no identifiable genre, the word "bâtard" also defiantly underlining her own presumed illegitimate status (*MI* 50). As a child of unknown origins, Isabelle is free to participate in the Freudian "family romance" of the "foundling plot,"[13] creating an imaginary mother more exalted than the frivolous Suzanne.

While the daughter's rebellion can be something of a cliché in contemporary Quebec writing, the mother's rebellion against maternity is more startling. In Poulin's novel *La Couronne d'oubli*,[14] the mother's refusal of her traditional nurturing role is all the more surprising to her children because she has been such a dominant force in their lives. Suffering from a stroke following a heart attack, Florence Duchesne awakes with aphasia and amnesia, unable to recognize any of her children. Angrily, she rejects their attempt to restore her speech and memory: "I didn't know what they were going to make of me, but I was determined not to let the Duchesne children pose on my face the mask of their mother. They would not burden me with their past" (*CO* 20).[15] Her son Julien, a priest, is particularly obsessed with the image of Florence as a saintly mother: "You are the virgin who sympathizes, the merciful mother who calms God's anger" (*CO* 92).[16] Her response to his sermonizing is acerbic: "Why did his pious mother, if it is true that her ghost lingers in this room, not shut him up?" (*CO* 88).[17] As one by one her children bring their concerns to her, she refuses to play the role of the nurturing, self-sacrificing mother suggested in the Christian ideal of the *mater dolorosa*.

When her memory begins to return, her first thoughts do not relate to her children. Although her daughter Céline coaxes her to pronounce the name "Céline," the first word she latches on to is her own name, Florence. She remembers her own childhood in l'Auberge du Torrent, a former convent that her grandfather had transformed into an inn. Florence is aware that the disjointed nature of her narrative goes against the conformist models that her husband and children expect from her: "They can relax, the dears! The very spirit of their father has decided to intervene. Edgar Duchesne haunts the room. He seeks to take charge of my rambling memory.... He'll teach her how to tell the story of a life. A normal life, with a beginning, a middle and an end" (*CO* 113).[18] The relevant intertext here is Sleeping Beauty; memories of the prince coax Florence from her deep sleep. Florence focuses on mentally reliving the year in which she took a lover, an artist and defrocked priest ironically dubbed Barberousse, evoking the famous Holy Roman emperor, a name suitable enough for their early impassioned love but clearly ironic in the face of his evident narcissism. In this instance, the mother's mental narrative is triggered by that of her two daughters. Louise, the artist of the family, first speaks to her mother about Barberousse from the point of view of an adolescent daughter awakening to her own sexuality and becoming aware of her mother as a sexual being. Florence's eldest daughter, Mylène, condemned by the other siblings for her many lovers, also confronts her mother with her knowledge of the artist lover. In fact, she credits this knowledge with having saved her from true promiscuity; if her love affairs do not last, it is because she is still searching for the great passion that her mother experienced with Barberousse. In turn, the mother's memories of her love affair lead her back to memories of her children, as she concludes her mental account of that fateful year with the birthday party that her children had given her the evening her lover announced his intention to leave. As Florence remembers Barberousse pouring out the story of his life to her, she is resentful of his demand that she nurture him as she does her own children: "Why does the artist insist on making me enter the murky universe where he has struggled for so long? Don't I have enough of the seven children clutching to my skirts without having to feel sorry for this one?" (*CO* 156).[19] Barberousse, unworthy of his exalted name, announces that he must leave, and the "prodigal mother" (*CO* 157) returns to the party that her children have prepared for her. Despite the suggested incompatibility between maternity and passion here, it is evident that the awareness of Barberousse as the mother's lover unifies the tales of the mother and her adult daughters.

In *Le Livre de déraison*,[20] Virginie Sansterre does not direct her anger toward the maternal role in general but toward her daughter, Rolande. In part, this hostility stems from the patriarchal mother's favouritism toward the son, which continues from one generation to the next; Virginie's granddaughter Michelle accuses her own mother of preferring her brother. Virginie states explicitly that she chose an emperor's name for her son, although she hadn't been thinking of the emperor Frédéric Barberousse (*LD* 138). The other man in her life, Gabriel Lavoix, whom she meets in the retirement home, is also associated with royalty; he is "Barbefleurie," like the emperor Charlemagne. Again, the exalted male names contradict reality; although these male figures are greatly idolized, they are far from being powerful protectors, as Virginie will outlive them both. Virginie blames herself for her indifference toward Rolande after her husband's death, preoccupied as she was with her son and the memory of her husband: "After the death of my husband, I think I forgot that I was the mother of the girl who had always treated me as a rival. She must have been devastated" (*LD* 141).[21] Virginie's indifference turned to hatred when Frédéric contracted pneumonia and died after Rolande had abandoned him during a Halloween storm so that she could spend time with a boyfriend. Rather than accuse Rolande of having caused her brother's death, Virginie simply ignored her. She wonders if the tragedies in her life are punishment for the abandonment of the vows she had taken as a novice; on her departure, one of the nuns had foretold a horrible future for her (*LD* 147–48). She struggles to shake off her sense of guilt for having exchanged the role of bride of Christ for marriage and maternity. Her daughter, Rolande, now middle-aged with a younger husband, plays a maternal role toward her mother, securing her accommodation in a convent turned retirement home in this more secular age, but scolding her like a "Mother Superior" (*LD* 98). The reconciliation with the daughter seems to result from a belated appreciation of Rolande's pragmatic manner, which sustains her aging mother. Virginie's new tenderness toward her daughter may also be seen as a function of the power of narrative. Virginie's "livre de déraison" ("book of unreason"), in contrast to the traditional "livre de raison," an official chronicle of family history traditionally written by women of her generation, is jotted down in a journal given to her by her granddaughter Michelle, who will one day become a writer. It is by writing this journal, particularly the story of her son's death, that Virginie comes to resolve some of her ambivalence toward the mother-daughter bond.

While her previous novels presented the theme of the patriarchal mother primarily through the perspective of mothers and daughters, in her most recent novel, *Qu'est-ce qui passe ici si tard?*[22] Poulin presents the mother through the eyes of a son caught in the web of the Oedipal complex. Invigilating his final exam before his retirement, Professor Jacques Durocher drifts away into a long reverie, filled with memories of his jealousy toward his brutal father and his attraction to his mother, who would permit him as a child to kiss her breasts, calling him "my man," "my angel," "my little lover" (*QQP* 66).[23] It is evident that the desire to seduce the mother has dominated his many love affairs. His carefully planned seduction with his candlelit apartment as centre stage has failed in only one instance. After having picked up a woman of colour in a bar, he is so overwhelmed by this "black goddess" (*QQP* 87) that he is at first impotent, and she must take the initiative to seduce him and reduce him to a state in which he feels "swallowed up in an unbearable sea of pleasure" (*QQP* 88).[24] The reference to the woman's origins in Africa, the cradle of humanity, suggests a fascination with the Great Mother archetype. Referred to as "Don Quichante" by his students, Jacques Durocher is evidently on a quest to return to the pre-Oedipal state of fusion with the mother.

Written in counterpoint to the professor's wandering thoughts is the exam paper of Marie-Eve Vallée, the student who desires Jacques Durocher and is desired in turn, although neither has spoken of this attraction. Born in a secular age in which modern mores and contraception make maternity a choice rather than an obligation, Marie-Eve paradoxically bears a name that evokes maternity and the origins of humanity, as she herself notes: "I who have no children, who will perhaps never have any, I who bear the name of the Mother of the living, I hear almost every night the cry of the unborn child" (*QQP* 99).[25] Jacques Durocher sees her as "the recreated Mother" (*QQP* 52) whose arms offer him pleasure and comfort, while Marie-Eve in turn sees him as her "reinvented father" (*QQP* 76),[26] her Electra complex echoing his Oedipal complex as she must reject his cherished insistence on the necessity of parricide. While following his instructions to use selected lines of surrealist poetry as the "epicenter" of her text (*QQP* 21), Marie-Eve breaks with the protocol of exam-writing to address a very personal letter to her professor. Despite her attraction to him, she reproaches his ignorance of women: "In your courses, you have never spoken of childhood or the mother. You like women, I'm sure of it: everything in your attitude betrays your desire. But our most secret urges have never found a place in your lectures."[27] In the Oedipal complex, the son can see the mother only as object of desire, never as subject.

Ultimately the son's subjective reconstruction of the Mother archetype comes to an end, as Jacques Durocher dies suddenly of a heart attack. Marie-Eve takes her exam home, unable to hand in such a personal document. She muses over the power of words: "It's thanks to them alone, to their gratuitousness and daring, that you could remain the other protagonist, forever alive, of this story. My story. The story of one of my follies" (*QQP* 124),[28] the last two sentences being taken from Arthur Rimbaud's "Alchimie du verbe." To underscore the power of the imagination, Poulin also borrows the title of the second section from a line in Paul Eluard's poem "Au défaut du silence": "Which one of us two invented the other?" (*QQP* 111).[29] Is Marie-Eve the woman Jacques Durocher had dreamed of—the 30-year-old virgin who would embody the Mother and lover? Does the image of the father/lover constructed by Marie-Eve Vallée really correspond to Jacques Durocher— the professor who each year has his students write a dictation from which he concludes "not without irony" which women are "virginal," based on the purity of their syntax and spelling (*QQP* 43)? Marie-Eve dreams of having a child, but Jacques Durocher desires only to possess the Mother by killing the Father.

In his analysis of Poulin's novels, Robert Viau has pointed out that the female protagonists engage in two opposing modes of writing: one that is irrational, sincere, and nonconformist; the other rational, insincere, and conventional. Sister Anna/Rachel Delisle has her notebook but also the rules of her religious order; Isabelle has her two sets of notebooks; Virginie has her "book of unreason" and her "book of reason" (Viau 385). In one set of writings, the narrator pretends to conform to a certain ideal of womanhood; in the other, she is free. This opposition unravels in *Qu'est-ce qui passe ici si tard?* where the exam paper itself, normally intended to be the most rational of documents, is transformed into a personal meditation, a love letter. Awakening like Sleeping Beauty to the experience of sensuality condemned by the repressive Quebec society of the past, characters such as Rachel Delisle, Florence Duchesne, and Virginie Sansterre tell their tales of traversing an emotional desert; while Françoise Martin, punished for her sensual nature, transmits her maternal heritage through the life story she communicates to her niece. Isabelle expresses the ambiguities of her social status in her *écriture bâtarde*. Marie-Eve Vallée is, like Demeter, a reflection of the Mother of all humanity, but also Freud's Electra searching for the Father in the arms of her male lovers. Both sensual and maternal, she undermines the impossible ideal of the Virgin mother through the humanizing reality of the imperfect Eve. In Poulin's post–Quiet Revolution world, the traditional Catholic ideals of womanhood that once dominated Quebec society give way to a more holistic model in which women are free to follow their own desire as mothers, lovers, daughters and to transmit their stories from generation to generation as a liberating force.

Notes to Chapter 7

1 "Je sentis se réveiller une nostalgie et un regret que je croyais pourtant disparus: je n'avais pas d'enfant, je n'en aurais pas, sinon dans mes rêves. Mais, en moi, une voix plus forte protesta: 'Rien n'est impossible à qui peut écrire!' ... je pouvais compter sur la volonté de vivre de personnages inespérés: les enfants du désir et de la promesse" (Poulin, *La vie l'écriture* 346). Subsequent references to this book will appear as *VE*.

2 Hirsch borrows the term "emancipatory strategies" from Patricia Yaeger's *Honey-Mad Women: Emancipatory Strategies in Women's Fiction* (New York: Columbia University Press, 1987).

3 The author attributes the term "patriarchal mother" to Nicole Brossard in *L'Amer* (Montreal: Quinze, 1977) 24.

4 Saint-Martin quotes Adrienne Rich in *Of Woman Born: Motherhood as Experience and Institution* (New York: Norton, 1976) 235.

5 Subsequent references will appear as *MI*.

6 "Que les autres se débrouillent avec les fantômes noirs des mères, prisonnières des mots et des formes du passé."

7 Quotes in English are taken from Jane Pentland's translation *All the Way Home* (Toronto: Oberon Press, 1984). Subsequent quotes will be marked *AWH*.

8 "Anna, la mère de Rachel, applique aux complexités morales de la vie une philosophie de couturière: 'C'est comme pour la couture: moi, il m'a toujours fallu un bon patron, mais je sais bien qu'il y en a qui réussissent à faire tout leur linge sans ça' [*Cogne la caboche* 12]. Les patrons gouvernent l'imagination des mères déterminées surtout à préserver l'ordre établi."

9 Subsequent references will appear as *CTG*.

10 "La figure dominante du monde de la sexualité, c'est le père. De même que la mère représente la répression, de même le père transmet la liberté, la perte des inhibitions."

11 See Hirsch's discussion "Discovering the Pre-Oedipus" 98–103; also p. 55.

12 "Les religieuses, au contraire, me paraissaient des anges de perfection. Elles mangeaient à peine, ne buvaient pas, s'habillaient d'étoffes grossières, se déplaçaient en silence, sans bruit de talons, n'allaient jamais dans les magasins ni dans les banques, ne recevaient pas pour le thé ni ne jouaient au bridge."

13 See Hirsch on Marthe Robert's notion of "the foundling plot" in the "family romance" postulated by Freud: 54–55. Marthe Robert, *Origins of the novel*, trans. Sacha Rabinowitch (Bloomington: Indiana University Press, 1980).

14 Subsequent references will appear as *CO*.

15 "Je ne savais pas ce qu'on allait faire de moi, mais j'étais décidée à ne pas laisser les enfants Duchesne poser sur ma face le masque de leur mère. Ils ne me chargeraient pas de leur passé."

16 "Vous êtes la vierge qui compatit, la mère miséricordieuse qui apaise la colère de Dieu."

17 "Pourquoi sa pieuse mère, s'il est vrai que son fantôme traîne dans cette chambre, ne le faisait-elle pas taire?"

18 "Qu'ils se détendent, les chéris! L'esprit même de leur père a décidé d'intervenir. Edgar Duchesne hante la chambre. Il cherche à s'emparer de ma mémoire divagante.... Il va lui enseigner, lui, à raconter sa vie. Une vie normale, avec un commencement, un milieu et une fin."

19 "Pourquoi l'artiste tient-il à me faire pénétrer dans l'univers trouble où il se débat depuis si longtemps? N'ai-je pas assez de sept enfants accrochés à mes jupes que je doive encore m'apitoyer sur celui-ci?"

20 Subsequent references will appear as *LD*.

21 "Après la mort de mon mari, je crois que j'avais oublié que j'étais la mère de cette fille qui m'avait toujours traitée comme une rivale. Elle a dû être désemparée."

22 Subsequent references will appear as *QQP*.

23 "Mon homme," "mon ange," "mon petit amant."

24 "L'orgasme avait été instantané d'une violence telle qu'il s'était senti rejeté du sein de la terre, telle une lave incandescente, enseveli dans une mer insoutenable de volupté."

25 "Moi qui n'ai pas d'enfant, qui n'en aurai peut-être jamais, moi qui porte le nom de la Mère des vivants, j'entends presque toutes les nuits le vagissement de l'enfant jamais né."

26 "La Mère recréée"; "mon propre père réinventé."

27 *QQP* 98. "Dans vos cours, vous n'avez jamais parlé de l'enfance ni de la mère. Vous aimez les femmes, j'en suis sûre: tout dans votre attitude trahit votre désir. Mais nos plus secrètes pulsions n'ont jamais trouvé de place dans vos discours."

28 "Les mots en liberté sont toujours sûrs, Professeur, de votre parfaite complicité. C'est grâce à eux seulement, à leur gratuité et à leur audace, que vous pourriez de-

meurer l'autre protagoniste, toujours vivant, de cette histoire. A moi. L'histoire d'une de mes folies."

29 "Qui de nous inventa l'autre?"

Works Cited

Dumont, Micheline. "Vocation religieuse et condition féminine." *Travailleuses et féministes: Les femmes dans la société québécoise.* Ed. Marie Lavigne and Yolande Pinard. Montreal: Boréal Express, 1983: 271–92.

Hirsch, Marianne. *The Mother/Daughter Plot: Narrative, Psychoanalysis, Feminism.* Bloomington: Indiana University Press, 1989.

Jones, Grahame C. "La Recherche de la liberté chez les héroïnes de Gabrielle Poulin." *Revue d'histoire littéraire du Québec et du Canada français* 12 (1986): 265–78.

Poulin, Gabrielle. *Cogne la caboche.* Montreal: Stanké, 1979. Rev. ed. Montreal: VLB Editeur, 1990.

——. *All the Way Home.* Trans. Jane Pentland. Toronto: Oberon Press, 1984.

——. *La Couronne d'oubli.* Sudbury: Prise de parole, 1990.

——. *Un cri trop grand.* Montreal: Bellarmin, 1980. Rev. ed. Ottawa: Vermillon, 1999.

——. *Le livre de déraison.* Sudbury: Prise de parole, 1994. Rev. ed. Sudbury: Prise de parole, 1996.

——. *Les Mensonges d'Isabelle.* Montreal: Québec/Amérique, 1983.

——. *Qu'est-ce qui passe ici si tard?* Sudbury: Prise de parole, 1998.

——. *La vie l'écriture: Mémoires littéraires.* Ottawa: Vermillon, 2000.

Saint-Martin, Lori. *Le Nom de la mère: Mères, filles et écriture dans la littérature québécoise au féminin.* Montreal: Nota Bene, 1999.

Viau, Robert. "Un cri trop grand: L'oeuvre romanesque de Gabrielle Poulin." *La création littéraire dans le contexte de l'exiguïté.* Beauport, PQ: Publications MNH, 2000. 365–94.

8

"Opaque with confusion and shame":
Maternal Ambivalence in Rita Dove's Poetry

BY ELIZABETH BEAULIEU

When Rita Dove received the Pulitzer Prize for Poetry in 1987 for *Thomas and Beulah*, it established her as a significant American poet. *Thomas and Beulah* proved to be the first volume in a trilogy of poetry about motherhood; companion volumes *Grace Notes* (1989) and *Mother Love* (1995) followed. In these works we see Dove grappling with the notion of maternal ambivalence, something many women experience but are loathe to talk about. Dove interrogates maternal ambivalence from several female vantage points in her poetry and ultimately celebrates the creative powers it bestows upon the women who embrace their struggle with it. This essay looks at a number of Dove's poems and argues that it is only through acknowledging and dealing with maternal ambivalence that women, especially Black women, can truly embrace motherhood in all its complexity.

Rita Dove's *Thomas and Beulah* has been with me for a long time. I first encountered the 1987 Pulitzer Prize–winning volume of poetry in a graduate seminar on Black women writers, and since that time my second-hand copy has grown tattered with rereading. Dove's maternal grandparents have always seemed somehow familiar to me; perhaps it speaks tellingly of Dove's gifts as a poet that a thirtysomething Caucasian woman related so easily to the lives of Depression-era Black folks. But more than a sense of the familiar kept urging me back to *Thomas and Beulah*. Since my initial reading of the text, the poem "Motherhood," which stands approximately at the centre of Beulah's section of the volume, has profoundly disturbed me. As I immersed myself further in African American literature, I encountered numerous portraits of heroic mothering; most of the women whose lives and works I studied combined the pride of Sojourner Truth with the stamina of Harriet Jacobs.[1] Indeed, this was the one enduring quality that drew me to the formal study of African American literature.

And so I found myself returning again and again to Beulah and "Motherhood." I wondered why she, as a new mother, dreamt such horrible dreams, and I particularly questioned her unmitigated ambivalence toward mothering. Cultural norms dictate that women are expected to have children and also perpetuate the notion that the children we have will be soft bundles of joy. Further, women are expected to love their children no matter what and to willingly sacrifice for their offspring. So, while I was educated enough to think critically about society's mandates, I nevertheless found myself continuing to judge Beulah. What was she thinking? Why couldn't she be more like Harriet Jacobs, a woman who was just the kind of mother I fancied that I myself would one day be? The questions bothered me. And then one day I became a mother.

This essay, then, is a bit of a personal odyssey. When my son was born my life took on a new rhythm; his needs became mine as I struggled to understand him. At the same time I was entering the professional arena after years in graduate school. My life was fraught with anxiety and ambivalence; every act, from getting up in the morning to answering a plaintive wail in the middle of the night, seemed to demand something new of me. Mundane professional responsibilities became obstacles to overcome. I turned again to what I had come to view as Beulah's "signature" poem, and I began to understand. Like the "promised land" that her name evokes, Beulah—who had so perplexed and disturbed me—now beckoned encouragingly. I discovered in Dove's elegant lyricism a portrait of endurance, a message of hope addressed specifically to those who mother. This reading invites Beulah into the company of those mothers responsible for the uplift and the survival of the human race.[2]

Dove opens the "Beulah" section of *Thomas and Beulah* with several lines from "Lines to a Nasturtium," by Harlem Renaissance poet Anne Spencer: "Ah, how the senses flood at my repeating, / As once in her fire-lit heart I felt the furies / Beating, beating." The poem, subtitled "A Lover Muses," parallels the beauty of the "flame-flower" with the beckoning of the beloved. The attraction to both, Spencer dramatizes, is paradoxically fulfilling and destructive. The lines from Spencer's poem set the tone for Dove's depiction of Beulah as wife and mother, roles that are both comforting and confining to Beulah. As Emily Walker Cook argues, both Thomas and Beulah adhere to conventional gender expectations typical of Depression-era America. Both, however, feel constrained by society's definitions; Thomas is frequently frustrated by his inability to maintain a comfortable lifestyle for his family, and Beulah chafes under her ever-present domestic obligations.

When I teach this volume of poetry to students in my Black literature and women's studies classes, I pose the following question near the end of our discussion: Who had the happier life, Thomas or Beulah? Inevitably the class members rush to take sides: some argue that Thomas was ultimately able to provide for his family, while Beulah never fulfilled her dreams; others counter that at least Beulah had dreams. Commenting on the process by which she assembled the poems, Dove notes, "Then this poem 'Dusting'appeared, really out of nowhere. I didn't realize that this was Thomas's wife saying, 'I want to talk. And you can't do his side without doing my side'" (Kitchen et al. 236). Indeed, many readers view "Dusting" as typical of Beulah's "side" of her life with Thomas—fraught with frustration, lost promise, suffocating routine. Beulah's heart, once "fire-lit" with dreams of travel and romance, now beats only to the dull rhythm of domestic life.

Consonant with Beulah's domestic duties is her position as primary care-giver of the couple's four daughters, a role Beulah approaches with decided ambivalence. Many, students and scholars alike, who argue that the Beulah section is characterized by despair (as the lines from Spencer's poem initially seem to suggest) turn to the poems about motherhood to support their interpretation. It is my contention, however, that the poems concerning motherhood are the richest in Beulah's section and serve to provide the very measure by which we are able to chart Beulah's growth and development.

As she does in Thomas's section, Dove begins Beulah's section by dramatizing a formative experience. In "Taking in Wash," the narrator tells us that Beulah was "Papa's girl / black though she was." The dream that transforms "Papa's girl" into a "beast / with stricken eyes" suggests that the young Beulah is a victim of sexual abuse, possibly even rape, at the hands of her father[3] and also establishes the motif of dreaming that will structure the entire section. Beulah's mother figures prominently in the first poem as well. "Mama never changed," the narrator tells us; she attempts to act proactively each time her husband comes home drunk, hiding the laundry and hushing the dog, but the third stanza indicates that her efforts are insignificant. A grim, unaffectionate woman described as a "tight, dark fist," her complicity in Beulah's abuse is implied in the warning she offers in the closing lines of the poem: *"Touch that child / and I'll cut you down / just like the cedars of Lebanon."*

Beulah's relationship with her mother is as formative as her relationship with her father and, although significantly different, no less destructive. The title of the first poem, "Taking in Wash," refers, in fact, to Beulah's mother, who presumably takes in laundry to supplement her husband's income. It is the first of numerous homely images that will serve to structure Beulah's section, suggesting that Beulah is heir to her mother's domestic realm and its attendant powerlessness.[4] In particular, the ineffectual nature of the protection Beulah's mother offers her weighs heavily as Beulah contemplates becoming a mother herself. In assessing what she has to offer her own children, Beulah fears that she will let them down because this was her experience as a child.

Offsetting the anxiety Beulah feels toward impending motherhood is the expectant joy she shares with Thomas as they prepare for the birth of their first child. The poem "Weathering Out" conveys Beulah's tremendous anticipation as she enjoys the final months of pregnancy. Her coffee, "flushed with milk," tastes just right; she "float[s]" from room to room and feels "large and placid" like the zeppelin she and Thomas go to view at the new airdock. Although Thomas is discouraged in his job search, he is attentive to Beulah and the unborn child: *"Little fellow's really talking,"* he'd say, as he listened to her belly in bed at night. In fact, the only indication of Beulah's hesitancy in this poem occurs when she mentally contradicts Thomas's interpretation of the baby's attempts to communicate with them: *"to her it was more the pok-pok-pok / of a fingernail tapping a thick cream lampshade."* The poem's tone is optimistic; in keeping with the spirit of the volume, the couple's hardships are alluded to, but the concluding image of the clover between the cobblestones that hangs "stubbornly on" in spite of the winter frost suggests that the young family will "weather out" their storms together. The ellipses with which Dove ends the poem suggest that there will indeed be storms.

The next poem, entitled simply "Motherhood," dramatizes one such storm. Powerfully evocative of both a fairy tale and a nightmare, the poem's imagery implies that for Beulah the act of becoming a mother has the potential to be both fulfilling and destructive. Significantly, the first verb in the poem is "dreams." Furthering the dream motif begun in the second poem, "Magic," which articulates Beulah's dream of trading life in her parents' home for the wonders of Paris, the first stanza describes Beulah's literal dreams as a new mother: first she misplaces the baby, then she drops it and it disappears. Finally, the baby explodes before her eyes. The early lines of this poem clearly reflect the feelings of inadequacy and overbearing responsibility that bombard Beulah upon the birth of her child.

The movement into the second stanza deflects Beulah's anxieties as we journey with the new family on an outing to the countryside. Indeed,

Dove depicts a pastoral moment, only to shatter it with the appearance of the three men "playing rough with a white wolf." Here the poem takes on a surreal quality, as Beulah helplessly shouts a warning and then must fight the wolf herself to protect her child. Interestingly, Thomas and the three men disappear entirely from the poem; with her baby on her back, Beulah "straddles / the wolf and circles its throat." She tames the wolf into submission, bloodying its fur, and the poem ends with perhaps the most ambiguous image in the volume: "The small wild eyes / go opaque with confusion and shame, like a child's."

So whose eyes are these? Literally they are the wolf's; in her panic, Beulah sees them as "like a child's," suggesting her mixed emotions at conquering the white wolf. Metaphorically the eyes are not only the child's, looking reproachfully at the new mother, but also Beulah's own, reflecting the overbearing and solitary responsibilities of motherhood her nightmare picnic evokes. The poem "Motherhood," then, is deeply disturbing to many readers for the degree to which it portrays Beulah's ambivalence. In this reading motherhood becomes, simply, a nightmare.

This reading becomes all the more troubling when viewed through the lens of race. Beulah is, after all, a Black woman only a couple of generations removed from slavery. She would have been extremely conscious of the lengths to which her enslaved maternal ancestors went to resist the biological contradictions of enslaved motherhood; Beulah's heritage would almost certainly have included stories of heroic mothering—women who learned to read and sometimes tutored their children; who instilled in their children a sense of self-worth that served to contradict their enslaved condition; who fought to keep their families together; who served as othermothers to slave children separated from their own mothers; who developed extended kin networks to provide and receive support, encouragement, and everyday assistance; and who sometimes, as in the case of Margaret Garner,[5] resorted to violence. These facts are the legacy of slavery bequeathed to the twentieth-century Black woman. Beulah would have been aware, too, of the high value placed on motherhood in the contemporary African American community.[6] And so, aware of her privilege and her duty to claim her children fully as her enslaved maternal ancestors never could, Beulah's racial consciousness would certainly have painfully magnified her feelings of ambivalence.

Recent scholarship, however, sheds interesting light on the nature of Beulah's ambivalence and offers an alternative to reading Beulah's life as dominated by guilt and despair. In her 1995 book *Mother Love / Mother Hate: The Power of Maternal Ambivalence*, Rozsika Parker emphasizes the potentially creative aspect of maternal ambivalence. Building on Jane Lazarre's theory that ambivalance is the most eternal and natural emotion in mothers, Parker argues that a mother's capacity for nurturing both herself and her offspring is greatly augmented once ambivalence is acknowledged. In other words, conflict and conflicting emotions can serve to catalyze self-awareness and can bridge the understanding gap that necessarily exists between mothers and their children.

Cultural representations of the mother, of course, eschew ambivalence; the mother who straps her child on her back and fights off the big, bad wolf not only takes great pride in her accomplishment—proof of her maternal instinct—but is valorized by a society intent on maintaining her position with children within the domestic sphere. But Parker contends that ambivalence is, in fact, crucial both for the development of a healthy maternal identity and for the eventual process of separation that children must undergo:

> The experience of maternal ambivalence ... provides a woman with a sense of her independent identity. The pain of ambivalence, the distress in recognising that the child hates her for frustrating its desires, and that she hates the child for frustrating her independent needs, can be a force for affirming her independent identity. Both mother and child need the mother's affirmation of her own needs, desires, opinions, rage, love and hatred if separateness is to be established—and thus relationship. (137)

This theory brings us to the opening line of Dove's poem "Daystar," which almost immediately follows "Motherhood": "She wanted a little room for thinking." Here Beulah articulates a strategy for coping with children; like Virginia Woolf and all other women leading multifaceted lives, she recognizes the need for a place of her own.[7] That she wants to "think" while the children nap rather than do laundry (as her mother may have done) or pick up toys indicates that Beulah recognizes the importance of maintaining some semblance of cognitive activity and stimulation while surrounded by infants and toddlers. Sitting in her quiet spot behind the house in the lawn chair she has "lugged," Beulah rests, observes nature, and sometimes simply gets in touch with herself: "Star[ing] until she was assured / when she closed her eyes / she'd see only her own vivid blood." When her daughter appears, calling her back to her domestic duties and inquiring what in the world she is doing, Beulah's answer is significant: "Why, / building a palace." Beulah's dreams have returned.

The concluding stanza of the poem suggests that Beulah can revisit her special place via her imagination whenever she chooses. When Thomas "roll[s] over and / lurche[s] into her" at night, she retreats to the essential self she has discovered in the yard behind the house and becomes "nothing / pure nothing." The lines may suggest the lack of fulfillment Beulah experiences in her sexual relationship with her husband; as Cook argues, "sexual domination ... comprised a part of Beulah's gender role that she must accept, even if she never became completely resigned to it" (326). I choose to read Beulah's becoming "nothing" during sex with Thomas as an affirmation of her newly emerging self; the Beulah in the final stanza of "Daystar" is a woman who has found some healthy measure of freedom not only from the demands of motherhood and household management but also from the baggage of her childhood encounters with her father.

Immediately following "Daystar" is the short poem "Obedience," which my reading privileges as the climax of Beulah's section for the way in which it dramatizes Beulah's relationship to the world around her and recontextualizes her relationship with her children. The tentativeness of the first stanza is established by two words: "if" and "perhaps": "That smokestack, for instance, / in the vacant lot across the street: / if she could order it down and watch / it float in lapse-time over buckled tar and macadam / it would stop an inch or two perhaps / before her patent leather shoes." Perhaps Beulah sees her own children reflected in the stubborn unwillingness to yield that characterizes the smokestack; in any event, the smokestack does not "obey."

The final two stanzas, however, affirm the powers Beulah does possess. First, "her mind is free." In other words, she still has her dreams. The following lines conjure up a wonderful twilight—colourful, peaceful, homey. But she revises her imaginative rendering of the twilight scene in the first line of the last stanza: "but she would never create such puny stars." One wonders what has prompted this implied critique of God, but the moment is again revised as Beulah's thoughts turn to her home and its inhabitants. In what I read to be the most moving lines in the entire volume, Beulah reflects on her children: "those tight hearts breathing inside— / she could never invent them." Here Beulah acknowledges the miracle her children are in her life—individuals so wonderful and complex that even in her cherished, carefully cultivated dream life she could not have imagined them. These lines signal Beulah's acceptance of her role as mother—a role enhanced by the ambivalence she has struggled with throughout her adult life.

I do not mean to suggest at this point that Beulah has completely conquered the feelings of ambivalence that characterize her relationship with her children, merely that she has channelled those feelings in constructive, creative ways that enable her to find fulfillment in her everyday life amid the sacrifice and loss of self inherent in motherhood. In naming the section "Canary in Bloom," Dove tips the scales in Beulah's favour, I think, implying from the beginning that Beulah, like her beloved bird, will one day "bloom." The tension that propels the "Beulah" section develops from the conflicting desires portrayed: the canary, with its suggestions of beauty, song, and intended flight, and the womb, which serves to anchor Beulah to her home and family. The ambivalence motherhood evokes in Beulah initially exacerbates what Beulah perceives to be impossible drives at work within her; she loves her children, but she will never get to Paris. Only when she renegotiates her relationship with herself does she come to understand that her dreams may find many expressions. The canary is, after all, a caged bird, its song notwithstanding.

The poems that follow "Obedience" reflect Beulah's contentment with her life; she exhibits pride in her handiwork in "Headdress," and recalls her mother with a new fondness in "Sunday Greens." And her own "compendium"—her final assessment of her life with Thomas in the poem "Company"—is tender: *"listen: we were good / though we never believed it."*[8] It seems, following "Obedience," that Beulah has made her peace with her children and with herself; these poems do not merely indicate that her life goes on but rather suggest that she has successfully integrated the many complex aspects of her personality and the many conflicting demands she feels as a woman living in the twentieth century. Dove alludes to the measure of Beulah's success as a mother by including Joanna's proud statement in the poem "Wingfoot Lake": "Mother, we're Afro-Americans now!" No longer confused or ashamed—this is the gift that Beulah has allowed herself to receive from her children; this, too, is the gift she gives back to her daughters.

Lotta Lofgren, in an article entitled "Partial Horror: Fragmentation and Healing in Rita Dove's *Mother Love*," argues that *Thomas and Beulah* and Dove's next two volumes of poetry, *Grace Notes* (1989) and *Mother Love* (1995), constitute "a kind of trilogy of the cycles of human existence" (142). Lofgren maintains that Dove's overriding subject matter has been the nuclear family, which she examines from a variety of perspectives. In *Thomas and Beulah* Dove begins with the foundational relationship between a husband and wife, specifically that shared by her maternal grandparents; in *Grace Notes* the poetry becomes even more personal, as she includes a number of poems written in the voice of a new mother, poems that reflect her own experiences as the mother of a daughter. *Mother Love*, then, finishes the cycle. This volume—Dove's most complex to date—is her reworking of the Demeter/Persephone myth.[9] According equal time to both mother and daughter, Dove takes as her theme the process of individuation, that moment of final separation that every mother both anticipates and fears. In the last poem of the volume the speaker articulates the moment of awareness toward which the volume has been inexorably moving:

> Through sunlight into flowers
> she walked, and was pulled down.
> A simple story, a mother's deepest
> dread—that her child could drown
> in sweetness.

Lofgren contends that *Mother Love* "complete[s] the journey, finding regeneration through fragmentation as the newborn daughter of *Grace Notes* grows up and the cycle begins anew" (142).

Indeed, the poetry in *Mother Love* seems to move some of Dove's concepts in *Grace Notes* to a higher level. Many of the poems in the earlier volume celebrate motherhood unabashedly; there is little evidence of the ambivalence I noted in *Thomas and Beulah*. For example, in "Pastoral" the speaker marvels at the joy she feels while breast-feeding; although she is "diminished / by those amazing gulps," she is at peace, dozing as contentedly as her newborn in the final lines of the poem. "After Reading *Mickey in the Night Kitchen* for the Third Time Before Bed" is also life-affirming and exuberant, as the speaker shares her daughter's innocent explorations of the female body. This poem dramatizes the mother's relaxed attitude and sheer delight in her daughter's curiosity, but it must be noted that their relationship is not all giddiness. The mother has clearly prepared her daughter for the dangers inherent in growing up female. She also is aware that as the mother of a biracial child she must invest her child with a healthy sense of self and racial identity. The menstrual blood alluded to in the final stanza of the poem prefigures the bond of womanhood these two will one day share, the bond that is already taking shape and being shaped. And the tone is similar in "Genetic Expedition," as the speaker contemplates the beauty of her own abundant breasts and spreading buttocks before going on to seek genetic evidence of herself in her toddler daughter. This poem, in my estimation, is a near-perfect parallel to "Obedience" in *Thomas and Beulah*, in the wonder evoked at the creation of a child. The sentiment is also expressed in "The Breathing, The Endless News":

> Children know this: they are
> the trailings of gods. Their eyes

> hold nothing at birth then fill slowly
> with the myth of ourselves.

With *Mother Love*, however, Dove reintroduces the notion of maternal ambivalence.[10] The title itself suggests the volume's theme,[11] and Dove dedicates
the poetry "FOR my mother TO my daughter." In the foreword, entitled "An
Intact World," Dove discusses her attraction to the Demeter/Persephone
myth. Calling the myth "a tale of a violated world" (i), she goes on to characterize the story as "a modern dilemma as well—there comes a point when a
mother can no longer protect her child, when the daughter must go her own
way into womanhood" (i). Robert McDowell points out that one of Dove's
great strengths as a poet is "understand[ing] the opposing sides of conflicts
she deals with. She tells all sides of the story" (294). Nowhere is this more
apparent than in *Mother Love*.

In a sense, writing *Thomas and Beulah* (more so than *Grace Notes*) has
prepared Dove for her ambitious analysis of the complex relationship
shared by mothers and daughters. Not only has she told the story of her maternal grandparents' marriage from both perspectives, but she has resisted
the temptation to present Beulah as the stereotypically content mother. As
I have noted, the couple's four children are noticeably absent from the volume; *Mother Love*, then, picks up where *Thomas and Beulah* leaves off, giving
voice to both sides of the conflict. The mother remembers her own mother
in "Party Dress for a First Born": "When I ran to my mother, waiting radiant /
as a cornstalk at the edge of the field, / nothing else mattered: the world
stood still." The daughter calls plaintively for her mother in "Persephone
Abducted" but soon is ready to be free of her mother's protective instinct;
in Part II of "Persephone in Hell" she says,

> Mother worried. Mother with her frilly ideals
> gave me money to call home every day,
> but she couldn't know what I was feeling;
> I was doing what she didn't need to know.

The struggle to separate does not come easily for either, and Dove infuses
her speakers—mothers and daughters sometimes indistinguishable from
each other—with a wide range of emotions.

By far, though, the rawest emotions belong to Demeter and the other
mother figures in the collection. For the daughters, maturation is a time
of celebration; they look only ahead to a future beckoning brightly. For the
mothers, the pride they feel in their maturing daughters is muted by feelings of incompleteness, helplessness, and, frankly, devastation. Such mixed

emotions are alluded to in a number of poems narrated from the mother's perspective. In "The Bistro Styx," a mother joins her daughter abroad; they meet for lunch and the speaker discovers that her daughter has grown beyond the limits of her imagination. The generation gap manifests itself in the mother's inability to appreciate her daughter's new lifestyle, and the poem concludes with the mother's desperate thought: *"I've lost her...."* "Demeter Waiting" expresses the mother's anger vehemently; these are perhaps the strongest lines in the collection:

> She is gone again and I will not bear
> it, I will drag my grief through a winter
> of my own making and refuse
> any meadow that recycles itself into
> hope. Shit on the cicadas, dry meteor
> flash, finicky butterflies! I will wail and thrash
> until the whole goddamned golden panorama freezes
> over. Then I will sit down to wait for her. Yes.

"Demeter Mourning" begins with the line "Nothing can console me," and concludes with the mother's acknowledgment that nothing will make her happy again, "for I have known that." Juxtaposed nicely to "Demeter Mourning" is "Exit," which offers "Reprieve ... 'provisionally'" from the anguish of loss that monopolizes the mother's thoughts. Here she admits to herself that her daughter has become an independent woman and even congratulates herself for the role she has played in her daughter's development. And in "Demeter's Prayer to Hades," which may be read as conciliatory, Demeter offers the benefit of her own insight to Hades, cautioning him to recognize that "we are responsible for the lives / we change. No faith comes without cost, / no one believes without dying."

Indeed, the volume is filled with images of death and dying; Dove implies that the inevitable growth of the child to survival on her own is a life-blow to the mother. Lofgren contends that "Demeter's hardest lesson in the cyclical process of growth and change in which she and Persephone participate involves recognizing her own monstrous selfishness in wishing to keep her daughter with her. She must acknowledge that her excruciating sense of fragmentation at her daughter's departure is not only inevitable but crucial to the cyclical nature of human existence" (140). In dramatizing Demeter's struggle to accept the loss of what is essentially a part of herself, Dove brings us back to Beulah's lesson: that to mother means to give up an essential part of the self. We meet Beulah at the beginning of the journey of mothering; although she resents the loss of self inherent in mothering, it is her negotiation of these feelings that ultimately enables her to flesh out an inner, private self, one filled with dreams and noticeably devoid of ghosts. Demeter represents the logical conclusion to Beulah's story; the woman who has found her self (through loss of self) in the life-giving relationship with her child (or children) then must deal with the betrayal she feels when the life-sustaining force separates.

The loss of the child—a constant motif throughout the volume—is graphically portrayed in the title poem. The reader might easily envision this as one of Beulah's poems, placed close in sequence to "Motherhood." "Mother Love" begins with the powerful question, "Who can forget the attitude of mothering?" and goes on to dramatize the maternal cues that quickly become second nature to any mother: holding the child comfortably "on the hip," "bar[ing] the nipple," "hum[ming] at bedside." The poem transforms, however, in the second stanza, becoming a nightmarish vision akin to Beulah's in "Motherhood." Of the child she has been given to raise, the speaker says,

> I decided to save him. Each night
> I laid him on the smoldering embers,
> sealing his juices in slowly so he might
> be cured to perfection.[12]

The image of the mother preserving the child by curing him over the fire grotesquely perverts the ideal of the nurturing, protective mother. This poem dramatizes the dangers of narcissistic mothering; Lofgren argues that if mother love becomes preoccupied with self-gratification it turns destructive.

No one can achieve perfection for another human individual, even a child; the child must strive for—and fail at—itself. Any attempt to "seal the juices" of the child, to "cure" the child by isolating it from the outside world, is brutality. Such an attempt at false autonomy will kill the child, spiritually if not physically. The greatest potential betrayal consists not in Olympian deception but in Demeter's refusal to allow Persephone regeneration (140). The central poem clearly stands as a warning of the costs of "motherlove too thick" (164), to borrow a phrase from Toni Morrison's 1987 best-selling novel *Beloved*.[13] Yet the volume quickly distances itself from the explicit violence of the title poem; Demeter grieves loudly, becomes hopeful, sulks, but commits no violence against the self or the other. Just as Beulah must resolve the shame and confusion motherhood thrusts upon her, so Demeter must learn to make the ultimate sacrifice—to let her child go. The loss of the child, beginning at birth, is a reality that she will always be forced to remember, as the final line of the poem makes clear; the child's process of individuation becomes one of the "attitudes of mothering" ingrained in the mother's being.

We do not see the transformative power of maternal ambivalence as clearly in *Mother Love*, but it is there. *Thomas and Beulah* becomes the lens through which to interpret Demeter's crisis in the later volume, illustrating that maternal ambivalence is the foundation on which the healthy relationship with the daughter has been built, and as such it is the coping mechanism that will finally allow Demeter to confront "a mother's deepest dread" and to wish her daughter, who we learn in the poem "History" is herself an expectant mother, the joy she herself has known. *Mother Love* complements *Thomas and Beulah* by allowing us to see the intimate and sometimes stormy relationship between mother and daughter that of necessity is missing in the earlier volume. And again it is very human poetry, poetry that speaks to mothers from all walks of life. Even those mothers unfamiliar with Greek mythology can recognize something of themselves in the mother who provides her grown daughter with money to phone home, in the mother who may endanger her child's life in the name of protecting him, in the difficult process of growth and separation for two humans who were once so intimately connected. "No story's ever finished," Dove tells us near the end of the volume's final poem, just as the privilege of mothering is never fully resolved, the responsibility never completely relinquished. Dove's poetry, then, celebrates the privilege and the responsibility, affirming motherhood in all its terrible beauty.

Notes to Chapter 8

1   Sojourner Truth (c. 1799–1883) was enslaved until she was legally emancipated in 1827. She subsequently became a preacher and an abolitionist and is known especially for the speech she gave at an Akron, Ohio, women's rights meeting in 1851, during which she asked, "Ar'n't I a woman?" Harriet Jacobs (c. 1813–1897) was enslaved in Edenton, North Carolina, until she escaped by hiding in her grandmother's attic for almost seven years. She chose to hide locally rather than flee to the North so that she could remain close to her two children. Purchased and set free finally in 1853, she published her slave narrative *Incidents in the Life of a Slave Girl* in 1861.

2   Although Thomas and Beulah are African American, Dove is not particularly race conscious in her depiction of their life together. Therefore, my comments here refer to Beulah simply as a mother. Later in this essay, however, I will discuss the legacy of slavery as it affects the twentieth-century Black mother.

3 While it is not my intention here to make the argument that Beulah was definitively the victim of sexual assault or rape at the hands of her father, I will point out that the poems in which Beulah's father appears have an ominous quality; for example, on Beulah's wedding day ("Promises") her father is depicted as a "mountain of shame" and as a "hulk" in the vestibule whom she tries to "forget" and literally turns her back on. The poem "Anniversary" ends with Beulah's father winking suggestively at her. One might interpret Beulah's recurrent nightmares as a symptom of abuse and her daydreams of travel as an attempt to escape. Her mother's role is unclear; although she threatens her husband, the cumulative effect of the poems suggests that she never follows through on her threats, thus allowing the abuse to continue.

4 In this same spirit, Cook points out that Beulah's section appears after Thomas's, is shorter than Thomas's, and lacks the "in-control" types of titles found in Thomas's section.

5 Margaret Garner (1833–1858) was a Kentucky slave who fled to Ohio with her four children. When slave catchers approached, Garner attempted to kill her children; she succeeded in wounding three of them and in nearly decapitating her two-year-old daughter. Garner is the historical model for the protagonist Sethe in Toni Morrison's 1987 novel *Beloved*.

6 See Patricia Hill Collins's 1987 article "The Meaning of Motherhood in Black Culture and Black Mother / Daughter Relationships" (*Sage* 4, 3–10) for further discussion.

7 It is interesting to note that Beulah has to go outside of the physical confines of the home itself to create her own place. Dove perhaps suggests that it is impossible within the confines of domestic space for Beulah to develop a perspective that is distinct from that cultivated by her roles as wife and mother.

8 Peter Harris, in a review of *Thomas and Beulah* (*The Virginia Quarterly Review* 64, 262–76), offers a significantly different reading of these lines, arguing that after Thomas's death Beulah leads a "dignified, though sadly reduced widowhood, where the best that she can say about her marriage is 'we were good, / though we never believed it'" (272).

9 Dove not only modernizes the Demeter/Persephone myth, but she chooses the sonnet, which she calls "an intact world" (*Mother Love* i), as her primary form of creative expression in this volume. For an excellent analysis of the function of the sonnet form in *Mother Love*, see Stephen Cushman's article "And the Dove Returned" (*Callaloo* 19, 131–34).

10 It is not my intention here to offer a detailed analysis of maternal ambivalence in *Mother Love*. Lofgren provides a fine explication of the complexities of the mother–daughter dynamics that underpin the volume.

11 However, as Alison Booth points out in "Abduction and Other Severe Pleasures: Rita Dove's *Mother Love*" (*Callaloo* 19, 125–30), the title is deceptive. She states, "Mother love can mean 'Protection,' tutelage in fatal gender roles, possessive grief, devouring rage, deceptive or strategic calm" (128).

12 Lofgren points out that Dove borrows the image directly from the original myth: "in gratitude for hospitality offered her, Demeter roasts the boy Demophon to make him immortal, but the process is interrupted, and he dies" (140).

13 Dove's poem and Morrison's novel both comment on the dangers of loving the "beloved" too intensely. In the poem it is the child who is sacrificed; in Morrison's novel, although the child dies, it is the mother who makes the greater sacrifice, both in the loss of the child and in her refusal to recognize that her self is her "best thing" (273).

Works Cited

Cook, Emily Walker. "'But She Won't Set Foot / In His Turtledove Nash': Gender Roles and Gender Symbolism in Rita Dove's *Thomas and Beulah*." *College Language Association Journal* 38 (1995): 322–30.

Dove, Rita. *Grace Notes*. New York: W. W. Norton & Company, 1989.

——. *Mother Love*. New York: W. W. Norton & Company, 1995.

——. *Thomas and Beulah*. Pittsburgh: Carnegie-Mellon University Press, 1986.

Kitchen, Judith, Stan Sanvel Rubin, and Earl G. Ingersoll. "A Conversation with Rita Dove." *Black American Literature Forum* 20 (1986): 227–40.

Lofgren, Lotta. "Partial Horror: Fragmentation and Healing in Rita Dove's *Mother Love*." *Callaloo* 19 (1996): 135–42.

McDowell, Robert. "The Assembling Vision of Rita Dove." *Conversant Essays: Contemporary Poets on Poetry*. Ed. James McCorkle. Detroit: Wayne State University Press, 1990. 294–302.

Morrison, Toni. *Beloved*. New York: New American Library, 1987.

Parker, Rozsika. *Mother Love / Mother Hate: The Power of Maternal Ambivalence*. New York: Basic Books, 1995.

9

Maternal Blitz: Harriet Lovatt as Postpartum Sufferer in Doris Lessing's *The Fifth Child*

BY DENYS LANDRY

This chapter deals with postpartum depression and how the illness manifests itself in the character of Harriet Lovatt, the overwhelmed mother of five in Doris Lessing's *The Fifth Child* (1988). The story, which takes place in suburban England from the 1960s to the 1980s, focuses on Ben, the titular fifth child, and his negative impact on his parents (mostly his mother) and his four siblings. Unlike most analyses of Lessing's *The Fifth Child*, this paper does not attempt to determine what Ben actually is or provide explanations as to why he turns out the way he does. At the end of novel, Ben, now 15 years old, spends most of his time away from home with an "alienated, non-comprehending, hostile tribe" of teenagers (154). In her sequel to *The Fifth Child*, entitled *Ben, in the World* (2000), Lessing reintroduces her character who, at 15 years of age, has severed all ties with the Lovatts by running away to South America. I will draw attention away from the "poor little chap" and place it instead on "poor Harriet," though I realize that both are inextricably linked (65). I will argue that Harriet Lovatt is the prototypical postpartum sufferer. Since scant critical attention has been given to examining the topic of depression (let alone postpartum depression) in *The Fifth Child*, this paper will use recent scientific studies of postpartum depression to explain Harriet's confounding behaviour. I will provide important scientific evidence in conjunction with a textual analysis of Lessing's novel to illustrate both the progression of Harriet's malady and the detrimental impact each pregnancy has on her mothering and on her physical, mental, and emotional health.

The Fifth Child is a modern gothic text that deals explicitly with the perverse, violent, and uncanny aspects of domestic and familial relations (marriage, pregnancy, and motherhood). Since its publication, many scholars have ventured opinions on Lessing's powerful fable. Some critics have focused their attention on the character of Harriet Lovatt, viewing her positively as an embodiment of the nineteenth-century persona of, to use Virginia Woolf's expression, "the angel in the house," who unfortunately gives birth to a genetic throwback (qtd. in Gilbert and Gubar 17). Others have portrayed her rather negatively as a gothic villainess, "a madwoman in the attic" who, by overextending herself physically and emotionally in the pursuit of the perfect family, ends up poisoning her familial relations (Gilbert and Gubar 425). In the same way as women face a double standard in society (they are seen as either madonnas or whores), mothers are held to a higher standard than fathers because of women's traditional association with, and relegation to, the so-called private sphere and the assumption that women are innately nurturing. Consequently, a woman who does not sufficiently display this innate maternal instinct is seen as an anomaly, a monster.

In the past two decades, there has been a proliferation of news stories, books, and movies that deal with the strangest perversity: mothers hating—even killing—their children. Among these sensationalistic accounts of real-life incidents of maternal infanticide one remembers the case of Andrea Yates, who now serves as the new millennium's gothic villainess. In 2001, the 37-year-old Texas mother drowned her five children (Noah, 7; John, 5; Paul, 3; Luke, 2; Mary, 6 months) in quick succession in the family bathroom. During the trial, defence attorneys and medical experts insisted that Yates had committed maternal infanticide because of postpartum psychosis, an extremely rare form of the more commonly diagnosed illness known as postpartum depression.[1] Yates was initially sentenced to life in prison for 40 years without the possibility of parole. However, because of some erroneous testimony in the 2002 trial, the verdict was overturned. Yates was later retried on the same counts, and on 26 July 2006, she was found not guilty of murder by reason of insanity. Partly because of the intense media scrutiny of the Yates murder trials in the last seven years, there has been much public discourse on the misunderstood malady that is postpartum depression, its various symptoms, possible causes, and potential treatments.

Before I develop the argument that Harriet Lovatt exhibits the classic signs of postpartum depression, it is important to note that the illness is not a late-twentieth-century phenomenon. While there has never been more attention given to this postnatal disorder than now (one has the impression that every psychiatrist, psychologist, political pundit, and talk-show host has weighed in on the subject), Johnson and Apgar point out that, "historically, the connection between childbirth and psychiatric illness has been well-recognized.[2] In 460 BC, Hippocrates described 'puerperal fever,' theorizing that suppressed lochial discharge was transported to the brain, where it produced 'agitation, delirium, and attacks of mania'" (1). Furthermore, they state that "attempts to describe and classify postpartum mental illness became more systematic in the mid-nineteenth century, when Esquirol wrote of the 'mental alienation of the recently confined and of nursing women'" (1).

In current medical discourse, there are conflicting reports as to what actually qualifies as postpartum depression, and researchers are even raising questions about the terminology used to describe the illness. Sometimes called "baby blues," "postpartum blues," "transitory minor affective disorder," "chronic depressive syndrome," "moderate depression disorder," or, mistakenly, "postpartum psychosis," postpartum depression (the acronym PPD will appear henceforth) is a biochemical brain disorder "characterized by feelings of sadness in the new mother, extreme emotional instability, weeping, irritability and fatigue" (Johnson and Apgar 2, 1–14). By relying on the previous definition of PPD, one is able to diagnose Harriet not as a victim of postpartum psychosis (an acute but rare form of postnatal depression that affects 0.1 to 0.2 percent of mothers) but instead as a sufferer of PPD, which is, according to Harvard psychiatrist Deborah Sichel,[3] a brain illness that afflicts one-third of mothers (Johnson and Apgar 3). Although they fight over the terminology and the incidence rates of PPD, researchers agree on the following physical symptoms and mental states associated with the illness: headaches, numbness, fatigue, eating and sleeping problems, tearfulness, irritability, violent mood swings, dark thoughts, feelings of hopelessness and incompetency (especially as a mother), and loss of interest in leisure activities and social outings (Johnson and Apgar 4–5; Herz 72).

In this regard, critics who argue that Harriet becomes ill as a result of giving birth to a demon spawn fail to recognize that her deterioration occurs well before her fifth pregnancy. Indeed, the first warning signs of Harriet's affliction with PPD are manifested after the birth of her second child, Helen. Though Harriet suffers from morning sickness and looks pale during her first pregnancy with Luke, she is able to avoid postnatal distress because "Luke was an easy baby" (24). Within a year of her son's birth, Harriet delivers Helen, and it soon becomes obvious that Harriet is in the preliminary stage of PPD. Even her mother, Dorothy, notices her daughter's fatigue: "Though Harriet was tired—indeed, worn out—the Easter party took place. Dorothy was against it. 'You are *tired*, girl,' she said. 'You are bone tired.' Then, seeing Harriet's face: 'Well, all right, but you aren't to do anything, mind'" (27). The physical discomfort that Harriet experiences is a symptom that is common to many parturients; however, the sudden change in her mental state is definitely atypical.

Harriet's worsening mental health is evidenced not only by her constant pangs of guilt following the birth of her third child (Jane) in four years but also by her occasionally bizarre thoughts, such as her musings to her husband about her sister's mentally challenged child:

> Harriet said to David, privately, that she did not believe it was bad luck: Sarah and William's unhappiness, their quarrelling, had probably attracted the mongol child eyes, yes, of course she knew one shouldn't call them mongol. But the little girl did look a bit like Genghis Khan, didn't she? A baby Genghis Khan with her squashed little face and her slitty eyes? David disliked this trait of Harriet's, a fatalism that seemed so at odds with the rest of her. He said he thought this was silly hysterical thinking: Harriet sulked and they had to make up. (29)

This passage also shows that Harriet feels both superior to and jealous of her sister Sarah. Harriet reproaches her mother for spending more time at Sarah's place than at the Lovatt home, and though her criticism of her mother is unfair, it is entirely understandable considering Harriet's personality. After all, she pursues a hubristic goal of creating an idyllic family environment for her husband and children as well as for her relatives. Ultimately, she overextends herself physically, mentally, and emotionally by transforming her home into a hotel and tending to everyone's needs. Even after delivering her fourth child in six years, Harriet neither abandons her hosting duties and perfectionistic ways nor confesses her mounting exhaustion to anyone.

This secretiveness on Harriet's part is a trait common to the vast majority of postpartum sufferers. In "The Pathway to Care in Post-Natal Depression: Women's Attitudes to Post-Natal Depression and Its Treatment," Whitton et al. find that "over 90% recognized there was something wrong, but only one-third believed they were suffering from post-natal depression. Over 80% had not reported their symptoms to any health professional" (427). But, if these mothers are aware of their progressing lethargy, why do they not reach out to a family member, friend, or doctor? One possible explanation is that motherhood is still romanticized in contemporary popular culture, so much so that a mother who finds her maternal experience simply overwhelming (or underwhelming) must hide her negative feelings or run the risk of being called an unfit mother or a monster (Johnson and Apgar 12). Both David and Harriet romanticize parenthood, and after having their fourth child (Paul), the couple become even more dependent on their relatives to organize and finance their lavish gatherings. As David starts to work extra hours to support his expanding family, Harriet begins to experience violent mood swings. This is quite evident during a dinner party when she snaps at the children, berates herself for her irritability, and defends her and David's future childbearing plans against her relatives' criticisms. However, the hostile exchanges are soon forgotten, and a few months later, Harriet announces that she is pregnant yet again (30, 33–41).

Since Harriet displays many of the symptoms associated with PPD after her second, third, and fourth pregnancies, I contend that her extremely difficult fifth pregnancy has as much to do with her recurring battle with PPD as with the development of her so-called monstrous foetus. Undoubtedly, Harriet's perinatal experience with Ben is horrific, and the toll it takes on her is devastating. Harriet's behaviour becomes progressively more erratic; her actions include weeping constantly, arguing with her relatives, ignoring her children's needs, and ruminating over her difficult pregnancy (41–47). During her second trimester with Ben, Harriet suffers from insomnia and major discomfort; as a result, she seeks the help of Dr. Brett, who does not properly diagnose her as a postpartum sufferer. Also, he does not confirm her belief that her latest pregnancy is highly unusual. Instead, Dr. Brett gives Harriet a sedative to help her sleep (48–49). His misdiagnosis, not to mention his treatment option for insomnia, is partly responsible for Harriet's growing secretiveness and drug consumption:

> Now, afraid of asking Dr. Brett, she begged tranquilizers from friends, and from her sisters. She did not tell David how many she was taking, and this was the first time she had hidden anything from him. The foetus was quiet for about an hour after she dosed herself, and she was given a respite from the ceaseless battering and striving. (49)

Eventually, Harriet begins to view her foetus as a mortal enemy, and in her last trimester, she continues to wage a war with it by increasing her drug-taking, which affects both her temperament and her familial relations (51–53). This passage sheds light on Harriet's problematic perinatal experience with her fifth child:

The seventh month was better, and this was because of the amount of drugs she took. Appalled at the distance that had grown up between her and her husband, between her and the children, her mother, Alice, she now planned her day for one thing: that she would seem to be normal between the hours of four, when Helen and Luke ended school, until eight or nine, when they went to bed. The drugs did not seem to be affecting her much: she was willing them to leave her alone and to reach the baby, the foetus this creature with whom she was locked in a struggle to survive. And for those hours it was quiet, or if it showed signs of coming awake, and fighting her, she took another dose. (52–53)

Harriet's drug-taking has undeniably harmed Ben, and the latter's violence has obviously triggered his mother's recurring bouts of PPD. Sharon L. Dean points out that some scholars "locate the child Ben's behavior in the facts [sic] that his mother took drugs and was tense during an unwanted pregnancy and his father, along with the rest of the family, rejected him from the time he was born, exacerbating his drug-induced genetic problems" (120). Harriet creates a precedent with Ben: she delivers him in a hospital rather than at home as she did with her other children. Trying to bond with her newborn, her fifth child in seven years, she is so horrified by his abnormal physical appearance and ravenous appetite that she addresses him with derogatory terms, such as "troll," "goblin," and "Neanderthal baby" (60–65). Whatever Ben is—an alien, a genetic throwback, a mentally challenged baby—remains unclear. What is certain, though, is that Harriet's PPD resurfaces with the arrival of the fifth child.

The first tell-tale signs pointing to Harriet's recurring depression are her conflicting feelings toward Ben. At times, Harriet defends her youngest child from the harsh comments of those in her entourage, and at other times, she is guilt-ridden because she despises him too (67–69). Dr. Brett manages temporarily to assuage her feelings of guilt, telling her that "it is not abnormal to take a dislike to a child. I see it all the time. Unfortunately" (67). But one day, after overhearing her relatives denigrate Ben, Harriet decides to make a concerted effort to foster the mother–son connection:

[Her sister's disparaging remarks about Ben] afflicted Harriet with remorse: poor Ben, whom no one could love. She certainly could not! And David, the good father, hardly touched him. She lifted Ben from his cot, so much like a cage, and put him on the big bed, and sat with him. 'Poor Ben, poor Ben,' she crooned, stroking him. He clutched her shirt with both hands, pulled himself up, and stood on her thigh. The hard little feet hurt her. She tried to cuddle him, persuade him to soften against her.... Soon she gave up, put him back in his pen, or cage ... a roar of frustration because he had been put down, and she held out her hands to him. 'Poor Ben, dear Ben,' and he grasped her hands and pulled himself up and stood grunting and roaring with triumph. Four months old.... He was like an angry, hostile little troll. (69)

Other striking signs of Harriet's postpartum distress are her intermittent dark thoughts, most of them involving Ben's death. Before giving birth to him, she "fantasized that she took the big kitchen knife, cut open her stomach, lifted out the child, and when they actually set eyes on each other, after this long blind struggle, what would she see?" (59). A few months after delivering Ben, Harriet meets with her family doctor for a prescription for her son's diarrhea, and makes this bizarre statement: "After all, I don't want to kill the nasty little brute" (67).

From a Freudian perspective, Harriet's extempore remark constitutes a wish-fulfillment. A few weeks after her remark in the doctor's office, Harriet reluctantly saves Ben from a fall from a window ledge, and she feels no remorse for hoping that he fall and die: "Harriet was thinking, What a pity I came in ... and refused to be shocked at herself" (73). Another example that illustrates Harriet's mental fragility is when she loses sight of Ben but eventually finds "that stubby squat little figure going through traffic lights, ignoring cars that hooted and people who screamed warnings at him. She was weeping, panting, half-crazed, desperate to get to him before something terrible happened, but she was praying, Oh, do run him over, do, yes, *please*" (77). Harriet dreams of her son's demise, believing incorrectly that he is solely responsible for her ennui. What she fails to recognize is that her mental and physical collapse is due to an illness, PPD.

But what exactly are the causes of and treatment options for PPD? Researchers generally try to analyze postnatal distress by appeal to biological theories or psychosocial factors (such as personality, demographic, and interpersonal variables). The studies that attempt to explain PPD on biological grounds focus on hormonal shifts in women during and after pregnancy. However, in their investigation of a hormonal link to PPD, Harris et al. report that, in fact, there is "no support for a direct association of progesterone with postnatal mood at 6 weeks postpartum" (743). This idea is corroborated by Gregoire et al., whose study concludes that "links between absolute or changing concentrations of steroids such as cortisol and progesterone and maternity blues have not, so far, led to any positive associations with postnatal depression" (930). For their part, Hendrick et al. maintain that "studies have been negative or contradictory for most biological variables thought to be etiologic. Thus, the literature to date does not consistently support any single biological etiology for postpartum depression" (98). Instead of looking for a definite biological explanation for PPD, these researchers suggest concentrating on "psychosocial stressors" that affect many PPD sufferers, such as "lack of support, marital conflict, unemployment, an unplanned pregnancy, single motherhood, and young age" (98). Hendrick et al. stress the importance of these social and psychological factors on the scientific investigations of PPD: "Future research on the biological factors that may underlie postpartum mood disorders should attempt to control for [psychosocial] variables, as they otherwise are likely to confound the data" (98).

Other scholars are already studying psychosocial variables in the hope of linking them with PPD. In terms of personality variables, the scientific literature is consistent in suggesting that a woman's attitude toward her pregnancy, especially if it is ambivalent or predominantly negative, is strongly linked with depression. Needless to say, the previous explanation certainly applies to Harriet Lovatt, who registers surprise, apprehension, and shock after each new pregnancy. Regarding demographic variables, pregnant women appear susceptible to postpartum illness if they worry about such things as money or job security. Harriet does share these preoccupations along with her husband as both rely more and more on their parents' financial support to make ends meet.

At first, one might not think that interpersonal variables can be linked to Harriet's bout with PPD because she has a substantial support network. Nevertheless, researchers claim that marital discord can be an important factor leading to PPD, so Harriet and David's clearly dysfunctional relationship may contribute to Harriet's malady (Johnson and Apgar 6). In her study on obstetric variables, Herz underscores another aggravating factor. She states that "long and very short intervals between pregnancies may be potential risk factors for postpartum illness" (68). Her conclusion is particularly convincing when one thinks of Andrea Yates and Harriet Lovatt, who both had five children in just seven years. Basing their findings on a 1995 study titled "Effects of Postpartum Psychiatric Illnesses on Family Planning" by Peindl et al., Johnson and Apgar are convinced that the aforementioned psychosocial variables play a crucial role in PPD:

> Depressed mothers often show a more negative attitude toward their children, and a debilitated new mother puts significant emotional and perhaps economic burdens on family relationships. The patients themselves are often the most sensitive to these consequences. A recent study [4] reports that 32% of women who suffered an episode of postpartum depression dramatically changed their future

childbearing plans, resorting to adoption, abortion, or in some cases even sterilization. (4)

Like almost one-third of the women mentioned in Peindl et al.'s study, Harriet abandons her and her husband's plan of having "six children at least" (14). She regretfully tells David that she has started to use birth control: "Harriet informed him that she was now on the Pill: for both it was a bleak moment, because of everything they had been, had stood for, in the past, which had made it impossible for her to be on the Pill. They had felt it deeply wrong so to tamper with the processes of Nature!" (111).

There is not one agreed-upon cause of PPD in the scientific literature, as researchers offer several potential and often conflicting explanations. However, they do agree not only on the treatment options for postpartum sufferers but also on several practical tips for depressed mothers. In order not to fall prey to the illness, mothers need to keep their strength up by getting plenty of rest and sleep and must admit to their spouse, family members, close friends, or health care providers if they suddenly become overwhelmed (overtired and overanxious). Also, parturients must not overburden themselves with trivial household chores, take care of additional people such as relatives or friends, or abandon weekly or monthly social outings (Herz 73–75).

In addition to these suggestions, some researchers advocate psychopharmacological interventions. In his study, Jermain explains that antidepressants such as Prozac, Zoloft, and Paxil are "the drugs of choice for first-line treatment of depression" (36). Other studies focus less on antidepressant therapy and more on prevention. For example, Walther argues that

> the treatment of postpartum depression can be greatly enhanced by an ounce of prevention. With multifactorial causation, reducing any of the contributing factors may lessen the likelihood that a serious psychological problem will develop following birth. New prospective studies have suggested that rates of depression during pregnancy are similar to those developed and diagnosed after pregnancy. Furthermore, prenatal depression has been found to be a predictor of postpartum depression. (109)

Walther's claim that there may exist a causal link between perinatal and postnatal depression is certainly validated by Harriet's depressive episodes, which are exacerbated by sleep deprivation. During her first pregnancy, Harriet "slept badly from indigestion" and kept on losing sleep by mothering so many young children (23). David notices the toll that sleep deprivation has taken on his wife: "He looked instead at Harriet, who sat nursing Paul, two months old, in the big chair that was hers because it was comfortable for this function. She looked exhausted. Jane had been awake in the night with her teeth, and had wanted Mummy, not Granny" (33). As mentioned earlier, Harriet, suffering from insomnia during her fifth pregnancy, does consult her family doctor, but he simply prescribes her a sedative (48–49).

In this case, who is more to blame: the patient or the physician? It is undeniable that Harriet does not volunteer pertinent information about her mental state, but Dr. Brett does not even attempt to elicit such information from her. He is the one who should be seriously reprimanded for his unprofessional and condescending behaviour. The physician cavalierly dismisses his patient, unwilling to take the basic measures to properly diagnose her malady (48–49). As a result, Harriet's illness goes undiagnosed, and it seriously affects her physical and mental health. Johnson and Apgar insist that "postpartum depression is a common, frequently unrecognized, yet devastating disorder. The keys to successful treatment are early identification and intervention, both supportive and pharmacologic. These treatments are effective, and the ability to lessen the impact of this disease is congruent with the primary care provider's role" (12).

In conclusion, this paper has used recent scientific evidence in conjunction with a close reading of Doris Lessing's novel *The Fifth Child* in order to show how Harriet Lovatt is a postpartum sufferer. It has not portrayed Harriet and Ben as gothic monsters who are solely responsible for the destruction of the Lovatt household. However, Harriet's secretiveness and excessive pride prevent her from being properly diagnosed. Consequently, she wastes away and arguably becomes an unfit mother. Those who hold the view that Harriet is a dastardly figure cite the fact that she never accepts Ben from the day he is born, thus preventing the all-important mother–child bond. They also mention the fact that she allows her son to be institutionalized. In fairness to Harriet, she is both coerced by all members of her family into accepting that decision and victimized by a medical establishment that has not recognized her malady, even though the scientific literature has addressed the insidious effects of PPD for over a century and a half (Rowe 105–06).

In gothic stories such as *The Fifth Child*, the domestic sphere becomes a dangerous place, and in Lessing's novel, the scariest elements are the Lovatts themselves. David transforms from loving husband and doting father to stoic partner and distant patriarch. Harriet, initially an "angel in the house," metamorphoses into a "madwoman in the attic" (Gilbert and Gubar 17, 425). Luke, Helen, Jane, and Paul start out as loving children, but they become resentful of their mother when she retrieves Ben from the institution. They eventually and quite willingly leave home. As Rowe points out, Harriet pays a high price for rescuing Ben and trying desperately to establish a loving bond with him; she does not completely civilize her fifth child and ruins her relationships with her four other children and her husband in the process (107–09). By relegating herself to the private sphere, Harriet unwittingly invents a modern female gothic persona: the postpartum sufferer. Scholars interested in representations of mothering in literature may wish to investigate other literary manifestations of postpartum depression in fiction and life writing. Future studies dealing with postpartum sufferers could highlight how their perinatal and postnatal experiences are similar to, or different from, Harriet Lovatt's. Further analyses, scientific and theoretical, of PPD are needed, and doctors must not only diagnose and treat these women but also work on early prevention and education. Otherwise, more children will be harmed, and severely depressed mothers—real ones such as Andrea Yates and literary ones such as Harriet Lovatt—will continue to be vilified as monsters.

Notes to Chapter 9

1   Russell Yates, interview with Oprah Winfrey, *The Oprah Winfrey Show*, ABC, WLS-TV, Chicago, 20 Mar. 2002.

2   V. Thurtle, "Post-Natal Depression: The Relevance of Sociological Approaches," *Journal of Advanced Nursing* 22 (1995): 416–24.

3   Deborah Sichel, interview with Oprah Winfrey, *The Oprah Winfrey Show*, ABC, WLS-TV, Chicago, 9 Jan. 2002.

4   K. S. Peindl, E. J. Zolnik, K. L. Wisner, and B. H. Hanusa, "Effects of Postpartum Psychiatric Illnesses on Family Planning," *The International Journal of Psychiatry in Medicine* 25 (1995): 291–300.

Works Cited

Dean, Sharon L. "Lessing's *The Fifth Child*." *Explicator* 50 (1992): 120–22.

Gilbert, Sandra M., and Susan Gubar. *The Madwoman in the Attic: The Woman Writer and the Nineteenth-Century Literary Imagination*. New Haven and London: Yale University Press, 1979.

Gregoire, A. J. P., et al. "Transdermal Oestrogen for Treatment of Severe Postnatal Depression." *Lancet* 347 (1996): 930–33.

Harris, B., et al. "Postnatal Development at 5 to 6 Weeks Postpartum, and Its Hormonal Correlates Across the Peripartum Period." *British Journal of Psychiatry* 168 (1996): 739–44.

Hendrick, V., et al. "Hormonal Changes in the Postpartum and Implications for Postpartum Depression." *Psychosomatics* 39 (1998): 93–101.

Herz, E. K. "Prediction, Recognition, and Prevention." *Postpartum Psychiatric Illness: A Picture Puzzle.* Ed. J. A. Hamilton and P. N. Harberger. Philadelphia: University of Pennsylvania Press, 1992. 68–75.

Jermain, D. M. "Treatment of Postpartum Depression." *American Pharmacy* 35 (1995): 33–38.

Johnson, Timothy R. B., and Barbara Apgar. "Postpartum Depression." *OBGYN.net.* 1996–2001. 22 Mar. 2002, http://www.obgyn.net/femalepatient/femalepatient .asp?page=leopold.

Lessing, Doris. *The Fifth Child.* 1988. London: Flamingo, 1993.

Rowe, Margaret Moan. *Doris Lessing.* New York: St. Martin's Press, 1994.

Walther, V. N. "Postpartum Depression: A Review for Perinatal Social Workers." *Social Work in Health Care* 24.3–4 (1997): 99–111.

Whitton, A., et al. "The Pathway to Care in Post-Natal Depression: Women's Attitudes to Post-Natal Depression and Its Treatment." *British Journal of General Practice* 46 (1996): 427–28.

10

We Need to Talk about Gender: Mothering and Masculinity in Lionel Shriver's *We Need to Talk about Kevin* | BY EMILY JEREMIAH

Feminist debates about maternity have proliferated wildly over the past few decades. Underlying many such discussions is the conviction that mothering is widely dismissed and undermined. Naomi Wolf, for example, contends that modern American motherhood is "undersupported, sentimentalized, and even manipulated at women's expense" (1). This critique is echoed in Lionel Shriver's 2003 novel *We Need to Talk about Kevin*, a work that forms a valuable, if reluctant,[1] contribution to feminist thinking about mothering. In particular, as we will see, the text offers complex conceptions of corporeality, gender, and family—all sites of power—in the context of (American) postmodernism.

The novel also exposes and challenges the traditional conflation of "maternity" and "femininity"; women, it suggests, are not naturally or necessarily able parents. Nor are they always very "feminine." The text implies, in fact, that femininity is a rather undesirable condition. In challenging traditional assumptions to the effect that women are, or should be, both feminine and maternal, the work aligns itself with queer theory, which posits that gender and sexuality are not fixed givens that exist in a stable relationship to each other. It overturns, or "queers," dominant ideas about gender, then, paving the way for new conceptions of sex and of parenting. It calls into question the gender of mothering—a term that will now be investigated—and, in so doing, the nature and function of gender in general.

The Gender of Mothering

The feminist exposure of and challenge to "the feminine mystique" (Friedan) is not new; Simone de Beauvoir observed in 1949 that "one is not born, but rather becomes, a woman" (295). Gender is a construct, then—this goes, of course, for masculinity as well as for femininity. The sex/gender opposition is problematic, though, for it may suggest that gender is simply imposed onto sex, or society onto biology, where the latter is an immutable entity. In fact, as Judith Butler has pointed out, the body is itself a construct and by no means a simple or stable affair (6). In addition, the notion of constructed-ness needs to be treated with caution. Butler describes construction as "a temporal process which operates through the reiteration of norms; sex is both produced and destabilized in the course of this reiteration" (10). Con-struction is an ongoing process; sex is fabricated by means of repeated acts that affirm norms, but that also allow for deviation and disruption.

This is a "performative" view of sex. Performativity is "the reitera-tive and citational practice by which discourse produces the effects that it names" (Butler 2). Gender, according to this understanding, is a series of acts that congeal over time to produce an effect of "natural" maleness or femaleness. Maternity has been viewed similarly: "To be a mother is to en-act mothering" (Chandler 273). Such an understanding of parenting might seem to free women from oppressive models of mothering, such as those evoked by Wolf; or, indeed, from mothering altogether. If maternity is a performance or a mode of cognition—philosopher Sara Ruddick writes of "maternal thinking" (44)—then men can do it just as well. There is a danger here, it should be noted: in granting men the status of mother there is a risk that the work still done primarily by (female) mothers is overlooked. There is also the risk that the significance of women's experiences of pregnancy, childbirth, and breastfeeding is trivialized or ignored.

The issue of men as mothers also raises a troubling question: Why, if we can accept this notion, are we so resistant to the idea of women as "fa-thers"? For as queer theorist Judith Halberstam notes, gender is apparently reversible only in one direction (269). This is perhaps particularly so where parenting is concerned; in the course of her discussion of masculinity in women, Halberstam speculates: "Presumably, female masculinity threatens the institution of motherhood" (273). Indeed, the ideologies of motherhood and femininity are closely intertwined, even interdependent. To disrupt one—to suggest, for example, that women might not be naturally caring and selfless—is to disrupt the other, in, one hopes, productive and interesting ways. This is what Shriver's novel does.

But what, first of all, *is* "masculinity"? As Halberstam points out, masculinity "becomes legible as masculinity where and when it leaves the white male middle-class body" (2); that is, it is normalized to the point of invisibility. Masculinity is seen as something that "just is"; femininity, on the other hand, is perceived as elaborate and artificial (Halberstam 234). And yet, as Halberstam points out, massive amounts of time and money are spent ratifying versions of masculinity that we support and trust (1). Masculinity, for Halberstam, has connotations of legitimacy, privilege, and wealth, and for her, female masculinity is empowering. She describes the figure of the stone butch as "viable, powerful, and affirmative" (126) and argues that masculinity in heterosexual women, too, has health benefits, traditional models of femininity being in many cases constraining and debilitating. Shriver's *Kevin* echoes and reinforces such challenges, as we will see.

Challenging Motherhood, Challenging Femininity

Shriver's dense, complex novel takes the form of a series of letters from Eva Khatchadourian to her husband, Franklin. Eva is the mother of Kevin. Aged 15, Kevin carries out a high-school massacre, killing nine people—seven fellow students, a teacher, and a cafeteria worker—with the aid of a bow and arrow. Eva begins her correspondence in November 2000, one year and eight months following her son's killing spree, and ends it in April 2001. Kevin is now nearly 18 and soon to be transferred from the juvenile correctional facility where he is currently detained to an adult prison.

In her letters, Eva reflects on the events leading up to her son's crime, in particular on her decision to become a mother and on her hostility toward her son, who appears sinister from birth. A series of malicious acts committed by Kevin is described. Although in some cases ambiguity surrounds these acts (for example, did Kevin cause the disappearance of the family pet?), the overall impression is one of malevolence. Interspersed with the account of Kevin's birth and development are descriptions of Eva's current abject, isolated life in Nyack, including her regular visits to Kevin in the Claverack institution where he is held. We also learn how Eva has been treated by neighbours and by the authorities following her son's crimes. Her house has been vandalized; she has been shunned, gawped at, or prayed for, and accused in a civil trial of "parental negligence." Halfway through the text it is revealed that Kevin had a younger sister, Celia. It also emerges, toward the end of the book, that both Franklin and Celia are dead: murdered by Kevin the same day he committed the high-school killings.

Already it is apparent that this novel challenges any residual notions of maternity as an instinctive and unproblematic affair. The work has indeed been described as a "resolutely anti-parenthood and anti-children book" (Smith). Given this bleakness, the novel's popularity is interesting. Despite the author's initial difficulties in finding a publisher (see Cusk, "Darkness"), the novel (Shriver's seventh) has been a critical and commercial success in the United States and in Britain, where it won the 2005 Orange Prize for fiction.[2] Clearly, Shriver's multilayered depiction of contemporary mothering offers something useful. In particular, I would suggest, it poses a welcome challenge to idealizations of maternity, and to assumptions that all women can and should mother; Eva's existence is in fact destroyed by maternity.

Perhaps unsurprisingly, the novel has been criticized for its negative depiction of mothering. It has been suggested that in focusing on an extreme case, Shriver is being somehow dishonest: Jennie Bristow states that "most children are not Kevin, and we don't need to talk about them as if they were," an interestingly defensive position. Another critic wonders why Kevin and his family were not referred for assessment and counselling (Curtis), being unable, apparently, to accept the story that is presented. Sarah A. Smith thinks Shriver "has rendered her exploration of motherhood futile by linking it to such black events." Another critic opines similarly: "It would have been a braver, more interesting ... novel had Shriver steered clear of the headline-orientated denouement altogether" (Tripney). Shriver has herself commented on the anxious responses to her book, noting, "[Kevin] has drawn fire from Catholic websites for being hostile to 'family,' while grotesque distortions of the book's underlying theme ... have spored from article to article like potato blight" (Shriver, "No Kids" 38).

A further criticism that has been levelled at the novel is that it is unoriginal, because "there is nothing taboo about whingeing in print about the everyday grind of maternity"; here, this commentator cites Rachel Cusk, Kate Figes, and Naomi Wolf (Bristow). Two points are worth raising in response. Firstly, the fact that Eva's is an extreme case does not render her, or Shriver's, insights any less valuable (or uncomfortable). It would in any case be odd to expect that literary texts should present only typical stories with which one can easily identify. Secondly, it is a relatively recent development that women have been able to indulge in public "whingeing" about mothering, and a luxury not to be scorned. Shriver's "whinge," incidentally, does not arise from her personal experience—the author is not herself a mother—which renders the charge of self-indulgent moaning even weaker.

Let us look now at the content of this "whinge." Before becoming a mother, Shriver's Eva is a wealthy and successful businesswoman who runs a company producing guidebooks and who travels frequently; as such she is "masculine" in Halberstam's sense. Her initial worries about mothering—"I was afraid of being the steadfast, stationary anchor" (Shriver, *Kevin* 31)—are soon borne out. Her independence is gradually eroded and replaced with a life of boredom and entrapment. Eva and Franklin move away from Manhattan when Kevin is four, to a house of Franklin's choosing in Nyack, which is "woodsy and right on the Hudson" (131). The house seems to Eva bare and open: "I panicked, thinking, *There's nowhere to hide*" (132). It can be seen as an emblem of maternity: an institution that leaves Eva both confined and exposed. Eva's identity evaporates, as her knowledge and skills are proved useless in motherhood (153, 193). The destructive Kevin ruins the wallpaper Eva assembles from maps (157–58); her experience and memories are thus symbolically erased.

Eva's mother, in contrast to her globe-trotting daughter, is an agoraphobic. While this Armenian widow constitutes a complex character in her own right, she could be also seen as an extreme representative of a previous generation of women: cloistered and fearful (see Friedan 18). The differences between Eva and her mother tell of a generational shift, one that Gloria Steinem has seen as a move toward female masculinity: "we are becoming the men our mothers wanted us to marry" (qtd. in Wolf 102). Eva is, or was, affluent, attractive, and ambitious—and, as noted, "masculine."[3] Eva's mother's housebound condition also calls to mind the feminist critique of the public/private divide, which served historically to isolate and confine women to the domestic sphere, while men were free (or bound) to participate in education, politics, and business (e.g., Badinter 145). At the time of her letter-writing, Eva herself is leading an isolated life, cut off from politics and from most forms of human interaction. "Having it all" has clearly not worked out for her (see Benn 45–47; Buxton 6), and retreat into isolation is the only possible option: a damning indictment of contemporary motherhood.

Shriver's novel also deals with the (relatively recent, Western) idea of maternity as a "choice," one that here appears perverse. Indeed, it would seem more natural for women *not* to become mothers, given that parenting involves such factors as "dementing boredom," "social demotion," "unnatural altruism," and a "worthless social life"—not to mention the unforeseen risk "son might turn out killer," as Eva wryly reflects (Shriver, *Kevin* 26, 25). And the assumption that women are naturally inclined to be mothers is damaging:

> For years I'd been awaiting that overriding urge I'd always heard about, the narcotic pining that draws childless women ineluctably to strangers' strollers in

parks. I wanted to be drowned by the hormonal imperative.... Whatever the trigger, it never entered my system, and that made me feel cheated.... By the time I gave birth to Kevin at thirty-seven, I had begun to anguish over whether, by not simply accepting this defect, I had amplified an incidental, perhaps merely chemical deficiency into a flaw of Shakespearean proportions. (27)

It is thus suggested that it would have been better for Eva to have accepted the lack of maternal urge (see Badinter xxi). Shriver can here be seen to criticize biologism: the assumption that the body—understood as "pure" and "natural"—conditions and constructs the self; in Eva's case, it is societal and cultural factors that shape her decision. In retrospect, though, the choice to become a parent makes no sense to Eva, philosophically or psychologically; she considers the erroneous view that having a child gives meaning to life, for: "if there's no reason to live without a child, how could there be with one?" And if one seeks purpose in a child, then the meaning of life is simply transferred to the next generation in "a cowardly and potentially infinite delay" (Shriver, *Kevin* 255).

Eva's views, of course, are not to be taken as Shriver's own. In a 2005 article for *The Guardian*, Shriver discusses her own and many of her contemporaries' choice not to have children, problematizing and, to an extent, critiquing this decision. Declaring "I've had it with being the Anti-Mom," she explores the declining fertility rate in the West and argues: "baby boomers and their offspring have shifted emphasis from the communal to the individual, from the future to the present, from virtue to personal satisfaction.... We will assess the success of our lives in accordance not with whether they were righteous, but with whether they were interesting and fun" ("No Kids" 41). Thus, Shriver criticizes widespread, rampant individualism. Shriver's earlier novel *Game Control* likewise offers a thoughtful treatment of the issue of reproduction. It deals satirically, and often grotesquely, with the question of population control in Africa, investigating its political and ethical dimensions. At the end of the novel, we learn of the main female protagonist's desire to have children, a wish that is perhaps to be read as ironic and absurd, but which might also be seen as a celebration of procreation—this is a typically ambiguous touch on Shriver's part.

To return to *Kevin*: like Butler and such postmodernist theorists as Jean-François Lyotard and Jean Baudrillard, Shriver understands (maternal) experience as constructed, or performed. During discussions about possible parenthood, Eva and Franklin engage in role-play: "These talks of ours had a gameliness.... This time I bid for the more daring role: 'At least if I got pregnant, something would happen'" (Shriver, *Kevin* 16–17). As well as recalling Lyotardian notions of "just gaming," these references to play and performance also bring to mind Butlerian performativity. Eva performs pregnancy; she "assemble[s] [herself] into the glowing mother-to-be" (52). She deliberately styles herself as a "mother-to-be," then, drawing on the stock of cultural associations and imperatives (asexuality, radiance, sobriety) that attach themselves to that figure. Eva's performance recalls Wolf, who notes that the pregnant woman is supposed to express only a blossoming sense of joy and anticipation (53); ambivalence is not permitted her. Shriver's Eva, having just given birth to Kevin and disappointed by her own lack of a response, "reache(s) for a line from TV" (82); again, there is a sense of performance, of inauthenticity.

Thus Shriver rejects biologism and embraces constructivism, or performativity. But while the novel critiques biologism on the one hand, it also, on the other, endorses it, by suggesting a view of the female body, particularly the pregnant body, as all-engulfing and all-powerful. Shriver states in an interview: "There are downsides to both sexes, and the downside to being female is pretty obvious. We haven't run the world. It's hard not to have some misgivings about the whole process of pregnancy and motherhood. It's a tremendous imposition." In the novel, pregnancy is indeed viewed as an imposition. It changes Eva's view of her own body, rendering it animalistic. Her body becomes a resource: "I felt expendable, throw-away, swallowed by a big biological project that I didn't initiate or choose.... I felt used" (Shriver, *Kevin* 51). Pregnancy constitutes an invasion; Eva refers to the "humbling price of a nine-month freeloader" (58). And childbirth, Eva states, is "awful," and akin to "ramming a watermelon through a passage the size of a garden hose" (74, 76). In this way, the novel is reminiscent of early second-wave feminist rejections of motherhood. It brings to mind, for example, Simone de Beauvoir's description of the pregnant woman as "life's passive instrument" and "the prey of the species" (513, 515). The evocation of childbirth echoes radical feminist Shulamith Firestone's reports of "shitting a watermelon" (189).

Eva's discomfort with the biological facts of pregnancy, with her body, ties in with Western ("masculine"?) ideals of individualism and rationality. Eva's agency is undermined by pregnancy: "I had demoted myself from driver to vehicle, from householder to house" (Shriver, *Kevin* 58). Such a challenge to individualism has been seen as productive and subversive by feminist theorists. Pregnancy, it has been pointed out, poses a challenge to the unified subject of humanist discourse (Cosslett 117). Mothering in general challenges Western capitalist ideals of individualism (Chandler 272; DiQuinzio xv). Shriver's assertion of female corporeality, of natality, can also be seen as subversive. When Eva looks round her on the street and registers with incredulity that "every one of these people came from a woman's cunt" (Shriver, *Kevin* 58), she is posing a challenge to a culture that routinely suppresses the mother's body, that, according to Luce Irigaray, practises matricide (47).

But more obviously, the novel is interested in how the female body, in particular the pregnant body, is constrained and controlled, in line with numerous feminist analyses, including that of Wolf (see also Rich 176). When Eva is pregnant, Franklin closely monitors her behaviour, disapproving, for example, of her drinking a glass of wine (Shriver, *Kevin* 51). He displays a proprietary protectiveness toward his unborn child; when Eva goes out it is "as if I were bearing away one of your prized possessions without asking" (63). Eva challenges foetalism, then, the stress on the unborn child at the expense of the desires, experience, and well-being of the mother (Faludi ch. 14). Eva's critical reflection that "the right to boss pregnant women around was surely on its way into the Constitution" (Shriver, *Kevin* 52) accords with contemporary feminist anxieties to that effect (see also Cusk, *Life's Work* 34).

Eva's most explicit challenge to traditional femininity, and to the very notion of "tradition," comes during a discussion between Eva and Franklin about the surname of their unborn child. Franklin appeals to "tradition" when arguing that the child should take his surname: "since somebody's gotta lose, it [*sic*] simplest to stick with tradition." Eva replies: "'According to *tradition*, women couldn't own property until, in some states, the 1970s. *Traditionally* in the Middle East we walk around in a black sack and *traditionally* in Africa we get our clitorises carved out like a hunk of gristle—' You stuffed my mouth with cornbread" (Shriver, *Kevin* 59). Eva thus parodies and undermines the notion of tradition as a guarantor of rightness. She is then silenced; it is suggested that such critiques have limited power.

Further criticism of traditional femininity is to be found in the figure of Kevin's sister, Celia, a "girl-girl" whose "feminine diffidence and delicacy were foreign to (Eva)" (Shriver, *Kevin* 226). (Eva does, nonetheless, display care and connectedness in relation to her daughter.) Celia is squeamish and sensitive, and Kevin exploits her. A shocking manifestation of this dynamic—which may be expressed in terms of masculine dominance versus feminine submissiveness (see here Dinnerstein 40)—occurs when Kevin apparently pours cleaning fluid in Celia's eye. Kevin's murder of Celia is its horrific culmination. Shriver's portrayal of an exaggeratedly "feminine" femininity stands at odds with the "masculinity" of the maternal protagonist and brings to mind Halberstam's view that femininity is unhealthy.

(American) Masculinity in *Kevin*

"Masculinity" (in men or women) is not unquestioningly celebrated in the novel, however. We see this most obviously in the depiction of Kevin. Eva's reaction to discovering the sex of her first child is disappointment. She associates boys with menace:

> For all our squinting at the two sexes to blur them into duplicates, few hearts race when passing gaggles of giggling schoolgirls. But any woman who passes a clump of testosterone-drunk punks without picking up the pace, without avoiding eye contact that might connote challenge or invitation, without sighing inwardly with relief by the following block, is a zoological fool. A boy is a dangerous animal. (Shriver, *Kevin* 62)

Eva again indicates a biologistic view of sexual difference here; sex, for her, is not a construct—"squinting" gender/queer theorists are dismissed—but a "zoological" affair. Such a view might be termed reductionist. But in any case, what is interesting here is the understanding of masculinity as threatening and violent.[4] Eva finds boys to display an aggressive sexuality; and indeed, aged 14, Kevin masturbates openly in front of her, something Franklin refuses to take seriously (297).

Kevin uses his sexuality to hurt and humiliate others. Aged 15, he accuses his drama teacher, Miss Pagorski, of sexual harassment (Shriver, *Kevin* 331). Although it is never proven whether his charges have any real foundation—throughout the text, truth and blame emerge as uncertain terms—enough doubt is cast on his account by Eva for us to suspect that it is a malicious fabrication. It results in the demotion of the teacher in question, who is portrayed as inept and vulnerable. Again, masculine dominance over women is played out (see Benjamin 190), albeit in a stereotypically "feminine" (sly, indirect) way. A comparable slant is taken in Shriver's earlier novel *The Female of the Species*, in which a young man seduces an older woman, a respected anthropologist, eventually to reject and humiliate her.

Kevin also suggests how masculinity is bound up with nationalism, in particular Americanness. Kevin could be seen as standing for the United States in general. He defines himself firmly as "an American," rejecting any link to Eva's Armenian background, and his gung-ho militarism, which Franklin finds "adorable," is perhaps also to be read as typically "American" (Shriver, *Kevin* 214, 219). The terminally bored Kevin, lacking in interest in others and murderously jealous of those with passions, like those he kills, can be seen as representing a deadly, glutted empire; he has everything, and yet he "hated being here so much" (90). Kevin's teacher speculates that it is affluence itself that makes him feel superfluous and destructive (333–34). The suggestive linkage between Kevin and the United States is affirmed when the patriotic Franklin defends his country: "Sure it was imperfect, you would add, with the same hastiness with which I observed before Kevin was born that of course some children 'had problems'" (37–38).

America, it is implied, breeds violence, on which it thrives; Kevin's crimes offer excitement and interest (Shriver, *Kevin* 96, 357), just as his birth had promised eventfulness and distraction to his parents. This is a hollow and materialistic place, a country in which "materials are everything," as Franklin's father opines (4, 136), and in which nothing is authentic. Franklin, a locations finder for an advertising company, boasts that he can "find you the Rhone Valley in Pennsylvania" (37).[5] Eva reflects on the design of a Campbell's soup tin, recalling Warhol; this is a telling detail, for as Eva muses, "The whole country's lost, everybody copies everybody else, and everybody wants to be famous" (3, 314). Nothing in Eva's current life is stable or authentic: "This tremulous little house—it doesn't feel quite *real*, Franklin. And neither do I" (5). The country itself seems unreal, ridiculous. Eva writes her letters against the backdrop of the hung election of 2000, a detail that implies the impossibility of change, the absurdity of the political process.

Franklin does not offer an entirely positive model of masculinity, either. Unlike Eva, Franklin embraces the role of parent with a simple-mindedness that occasionally strains the reader's good will. Eva reflects that in general Franklin "seemed to be able to squint and blur off the rough edges" (Shriver, *Kevin* 135). As a father, he "buy[s] into all that stuffed-bunny schlock" (75), as his view of Kevin, so radically at odds with Eva's (and the reader's), also implies. Paternity here appears unquestioning, and even ridiculous, though not unmoving. In the end, Franklin is destroyed.

What of Eva, then? Is there in her "female masculinity" (Halberstam) something to be celebrated? What can be salvaged from this story? Eva is certainly not an obvious role model. While she may be subversively "feminist" in her rejection of traditional ideals of women as nurturing and caring, her ("masculine") individualism and pragmatism are not attractive. Without telling Franklin, Eva has the foetus she is carrying tested for Down Syndrome, and the reasons she gives are brutal: "I did not want to mother an imbecile or a paraplegic; whenever I saw fatigued women wheeling their stick-limbed progeny ... my heart didn't melt, it sank" (Shriver, *Kevin* 72). As Kevin will later point out, Eva can be "kind of harsh" (273). This harshness is manifested most awfully in her methods of mothering, as we will see.

Eva is as much a product of America as her son is. Her nomadism (Braid-otti), her endless quest for novelty, is as much symptomatic of American excess and boredom as are Kevin's apathy and violence. In this, Eva is like Estrin Lancaster in Shriver's *Ordinary Decent Criminals*, with her "avaricious crackling of maps" (60). When Kevin challenges Eva regarding her anti-Americanism, her mind goes blank: "I ... worried that maybe I hadn't kept the U.S. at arm's length from sophisticated cosmopolitanism, but rather from petty prejudice" (Shriver, *Kevin* 276). Kevin also observes that Eva falsely "others" Americans (307). When it is revealed that Kevin admires and is proud of his mother, Eva's detachment, from her son and her country, is further challenged. She has to acknowledge: "I live here" (307).

Eva's mothering is certainly not ideal. Recent feminist theories of maternity stress "mutuality" or "interdependence" between mother and child (Benjamin 19; Everingham 6). As mentioned before, mothering has been seen to pose a challenge to the individualism prized by Western capitalism. Maternity has been viewed as a key site of ethical behaviour (e.g., Kristeva 182); indeed, the mother–child dyad could be theorized as the source of, or model for, *all* ethical behaviours. This view is not without risks; it could be dangerous to reinscribe women as "angels of the house," guardians of morality. But in any case, this risk is not run in *Kevin*, in which Eva is a self-confessed "rotten mother" (Shriver, *Kevin* 250). While she might resolve to "[meet] Kevin halfway" (120), her attempt at mutuality fails in the face of Kevin's intractable awfulness. There are hints of maternal sadism; Eva feels a "gush of savage joy" when confiscating Kevin's squirt gun (150). Most shockingly, she throws the six-year-old Kevin across the room in a rage, causing his arm to break (194). Such a reminder of maternal power is on the one hand useful—it brings to light the importance of mothers' care and protection—but on the other hand, this is of course no way to behave.[6]

Power, Blame, Ethics

As implied, blame is a complex issue here, for the "truth" is manipulable and even inaccessible (Shriver, *Kevin* 68, 70). As we have only Eva's perspective on events, we cannot easily reach judgment. Shriver's treatment of the issue of responsibility is nuanced. While Eva is widely shunned and blamed for her son's crimes, she herself is wary of that side of her account that renders her accountable. Guilt can be self-indulgent, she points out: "There's a self-aggrandizement in these wallowing mea culpas, a vanity" (65). Eva critiques the phenomenon of mother-blaming, then (see 157), highlighting the fact that mothers are not isolated from their societies. As philosopher Ruddick expresses it, mothering is a practice that "begins in response to the reality of a biological child in a particular social world" (17). At Eva's civil trial, Eva is asked by her lawyer if she monitored Kevin's toys and television and video viewing:

> "We tried to keep Kevin away from anything too violent or sexually explicit, especially when he was little. Unfortunately, that meant my husband couldn't watch most of his own favorite programs. And we did have to allow one exception."
>   "What was that?"…
> "The History Channel." A titter; I was playing to the peanut gallery. (Shriver, *Kevin* 144)

Childhood and adulthood are constructs, Eva notes, and when people "protect" their children, they are simply boosting their own self-importance by holding on to an idea of some adult mystique (147).

Mothers might be powerful, but so, in Eva's view, are children (Shriver, *Kevin* 107, 302). Parental authority is fragile and dependent on threat (202). In addition, as Eva observes, all children are different and present varying challenges; she is puzzled as to how anyone can claim to "love children," as if they were all the same (180). Eva points out to her lawyer that she herself was unprotected from Kevin's "coarsening influence" (144), a claim that highlights the agency and particularity of the child. While for Franklin, who has "that insouciant boy-thing going," Kevin is a simple creature, a blank slate, for Eva he is "pre-extant, with a vast, fluctuating interior life" (116). The question of nature versus nurture, like that of blame, is subtly explored here. As Shriver states, "Clearly, both nature and nurture have an effect [in the shaping of the self]."

Shriver, then, presents a complex view of mother–child relationships and their interaction with particular societies. She also critiques the heterosexual family. Although her novel is not explicitly interested in queerness—there is, for example, a dismissive reference on Franklin's part to "the fag" downstairs (Shriver, *Kevin* 92)—and nor is Shriver herself (see note 1),[7] the dissection of heterosexual relationships offered here could usefully be harnessed for a queer agenda. As we have seen, Shriver's work challenges the assumption that sex and gender are stable and unquestionable, and it undermines dominant ideals regarding women's capacity for mothering. In questioning the idea of the "family," it contributes even more powerfully to feminist and/or queer debates.

Eva questions patriarchal "tradition," as shown. She also views the notion of "family" with suspicion: "We were no longer Eva and Franklin, but

Mommy and Daddy; this was our first meal together as a *family*, a word and a concept about which I had always been uneasy" (Shriver, *Kevin* 54; see also Shriver, *Perfectly Good Family* 116). After Kevin's birth, Franklin appears to prioritize his son over Eva, not, for example, noticing that she is seriously ill (Shriver, *Kevin* 94). Gradually the relationship between Eva and Franklin is destroyed. We are told that Eva defies "heterosexual norms" when she reveals her sexual fantasies to Franklin (64)—but when she wants to talk about her ambivalence as a mother this is not permitted. This is an interesting detail, suggesting that motherhood, in contrast to sex, is still surrounded by taboo. Similarly, Eva vows she will never reveal to anyone that childbirth left her unmoved (83). This detail recalls Halberstam's observation regarding the closely linked ideologies of motherhood and femininity.

But while maternity and the family are subject here to deconstruction and suspicion, the mother–child bond is powerfully, if disturbingly, affirmed; Eva maintains a relationship with her son and keeps a room ready for him in her house for when he is released from prison, so that "perhaps what comes across most strongly [in the novel] is the sheer power of the parent-child bond—for better or for worse." Eva reflects that "it must be possible to earn a devotion by testing an antagonism to its very limit" (Shriver, *Kevin* 400). In testing maternal ambivalence to the limit, the novel earns serious attention, ultimately promoting respect for the intensity of the mother–child relationship. And in its very "harshness," even perversity, it triggers questions that a sentimental, glossed-over treatment of motherhood could not do. Eva notes that "for Kevin, progress was deconstruction" (397); the novel's deconstruction of mothering—particularly the gender of mothering—likewise constitutes progress, enriching existing debates about parenthood and opening up new lines of inquiry.

In conclusion, although *Kevin* is not concerned with offering ethical guidance as to the issue of parenting, its very complexity and ambivalence can be seen as ethical; the work calls for a necessary reappraisal of current social arrangements. In particular, it asks that we look again at traditional assumptions about gender, sex, and parenting, as argued. A perverse reading of the novel might even say that it is profoundly "maternal," where "maternity" is understood as connoting relationality, dialogue. As Cusk puts it, this is a book "about the dangerous distance that exists between what we feel and what we are actually prepared to admit when it comes to family life ... about what we need to talk about, but can't" ("Darkness").

Notes to Chapter 10

1 Shriver is not keen on the term "feminist": "I'm uneasy with the label 'feminist,' which is unfortunate. What the word means on the face of it I should be able to embrace. But the connotations of the term have soured. These days if you say you're a feminist people hear that you are A) ugly, B) probably a dyke, C) shrill, touchy, and eager to bring you to book on some minor infraction of political correctness, and—worst of all, in my view, D) utterly lacking a sense of humour" (Lawless). Shriver's fear of being perceived as a "dyke" is interesting, smacking as it does of homophobia, as is her general fear of others' perceptions, which seems uncharacteristic.

2 As Shriver herself notes: "In the context of my hitherto doomed literary career, the novel that won last year's Orange Prize was already selling bizarrely well by the time it made the shortlist. Nevertheless, the prize gave those sales long legs, and raised my public profile to the point of embarrassment" (Shriver, "It Pains Me").

3 Like Shriver, "a woman writer with a man's name" (Cusk, "Darkness"). Cusk reports: "Lionel Shriver changed her name from Margaret Ann when she was 15. She was, she says, a tomboy, but there was more to it than that. 'Lionel' isn't a pseudonym, or an alternative identity. It's an alias that frees her in a small but important sense. As a child, everywhere she looked—among her peers, in her parents' marriage, on the shelves at the bookshop—boys, men, had a better time. So, on the threshold of womanhood, she declined."

4 Eva does, however, enjoy the company of men, as the rather barbed explanation follows: "I liked their down-to-earth quality, I was prone to mistake aggression for honesty, and I disdained daintiness" (Shriver, *Kevin* 62).

5 "That was one of your favourite themes: that profusion, replication, popularity wasn't necessarily devaluing," Eva recalls (Shriver, *Kevin* 37).

6 At a reading on 13 Dec. 2005, in the Purcell Room on the South Bank in London, Shriver chose to read out the passage in which Eva injures her son. She prefaced the reading by assuring us that she would never publicly advocate child abuse, "at least not in this country"; but, she added provocatively, in scenes of mother–child conflict "violence can present itself as an almost refreshing opportunity."

7 See also the following squeamish passage in an earlier novel: "There had been times in a public bath when she had stared at a handsome woman in a way that made the other uncomfortably assume Constance was—no, it wasn't that" (Shriver, *Ordinary Decent Criminals* 77). See also a review by Shriver of Norah Vincent's *Self-Made Man*, which describes the year the author spent passing as a man: "Gay or not, [Vincent is] still a woman with a woman's perspective," she observes unnecessarily ("Stubble").

Works Cited

Badinter, Elisabeth. *The Myth of Motherhood: A Historical View of the Maternal Instinct.* Trans. Roger DeGaris. London: Souvenir, 1981.

Baudrillard, Jean. *Simulacra and Simulation.* Trans. Sheila Faria Glaser. Ann Arbor: University of Michigan Press, 1995.

Beauvoir, Simone de. *The Second Sex.* Trans. Howard Madison Parshley. London: Vintage, 1997.

Benjamin, Jessica. *The Bonds of Love: Psychoanalysis, Feminism, and the Problem of Domination.* London: Virago, 1990.

Benn, Melissa. *Mother and Child: Towards a New Politics of Motherhood.* London: Cape, 1998.

Braidotti, Rosi. *Nomadic Subjects: Embodiment and Sexual Difference in Contemporary Feminist Theory.* New York: Columbia University Press, 1994.

Bristow, Jennie. "We Don't Need to Talk about Hating Our Kids." Rev. of *We Need to Talk about Kevin*, by Lionel Shriver. *Spiked* 14 June 2005. 26 July 2005, http://www.spiked-online.com/index.php?/site/article/829/.

Butler, Judith. *Bodies That Matter: On the Discursive Limits of "Sex."* New York: Routledge, 1993.

Buxton, Jayne. *Ending the Mother War: Starting the Workplace Revolution.* London: Macmillan, 1998.

Chandler, Mielle. "Emancipated Subjectivities and the Subjugation of Mothering Practices." *Redefining Motherhood: Changing Identities and Patterns.* Ed. Sharon Abbey and Andrea O'Reilly. Toronto: Second Story, 1998. 270–86.

Cosslett, Tess. *Women Writing Childbirth: Modern Discourses of Motherhood.* Manchester: Manchester University Press, 1994.

Curtis, Sarah. "Would Therapy Have Helped?" Rev. of *We Need to Talk about Kevin*, by Lionel Shriver. *TLS* 8 April 2005. 26 July 2005, http://www.the-tls.co.uk/archive/story.aspx?story_id+2110770.

Cusk, Rachel. *A Life's Work: On Becoming a Mother.* London: Fourth Estate, 2002.

——. "Darkness at the Heart of the Family." Rev. of *We Need to Talk about Kevin*, by Lionel Shriver. *Guardian* 4 Oct. 2003. 26 July 2005, http://www.guardian.co.uk/weekend/story/0,,1054139,00.html.

Dinnerstein, Dorothy. *The Mermaid and the Minotaur: Sexual Arrangements and Human Malaise.* New York: Harper Perennial, 1991.

DiQuinzio, Patrice. *The Impossibility of Motherhood: Feminism, Individualism, and the Problem of Mothering.* New York: Routledge, 1999.

Everingham, Christine. *Motherhood and Modernity: An Investigation into the Rational Dimension of Mothering.* Buckingham: Open University Press, 1994.

Faludi, Susan. *Backlash.* London: Vintage, 1992.

Figes, Kate. *Life after Birth*. London: Viking, 1998.

Firestone, Shulamith. *The Dialectic of Sex: The Case for Feminist Revolution*. London: Women's Press, 1979.

Friedan, Betty. *The Feminine Mystique*. London: Penguin, 1992.

Halberstam, Judith. *Female Masculinity*. Durham: Duke University Press, 1998.

Irigaray, Luce. "Women-Mothers, the Silent Substratum of the Social Order." Trans. David Macey. *The Irigaray Reader*. Ed. Margaret Whitford. Oxford: Blackwell, 1991. 47–52.

Kristeva, Julia. "Stabat Mater." Trans. Leon S. Roudiez. *The Kristeva Reader*. Ed. Toril Moi. Oxford: Blackwell, 1986. 160–86.

Lawless, Andrew. "We Need to Talk about Kevin—Lionel Shriver in Interview." *Three Monkeys Online* May 2005. 26 July 2005, http://www.threemonkeysonline.com/threemon_article_we_need_to_talk_about_kevin_lionel_shriver_interview.htm.

Lyotard, Jean, and Jean-Loup Thébaud. *Just Gaming*. Trans. Wlad Godzich. Minneapolis: University of Minnesota Press, 1985.

Page, Benedicte. "A Rotten Bond." *The Bookseller* 22 Oct. 2004: 25.

Rich, Adrienne. *Of Woman Born: Motherhood as Experience and Institution*. London: Virago, 1977.

Ruddick, Sara. *Maternal Thinking: Toward a Politics of Peace*. Boston: Beacon, 1995.

Shriver, Lionel. *The Female of the Species*. New York: Farrar, Straus & Giroux, 1987.

——. *Game Control*. London: Faber & Faber, 1994.

——. "It Pains Me that I Can No Longer Feel Sorry for Myself." *Guardian* 13 Mar. 2006. 10 Apr. 2006, http://books.guardian.co.uk/orange2006/story/0,,1729668,00.html.

——. "No Kids Please, We're Selfish." *Guardian* 17 Sep. 2005: Magazine 38–44.

——. *Ordinary Decent Criminals*. London: HarperCollins, 1992. Rpt. of *The Bleeding Heart*. New York: Farrar, Straus & Giroux, 1990.

——. *A Perfectly Good Family*. London: Faber & Faber, 1996.

——. "The Stubble Diaries." Rev. of *Self-Made* Man, by Norah Vincent. *Guardian* 1 Apr. 2006: Review 10.

——. *We Need to Talk about Kevin*. London: Serpent's Tail, 2005.

Smith, Sarah A. "Not Mad about the Boy." Rev. of *We Need to Talk about Kevin*, by Lionel Shriver. *Guardian* 15 Nov. 2003. 26 July 2005, http://books.guardian.co.uk/review/story/0,,1084448,00.html.

Tripney, Natasha. "We Need to Talk about Kevin." Rev. of *We Need to Talk about Kevin*, by Lionel Shriver. *Pixelsurgeon* 2005. 26 July 2005, http://www.pixelsurgeon.com/reviews/review.php?id+756.

Vincent, Norah. *Self-Made Man*. London: Atlantic Books, 2006.

Wolf, Naomi. *Misconceptions: Truth, Lies and the Unexpected on the Journey to Mother-hood*. London: Vintage, 2002.

Part 3: Maternal Agency

11

Narrating Maternal Subjectivity: Memoirs from Motherhood | BY JOANNE S. FRYE

In a paper presented in 1997, at the first conference of the Association for Research on Mothering, I posed a question: "What does it mean to write as a mother?" And I began by reframing the question in terms that were familiar to most feminist literary critics of the time: "Why do we so rarely hear the voices of mothers in narrative form? Why is it that even women who are both mothers and writers are unlikely to portray mothers as active subjective presences? Why is it so difficult to find in narrative form the kinds of experiential insights that we assume derive from living as a mother?" (Frye 1). More than a decade later, I return to these same questions, aware that we are in the midst of an explosion of books by mothers, even as we continue to struggle with the meanings of maternal subjectivity and the difficulties of portraying it. For this undertaking, I find particularly valuable the resources of memoirs by mother-writers, autobiographical forms that set out to explore the experiences a woman undergoes as a mother and to render those experiences freshly through a heightened self-awareness.

I am convinced of the value of maternal memoir, despite the thematic difficulties that Ivana Brown has accurately identified in her reading of contemporary examples: "gender essentialism and dichotomous categorization

An earlier version of this essay was presented at the Association for Research on Mothering Conference, York University, Toronto, October 2004.

of gender" (209), by which memoirs "naturalize the social origins of gender inequalities" (210). But in my view, this is often only an *apparent* naturalizing, part of the long struggle to articulate what has been silenced from within a culture that continues to insist on motherhood as a ground for gender inequality. Thus I wish to join in a project that Laura Major has attributed to poet Alicia Ostriker: "re-imagining and confronting maternity ... tackl[ing] the problematic areas of reproduction and their representation" (193). Though some maternal memoirs do participate in perpetuating essentialism and gender dichotomies, I find in a select group the ability of language and narrative form to extend our understandings of the actual lives of women who mother and to initiate alternative understandings that resist the hazardous cultural constructions with which we continue to wrestle.

I begin my analysis by identifying the reasons why narrating maternal subjectivity is such a difficult task, so long in coming to fruition. I then discuss the particular problem of "representation" for maternal narratives and point toward possible ideas of "self" that may have special utility for this project. Finally, I examine three examples of mother-memoirs: Carole Maso's *The Room Lit by Roses*, Rachel Cusk's *A Life's Work*, and Anne Enright's *Making Babies*. Even though they cannot entirely elude the problems that remain embedded in the cultures they portray, these mother-writers point valuable directions for revisioning our ideas of maternal subjectivity.

In 1997 when I initiated this project, the questions I posed were already familiar to feminist literary inquiry into motherhood. Beginning in the 1970s, when Tillie Olsen's *Silences* and Adrienne Rich's *Of Woman Born* insistently reminded us of the missing insights caused by maternal silence, feminist critics had been posing and re-posing these same concerns. In Olsen's words, "Not many have directly used the material open to them out of motherhood as central source for their work" (32). And the same concerns had persisted into the 1990s, for example, in such collections as *Narrating Mothers: Theorizing Maternal Subjectivities* (1991), edited by Brenda Daly and Maureen Reddy, and *Mothers: Twenty Stories of Contemporary Motherhood* (1996). The editors of the latter, Katrina Kenison and Kathleen Hirsch, echoed Olsen's statement from 20 years earlier: "Invariably, we found ourselves asking, 'Why aren't more women writing about motherhood?'" (7). Before that, Marianne Hirsch had, in 1989, already provided a compelling analysis of what she called "the mother/daughter plot," reaching—toward the end of her analysis—a series of germinal questions: "Do mothers write their own experience *as mothers*? What shapes and plots accommodate those experiences, and what is the relationship of maternal narratives to ... cultural projections...? To what extent do women writers who are mothers co-conspire in their own silence...?" (*Mother/Daughter Plot* 176).

In my analysis in 1997, I focused a good deal of attention on a list of reasons for the dearth of mother-writers, centred in the difficulties that women writers who are mothers faced in conveying maternal experiences. Somewhat arbitrarily, I had identified seven of them. First—and this observation reaches back at least to Virginia Woolf's *A Room of One's Own* (1928)— the material circumstances of motherhood, the requirements of time and energy and interruptibility. Second, the apparent conflict between the terms—"writing" and "mothering"—so that these two activities were still largely perceived to be mutually exclusive, particularly because of the relationship that mothers have to discourse and to cultural authority. Third, the notion that mothers are by definition objects—embedded in the imaginings of their children rather than active agents, able to speak for themselves; this view has been strongly reinforced by psychoanalytic perspectives: the "mother exists only in relation to her child.... She cannot be the subject of her own discourse" (Hirsch, "Maternal Voice" 252). Fourth, the widespread cultural notion, as Shirley Garner says, that mothers "are not interesting or not the proper subject of literature" (87). Fifth, the difficulty of speaking honestly *as a mother*, in part because of the maternal role as protector of children and in part because of the prevailing idea of Mother as a singular identity, without complexity or ambivalence—without a sexual identity or concerns beyond her children. Sixth, the tension between *self* and selflessness, which automatically labels a mother as "bad" when she asserts her own maternal complexity. And finally, the understanding that the forms for mother-writing are simply not there; in Jane Smiley's words, "The paradox of literary composition is that our work, even our most 'realistic' work, is based on literary models ... it is literature that tells us how to make literature" (10).

Most of these problems persist, even in the first decade of the twenty-first century, particularly for women who live in difficult economic circumstances, whose insights continue to suffer a constraining silence. As Suzanne Juhasz puts it in her recent essay, "The paucity of mother-writing— even today, when we might think that feminism had paved the way for maternal writing as well as for maternal subjectivity—is a clue not only to the elusiveness of an identity that initially seems so self-evident but also to the difficulties inherent in both understanding and affirming it" (398). Juhasz, too, sees this silencing—even in 2003—as integral to the problem of maternal self-definition: "The cultural consensus, usually well internalized by individual women, is that there is only one identity: Mother" (405).

The effort to trace maternal subjectivity—for women to write as mothers—is important work, for feminist theory of motherhood requires the particularities of women's lives to help fend off the dual threats that Patrice

DiQuinzio has identified in her aptly titled *The Impossibility of Motherhood*: essentialism and individualism. On the one hand, we are threatened by essentialism, the peril of defining women yet again through our bodies and our reproductive systems or through our culturally assigned roles—which includes an embrace of motherhood as *the* definition of woman. Equally, we are threatened by the peril of blindness to the differences among women and by the individualist notion that a woman should aspire to being a rational, autonomous human being, making self-defined choices. As DiQuinzio points out, this idea of individualism—desirable to many—has additional hazards as it underpins a number of the binaries that have forestalled feminist inquiry: self and other, mind and body, public and private, nature and culture—and, of course, male and female (see esp. 7–11). Because both of these views of selfhood are inadequate to constructing maternal subjectivity, the task itself becomes virtually impossible in DiQuinzio's view: "Individualism and essential motherhood operate together to determine that women can be subjects of agency and entitlement only to the extent that they are not mothers, and that mothers as such cannot be subjects of individualist agency and entitlement" (13). A dire result indeed.

I agree with DiQuinzio in most of her analysis of feminist theory, as it oscillates between these two hazards. And I further agree with her assessment that—despite these hazards—"feminist theory must consider the specificity of female embodiment, of women's situations, experiences, and consciousness, and of women's social relations and contexts" (13). But I resist when she also rejects the possibility that autobiography (memoir, in my terminology) might be a useful source of maternal insight—a way to explore maternal subjectivity rather than to accept its impossibility—because of what she calls the "paradox of representation" (226). This is the notion, in the words of Domna Stanton, that "either we name and become entrapped in the structures of the already named; or else we do not name and remain trapped in passivity, powerlessness, and a perpetuation of the same" (qtd. in Siegel 153). DiQuinzio takes this insight a step further and argues directly against the usefulness of autobiography: "Since it suggests that what the author presents is not an interpretation, but simply a truthful report, it ... may tend to imply that it is not open to critical analysis because it is a report of the author's own experience" (226). In this observation, she joins a strong feminist critique of "experience" as always already constructed, embedded in cultural norms and expectations—impossible to free from the interpretive frameworks that we all inherit from our culture.

By contrast, my own reading suggests that *memoir*—including published journals—might be one of the ways in which mother-writers can actually break open some of these interpretive frameworks and provide us with new and resistant understandings of maternal subjectivity: incorporating work and sexuality, for example, and attending to the distinctive relational features of motherhood as well as the marked physiological realities. From these renderings, then, we might be able to resist the simplistic notions of "good" mother as selfless, "bad" mother as selfish, and develop instead a fuller understanding of human mother as an active and thinking self.

And this *is* beginning to happen. Despite the difficulties and the ongoing relative dearth of mother-writing, I can see that some of my earlier observations about the prohibitions on mother-writing have begun to break down in the intervening years. Indeed, in the last decade or so, there has been a small explosion of maternal narratives and most particularly of maternal *memoirs*—mother-writers resisting the restrictions that have made this work so difficult. Emerging in conjunction with what some have called the "age of memoir" (see, e.g., Eakin 144), these memoirs by mothers are beginning to provide different angles on the old questions of maternal silencing. From them, we can begin to identify strategies for rendering maternal subjectivity that, at least in part, elude the constraints of narrative form and cultural dismissal. Among these, I have found particularly compelling the memoirs of mothers who define themselves centrally as writers—usually novelists—and who draw upon their previous attunement to language and narrative form in order to convey their own distinctive experiences of being mothers. What *does* happen when—in Hirsch's words—"mothers write their own experience *as mothers*" (*Mother/Daughter Plot* 176)? And how *are* they finding ways in which to do so without falling into the paradox of representation?

After all, this is not an entirely new enterprise. Though she was nearly a singular voice at the time, Jane Lazarre—in her 1976 memoir, *The Mother Knot*—initiated a set of questions about narrating maternal subjectivity that persist as part of the current memoir explosion. There she portrayed her own experience of motherhood as "knotted," necessarily premised on contradictions. From that early memoir, many of us have taken the distilled observation: "We learned always to expect sentences to have two parts, the second seeming to contradict the first, the unity lying only in our growing ability to tolerate ambivalence—for that is what motherly love is like" (70). Her work then was groundbreaking, as it joined the pleas of Tillie Olsen and Adrienne Rich that we needed to fill the gaps caused by maternal silences. These pleas—and Lazarre's work—in many ways continue to set the parameters for the work we need yet to do, teasing out the "knot" of motherhood by writing the experiences of mothering. Lazarre calls this "a central passion of my life" (*Beyond*, 128) and claims it as her lifelong writing passion as well. Already in 1976 she was pursuing these passions and beginning to break free of the constraints of "representation" through her embrace of contradiction and her use of novelistic techniques.

Now she has also joined the more recent work in maternal memoir, and again she helps to point the way. In the concluding pages of her 1996 memoir—*Beyond the Whiteness of Whiteness: Memoir of a White Mother of Black Sons*—she returns us to the ongoing imperative of maternal narratives when she reclaims her initial reasons for writing about her mothering experiences: "to name them more accurately, to understand them, to convey meaning to others, to use one's own life to think about life itself" (128). But here she adds another dimension as she speaks of what it means to prepare to write: "I felt blank inside, empty of language, filled with presences that can be called neither thought nor feeling, nothing so exact, but rather a sense of fullness without shape, of being blown up beyond my usual contours with something that feels familiar and important as yet unknown and unnamed" (129). She continues: "Only at the end of the sentence do I realize I am describing pregnancy" (129).

How familiar this sounds to many of us, trying to write—the emptiness of language; the fullness that lacks a shape; the need to name; even the finding of metaphor in the very act of writing. And it is in finding her metaphor—a motherhood metaphor—that Lazarre highlights the potency of her undertaking: experience and language entangle in a vast emptiness; the pregnant body—like the activities of caring for children—is literal, yet nearly indefinable; motherhood eludes narrative form, even as it demands a shape and provides a metaphor. She returns us to the great difficulty: how to render maternal subjectivity. But in doing so, she has also pointed the new/old direction that she herself initiated in *The Mother Knot*: to draw upon the capacities that she has developed as a writer committed to extended narrative and attuned to language and metaphor even as she probes the particularity of her experiences as a mother, including her experience as *body*. As a writer, she embraces the notion of a self who is much more complex than either an essentialist Mother or a unitary rational individual. What's more, she self-consciously resists the idea that experience is transparent *and* the idea that language itself is stable and referential.

In my own investigation, I have found some guidance in the work of cognitive psychologists and narrative theorists, especially Ulric Neisser, Jerome Bruner, and Paul John Eakin. Though these theorists tend to omit or minimize specifically female experiential concerns, I am drawn to the idea of the narrative construction of self, as well as overt concerns with discontinuity, body, and relationality—all notions that are inherent in experiences of mothering. I have found Neisser's concept of plural selfhood especially relevant to thinking about maternal subjectivity. This is, to paraphrase Eakin's summation of Neisser's work, a "self" that is not an essence but a perceiver, responsive to her environment, both social and material; a self that is interpersonal in its construction; that is formed through memory and anticipation; that is private in its interiority and that negotiates the surrounding culture through taking on and resisting imposed concepts (see Eakin 22–23). In such a subjectivity, the body is integral but not defining—a location of self-awareness—and the resulting self is "dynamic, changing, and plural" (Eakin 98). Patricia Williams echoes some of these understandings when she affirms a need to inquire into relational selfhood—"Very little in our language or culture encourages looking at others as parts of ourselves" (62)—and sees in pregnancy a distinctive access to understandings of relational selfhood (e.g., 226).

My own concern is, then, also with the linguistic and narrative strategies through which mother-writers find ways to write experiences that many have seen as unnarratable. Though Juhasz takes an explicitly psychoanalytic approach and speaks primarily to *fictional* renderings, I find an intriguing commonality in her analysis: "I am proposing that writing can serve as an agent for constructing maternal subjectivity, because the transitional space of language allows for representation that is inventive as well as mimetic. Art is not exactly like life because it can transform as well as describe" (422). This, it strikes me, is also what we can seek in maternal memoirs, as they struggle to escape the paradox of representation. Kristi Siegel says, "A mother who would ... focus her reflective planes inward to see herself, to consider her own desires, literally has to create space for herself within our existing family structures" (143). A key step in creating such a space is to begin to create alternative *literary* space, a space committed to "transform as well as describe," even while holding to the imperative of experiential understanding.

Though I do not have space to go into them in depth, I want at least to sketch out some of the ways in which three contemporary mother-memoirists have taken on this challenge of maternal self-representation: Carole Maso, Rachel Cusk, and Anne Enright. All three of these writers were already established novelists before they became mothers. Each published a memoir in the first flush of new motherhood. And though the narratives that they have published differ markedly from one another, each has found a way to draw upon her craft as novelist to render maternal experience without relinquishing critical consciousness. None of them, in my view, completely eludes the constraints of cultural assumptions about mothers—indeed, I doubt that is possible—but all participate in the feminist project of disrupting old certainties and moving toward alternative understandings—beyond the outworn polarity of good mother/bad mother, beyond the hazards of essentialism and individualism.

Carole Maso, first. Titled *The Room Lit by Roses* (2000), her memoir is a public version of her private self-narration, identified in its subtitle as "a journal of pregnancy and birth." The immediacy of the journal form also puts her at risk for seeming simply to transcribe experience, relinquishing the critical consciousness necessary to negotiate the paradox of representation. Maso herself lays claim to direct transcription: "To simply record, without embellishment, without conscious intervention or formalization, as much as possible. Free for once of fiction's incredible demands" (18). Repeatedly, she asserts that this effort is immediate, unmediated—"To not invent a single thing" (18).

But even as she claims "to be freed for once of the burden and joy of making artful shapes. To just write"—she interrupts herself immediately: "as if, after all these years, one could." And she follows with: "How to describe these feelings as they come on—they resist description. A humbling experience—yet again—what refuses to pass into 'writing'" (18). If she intends to provide direct experience, she does not so easily relinquish her habits as a self-conscious writer. In addition to making periodic meta-commentary on the impossibility of writing, she also regularly plays with words and their root meanings, undermining any sense of linguistic transparency: amniotic, meaning lamb (4); placenta, meaning cake (6); or, addressing the baby, "You are covered now in a coat of grease like a channel swimmer. It is called *vernix*—that is Latin for varnish" (102).

Maso also reminds herself—and by extension us as readers—that she has lived her life in resistance to conventions: as a lesbian now pregnant by a one-time encounter with a male sexual partner and living in long-term commitment to Helen, her life partner. She says of Helen, "She wishes I were more romantic. But I have always distrusted such conventions.... The buying into a pre-fabricated value system" (115). And she speaks ironically of the way in which pregnancy earns her what she calls "Normal Person credits" (97). In other words, in her relation both to language and to cultural convention, she periodically invokes a critical self-consciousness that implicitly critiques the notion of transparent narrative along with the notion of "good mother" and gender polarity.

What's more, Maso has woven into these observations a pattern of attention to work, her teaching and her writing, especially a current biographical project on Frida Kahlo, with whom she carries on an internal dialogue about having children. In these interwoven observations, she explicitly enacts a complex and multiple subjectivity, even as she explores and resists the identity of "Mother."

Still, she takes that other risk, too, the risk of essential motherhood and a sentimental embrace of the female body and the anticipated baby. Of pregnancy she says, for example, "I feel the pure life force, pounding in me" (58); or "It's lovely to be in this gorgeous fog carrying all this miraculousness inside" (65). And she idealizes her hypothesized child as an "angel," thinking of her hyperbolically as "Rose in waiting. Rose on the verge" (108). But even here, the hyperbole itself has a way of undercutting any full embrace of sentiment, and it has been her habit as a novelist to push the boundaries of language by occasional and deliberate extravagance, an excess that is purposefully unsettling. She incorporates, as well, other physiological observations that serve to undercut sentiment: "I feel claustrophobic. That the two of us can't do this together anymore. Share the same body.... I can't breathe" (67). Unlike some other recent examples of mother-memoirs, which seem to embrace the necessity of selflessness for a mother, identify the female body with mothering, and capitulate to essentialist notions of womanhood, Maso's verbal resistances open on to an alternative maternal subjectivity by which to disrupt, at least partially, a sentimentalized notion of "Mother."

Rachel Cusk's *A Life's Work: On Becoming a Mother* (2001) is not only markedly lacking in the sentimentality that threatens many mother-memoirs; it is also, on the face of it, very different from Maso's lyrical and complex engagement with mothering. It is, in fact, so different that when I went looking for it in a local Barnes and Noble, I found it shelved as a "self-help" book. This mostly suggests a failure of understanding on the part of those who categorize, but it also hints at a feature of its commitment to speak to "reality"—again taking the risk of direct representation.

But like Maso, Cusk is centrally committed to probing her own distinctive experience, tracing out the peculiarities and resistant edges of her individual mother-life. In rendering her struggles to "become a mother," Cusk's narrative goes considerably beyond birth and into her daughter's early childhood, and, unlike Maso's, it has none of the day-by-day immediacy that a journal relies upon; indeed, it tends toward a more conceptual organization of its experiences. Nonetheless, it too is committed to "representation" of an individual maternal subjectivity, framed by a critical consciousness. For Cusk, the task is to write as rawly and negatively as she can about the shock of new motherhood and the culture's failure to prepare her for it—even as she explores new ways to love, learned by being a mother. She examines her own experiences through a dual lens of chafing honesty and a cultural norm that belies her individual experience.

In an initial reading, Cusk seems to endorse a problematic individualism as the memoir explicitly embraces the notion of a self that pre-exists motherhood and is now lost: the mind and prior self suppressed by the urgencies of body and baby. She overtly grieves this lost self and speaks in terms of a new self-alienation following the birth of her baby. And yet the very act of making this split overt is crucial to the memoir's investigation of the ways in which mothering can lead to an expanded and redefined sense of self. Like Maso, Cusk draws her work as a writer into the narrative process, implicitly using it to negotiate a newly defined self that comes to her as both a return to her previous self and an embrace of a self that has channelled into "Motherbaby" and then split anew. Her use of a conceptual structure—with each chapter labelled according to an idea inherent in her mothering experience, rather than a temporal progression—reinforces the possibility of multiple dimensions to a self. And she overtly draws together the shifts in selfhood and the complexities of time during new motherhood: "The days pass slowly. Their accustomed structure, the architecture of the past, has gone" (102).

Cusk's investigation of her own mothering further embraces both her literary profession and her writing processes by using two different discourses to frame her experience: the discourse of actual self-help literature—Benjamin Spock, Penelope Leach, and pamphlets from the doctor's office—and the discourse of literary renderings of maternal life—Coleridge, Edith Wharton, D. H. Lawrence. Though literature is much more resonant for her, neither discourse is a match for her individual experience. She comes eventually to a stark realization: "I wonder how I could have read so much and learned so little.... Could it be true that one has to experience in order to understand? I have always denied this idea, and yet of motherhood, for me at least, it seems to be the case" (122). In a book so given to literary parallels, spoken in the voice of a committed and accomplished novelist, the statement has a particular keenness. Her claim on the imperative of lived knowledge as she develops maternal understandings seems that much more potent.

Like Maso, Cusk also embraces a critical self-consciousness through her attention to language, though her techniques are different—a distinctive turn of phrase, a startling directness, as, for example, when she thinks of her mother-self as "a responsive unit, a transmitter" (98). Similarly, she comments on breastfeeding in markedly unromantic language that is even more unsettling for its echoes of the language of sentiment: "I imagine my solidity transferring itself to her, leaving me unbodied, a mere force, a miasma of nurture that surrounds her like a halo" (98). Her explicit attention to the marked shift in her identity joins her explicit attention to the physiology of early motherhood as markers of a distinctive maternal subjectivity. Her active resistance to the given descriptors of early motherhood opens on to alternative understandings. And the outline of maternal subjectivity that emerges is a self who is multiple, who critiques the notion of selflessness while tracing out the actual *process* of developing a loving maternal bond and thus acknowledging an interpersonal self. The interiority of the narrative is premised on a perceiving self, actively engaged in negotiating cultural assumptions.

As a third example of mother-memoir drawing explicitly on the play of language and form, I turn to Anne Enright's *Making Babies: Stumbling into Motherhood*. Like Cusk's memoir, Enright's takes the risk—even in its title—of being placed in the self-help section. But like Cusk and Maso, Enright goes beyond the strategy of generating commonality among women in pursuit of a collective consciousness about mothering—a strategy that is central and valuable in such mother-memoirs as Faulkner Fox's *Dispatches from a Not-So-Perfect Life* and Andrea Buchanan's *Mother Shock*. Instead, Enright overtly turns away from commonality, rejecting "toddler group" sharing, and draws on strategies of narrative and metaphor to open rifts in the understanding of her own mothering experience. Her first sentence announces her resistance: "Speech is a selfish act, and mothers should probably remain silent" (1). She then moves into a kind of mock apology—"So I'd like to say sorry to everyone in advance. Sorry. Sorry. Sorry. Sorry"—and includes in her list "readers who would prefer me not to think so much (because mothers just shouldn't)" (1).

Like Cusk's memoir—indeed, like many mother-memoirs—this one embraces a form that is both narrative and circular, drawing on a conceptual structure even as it embraces the importance of storytelling. As with Cusk, this approach yields a sense of multifaceted selfhood, premised on but exceeding maternal experiences. Also like other memoirists, Enright uses this structure to mimic the circular sense of time that is so integral to the experience of new motherhood: the daze of repetition, the oddly fluid notion of time that both passes and stands still. And she draws on a structure of brief elliptical pieces to render the fragmented sense of this early mothering experience.

For my purposes, I want to focus in particular on a section that takes on the question of maternal body. Titled "Milk," this section opens, "The milk surprises me," and continues with such observations as, "Women leak so much," followed by a wry observation, "Perhaps this is why we clean" (39). The last observation, like the overt embrace of body—"But what fun! to be granted a new bodily function so late in life" (39)—risks a kind of essentializing of both the maternal body and a "womanly" activity. But the effect is, to me, just the opposite: to find a way to speak such observations, to resist that ever-threatening "silence," without claiming it as one's essence. The thinking mother speaks: "I am faced with bizarre and difficult calculations— the weight of the groceries in a bag versus the weight of her nappies in a bag. Or my weight, plus a pint of water, minus four ounces of milk, versus her weight, plus four ounces, divided by yesterday" (39).

In continuing to discuss breastfeeding, Enright persists in walking the line between absurdity and thoughtfulness, essentialism and experience. She invokes Jonathan Swift as a reference point for a child's possible disgust with the breast, but then responds, "None of this seems *true* to me. I have no use for the child's disgust, as she has no use for mine. I am besotted by a being who is, at this stage, just a set of emotions arranged around a gut. Who is just a shitter, who is just a soul" (42). And then the thinking mother carries on, breaking the silence even as she remarks upon it: "Are all mothers Manicheans? This is just one of the hundreds of questions that have never been asked about motherhood. What I am interested in is not the drama of being a child, but this new drama of being a mother ... about which so little has been written. Can mothers not hold a pen?" (42).

In the final paragraphs of this chapter, Enright refers to the "occasional incontinence" of milk letting down at inconvenient times: "What I had not expected was that there should be some things that do not move me, that move my milk" (46). And then she weaves in the concerns of body and story and identity: "Do we need stories in order to produce emotion, or is an emotion already a story? What is the connection, in other words, between narrative and my alveolar cells?" And then,

> I suspect ... that I have found a place before stories start. Or the precise place where stories start. How else can I explain the shift from language that has happened in my brain? This is why mothers do not write, because motherhood happens in the body, as much as the mind.... A child came out of me. I cannot understand this, or try to explain it. Except to say that my past life has become foreign to me. Except to say that I am prey, for the rest of my life, to every small thing. (47)

The chapter's concluding single-word paragraph—"Damn"—resounds through the themes Enright has been exploring with such rich complexity, simultaneously embracing paradox and story, mind and body, language and silence.

Though I have barely touched on the strategies that these writers use—all three texts are rich in complexity and observation—I want now to conclude by suggesting the significance of such maternal narratives. The thematic concerns of these books include explicit reassessments of love and self, explorations of time and power and mortality, textured observations about female embodiment, and nuanced attention to the transmission of cultural values from mother to daughter. In these concerns, they participate in an ongoing effort to include bodily experience in our understandings of maternal thinking, as well as to deepen our insights into the intertwining of self and other that we can understand through maternal narratives. This effort is not unlike Sara Ruddick's call for "natal reflection" to participate along with other kinds of maternal thinking in " a distinctive construction of self and other ... material entanglement with an emergent being [that] challenges physically as well as conceptually the distinction between self and other" ("Thinking Mothers/Conceiving Birth," 42–43). The particular contribution of these mother-memoirs comes directly through their careful probing of highly individualized experiences, framed by repeated attention to intersections between writing and mothering. Along the way, it seems to me, these maternal narratives give us not only alternative and particular renderings of mothering experiences, but also alternative ways of resisting the binaries that threaten our capacity to understand the full and complex humanity of mothers.

I know that there is much more work to be done before we have the body of literature that Hilde Lindemann Nelson calls for: "'who' stories that don't insist that all and only women must mother, and a wider variety of 'how' stories that take the enormous diversity of mothers' circumstances, abilities, and resources into account" (146). I know that, in particular, we need to have stories of mothers whose resources are limited and whose experiences lie outside assumed norms. But this body of literature *is* growing—and increasingly it will include that chorus of diverse voices. From these maternal voices—if we read with the critical awareness with which some of the mother-memoirists are writing—we might not only find ways to move beyond the hazards of essentialism and gender polarity, beyond the paradox of representing maternal subjectivity; we might also develop a dynamic way of rethinking what it means to be a "self" at all. By *thinking as mothers*—to echo Sara Ruddick's urging and to embrace Jane Smiley's phrase—and then by *writing as mothers*, these recent mother-memoirists do, in fact, join Lazarre in her deepest goal: "to think about life itself" (*Beyond*, 128).

Works Cited

Brown, Ivana. "Mommy Memoirs: Feminism, Gender and Motherhood in Popular Literature." *Journal of the Association for Research on Mothering* 8.1 & 2 (2006): 200–12.

Bruner, Jerome. *Acts of Meaning*. Cambridge: Harvard University Press, 1990.

Buchanan, Andrea J. *Mother Shock: Loving Every (Other) Minute of It*. New York: Seal Press, 2003.

Cusk, Rachel. *A Life's Work: On Becoming a Mother*. New York: Picador, 2001.

Daly, Brenda O., and Maureen T. Reddy, eds. *Narrating Mothers: Theorizing Maternal Subjectivities*. Knoxville: University of Tennessee, 1991.

DiQuinzio, Patrice. *The Impossibility of Motherhood: Feminism, Individualism, and the Problem of Mothering*. New York: Routledge, 1999.

Eakin, Paul John. *How Our Lives Become Stories: Making Selves*. Ithaca: Cornell University Press, 1999.

Enright, Anne. *Making Babies: Stumbling into Motherhood*. London: Jonathan Cape, 2004.

Fox, Faulkner. *Dispatches from a Not-So-Perfect Life or How I Learned to Love the House, the Man, the Child*. New York: Harmony Books, 2003.

Frye, Joanne S. "Mothering, Narrative, and Cognition: What *does* it mean to write as a mother?" Unpublished paper presented at the ARM Conference, York University, Toronto, October 1997.

Garner, Shirley Nelson. "Constructing the Mother: Contemporary Psychoanalytic Theorists and Women Autobiographers." *Narrating Mothers: Theorizing Maternal Subjectivities*. Ed. Brenda O. Daly and Maureen T. Reddy. Knoxville: University of Tennessee. 76–94.

Hirsch, Marianne. "Maternal Voice." *Feminism and Psychoanalysis*. Ed. Elizabeth Wright. Oxford: Blackwell, 1992. 252–53.

———. *The Mother/Daughter Plot: Narrative, Psychoanalysis, Feminism*. Bloomington: Indiana University Press, 1989.

Juhasz, Suzanne. "Mother-Writing and the Narrative of Maternal Subjectivity." *Studies in Gender and Sexuality* 4.4 (2003): 395–425.

Kenison, Katrina, and Kathleen Hirsch, eds. *Mothers: Twenty Stories of Contemporary Motherhood*. New York: North Point Press, 1996.

Lazarre, Jane. *Beyond the Whiteness of Whiteness: Memoir of a White Mother of Black Sons*. Durham, NC: Duke University Press, 1996.

———. *The Mother Knot*. 1976. Rpt. Durham, NC: Duke University Press, 1997.

Major, Laura. "Alicia Ostriker's Propaganda for Motherhood." *Journal of the Association for Research on Mothering* 8.1 & 2 (2006): 190–99.

Maso, Carole. *The Room Lit by Roses: A Journal of Pregnancy and Birth*. New York: Counterpoint Press, 2000.

Neisser, Ulric. "The Self Perceived." *The Perceived Self: Ecological and Interpersonal Sources of Self-Knowledge*. Ed. Neisser. New York: Cambridge University Press, 1993.

Neisser, Ulric, and Robyn Fivush, eds. *The Remembered Self: Construction and Accuracy in the Self-Narrative*. New York: Cambridge University Press, 1994.

Nelson, Hilde Lindemann. *Damaged Identifies, Narrative Repair*. Ithaca: Cornell University Press, 2001.

Olsen, Tillie. *Silences*. 1978. Rpt. New York: Delta/Seymour Lawrence, 1979.

Rich, Adrienne. *Of Woman Born: Motherhood as Experience and Institution*. 1976. Rpt. New York: Bantam, 1977.

Ruddick, Sara. "Maternal Thinking." *Feminist Studies* 6.2 (Summer 1980): 342–67.

——. "Thinking Mothers/Conceiving Birth." *Representations of Motherhood*. Ed. Donna Bassin, Margaret Honey, and Meryle Mahrer Kaplan. New Haven: Yale University Press, 1994. 29–45.

Siegel, Kristi. *Women's Autobiographies, Culture, Feminism*. New York: Peter Lang, 2001.

Smiley, Jane. "Can Mothers Think?" *The True Subject: Writers on Life and Craft*. Ed. Kurt Brown. Saint Paul, MN: Graywolf Press, 1993. 3–15.

Williams, Patricia J. *The Alchemy of Race and Rights*. Cambridge: Harvard University Press, 1991.

12

The Motherhood Memoir and the "New Momism": Biting the Hand That Feeds You

BY ANDREA O'REILLY

After reading and rereading a dozen or more motherhood memoirs and many more articles on the subject, I, in a frustrating moment of writer's block, decided to Google the topic to see if someone else's insight would facilitate my own. While "motherhood memoir" yielded 545 hits, and "momoir" another 8900, the phrase "mommy lit" resulted in a staggering 33,400 entries. It seems that while I may have been at a loss for words, plenty had been written on "mommy lit." While the genre, to my knowledge, eludes a precise definition, there seems to be some agreement on its characteristics. In her recent article "You Are Not Alone: The Personal, the Political, and the 'New' Mommy Lit," Heather Hewett explains that "the only requirement seemed to be that it explored the 'real' experience of motherhood honestly, without sentimentality or idealization or judgement from the point of view of the mother. And more often than not, it circled around the issues of work, identity and motherhood" (121). And all agree that "mommy lit" is a very recent literary genre, emerging only within the last decade, at the turn of the millennium.

Stephanie Wilkinson and Jennifer Niesslein, editors of *Brain, Child*, open their 2005 article "Motherhood in Book Publishing" by referring to the initial mission statement of their magazine. "Motherhood," they wrote in their inaugural 2000 issue, "is worthy of literature." "It seemed an outrage to us," they go to say, "that there were probably as many literary books on bull-fighting as there were on the near-universal experience of raising kids" (1). Five years later, they concede that "anyone can go into a decent bookstore and find volumes of thought-provoking writing about mother-hood. In addition to the advice books and lite humor, you can find a smor-gasbord of serious books about motherhood" (1). In particular, they note, the mother-lit trend that began in the mid 1990s, "if not exactly a flood, seems a healthy stream" (3). Faulkner Fox, author of the best-selling *Dis-patches*, explains that when she started her book project in the fall of 2001, a book like hers did not exist: "If it had," she says, "I would have just read it, not written it" (qtd. in Wilkinson and Niesslein 4). Fast forward five years and Heather Hewett writes:

> As my due date quickly approached, I became more and more apprehensive. I found myself craving books on the subject of motherhood, but not books that made me feel worse.... I wanted something else: the stories of other mothers, their collective wisdom, and the bigger picture of motherhood in America. For-tunately, there were plenty of books to choose from. (121)

Indeed, a Google search of the words "motherhood/mothering/mothers" yields 438,000 hits. This abundance is indeed light years away from what was available to mothers 10 to 20 years ago. In 1983, when I first became pregnant, we would be lucky to come across a copy of Rich's *Of Woman Born* (1976) or Jane Lazarre's *The Mother Knot* at a book store, that is, if they had not gone out of print. And we certainly could not turn to the estimated 8500 parenting blogs for comfort and community. Again, if we were fortunate we had a mother-friend from the same apartment block whom we could meet in the playground after dishes were done and when the weather permitted.

Numerous explanations have been offered to account for the explosion of mothering literature, and in particular motherhood memoirs, over the last 15 years and most notably in the last eight years. Wilkinson and Niesslein point to several factors, one of which is feminism. They explain:

> This generation of mothers is the first to have grown up with the women's move-ment of the seventies in progress. At least some of us were told from the get-go that our opinions matter, that our experiences are valid. Growing up with the same sense of entitlement as our brothers played out in all sorts of well-documented ways. One less documented way that today's women's sense of entitlement has played out is in publishing. If football coaches and fishing enthusiasts could pen books about their experiences, why not mothers? (5)

Related to this sense of entitlement, as Wilkinson and Niesslein note, is the purchasing power of women: they buy 68 percent of all books and read 56 percent of all literary works (6). Another reason, not discussed by Wilkinson and Niesslein, is demographics. In 2000, the first group of third-wave feminists turned 35 and began having children. And while some third-wave writers and activists had their children at a relatively young age, notably Ariel Gore, most did not become mothers until their mid to late 30s at the turn of the millennium. Indeed, a review of current feminist third-wave writings reveals a baby boom among third wavers. These women, who were thinking and writing about other feminist issues in the 1980s and 1990s, turned their attention to motherhood as they became mothers themselves: hence, the appearance and appeal of "mommy lit" over the last seven to eight years.

This chapter will suggest reasons other than feminism, purchasing power, and demographics to account for the emergence of "mommy lit" at the turn of the millennium. (These three factors, however, do contribute to and support the explanation I develop below.) I argue that this literary genre was born from a new ideology of motherhood, what Sharon Hays has termed "intensive mothering" and Susan Douglas and Meredith Michaels call the "new momism." More specifically, I contend that, as this new ideology made possible a public voice on motherhood, it simultaneously limited what that voice could say about motherhood. Beginning with a discussion of intensive mothering and the new momism, the paper will go on to highlight several themes of the motherhood memoir from the perspective of this new discourse on motherhood. In particular, I will argue that as this discourse makes a critique of patriarchal motherhood possible, it simultaneously censors what can be said in that critique. More specifically, I argue that this discourse ultimately reinscribes, or more accurately naturalizes and normalizes, the very patriarchal conditions of motherhood that feminists, including the motherhood memoir writers themselves, seek to dismantle.

At the turn of the last century, maternal feminists relied upon the belief in innate gender difference, in particular the alleged moral superiority of mothers, to lobby for and make legitimate their claims for female suffrage. Similarly, motherhood memoir writers today draw upon, consciously or otherwise, the ethos of the new momism, in particular, the assumption that children are the all-consuming focus and purpose of a mother's life, to value and validate a public literature on motherhood. This use of maternal feminism and the new momism did make possible significant gender change: female suffrage in the last century and a de-privatization of motherhood in this century. However, it also serves to reify gender difference and hence reinforce traditional and patriarchal notions of womanhood and motherhood, most notably the private/public divide and the feminine/nurturer and masculine/producer gender dichotomy. This paper will examine the motherhood memoir's compliance and complicity with the new momism philosophy of mothering to argue that real challenge and change become possible only when this genre confronts and counters this discourse of motherhood.

Intensive Mothering and the New Momism

Intensive mothering is characterized by three interconnected themes. The first defines mothering as *natural* to women and essential to their being, conveyed in the belief, as Pamela Courtenay Hall notes, that "women are *naturally* mothers, they are born with a built-in set of capacities, dispositions, and desires to nurture children ... [and that this] engagement of love and instinct is utterly distant from the world of paid work" (59). The second theme provides that the mother is to be the central caregiver of her biological children, and the third that children require full-time mothering, or in the instance where the mother must work outside the home, the children must always come before the job. This model of mothering, as Sharon Hays explains in *The Cultural Contradictions of Motherhood*, "tells us that children are innocent and priceless, that their rearing should be carried out primarily by individual mothers and that it should be centered on children's needs, with methods that are informed by experts, labor intensive, and costly" (21). She emphasizes that intensive mothering is "a historically constructed *cultural model* for appropriate child care" (21; emphasis in original). "Conceptions of appropriate child rearing," she continues,

> are not simply a random conglomeration of disconnected ideas; they form a fully elaborated, logically cohesive framework for thinking about and acting toward children.... We are told that [intensive mothering] is the best model, largely because it is what children need and deserve. This model was not developed overnight, however, nor is intensive mothering the only model available to mothers. (21)

Sharon Hays argues that intensive mothering emerged in the post-war period. I contend, in contrast, that while the origins of intensive mothering may be traced back to this time, intensive mothering, in its fully developed form, came about in the early 1990s. Hays argues, as noted above, that intensive mothering is characterized by three themes: "the mother is the central caregiver," "mothering is regarded as more important than paid employment," and such mothering requires "lavishing copious amounts of time, energy, and material resources on the child" (8). I would suggest that while the first two characterize mothering from post-war to present day, only mothering of the last 15 years can be characterized by the third theme: namely, children require copious amounts of time, energy, and material resources.

The post-war discourse of good motherhood demanded that mothers be at home full time with their children; however this aspect did not necessitate the intensive mothering expected of mothers today. The ideology of good motherhood today demands more than mere physical proximity of mother–child: contemporary mothers are expected to spend, to use the discourse of the experts, "quality time" with their children. Mothers are told to play with their children, read to them, and take classes with them. As the children in the 1950s and 1960s would jump rope or play hide-and-seek with the neighbourhood children or their siblings, today's children dance, swim, and "cut and paste" with their mothers in one of many "moms and tots" programs. And today, children, as young as one month old, are enrolled in a multitude of classes, from water-play for infants, French immersion for toddlers, karate for preschoolers, and competitive skiing, skating, or sailing for elementary school children. (An article I read recently also recommended reading and singing to your child in utero.) Today, though, with fewer children and more labour-saving devices—from microwaves to take-out food—mothers spend more time and energy (and, I may add, money) on their children than their mothers did in the 1960s. And the majority of mothers today, unlike 40 years ago, practise intensive mothering while engaged in full-time employment. Mothering today, as in the post-war era, is "expert driven." However, mothering today is also, under the ideology of intensive mothering, more child-centred than the "children should be seen but not heard" style of mothering that characterized the post-war period. Indeed, as Susan Douglas and Meredith Michaels observe in *The Mommy Myth*, "intensive mothering [has become] the ultimate female Olympics" (6).

Douglas and Michaels term this contemporary discourse of motherhood the "new momism":

> The insistence that no woman is truly complete or fulfilled unless she has kids, that women remain the best primary caretakers of children, and that to be a remotely decent mother, a woman has to devote her entire physical, psychological, emotional, intellectual being, 24/7, to her children. The new momism is a highly romanticized and yet demanding view of motherhood in which the standards for success are impossible to meet. (4)

However, as Douglas and Michaels go on to explain, "the new momism involves more than just impossible ideals about women's childrearing, it redefines all women, first and foremost, through their relationships to children. Thus, being a citizen, a worker, a governor [and so forth] are supposed to take a backseat to motherhood" (22). "The new momism," Douglas and Michaels continue, "insists that if you want to do anything else, you'd better first prove that you're a doting, totally involved mother before proceeding. The only recourse for women who want careers, or to do anything else besides stay at home with the kids all day, is to prove they can 'do it all'" (22). A crucial dimension of the new momism which has particular relevance to the motherhood memoir is the concept of choice. Douglas and Michaels explain:

> Central to the new momism is the feminist insistence that women have choices, that they are active agents in control of their own destiny, that they have autonomy. But here's where the distortion of feminism occurs. The only truly enlightened choice to make as a woman, the one that proves, first, that you are a "real" woman, and second, that you are a decent, worthy one, is to become a "mom" and to bring to child rearing a combination of selflessness and professionalism.... Thus the new momism is deeply contradictory: It both draws from and repudiates feminism. (5)

Moreover, in its assertions of female agency and autonomy, the new momism denies and distorts the fact that most mothers have little or no choice in the making of their lives. The concept of choice, as feminist theory has shown us, is a liberal fiction that serves to disguise and justify social inequities, particularly those of gender.

The Motherhood Memoir

The contemporary motherhood memoir both draws from and disputes the new momism. As noted above, the emergence of this discourse on motherhood gave women permission to talk publicly on motherhood, in the vein that motherhood is so important and central to women that, of course, they can and must discuss it. At the same time, memoir writers critique many aspects of intensive mothering that make contemporary motherhood limiting to women. However, the motherhood memoir, because it is informed, if not created by, the discourse of the new momism, also often reinscribes the very gender roles that cause mothering to be oppressive to women and which are at the heart of the author's critique of patriarchal motherhood.

Motherhood memoirs are concerned with, to use the vernacular, "telling it like it is." Memoir authors examine, in Susan Maushart's words, "the mismatch between the expectations and the experiences [of motherhood]" (xi). Maushart uses a metaphor to signify what I term the cognitive dissonance between the reality and ideology of motherhood. To be masked is "to deny and repress what we experience, to misrepresent it, even to ourselves" (1–2). "The realities of motherhood," Maushart writes, "are kept carefully shrouded in silence, disinformation, and outright lies" (5). The mask of motherhood, she continues, "keeps women from speaking clearly what they know, and from sharing truths too threatening to face" (7). "It is not an emperor who is walking naked through the streets," writes Wendy Le Blanc in *Naked Motherhood: Shattering Illusions and Sharing Truths*, "it is our Mothers. All of us collude with the conspiracy by pretending we can see her fully clothed in all her mythological finery" (1). Andrea Buchanan asks in *Mother Shock*, "Why did no one tell me what motherhood is really like? Why had I never bothered to ask?" (xi). Each motherhood memoir, in one way or another, seeks to "unmask" motherhood: to speak honestly, authentically of what it means to become and be a mother.

Unquestionably, motherhood memoirs should be required reading for all mothers-to-be. We could begin a revolution in motherhood if we gave these books as shower gifts instead of the usual blankets and nappies. Motherhood memoirs prepare women for the truths of mothering and enables mothers to feel less guilt, anxiety, and stress about being a mother. In this, they are indeed revolutionary. However, I sense a hesitation in this mission of unmasking motherhood: Is it enough to identify and detail the differences between our expectations of motherhood and its realities, or to simply catalogue and critique the gender inequities of current family arrangements without seeking to change them? To be sure, to say that the boredom, exhaustion, ambivalence, guilt, loneliness, anxiety, and self-doubt mothers feel is normal and common—indeed more real than the contented, calm, and composed mother found in magazines—is therapeutic, indeed liberating. And documenting the day-to-day work of mothering makes real and public the second and third shifts of women's domestic labour and confirms the gender inequities of most households. At the same time, though, I think, we need to be asking more difficult questions: Why is there such a discrepancy between myth and reality? What purpose socially, economically, and psychologically does the ideology of perfect motherhood serve? Or more pointedly, in terms of the discussion of this paper, why are we content with only unmasking motherhood; should our aim not be to challenge and change patriarchal motherhood? It is my belief that while many

motherhood memoirs do expose motherhood as a patriarchal institution, they do not ultimately denounce or transform this institution. This is
because the critique is ultimately contained and constrained by the discourse of the new momism that creates and informs it.

In her highly perceptive article "Mommy Memoirs: Feminism, Gender,
and Motherhood in Popular Culture," Ivana Brown argues that the motherhood memoir is characterized by three themes: "emphasis on gender
dualism and gender difference in parenting; the significance of the bodily
experience of motherhood; [presence] of the 'natural mother' myth, which
assumes women's superiority and ability as natural caregivers" (202). Examples of such gender essentialism pervade the motherhood memoir.
Naomi Wolf, for example, writes: "We looked at the results [of the pregnancy
test] and gazed at each other. Then we reacted very differently. My husband
needed to run—and think; and I needed to sit still and not think. Male and
female ... we reacted spontaneously, like different elements" (15). And Susan Cheever writes: "For months and months ... it felt as if my daughter
and I were rejoined in our bodies as well as in our souls. Any separation was
indescribably painful. When I was with her I was whole—my two parts were
reunited." And in *Breeder*, an anthology edited by Ariel Gore and Bee Lavender, the natural mother myth is expressed in the valorization of attachment
parenting. As one writer notes, "Ben and I hold Ember all of the time, until
she freaks and needs her space. The first time I recognized that her crying
meant she just wanted to be put down, I was both heartbroken and relieved"
(113).

What Brown does not develop her article, and what is the focus of my research on the motherhood memoir, is that these three themes are precisely
the underpinning assumptions of the new momism discourse: namely that
mothering is a highly gendered and embodied experience that women are
naturally drawn to and prepared for. While memoir authors do critique the
consequences of these assumptions—i.e., women do all the work of mothering with little or no support—they do not challenge the assumptions themselves. Therefore, their challenge remains at the level of criticism and not
change. This is most evident in the authors' views on childcare. Of the memoirs I have read thus far, none of the authors consider childcare as a possible
option for allowing women to develop a selfhood outside of motherhood.
For some the reason is financial; however, for most it is because they sub-
scribe to the new momism belief in the necessity of full-time, natural, and
attachment mothering. They believe that they must be at home 24/7 for the
benefit of the child for at least the first three to five years, and to do otherwise would be unwise, if not unnatural, to both child and mother. Indeed,

as Brown noted in her conference paper, "while some authors challenge parts of the 'natural mother' myth, all of them are the primary caregivers of their children." She goes on to explain: "Mothers are the main caretakers of the children and fathers are more or less absent, appearing at the time of birth and then having a role in the background in financially supporting the family and helping the mother with certain tasks and responsibilities. The absence of fathers from the daily parenting tasks remains mostly unexplained." "This approach," as Brown noted, "contributes to the categorical differentiation between men and women [in the motherhood memoir]." Interestingly, but not surprisingly, in earlier motherhood memoirs, most notably Jane Lazarre's *The Mother Knot*, Mary Kay Blakely's *American Mom*, and Marni Jackson's *The Mother Zone*, works that predate the rise of the new momism discourse, childcare is a central theme.

For me the most worrisome part of the new momism, particularly as it is manifested in the motherhood memoir, is that being a stay-at-home mother is constructed as the mother's choice. Again, to return to Douglas and Michael's discussion of choice, they write:

> The mythology of the new momism now insinuates that, when all is said and done, the enlightened mother chooses to stay at home with the kids. Back in the 1950s mothers stayed home because they had no choice. Today having been to the office, having tried a career, women supposedly have seen the inside of the male working world and found it be the inferior choice to staying home, especially when their kids' future is at stake. It's not that mothers can't hack it (1950s thinking). It's that progressive mothers refuse to hack it. The June Cleaver model, if taken as a *choice*, as opposed to a requirement, is the truly modern fulfilling forward-thinking version of motherhood. (23)

While many of the authors expose the concept of choice for what it is—a fiction and a fallacy—they nonetheless see their full-time mothering as inevitable and necessary. Other memoir writers though do deflect and disguise the very real structural and familial inequities mothers face by way of a narrative of choice. A writer in the collection *Breeder* who practises attachment parenting as a college student, for example, explains that she decided to quit school when pregnant with her second child because "I was tired every day, tired all over, and the prospect of spending the next several months so impossibly tired was too much for me" (83). She goes on to explain, "Feeling that I faced a *choice* between my future and my present, I withdrew from my classes" (84; emphasis added). Later she writes, "My education has not been put on hold; on the contrary, I am a full-time student in an accelerated toddler studies program. My three-year-old is experimenting with wet-on-wet watercolours, and the baby will be walking soon. Now that's what I call progress" (85). As someone who gave birth to three children in five years while an undergrad and later a grad student, I can certainly understand being "impossibly tired." However, the *Breeder* writer's fatigue seems more the result of her adherence to the new momism discourse, which requires her to be the main caretaker of the children 24/7 via attachment parenting. Had she used some childcare, insisted upon shared parenting (her partner is mentioned only once), and renounced or reduced her "natural" and intensive mothering practices, she would have had, in all likelihood, the time and energy to combine motherhood with her studies. (This is not to minimize the real need for structural change in education and the workplace to enable women to combine work with motherhood.) But because of her adherence to the new momism philosophy of mothering, she simply cannot see these as possibilities and thus must accept societal and familial gender inequities as both inevitable and natural. More troublesome is that all of this is narrated and justified in the language of choice, and, even more problematically, as a feminist choice, as when she proclaims: "now that's progress."

Most motherhood memoirs, because of their identification with the new momism, cannot discern, let alone critique, the root causes of mothers' oppression; thus the genre remains one of complaint and not change. Some memoir authors, most notably Faulkner Fox and Marrit Ingman, do challenge. And not surprisingly, these authors also offer a critique of the new momism. We need more such memoir writers if we hope to move the genre from a rant to a revolution. But to do so, we must do away with the new momism and its naturalization of gender inequities. Indeed, memoir authors must bite the hand that feeds them.

Works Cited

Blakely, Mary Kay. *American Mom*. Chapel Hill, NC: Algonquin Books, 1994.

Brown, Ivana. "Mommy Memoirs: Feminism, Gender and Motherhood in Popular Culture." *Journal of the Association for Research on Mothering* 8.1&2 (Winter/Summer 2006): 200–12.

Brown, Ivana. "The Motherhood Memoir." Conference Paper, 10th annual conference of the Association for Research on Motherhood, Toronto, October 2006.

Buchanan, Andrea. *Mother Shock: Loving Every (Other) Minute of It*. Seattle: Seal Press, 2003.

Cheever, Susan. *As Good as I Could Be*. New York: Washington Square Press, 2001.

Douglas, Susan, and Meredith Michaels. *The Mommy Myth: The Idealization of Motherhood and How It Has Undermined All Women*. New York: Free Press, 2004.

Fox, Faulkner. *Dispatches from a Not-So-Perfect Life: Or How I Learned to Love the House, the Man, the Child*. New York: Harmony Books, 2003.

Gore, Ariel, and Bee Lavender, eds. *Breeder: Real-Life Stories from the New Generation of Mothers*. Seattle: Seal Press, 2001.

Hall, Pamela Courtenay. "Mothering Mythology in the Late Twentieth Century: Science, Lore, and Celebratory Narrative." *Canadian Woman Studies* 18.1–2 (1998): 59–63.

Hays, Sharon. *The Cultural Contradictions of Motherhood*. New Haven: Yale University Press, 1996.

Hewett, Heather. "You Are Not Alone: The Personal, the Political, and the 'New' Mommy Lit." *Chick Lit: The New Woman's Fiction*. Ed. Suzanne Ferriss and Mallory Young. New York: Routledge Press, 2006. 119–40.

Ingman, Marrit. *Inconsolable: How I Threw My Mental Health Out with the Diapers.* Berkeley, CA: Seal Press, 2005.

Jackson, Marni. *The Mother Zone: Love, Sex, and Laundry in the Modern Family*. New York: H. Holt, 1992.

Lazarre, Jane. *The Mother Knot*. New York: Dell Books, 1976.

Le Blanc, Wendy. *Naked Motherhood: Shattering Illusions and Sharing Truths*. Sydney: Random House, 1999.

Maushart, Susan. *The Masks of Motherhood: How Becoming a Mother Changes Everything and Why We Pretend It Doesn't*. New York: The New Press, 1999.

Wilkinson, Stephanie, and Jennifer Niesslein. "Tales from the (Mother) Hood: Motherhood in Book Publishing." *Brain, Child*. Spring 2005. July 2006, http://www.brainchildmag.com/essays/spring2005_niesslein_wilkinson.html.

Wolf, Naomi. *Misconceptions: Truth, Lies and the Unexpected on the Journey to Motherhood*. New York: Random House, 2003.

13

"I had to make a future, willful, voluble, lascivious": Minnie Bruce Pratt's Disruptive Lesbian Maternal Narratives | BY SUSAN DRIVER

In an era when lesbian motherhood has become normalized to the point of being framed in terms of heteroreproductive assimilation, it is easy to forget the rich and challenging legacies of lesbian mothering lives and life-writings. While legislative and cultural shifts in attitudes have rendered lesbian mothering visible and recognizable within mainstream public consciousness, the one-sided focus on acceptability and choice has obscured the fractured struggles and differences within and between mothers who exceed heteronormative ideals. Associated with the reformist and individualizing push of liberal equality rights and reduced to the logics of marital, reproductive, and familial lifestyle politics, lesbian mothering is increasingly cast in simple and universalizing rhetorics that erase the layered subjective histories that mark outlaw mothering. Commonly opposed to radical sexual edges of queer theories and cultures, lesbian mothers are cast as safe and predictable "breeders," who are reinforcing rather than undermining domestication. Within this context, is almost impossible to think about lesbian mothering in terms of heroic transgression and erotic risk-taking, as a practice that disrupts assumptions and spurs critical thinking and political action. Yet if the words of lesbian mother writers are remembered in all their intricacy and emotional intensity, stories emerge that defy static and binary logics. In this essay, I return to the poetic narratives of Minnie Bruce Pratt as a way of recollecting reflexive modes of life-writing through which the personal stakes of lesbian mothering are fleshed out as a process of ethico-political questioning and exchange. Pratt's *Crime against Nature* (1990) opens up possibilities for reading lesbian sexuality and mothering as dynamic experiential and historical relations. Moving beyond an individualizing liberal approach to lesbian mothering, Pratt's text solicits interpretations attuned to the ambiguities and intricacies of embodied knowledge.

My argument expands upon Chandra Mohanty and Biddy Martin's reading of Minnie Bruce Pratt's 1984 experiential text, "Identity: Skin, Blood, Heart," as a productive locus through which ideals of "family" and "home" are critically rearticulated according to specific legacies of race, gender, and class privilege. I take their interpretation further by exploring how the intimate edges of becoming a lesbian mother influence her rethinking of familial investments through and against sexual desires and identities. Drawing upon *Crime against Nature*, I show how the erotic dimensions of subjectivity become a basis for intense pleasure and resistance against the violent repudiation of the right to mother. Signifying her sexuality and motherhood as a dialogue, Pratt spurs her personal account of loss, survival, and passion in mobile relation with the voices of mothers whose histories refract intersecting power inequalities and sexual relations. Her text unfolds a self in transition: letting go of a stable sense of meaning and value, she reframes her own narrative in conjunction with those told by women whose own maternal status is jeopardized through sexual, racial, and class systems of domination. Becoming a lesbian mother opens up a contested set of interactions that are not reducible to a unified identity or realm of social belonging but on the contrary risk the impossibility of symbolic or material guarantees. Embracing ambiguity, Pratt moves lesbian mothering in the direction of open-ended and inter-subjective communication that compels readers to enjoin their own stories in the flux of self-knowledge and social understanding.

Pratt's texts are both highly unique literary works and urgently political discourses that reach beyond the sphere of poetic language. Her own life as an activist, academic, and poet from the 1960s to the present encourages an integrated approach bridging the practical contingencies of social justice movements, the finely tuned poetic articulation of words, and the aesthetic skills of storytelling. Involved in anti-racist resistance for several decades, Pratt hones her writing projects out of her lived political experiences that are formative of her everyday life as a woman, lover, writer, and mother. Her publication of six books of poetry and commitment to radical pedagogy as a university professor emerge out of her involvement in projects for political change along with the difficult work of un/learning privilege. She is a deeply engaged poet whose renderings of beautiful passages and socially resonant meanings are inseparable from the often painful and horrific realities of oppression that surrounded her growing up under conditions of racial segregation in the American South. Writing in a transformative mode that derives energy from grassroots involvement in civil rights, feminist, and transgender politics, Pratt strives to change consciousness without imposing truths or reifying interpretations. Her poetic style becomes politically charged as she writes out of the complexities of the world around her.

Reading Pratt's work within a broader context of lesbian mother life-writings written over the course of several decades,[1] I am keenly aware of how many fictional and experiential lesbian mothering narratives revolve around heroic overcomings of adversity and deprivation, as well as defiant acts that challenge the very system of maternal hierarchy structuring unequal relations of power. It is striking how much these texts foreground public revelations of sexual desires between women that have resulted in the loss of children, or even in the violent renunciation of the right to mother at all. The fear and actuality of losing custody pervade these experiential writings, overlaying accounts of psychic trauma and analysis of social injustice, private agony, and public struggles together in complex formations. Personal pain becomes inextricably political as a process of thinking and acting in the wake of histories of maternal dispossession and continuing accounts of unbelonging. Lesbian desire comes to signify daring contestations of moralistic norms of maternal goodness and legal entitlements. Exposing social inequalities and exclusionary precedents justified in the name of heterosexist and puritanical maternal ideologies, lesbian mothers affirm active independent sexual relations beyond patriarchal paternal controls and state regulations. Such pursuit of desires in the face of constant anxieties and actualities of losing children constitutes a locus of lesbian heroic subjectivity. Overcoming institutional obstacles and surviving traumatic loss are inscribed as part of a courageous assertion of desire and creative hopes for future relations. Lesbian mothers tell stories that rework the plot lines of masculine heroism in a plurality of ways.

Lesbian mother life-writings enact situated accounts of survival, resilience, and pursuit while challenging rationalistic single-minded paradigms of individual accomplishment for relationally and corporeally embedded models of heroic desire. Contrasted with models of disembodied phallic transcendence, it is interesting to return to how Adrienne Rich ends *Of Woman Born* with a call for a different model of reflexive subjectivity grounded in sensuous intellection: "thinking is an active, fluid, expanding process." The body becomes a dynamic signifying network of relations, a semiosis of experience that remarkably names the symbolic value of a mother's clitoris:

> There is for the first time today a possibility of converting our physicality into
> both knowing and power.... From brain to clitoris through vagina to uterus, from
> tongue to nipples to clitoris, from fingertips to clitoris to brain, from nipples to
> brain and into uterus, we are strung with invisible messages of an urgency and
> restlessness.... We are neither "inner" nor "outer" constructed; our skin is alive
> with signals; our lives and our deaths are inseparable from the release or blockage
> of our thinking bodies. (284)

Rich repeatedly links bodily pleasures and knowledge to envision a maternal subject situated and actively engaged in interpreting the world through rather than in spite of erotic desires and perceptions. Such a process of critical thought becomes interwoven into a sexual body and more specifically a lesbian body, crucial to the reinscription of maternal agency in Minnie Bruce Pratt's texts. Pratt takes Rich's notion of "thinking through the body" beyond its utopian and universalizing tendencies toward understanding how historical differences mark her engagements with others. Starting from her tactile impressions and located sensuous memories, she theorizes a process of conscious rebellion and social transformation by using poetic languages to bridge narrative dimensions of time and physical embodiments of space.

In the wake of Rich's textual explorations, Minnie Bruce Pratt's writings carry forth an attempt to perform heroic subjectivity in new configurations, as they detail the loss of children and the challenge of coming into her lesbian sexual identity. Desire spurs embodied pursuits for pleasure along with reflexive knowledge concerning the foreclosure and devaluation of subjects who exceed heteronormative boundaries. It is her dislocation from a position of privilege as an educated, married white woman into an experience of being deprived of those entitlements and comforts of "home" she had come to take for granted that compels Pratt to pursue new ways of imagining her family and political alignments. Her heroic quest is mapped within a landscape of different social histories in which she attempts to account for her past loss and suffering in relation to the present reconstruction of her life as a lesbian mother with grown children. Transforming denial and deprivation into an empowering story of ethical responsibility and connection, Pratt's writings move beyond the isolation of her pain to reposition herself within social webs of narratives. Heroic accomplishment is measured through the courage of changing a self over and over again through contacts with others. Pratt's willingness to relinquish herself as a fixed centre of social space and narrative action encourages multiple heroic selves to meet, argue, empathize, and desire with the aim of reciprocity, not synthesis.

Minnie Bruce Pratt's autobiographical essay "Identity: Skin, Blood, Heart" has been embraced by feminist theorists as a unique form of experiential interrogation. Mohanty and Martin claim that Pratt's narrative undermines abstract and unmarked assumptions of white identity by "resituating herself again and again in the social, by constantly referring to the materiality of the situation in which she finds herself" (194). They focus on the ways Pratt reflects upon the personal stakes of hegemonic meanings of "home" as a "safe" and insular domain which obscure structures of domination and psychic relations of fear and hatred. Through close and politicized readings of the geography, demography, domestic spaces, and architectures of her childhood, as well as various social sites and "scenarios" of her adult world, Pratt retraces her emerging desires as a spatial and temporal process. Unravelling nostalgic family beliefs perpetuating unequal privileges, Pratt's narrative offers a "pretext for posing questions" for considering "how such individual self-reflection and critical practice might translate into the building of political collectivity" (Mohanty and Martin 210). Mohanty and Martin appreciate the nonlinear collaborative style of Pratt's attempts to narrate her emerging personal and political consciousness as part of a provisional writing process—"tentativeness … consisting of fits and starts" (206)—through which multiple perspectives undergo continual revisions through and against each other. It is Pratt's willingness to renegotiate boundaries of her social and psychic life through past and present relations with others without appeal to a unified authorial identity or linear narrative text that aligns her permeable style of life writing with possibilities for coalitional politics.

What I am interested in pursuing further are Pratt's efforts to dislodge her emotional and social investments in "home" along with the illusory promise of a secure and self-contained subjectivity that dominant familial notions give rise to. How does such a risky interrogation of identity and belonging inflect her understanding of herself as a lesbian mother? Or perhaps more poignantly, how does becoming a lesbian mother shatter the psychic hold and social inertia of domesticating metaphors and myths of home? Mohanty and Martin discuss the transformative status of Pratt's lesbian sexuality:

A careful reading of the narrative demonstrates the complexity of lesbianism, which is constructed as an effect, as well as a source, of her political and familial positions…. What lesbianism becomes as the narrative unfolds is that which makes "home" impossible, which makes her self nonidentical, which makes her vulnerable, removing her from the protection afforded those women within privileged races and classes who do not transgress a limited sphere of movement. (202)

Although I agree with this framing of lesbian sexuality as a subversive force pushing open the edges of Pratt's text, Mohanty and Martin have little to say about the significance of Pratt's experience as a mother who loses custody of her children at the same time she publicly constitutes and embraces a lesbian identity. Despite Mohanty and Martin's interest in destabilizing normative familial conventions, they do not explore the ways Pratt struggles with the contradictions and convergences between her maternal and sexual identifications. Pratt's self-narrations are interesting precisely because of her efforts to read various levels of experience simultaneously. And this is no less the case when Pratt speaks about herself as a lesbian mother.

While motherhood becomes one strand of a web of social relations in Pratt's writing, it represents a personal site of trauma and rupture that marks a phase of Pratt's life as she begins to throw into question deeply embodied assumptions of stability, safety and possession. Pratt narrates a turning point in her life when she loses her children because she comes out as a lesbian, claiming that "the shell of my privilege was broken." What she had once taken for granted as a right to have a home and children was suddenly denied to her, forcing Pratt to come to terms with not only her personal loss but also the exclusionary social conditions that previously buttressed her status as an affluent white heterosexual mother. Such reinterpretations of childhood and family histories are concomitant with the destabilization of her maternal identity. Her violent experience of maternal dispossession forces radical re-evaluations of naturalizing and universalizing ideologies. At the same time, her self-analysis moves in several directions beyond privatized spaces congealed in nostalgic illusions of sameness into broader networks of political alliance that strive to come to terms with social differences.

Some of the most transformative ideas in "Identity: Skin, Blood, Heart" revolve around Pratt's fear of having to let go of stable and familiar conceptions of her self, and her assertion of the importance of confronting and mourning that loss as necessary for change. Having experienced the effects of prohibition and denial of tangible relations of love and care of her children, Pratt is compelled to rewrite her identity through the transgressive movements of her desires for love and community. Turning upon her own readings of herself, propelled by specific relations around her that loop back into her life-writings, Pratt practises a dialogical method of interpretation. Her dialogical approach hinges upon listening and responding to the multiple voices of mothers speaking from diverse historical locations. The personal stories of mothers inflect the tensions of racial and class hierarchies configured across time and space. While Pratt remains focused on the intimate details of her life, she weaves them into a layered tapestry of narrative fragments of mothers' lives. She retraces her survival of homophobic fear and repudiation through a process of awareness that connects her with the historical plights of other oppressed people.

Pratt's writings about lesbian sexuality and mothering begin with the visceral remembrance of her own bodily desires. In *Crime against Nature*, Pratt poetically narrates collisions between her lesbian longing and the loss of her children as a result of her defiant affirmations as "a pervert, a deviant … unnatural queer" (68). Writing 20 years after the events instigated by becoming a lesbian, she returns to her earlier experiences in the 1970s "of being declared an unfit mother of my children" by conjoining pieces of personal history, memories, dream work, and political events. Instead of reinscribing a "good" and selfless voice as a mother whose primary commitment is toward protecting and nurturing her sons, Pratt targets her anger at those powers and people reinforcing exclusive puritanical ideals. Affirming her survival and refusal of normative prescriptions of "goodness" while embracing an ethics of care, Pratt undermines moralistic judgments of "crime" and essentializing appeals to "nature." Pratt denaturalizes her desires as willed, embodied choices while avowing the contingency and mobility of her desires. Past choices and decisions become mediated not by abstract standards but by an interactive field of remembrance and ethical responsibility. Her text relays understandings in ways that do not revert back to any singular meaning that would justify her choices as a lesbian mother, calling out to others to question why such justifications are necessary in the first place.

Some of the most evocative features of Pratt's narrative trace out ephemeral encounters, positions, and lines of address. At times she attempts to converse intimately with her grown sons as a loving, empathetic mother who acknowledges the guilt she feels in the face of her choices. At other times she furiously directs her words toward those who attempted to regulate and punish her, turning attention onto heterosexist powers and critiquing the failures and hypocrisy of institutions of in/justice. In response, she seeks to support and confirm the voices of other women declared "unfit" as part of a political reconstructive process. Pratt also engages in strategies of resistance focused on the present and future in which she directly provokes readers to question their own biases:

My body of a woman, a mother, a lesbian.
And here,
perhaps you say: *That last word doesn't belong.*

Woman, mother: those can stay. Lesbian: no.'
Put that outside the place of the poem. Too
slangy, prosy, obvious, just doesn't belong.
Why don't you—? Why didn't you—? Can't you
say it some other way? (25)

Articulating her lesbian desire as that which continually unsettles her reader's presumptions of what constitutes a maternal self, Pratt plays up ambiguities that challenge the oxymoronic status of lesbian motherhood. The
point is not to resolve the tensions between her desires and identities but to
turn the problem onto those troubled by ambiguity. She provokes readers
to intervene in asking and answering questions from their respective locations of experience as to why her text upsets them. The borders of Pratt's
texts are permeable, speaking to a variety of audiences and assuming dif-
fering subject positions at various points in time. Pratt combines several
temporalities in her narrative, which enables her to rewrite her painful experiences of the past and actively envision alternatives within the here and
now. Yet the links between past, present, and future are shown to be highly
tentative and malleable—"the past repeats in fragments" that need to be
continually fictionally recomposed in an effort to "gather up the torn bits, a
path made of my own body, a trail to find what has been lost" (68). Adrienne
Rich states that *Crime against Nature* is remarkable insofar as "there is no
sentimental haze, no delusion that children as well as mothers do not suffer. These are not fluent, mellifluous poems. They are laden with mud, flint,
asphalt, blood, their field of energy is restless and impatient of resolutions"
(*What Is Found There* 157).

Pratt highlights socially enforced divisions between motherhood and
lesbian sexuality (and her refusals to sacrifice one for the other) as she
transgresses moralities prescribing the terms of maternal entitlement.
She describes being socially marginalized, and in her response of defiance
in terms of crossing spatial boundaries, she owns up to a "crime of moving back and forth between more than one self, more than one end to the
story," displaying the transitivity of her subjectivity. Although she follows
her erotic "freedom" at the expense of keeping her children, she refuses
to make a definite choice between one or the other in a world where "there
was no place to be simultaneous, or between" (18). Detailing her psychic
and social struggles to live as a desiring maternal and sexual subject, she
foregrounds the effects of her unwillingness to conceal or forgo her sexual
passions:

If I had been
more ashamed, if I had not wanted the world.
If I had hid my lust, I might not have lost
them. This is where the shame starts. (46)

Pratt stays close to, but does not remain solipsistically fixated upon, her own emotional shame, probing cultural and social conditions that enforce binary prescriptions experienced by many women as shameful. Shame becomes a departure point for reconstructing an empowering sense of pride in the refusal of restrictive norms and simplistic choices. Pratt transforms experiences of shame through the detours of painful wounds inflicted through moralities of maternal goodness/badness into an affirmation of erotic subjectivity that opens up understanding of maternal heterogeneity. Lust becomes a locus of shame and of joyful invention of future possibilities.

Pratt offers counter-narratives, criss-crossing intimate and social terrains of experience—"my love inverted history"—inscribing herself into a subversive maternal discourse that refuses to denounce or split off her non-maternal desires. Without offering a single correlation between motherhood and sexuality, she combines and separates them in unpredictable ways. At times she imbricates her lesbian sexuality and her maternal identity together as mutual dimensions of her subjectivity; at other times she calls attention to the gaps and incommensurable tensions that exist between them. Even non-narrative moments of her text configure loose constellations of fantasies, memories, and bodily pleasures as contextually meaningful, connected to the daily struggles of her life and the lives of those around her. When she explores the excesses and energetic movements of her desiring body, she does not ignore external forces that denigrate her "body shift" toward lesbian sexuality, or the ways her pleasures become solicited, defined, and judged by others. At other times, when Pratt inscribes her body as a site of loss, she is careful to track the historical underpinnings of that loss, grounding it within the fractured locations of her changing experiences.

Lesbian sexuality overlaps with her inconsolable maternal trauma—"reverberant pain, circular, endless" (31)—which drives and interrupts her narrative, a space in which Pratt attempts to verbalize memories that would otherwise remain painfully silent and impossible to communicate, while leaving gaps and moments of discontinuity at the discursive limits of her suffering. Writing through her memories and associative links, Pratt distinguishes the "dangerous" touch of lesbian sexuality from the sensual touch of mothering and the social preclusion of their mutuality at the same time as she interlaces images of maternal sensuality and lesbian sexuality at various point in her text. Lesbian fantasy, practice, and identity profoundly destabilize Pratt's world as a middle-class wife and mother, and as such they signify a process of change not only at the level of ethico-political consciousness but also through her assertion of bodily desires:

> how I began with her furtive mouth,
> her silences, her hand fucking me
> back of a van, beach sand grit
> scratch at my jeans, low tide. (46)

Pratt does not sever spontaneous sexual passions from her identifications as a mother but rather poetically overlays them. There is a fluid relationship between sexuality and motherhood in *Crime against Nature* that allows them to co-exist as different aspects of subjectivity capable of affecting each other. And one of the effects of her experiences of having lost her children is an interlacing of rage and willful desire into both her sexual and maternal narratives. Pratt creatively constructs a vision of maternal power, activating aggressive emotions rather than attempting to tame or resolve them. She voices her anger and critique as a forceful contrast to hegemonic images of maternal passivity and receptivity, asserting her resisting agency not only as a reaction to injustice but also as imaginative forces of desire and heroic defiance:

> I had to make a future, willful, voluble,
> lascivious, a thinker, a long walker,
> unstruck transgressor, furious, shouting,
> voluptuous, a lover, a smeller of blood,
> milk, a woman mean as she can be some nights,
> existence I could pray to, capable of
> poetry. (13)

This process of remembering and rewriting personal trauma figures a basis from which to project a future for herself as part of a collective movement, by eliciting the stories of other mothers whose circumstances differ from her own and indicate dispersed and prolific subjugated histories. Pratt does not seamlessly unite mothers in her attempts to gather experiential narratives together, but provides examples of sharp divisions and power relations (including the example of her own mother's homophobic refusal to help Pratt keep her children). Compiling disparate stories, images, and words of lesbian mothers marginalized for the ways their sexuality intersects with class and race, she expands the boundaries of her text. While she lost her children as an educated white femme, others might lose theirs for being poor and butch:

> Martha said she'd never see the baby again,
> her skinny brown arms folded against her flat breasts,
> flat-assed in blue jeans, a dyke looking hard as a hammer:
> And who would call her a mother? (31)

> the butch in black denim, elegant as ashes, her son
> perhaps sent back, a winter of no heat, a woman's salary. (32)

Specifying and interconnecting sexual, class, and racial powers shaping and dividing maternal experiences, this text challenges feminine maternal ideals of recognition and valuation, positioning gender as one piece of a larger terrain of maternal histories. Without equating the struggles of lesbian mothers at risk of losing their children, Pratt's efforts to provide space for maternal subjects who might not have institutional resources and access to write and circulate their own narratives is an important feature of *Crime against Nature*, which escapes individualistic enclosures of dominant heroic plots by juxtaposing a range of social struggles for agency, support, and belonging. It seems that Pratt is less concerned with consolidating maternal subjects than with expanding possibilities for listening to the stories of women who have been historically denigrated as bad or unfit mothers:

> her words sliding
> like a snapshot out of her billfold, faded outline
> glanced at and away from, the story elliptic, oblique
> to avoid the dangers of grief. (56)

Pratt enacts conversations with women—a commotion of voices"—while trying to position her own story among others whose lives are divided by the very social structures that deny them the right to mother:

> she inclines her head to signify us two
> in the long story of women and children
> severed. (57)

Pratt cuts into her personal narrative with multiple versions of maternal loss conditioned by slavery, war, racism, poverty, patriarchy. Yet it is not enough to track continuities between mothers deprived of their children, which would make it easy to smooth over fractious power relations between them. Pratt's writings problematize powers between women and the psychic fears that make it so difficult to confront them because they require recognition of social hierarchies dividing women in their struggles for reproductive choice and support. She shows on her own terms how such recognition calls for analysis and relinquishment of privileges as the basis for political alignments. Pratt makes it possible to speak about the courageous trials and survival as a lesbian mother, while exploring her privileged positions as a white middle-class woman. This self-reflexive understanding of inequality does not undermine the erotic focus of stories of suffering, survival, and transformation as a lesbian mother, but it does prevent them from closing in on themselves or valorizing a single individual heroic plot at the expense of others. At the same time, Pratt's respect for the complexity and unfinalizable work of narrating experiences as relational projects underlines her ethical and political challenge:

> Yes, that fear is there, but I will try to be at the edge between my fear and the outside, on the edge at my skin, listening, asking what new thing will I hear, will I see, will I let myself feel, beyond the fear. I try to say: To acknowledge the complexity of another's existence is not to deny my own. ("Identity" 35)

Note to Chapter 13

See works by Audre Lord and Adrienne Rich as well as collections of essays such as *Politics of the Heart* and Katherine Arnup, ed., *Lesbian Parenting: Living with Pride and Prejudice* (Charlottetown: Gynergy Books, 1995) for various accounts of oppressive conditions, homophobic threats, and struggles over custody faced by lesbian mothers.

Works Cited

Mohanty, Chandra, and Biddy Martin. "Feminist Politics: What's Home Got to Do with It?" *Feminist Studies/Critical Studies*. Ed. Teresa de Lauretis. Bloomington: Indiana University Press, 1986. 191–212.

Pratt, Minnie Bruce. *Crime against Nature*. Ithaca, NY: Firebrand, 1990.

——. "Identity: Skin, Blood, Heart." *Rebellion*. By Pratt. New York: Firebrand Books, 1991.

Rich, Adrienne. *Of Woman Born: Motherhood as Experience and Institution*. New York: Norton, 1996.

——. *What Is Found There: Notebooks on Poetry and Politics*. New York: Norton, 1993.

14

Lesbian Mothering in Contemporary French Literature | BY GILL RYE

In France, as elsewhere in the West, since the latter part of the twentieth century the contemporary family has been undergoing a process of accelerated change, with an increase in the number of lone parents, post-divorce "blended" families, and same-sex family groups, and a concomitant decline in the conventional nuclear model of the family (Roudinesco). France's "gayby-boom" (Cadoret 15; Gross 14) dates only from the mid 1990s (while that of North America took place in the early 1980s) even though lesbian and gay male parenting in France actually has a much longer history, and many parents who identify as homosexual originally became parents within a heterosexual marriage or partnership. Today, an increasing number of gay and lesbian couples in France are choosing to become parents, either alone, within their same-sex partnerships, or via co-parenting arrangements with other individuals or couples. These new family groupings not only contribute to ethnographic change but also call into question conventional notions of the family. In particular, lesbian families, which effectively consist of two mothers, cannot help but confront us with questions about the very meaning of "mothering" and about what it means to be a mother today.

This chapter engages with these very questions by considering two examples of what is proving to be an emerging trend, namely representations of lesbian mothering in French literature. The texts are Éliane Girard's novel *Mais qui va garder le chat?* (*But Who'll Look After the Cat?*) and Myriam Blanc's largely autobiographical *Et elles eurent beaucoup d'enfants ... : Histoire d'une famille homoparentale* (*And They [The Women] Had Lots of Children ... : The Story of a Same-Sex Family*), both of which were published in 2005.[1] Many of the issues with which lesbian parents in France are confronted echo those encountered in other cultures, but the dynamics of conformity and difference, normalization and transgression that lesbian families embody are particularly pertinent in the specific context of the French Republic. *Liberté, égalité, fraternité* (Liberty, equality, fraternity) may be its founding and defining principles, but France's model of egalitarian universalism eschews all forms of identity politics in favour of integration and assimilation into an inclusive notion of "Frenchness," and, moreover, the family in France is firmly conceived as a heterosexual unit. In this context, I explore how and to what extent Girard's and Blanc's texts each portray lesbian mothers as "normal," "ordinary," "just like other mothers," and how far they represent them as forging new terrain, experimenting with social forms, reinventing the family. The narrators in both texts themselves lay claim, alternatively, to normality, in their qualities as parents, and difference, in terms of carving out new family forms. My analysis, then, focuses on specific areas where these dynamics coalesce, namely, the issue of visibility, the question of the father, the figure of the second mother, and the problem of language. It then goes on, in the final section, to draw together the various strands of this analysis in an engagement with Élisabeth Roudinesco's suggestion that same-sex parenting may offer a model for the (French/European) family of the future (221–44).

First, though, I want briefly to outline the French socio-legal context in which my discussion is situated. European (EU) legislation and French national laws of the 1980s and 1990s on part-time work, maternity leave, and rights have done much to change working conditions for women as mothers in terms of equal rights and the work–life balance, and to alter expectations of how mothering in France can be lived. Yet, the effect of these laws is limited, as they actually tend to endorse rather than challenge conventional representations of women's mothering roles (Guerrina). The French PaCS legislation (Pacte civil de solidarité/Civil Solidarity Pact) of 1999 is a case in point.[2] By means of the PaCS law, the union of same-sex couples was legally recognized in France for the first time, in terms of taxation, inheritance, and social benefits. Such a law would seem to offer new horizons for forms and concepts of the family, but, although PaCS agreements are open to both heterosexual and homosexual couples and as such provide a legal framework for rights and responsibilities for unmarried, co-habiting couples, they make no provision for such couples with—or planning to have—children. Under French law, unmarried couples, those with or without a PaCS, whether hetero- or homosexual, cannot adopt children, although single individuals can.[3] Moreover, neither lesbian couples nor single women are allowed access to medicalized artificial insemination in France, whereas married and unmarried heterosexual couples who have been co-habiting for at least two years are (Doustaly; Gross). The PaCS law, applicable to both hetero- and homosexual couples, is a prime example of French Republican universalism in practice—in France it would be unconstitutional to pass a French law that would benefit only same-sex couples. Yet, since the impetus for the legislation emanated from gay and lesbian activism and lobbying, the law does also actually evidence recognition by the French state of the needs and demands of a particular identity grouping (Rosello). Despite, or perhaps precisely because of its exclusion of parenting rights, the PaCS law has fuelled public and political debate on same-sex parenting in France (Gross 17). The lack of legal recognition of gay and lesbian parents is an ongoing issue, since, in practice, lesbian and gay families with children increasingly exist alongside diverse heterosexual family groupings.

The two texts I have chosen to discuss, Girard's *Mais qui va garder le chat?* and Blanc's *Et elles eurent beaucoup d'enfants ...*, enable a preliminary study of how lesbian mothering is being represented in post-PaCS France. Both texts are first-person narratives, situating the mothers as subjects rather than objects of discourse (Hirsch). It is symptomatic of the political controversy surrounding same-sex parenting in France, as well as of its increasing visibility, that Girard and Blanc, although employing quite different genres, both focus on the complex process of *becoming* a lesbian mother rather than on its lived experience. They highlight, above all, the issues that their lesbian protagonists have to grapple with as they plan for parenthood and become mothers. Girard's novel gives voice to both mothers in a lesbian couple, the principal narrator being Cécile, the eventual birth mother, with the perspectives of her partner, Fanny, included by means of short sections interspersed throughout the text, entitled "Journal de Fanny" (Fanny's diary). The tone is light and humorous, but the novel nonetheless engages with both practical and political issues surrounding gay and lesbian families, since its characters and subplots serve to include different versions of same-sex parenting, against which Cécile and Fanny's venture is positioned, and the various debates on, and reactions to, gay and lesbian parenting are rehearsed by means of dialogue between characters. Blanc's text is quite different. Part autobiography, part ethnography, part fiction, and part political tract, the narrative combines humour, sarcasm, slang, and a storytelling mode with concrete facts and information, and it is divided into a series of short sections with headings. This structure, on the one hand, steers the narrative, and, on the other, serves to foreground the debates, attitudes, and issues that have an impact on the protagonists' experiences. Here, Myriam and her partner, Astrid, each give birth to a daughter, and thus they are both nonbiological as well as biological mothers within their family unit.

As Blanc's ironical title suggests, both texts are "happy ever after" stories with a difference. The narrative of Girard's *Mais qui va garder le chat?* unfolds as it follows through events from Cécile's desire for a child to its fruition. It also includes a series of flashbacks that flesh out the story line and subplots, and it ends in the present tense with the protagonists' son having just celebrated his third birthday. In contrast, in Blanc's *Et elles eurent beaucoup d'enfants*, the completed family (two mothers and two daughters) is presented on the very first page, and the narrative trajectory is retrospective. Thus, Girard's novel depicts, largely, a journey toward lesbian mothering, and Blanc's narrator approaches a similar journey with the benefit of hindsight and several years of mothering practice.

One of the key issues that gay and lesbian parents in France have to deal with is that they become visible "in a culture that doesn't recognize [their] primary intimate connections" (Benkov 121). Although becoming a mother may be considered a normalizing move on the part of a lesbian woman (Cadoret 148), the general sense is, however, that gay and lesbian parents are called upon to explain their choice to parent, indeed to justify themselves to a heterocentric, not to say homophobic, society. Thus, whether or not they see themselves as just like other families, others necessarily see them as different. In a British context, Jacqui Gabb argues for the integration of lesbian sexuality into lesbian motherhood in order to make lesbian sexuality visible in the very context of the lesbian family and thus to stress the difference of such families, but the women in Girard's and Blanc's texts reveal a more ambivalent negotiation with visibility. A mixture of clarity and discretion about Blanc's couple's relationship is designed to show the local community "that we are not ashamed of who we are, nor of our family" (15),[4] but the women are more ambiguous about their situation when dealing with the officialdom of French bureaucracy. Nonetheless, Blanc casts her text as a contribution to the politics of visibility—"Let's show ourselves, and let's show that we're happy, let's show off our radiant children, we owe them that!" (7)—and this activist element is reinforced by the inclusion of an appendix giving details, and promoting the role, of the APGL (Association des Parents et Futurs Parents Gays et Lesbiens/Association of Gay and Lesbian Parents and Future Parents) in lobbying for the visibility of same-sex parenting vis-à-vis French society and its legislators.[5]

Girard's novel portrays a rather different kind of negotiation with visibility. Cécile has not come out as a lesbian at work and, when her workmates discover she is pregnant, much to Fanny's disgust, she remains in the closet. Unprepared, she responds to the question, "Is your boyfriend pleased?" by mumbling, "Yes, he's pleased" (194). When she subsequently plucks up courage to be more open with her boss, admitting "there is no father" (200), he misunderstands and thinks she is embarking on single motherhood. Here, though, she chooses not to put him right, simply congratulating herself on having been honest, but then, ironically, she has to live with the consequences as he rapidly spreads *his* version around the office! Fanny, on the other hand, who normally tends to stay as much as possible within a gay milieu, realizes that increasingly she will have to engage with a wider, less sympathetic community:

How many times will I have to justify why I don't want to be pregnant yet do want to have a child?

How many times will people ask "And how did you decide who should carry the baby?"

How many times will people bug us with the question "If you aren't the mother then will you be the father?"

How many interrogations, assumptions and propositions will we have to put up with? (91)

Here, she foresees that the couple's inevitable visibility as lesbian parents will render them curiosities in society at large, with which, as parents, they will not be able to avoid interacting. Visibility is a particularly important issue for lesbian mothering in France, where identity politics are an anathema. Although visibility can be empowering, it renders lesbian women and their families different whether or not they wish to endorse lesbian identity politics, and whereas, on the whole, Blanc's couple do, Girard's Cécile, like many lesbians in France, does not. Even if lesbian mothers consider, or desire, themselves and their families to be just like other families—that is, like heterosexual families[6]—the simple fact of two women parenting together makes them visible and depicts them as different.

The question of a father and to what degree lesbian couples want a man to be involved in the parenting of their child is critical to the dynamics of normality and difference that this chapter is concerned with. In both texts, the women want to parent solely within their own couple, but the normative power of social conditioning is not negated. Girard's Cécile first has to confront and resolve her own guilt feelings that "a child needs a father and a mother" and that "it's selfish to bring a child into the world in a situation that is already not normal" (40), while Blanc, rehearsing the debate in a section "There's No Daddy" (35–37), ultimately, can do no more than to fall back on the evidence of her own experience, insisting that "you can have children without a father, even happy children" (37).

Blanc's couple, Myriam and Astrid, decide in favour of medicalized artificial insemination by an anonymous donor. The process is long and disruptive, since it is not available to lesbian couples in France and they have to go to Belgium for treatment, and Myriam takes almost a year to conceive, but donor anonymity is what is most important to them, allowing them to situate themselves as "the only parents of our daughters" (49), the donor being just that, "a donor, not a father" (49). This couple even takes the decision not to have the same donor for both their daughters, in order, the narrator declares, to avoid fantasy constructions of a "mythical father" (41), and to establish love rather than biology as the foundation of their family unit. In contrast, Girard's Cécile and Fanny reject the idea of an anonymous donor precisely because of what they see as the difficulty in answering their child's eventual questions about his father. They decide on conception by non-medicalized artificial insemination—or, as Fanny refers to it, "the syringe and yogurt pot method" (136)—by a known donor, their gay friend Gilles. Thus, Cécile and Fanny can point to Gilles as a biological father, even if not as an active or a present one. The absence of a father in these texts does not mean, however, that men are absent from the children's lives, and both couples interact with a larger community and extended families, in which men are present.

The lack of a father in a family unit is not new or revolutionary in itself, of course, although fatherless families may well still be designated as dysfunctional in normative discourses of the family. Even the choice to parent without a father is not confined to lesbian couples, since, in the West, an increasing number of heterosexual women choose to become single mothers (and, it should be remembered, single women may legally adopt in France) and other francophone cultures have different kinship traditions.[7] However, any women who choose to conceive without men are commonly positioned as a threat to the good functioning of the social order. Lesbian parenting, in particular, brings about a split in the different functions that have historically clustered around the father, and traditional gendered parenting roles do not apply. Above all, lesbian mothers confront society at large with the fact that (hetero)sexuality is no longer the only basis for the foundation of a family. Frequently, as is the case for the two couples in the texts discussed here, the social father is dispensed with completely—and, for Blanc, arguably also the psychological father, although children conceived by artificial insemination nonetheless tend to create "their own story about their father" (Gross and Peyceré 60). Anthropologists and sociologists in France, as elsewhere, are finding these new kinship structures interesting, and research showing that children in gay and lesbian families are as well adjusted as those in heterosexual families are widely quoted in their support,[8] but clinical psychoanalysts in France are still only just beginning to engage with the issue (Gross 103), and French law does not yet recognize the different notions of kinship that are being constructed by lesbian and gay families. Thus, the issue of the father that is resolved relatively easily in a personal context for Girard's and Blanc's narrators, in a broader frame, poses more questions than it answers.

The situation of the "second" (or co-) mother is perhaps even more complex. The nonbiological mother in lesbian families (and in many co-parenting arrangements) foregrounds two sets of issues: on the one hand, the place of this "second" mother in the family unit, and, on the other, her legal position vis-à-vis her children.[9] The situation of the nonbiological mother in lesbian couples who decide to have children together, like the protagonists in Blanc's and Girard's texts, is quite different from those in existing heterosexual family forms. For example, she is not in a similar position to a step-parent in post-divorce or post-bereavement "blended families," since she is involved in the planning of the family from the outset, nor is she like an adoptive mother whose role as social mother is modelled on that of a biological mother. Lesbian co-mothers have few points of reference to draw on and, largely, have to invent their own role and identity. Indeed, even in the North American context, in which lesbian families have a longer history, there is little research in existence on the role and identity of the second mother (Comeau 45).

In Girard's novel, the character Fanny, who chooses not to be the pregnant mother, reflects a great deal on her identity as co-mother: "the problem is that I'm the only one to have the honor of using this pretty title. Cécile is the mother. Period" (118). The relevant issues are worked through in scenes where the women announce the impending birth to their respective parents, who thus also function as figures of the opinion of society at large. Cécile's parents are very open-minded about their daughter's sexuality, to the point of boasting to their friends about their "daughter-in-law" (53), but, when it comes to the prospective baby, they find it difficult to think outside the heterosexual model and, in particular, have a problem with the concept of there being no father. For them, the biological father or donor *is* the father, and if, as Cécile explains, he will not take part in parenting the child, then "Fanny will act as Daddy, is that it?" (147). For them, there has to be a father. Fanny's parents, on the other hand, are more concerned about their status as grandparents than anything else. Fanny's mother fears, above all, that she will be less of a grandmother than Cécile's mother, who is "the mother of the real mother" (184), and her father is disappointed that Fanny is not the birth mother and that the child will not carry his name: "I didn't have a daughter so that she'd turn out to be a fake father" (185).

From all sides, then, Fanny is confronted with her lack of status: "'Completely ignored. That's it. If you don't have biological or legal rights, nobody will give them to you. I don't exist in relation to this child, you've just had proof'" (151). If Cécile's liberal parents have trouble placing Fanny as another mother to their future grandchild, Fanny's outburst reveals her own identity crisis; she has "no references or mirrors to view [her] reflection" (Dundas 37).

Similar dilemmas are also evoked in Blanc's text, with the difference that both women experience being the nonbiological mother as well as the pregnant mother. For Myriam, who gave birth to the couple's first daughter, "the second parent's torments" (93) are more to do with wondering whether she will love Astrid's baby as much as her own. On the whole, and with hindsight, Blanc maintains that any differences in the immediacy of the women's respective relationships with their children are more about who takes on most of the primary care and who devotes more time to earning money at any one time than about who is the biological mother.

As far as the legal status of the co-mother is concerned, Martine Gross is quite clear: "Whatever the structure, a social parent has no rights in France; s/he does not exist in the eyes of the law" (20). This situation has serious consequences for lesbian mothers. For Blanc, the lesbian co-mother is, in legal terms, a "non-parent" (28). In France, parental authority is conferred only on the father and the mother of a child and not on two parents of the same sex (Gross 31). This not only creates practical problems in dealings with schools or hospitals, but it also means that the co-mother has no custody rights to her children if her partner dies, and a child cannot inherit from his or her second mother. And if a lesbian couple split up, the co-mother has rights neither of custody nor even of access to her children. The adoption of the child by the co-mother, in an attempt to legalize her joint parenting, does not provide a solution in France, since French adoption laws mean the birth mother would be deprived of her parental authority. The law and its interpretation are continually evolving, however, and recent test cases suggest that the sharing of parental authority is beginning to become a real possibility for lesbian couples. The political thrust of Blanc's text means it dwells on the legal status of co-mothers more than Girard's novel does, but

Girard does not ignore legal issues. Indeed, Fanny is confronted with the stark implications of her lack of legal status when the couple's close friends Laetitia and Anne split up. This couple has a co-parenting relationship with a gay male friend, Serge, and when Anne leaves Laetitia for a new relationship, after 17 years, Laetitia, as birth mother, holds Anne to ransom over the children and refuses her access.

Thus, Girard's and Blanc's texts between them explore some of the personal, social, and legal implications for the lesbian co-mother in France. If she finds it hard even to figure her own role and identity in the family unit, this is partly because there are no preceding models. Moreover, as the confusion of Fanny's parents "between real and fake mothers, proper grandmothers and the father who isn't a father" in Girard's novel (184–85) and Myriam and Astrid's dilemma in Blanc's text of what to call "the other mother, the one who isn't THE mother" (114) serve to emphasize, there are as yet not even any conventions of language and terminology for them to describe who they are, and the vocabulary with which to name gay and lesbian parents in France is obviously still to be invented.

In Girard's novel, as we have seen, Fanny searches for a way of figuring her new identity: "A co-mother.... It's an ugly word. A co-parent, it's rather like being a joint owner or a member of a team" (118). The lack of language to name either her situation in the family structure or her relationship to her child, or even to Cécile, makes Fanny feel that she has no place. As the conversations with the couple's parents show, terms that are commonly in use in the gay and lesbian milieu have little meaning outside that circle: "The co-parent is a mystery to everyone, like a virtual parent that you can zap at any time" (118). Blanc's Myriam and Astrid, who are both co-mothers, experiment with made-up terms, but in the end resort to the more common solution of "Mom Myriam and Mom Astrid" (115). Language has a fundamental influence on the construction of family life, and, in this respect, lesbian mothers have it all to invent (Benkov).

These texts confirm that, although gay and lesbian families in France may be reinventing the family unit in their own private spaces and vis-à-vis their extended families and immediate communities, the lack of cultural accommodation of their different family structures, by way of language, names, or rituals, means their difference is figured in hierarchical terms, in which they are positioned as "abnormal" to the status quo. Blanc's narrator laments the paucity of French children's books portraying lesbian families: "Daddy is everywhere in our daughters' books but totally absent from their life" (117). There are as yet few cultural reflections of her children's different conceptions of gender relations and of what constitutes a family to them. Girard's and Blanc's texts individually do not come up with any firm solutions, but together they suggest that it is important that the work done within individual families on symbolizing new kinds of parental structures needs to enter the cultural arena in order, gradually, to make a place for gay and lesbian families "such as they are" (Roudinesco 238).

In their respective engagements with the issues of visibility, of the father, of the second mother, and of language, Girard's and Blanc's texts, then, contribute to the debate on the impact that same-sex parenting is having on the evolution of the family. Although the dynamic between the desire for integration and the assertion of difference is evident in each of the issues discussed, so that conformity is effectively the underside of difference and vice versa, the "new situation' (Girard 217) of lesbian families is never seriously in question in these texts. But, while lesbian mothers are represented here, literally, as "mother outlaws" (O'Reilly)—not against the law as such but not recognized by it either—to what extent do they represent the transgressive force that Roudinesco claims same-sex parenting potentially to be in her study of the contemporary family? Here, Roudinesco is referring to the fundamental challenge to the question of origins and to sexual difference that renders gay and lesbian families not simply a curiosity but also a threat to the social order (221–23). In comparison with co-parenting arrangements where the female–male/mother–father model is intact (although possibly multiplied), lesbian families destabilize sexual difference, on which the French social order is based (see Fassin), since they dispense with the social father. Yet, as we have seen in both Blanc's and Girard's texts, they do not eliminate sexual difference, neither as far as conception is concerned nor in a lack of male referents. Indeed, rather than transgression, we might see in this last point a revaluation of the extended family, which includes both women and men—a revaluation in counterpoint to the fragmentation that took place during the twentieth century. In the absence of fathers, other family members provide the couples' children with a "masculine presence" (Girard 159), and, moreover, both texts suggest that the whole concept of the extended family is enlarged and enriched by gay culture itself. By the inclusion of gay friends and networks, these new kinds of extended families not only provide practical help and support for lesbian mothers in the form of formal or informal "hands-on" godmothers and godfathers, but also, as Blanc's narrator emphasizes, enable their children to forge friendships outside a heterosexual framework.

This extended family notwithstanding, lesbian families do undoubtedly contribute to the contemporary decline and, for Roudinesco (243), crisis in paternal authority. Blanc's narrator's desire to eradicate even a "mythical father" (41) is perhaps the most transgressive move of all, since it raises questions about what happens to the Oedipal paternal function of psycho-analysis (as opposed to the biological or social fathering role) in families with two mothers and no father. French psychoanalysts have accepted for some time that figures of either sex can fulfill the Lacanian-Freudian paternal function of separator, but, in the texts discussed here, which focus on the process of becoming a mother rather than on its lived reality, it is not certain that this would be the co-mother, or, indeed, either mother: Girard's Fanny has yet to invent her role, and Blanc's couple, each of whom are both mothers and co-mothers, share primary parenting and other traditionally gendered roles. In their case, if the Oedipal function of separator survives within the family unit, it would seem to shift back and forth between them.

The narratives of the lesbian mothers discussed in this chapter suggest that the revolutionary potential of the lesbian family lies principally in the figure of the co-mother. It is in her role that the greatest challenge to concepts of the mother and of mothering lies. In Blanc's text, these innovatory aspects are displaced on to the couple—since they are both birth and non-birth mothers—and the two women not only share but also exchange traditional gendered roles, depending on the amount of paid work they each have at any one time. This sort of arrangement represents what Rose Croghan (244) suggests is "an alternative to current constructions of motherhood" and, in terms of the equality it engenders within relationships, offers a role model for heterosexual women. In Girard's novel, the way Fanny lives out her role as co-mother is left open-ended and thus open to speculation, but importantly, that speculation is written into the narrative itself. Cécile protests to her parents that "no, Fanny isn't a Daddy, isn't it obvious?" (148), but the counsellor from "Homoparents," Girard's fictional version of the APGL, reminds her that "it remains to be seen. Why should the father's role be held by a man?" (158). Rather than signifying a return to the father and conformity, however, this latter point is potentially more subversive than it might seem. Girard's novel, indeed, shows how Cécile's parents normalize the prospect of a lesbian family by conceptualizing Fanny as the father but, here, Girard suggests we should reflect on the innovative implications of women themselves appropriating—and, importantly, *necessarily* modifying—the paternal role, in the name of the mother.

As cultural narratives of lesbian mothering, Girard's and Blanc's texts are important in themselves. On the one hand, in their engagement with contemporary debates on same-sex parenting, they, in turn, also engage the reader in those debates. On the other hand, as broadly "happy-ever-after" stories, "in which lesbians and their families get to survive," they participate in "lesbian culture-building" (Agigian 168). Amy Agigian argues that such stories contribute to "a lesbian 'nomos'—a 'normative universe'" (167), which is not normative in the sense of integrating lesbian families into a heterosexual universalism. Instead, it "puts lesbians at the center, rather than trying to fit them into existing heteropatriarchal norms" (168). Although the two texts discussed do not negate the struggle and the problems involved in this process, the narratives nonetheless contribute to "a growing body of 'street theory'" (168) in France, which stands as an alternative to the official discourse of French Republican universalism and which, for Agigian, can serve as a platform from which to construct society differently. In this context, the irony—and, I would suggest, ultimate political point— of Girard's novel is in the twist at the end, when one of Cécile and Fanny's heterosexual women friends, in turn, uses them as role models for her own co-parenting project. Moreover, the humorous and light character of the narratives, in which Girard and Blanc both rewrite the "same old story" differently—the happy-ever-after story—work toward the project of remodelling concepts of the family in the French Republic in a particularly positive way. As Susan Suleiman has argued, in another context, *pace* Freud, laughter connotes both pleasure and rebellion, and a laughing mother at once asserts her own subjectivity and lightens "what otherwise could appear as too solemn a dream." Girard's and Blanc's lesbian mothers are, then, indeed, laughing with "subversive intent" (Suleiman 180).

Notes to Chapter 14

1   Éliane Girard is a director of radio programs at France Inter and has published books on youth culture as well as two other novels. Myriam Blanc lives in southern France with her partner and children and works in the media and in publishing. Other examples of the representation of lesbian mothers include Claire Altman's 2005 autobiographical account of a lesbian couple who adopted two baby girls from South America in the late 1980s and early 1990s, and Laurence Cinq-Fraix's 2006 novel about a co-parenting arrangement between a lesbian couple and a gay male couple. This chapter is an earlier version of a longer and more developed chapter that appears in my 2009 monograph (118-38).

2   For a description of the PaCS law in English, see http://www.france.qrd.org/texts/partnership/fr/explanation.html.

3   In 2002, the European Court of Human Rights narrowly voted not to condemn France for discrimination in a homosexual adoption case. See Gross (41–43).

4   All translations from the original French are my own.

5   See the APGL website: www.apgl.asso.fr.

6 Importantly, neither text negates the diversity of either heterosexual or homosexual families.

7 For example, serial single motherhood in French Caribbean cultures.

8 See, for example, Gross (75–92). For a detailed review of North American studies,
see Patterson. French studies are only just beginning to be carried out; see, for
example, Nadaud. Roudinesco (230–31) is of the opinion that recourse to studies
that compare homosexual families with heterosexual ones, as many of these do,
is misguided, on the grounds that psychoanalysis, at the very least, attests to the
effective dysfunctionality of the heterosexual nuclear family.

9 As Altman evidences, much of this discussion also relates to the "second" mother
in situations where lesbian couples adopt, so that, while both are nonbiological
mothers, only one of the mothers is the legal mother (since lesbian couples still
may not adopt in France).

Works Cited

Agigian, Amy. *Baby Steps: How Lesbian Alternative Insemination Is Changing the World*.
Middletown, CT: Wesleyan University Press, 2004.

Altman, Claire. *Deux femmes et un couffin: Une histoire d'adoptions homoparentales*.
Paris: Éditions Ramsay, 2005.

Benkov, Laura. *Re-Inventing the Family: The Emerging Story of Lesbian and Gay Parents*.
New York: Crown, 1994.

Blanc, Myriam. *Et elles eurent beaucoup d'enfants... : Histoire d'une famille homoparentale*. Manosque: Le bec en l'air, 2005.

Cadoret, Anne. *Des parents comme les autres: Homosexualité et parenté*. Paris: Odile
Jacob, 2002.

Cinq-Fraix, Laurence. *Family Pride*. Paris: Éditions Philippe Rey, 2006.

Comeau, Dawn. "Lesbian Nonbiological Mothering: Negotiating an (Un)Familiar
Existence." *Journal of the Association of Research on Mothering* 1.2 (Fall/Winter
1999): 44–57.

Croghan, Rose. "Sleeping with the Enemy: Mothers in Heterosexual Relationships
(Observations and Commentaries)." *Heterosexuality: A Feminism and Psychology
Reader*. Ed. Sue Wilkinson and Celia Kitzinger. London: Sage, 1993. 243–45.

Doustaly, Thomas. *Guide du PaCs*. Toulouse: Éditions Milan, 2000.

Dundas, Susan. "Lesbian Second Mothering," *Journal of the Association of Research on
Mothering* 1.2 (Fall/Winter 1999): 37–43.

Fassin, Éric. "The Politics of PACS in a Transatlantic Mirror: Same-Sex Unions and
Sexual Difference in France Today." *Sites, The Journal of 20th Century Contemporary French Studies* 4.1 (Spring 2000): 55–64.

Gabb, Jacqui. "Imag(in)ing the Queer Lesbian Family." *Journal of the Association for Research on Mothering* 1.2 (Fall/Winter 1999): 9–20.

Girard, Éliane. *Mais qui va garder le chat?* Paris: J. C. Lattès, 2005.

Gross, Martine. *L'Homoparentalité: Que sais-je?* 2nd ed. Paris: Presses Universitaires de France, 2005.

Gross, Martine, and Mathieu Payceré. *Fonder une famille homoparentale: Questions éthiques, juridiques, psychologiques... et quelques réponses pratiques.* Paris: Ramsay, 2005.

Guerrina, Roberta. *Mothering the Union: Gender Politics in the EU.* Manchester: Manchester University Press, 2005.

Hirsch, Marianne. *The Mother/Daughter Plot: Narrative, Psychoanalysis, Feminism.* Bloomington: Indiana University Press, 1989.

Nadaud, Stéphane. *Homoparentalité: Une nouvelle chance pour la famille.* Paris: Fayard, 2002.

O'Reilly, Andrea, ed. *Mother Outlaws: Theories and Practices of Empowered Mothering.* Toronto: Women's Press, 2004.

Patterson, Charlotte J. "Children of Lesbian and Gay Parents." *Child Development* 63.5 (October 1992): 1025–42.

Roudinesco, Élisabeth. *La Famille en désordre.* Paris: Fayard, 2002.

Rosello, Mireille. "Tactical Universalism and New Multiculturalist Claims in Post-colonial France." *Francophone Postcolonial Studies: A Critical Introduction.* Ed. Charles Forsdick and David Murphy. London: Arnold, 2003. 135–44.

Rye, Gill. *Narratives of Mothering: Women's Writing in Contemporary France.* Newark: University of Delaware Press, 2009.

Suleiman, Susan Rubin. "Feminist Intertextuality and the Laugh of the Mother." *Subversive Intent: Gender, Politics, and the Avant Garde.* Cambridge, MA: Harvard University Press, 1990. 141–80.

15

But She's a Mom! Sex, Motherhood, and the
Poetry of Sharon Olds | BY RITA JONES

When critics and reviewers describe the poetry of Sharon Olds, they tend to place her within one of two categories: a sexually explicit poet or a poet who is a daughter or a mother.[1] Although I will not be working with Olds's poems on being a daughter, I will explore some poems in which the mother considers her position as mother in terms of her daughter. More specifically, I argue that it is important to remove the sex/mother binary to put these "kinds" of poet within one category: a poet who writes about a sexually desiring woman who is also a devoted, sacrificing mother. It is no coincidence that in several of her collections, Olds has ordered the poems in such a way that poems about sex and poems about mothering often face one another or immediately follow one another, while still others, such as "New Mother" (*The Dead and the Living*, 1984), merge the two concepts into one poem. In this discussion, I examine, within the context of twentieth-century American constructs of proper motherhood, the impact of Olds's merging of the representations of a sexually desiring woman with those of a woman who is a caring mother. Specifically, I argue that the poetry of Sharon Olds, the bulk of which was published during the latter half of the twentieth century, refutes contemporary constructions of proper womanhood and mothering by offering a woman who is a loving mother and sexually satisfied. This woman reconstructs late-twentieth-century narratives of mothering by exploring and combining her sexual side with her mothering. An American poet born in San Francisco in 1942, Sharon Olds has been publishing collections of poems since 1980, when *Satan Says* appeared, and in this discussion, I will be addressing poems from three collections: *The Dead and the Living* (1984), *The Wellspring* (1995), and *Blood, Tin, Straw* (1999). As a white woman who has procreated, Olds in many ways represents the kind of woman targeted by millennial constructs of proper womanhood, and, thus, her poems often reference the American culture's tension between sexual satisfaction and motherhood, as Alicia Ostriker has noted.[2]

Before discussing the poems, I would like to examine contemporary notions of "good" mothers, those ideal constructs of mothering against which most women evaluate themselves and are evaluated. Certainly, these constructs rely upon typical markers of female identity—white, middle to upper middle class, heterosexual, and Christian—to impede the success of a great number of women. Several scholars have examined precisely how these markers function and have explored how even those women who meet the basic criteria still cannot meet the expectations of socially approved motherhood. In her important study on what she terms "intensive mothering," Sharon Hays thoroughly examines the contemporary status of mothering in America by examining social codes and mothers' self-evaluations. These evaluations, according to Hays, set up the basic criteria of intensive mothering: "one's 'natural' love for the 'inherently' sacred child [that] necessarily leads one to engage in child-centered, expert-guided, emotionally absorbing, labor-intensive, and financially expensive child-rearing" (129). Women argue that this role is best performed by women because men neither have the ability to multitask effectively and efficiently nor understand the nutritional, emotional, and developmental needs of the children (129–30). Importantly, Olds's poetry rarely emphasizes the male lover's or father's role in raising the children. Instead we see mothering from the eyes of the female speaker. Privileging this perspective would seem at the outset to represent a woman thoroughly grounded within the context of intensive mothering, and, certainly, escaping this narrative is a difficult task. The very echoes, however, of intensive mothering in Olds's poetry demonstrates how pervasive this narrative is.

In their daily lives, women witness narratives supporting intensive mothering that reinforce the basic tenets of good mothers by showcasing experts' knowledge, requiring significant sums of money and self-sacrificing love of women for their offspring. Susan J. Douglas and Meredith W. Michaels fully examine how the media have supported intensive mothering. Building upon Hays's notions of intensive mothering, Douglas and Michaels investigate what they term "the new momism," a contemporary form of mothering that seeks to eliminate all the advances feminism has afforded women since the 1950s (23). Importantly, they assert the new momism "redefines all women, first and foremost, through their relationships to children" (22), so, not surprisingly, those women who cannot or choose not to have children rank lowest. Of course, a woman who does spend a great deal of time with her children but also devotes time to satisfying her own sexual desires also rates as "suspect" in terms of contemporary narratives of mothering. We hear from this suspicious woman time and again in the poetry of Sharon Olds, but she is simultaneously represented as a caring mother. This woman refuses to lose the gains twentieth-century feminism has brought to women, specifically the realization that mothering, while often fulfilling and rewarding, is not the only role women desire and perform successfully. Further, by circulating this representation through her poetry, Olds acknowledges how these women, who refuse to follow the guidelines of contemporary mothering, move from the confines of the potential isolation of the private home into the public space.

Olds's poetry is important to consider within the context of American individualism because women who unquestioningly follow popular notions of successful mothering often remove themselves from many forms of social interaction. In doing so, they come into conflict with the basic contradiction of intensive mothering: women simultaneously exist within the frame of American individualism, where the individual's goals and desires are often weighted more heavily than the goals and desires of the community. As Hays points out, the ideology of intensive mothering exists alongside "one emphasizing impersonal relations between isolated individuals efficiently pursuing their personal profit" (97), and as the latter gains force, the former must either gain force or succumb. Hays discovers in her interviews with women that "the phrases used by these mothers is a measure of the deep and pervasive power of the ideology of intensive mothering" (98). Aware of their own ability to succeed or fail, aware of their own interest or lack of interest in contemporary standards of mothering, many contemporary women still incorporate the rhetoric of intensive mothering into their constructions of themselves, and, certainly, into how they evaluate other women. What remains significant about Olds's collections is how the woman in the poems acknowledges and often exhibits behaviours associated with intensive mothering, and then discusses self-serving acts that satisfy her sexual desires. This duality within one individual suggests, then, that contemporary American women can have it all, so long as they control definitions of successful womanhood for themselves.

Clearly, according to the tenets of intensive mothering or the new momism, a woman who is out enjoying herself sexually cannot possibly be devoting her energies to effective and loving childrearing. It is precisely this kind of discord that Sharon Olds's collections of poetry force readers to tackle, and what they discover is a woman who not only revels in her sexual self but also foregrounds her concern for the long-term well-being of her daughter and her son. Since the publication of her first collection (*Satan Says*, 1980), the bulk of Olds's poetry moves through stages of women's lives, particularly those who become mothers. While some critics describe Olds's work as "pumped up experience to such a heightened level it no longer resembles any reality a reader wants to participate in" (Brown-Davidson 4), these critics point to the importance of identifying in Olds's poems iterations of the everyday language and concerns of contemporary American women. The power of poetry characterized as confessional has been its ability to circulate similarities of experiences to a wide range of readers. Olds's poetry offers a kind of testimonial to late-twentieth-century women of the importance of maintaining control over their sense of "self" amidst the pervasive narratives of intensive mothering and new momism.

One of the main concerns apparent in the collections of Olds's poetry is how a woman can balance receiving sexual gratification with raising healthy, happy children. In *The Dead and the Living* (1984), Olds offers an unyielding look at a woman who enjoys sex and raising children, in spite of cultural requirements that she subdue her sexual acts once she becomes a mother. Instead, Olds represents a woman deliriously happy with sex *and* mothering. Olds breaks up the second half of the collection, "Poems for the Living," into three subsections, "The Family" (13 poems), "The Men" (5 poems), and "The Children" (20 poems). While the sheer number of poems in the first and last subsections greatly outweighs those in the middle section, "The Men" remains the connecting section between a "family" and "children." Using graphic language of the body in all three sections, Olds confines specific discussions of the woman's sexual activity to "The Men," but when understood together, the poems in the final section depend upon the sexual fulfillment the woman finds in the middle section.

Within the middle section Olds places "New Mother," where she complicates readers' expectations of intensive mothering by redefining successful womanhood and mothering. The title brings to mind the blending of mother and child—the birth of "mother" and the death of "woman"—consistent with intensive mothering and the new momism, but Olds quickly contradicts these expectations by altering the actors. The poem begins, "A week after our child was born," (l. 1) privileging the contemporary heterosexual, nuclear family, but then moves to the next lines with "you cornered me in the spare room / and we sank down on the bed" (ll. 2–3). For the remainder of the poem, the child disappears, to be replaced by the male lover, with whom the woman of the poem continues to experience intense sexual pleasure. Olds's poem refuses to back down from the discord it strikes in redefining "new mother," and the woman refuses to deny her old self ("woman") to become a "mother," one devoted only to her children. Even as she notes, "All week I had smelled of milk, / fresh milk, sour," the woman "began to throb" (ll. 6–7) as her lover's kisses sexually stimulate her. This woman, perhaps because she is new to the role of mother, refuses to deny her own desires and live only for her child. She may have little control over lactation, but she can control her responses to the sexual stimulation of her lover. After remembering the intense pain she experienced during and after childbirth, she describes how her lover does not have sex with her, but, instead, waits for her to heal from the painful stitches. The tenderness exhibited between the two furthers the dissonance readers feel because this sexual stimulation occurs with a combination of fondness, desire, and restraint. Although her lover initiates sexual activity, the woman freely responds, and, perhaps, she responds in this way because she understands he will not harm her but will stay to protect and nurture her while she recovers from delivering a child vaginally. She exhibits and satisfies her own sexual desires; she keeps instead of loses these desires and their accompanying actions even as she becomes a mother.

Unashamedly and unabashedly, Olds's poem presents this redefinition of "new mother" for the readers, and many of us may wonder why a woman who embodies successful mothering and sexual desires can be considered a contradiction in the first place. After all, women typically must initially have sexual intercourse to become mothers, but, once becoming mothers, sex for pleasure becomes an impediment to fulfilling the requirements of narratives of contemporary motherhood. These sorts of activities move from selfless acts of procreation to selfish, irresponsible wastes of time. Within the context of American culture, we note the impact of Christianity in forming the "virgin" mother stereotype, examined at length by Cristina L. H. Traina, who explains that while many contemporary Christian religions "support passionate marital sexuality," they nonetheless limit these experiences to heterosexual couples and argue "sexuality is the divinely created and elemental urge of men and women toward each other for the purposes of psychic completion and procreation in marriage" (380). According to this analysis, sexual pleasure is really only a byproduct of a heterosexual relationship, and, by extension, most heterosexual American couples should be focusing on childrearing rather than childmaking.

Olds refuses to confine sexual activity to procreating by interweaving poems about a woman's sexual pleasure with a woman's celebration of and concern for her children in two of her later collections, *The Wellspring* (1995) and *Blood, Tin, Straw* (1999). In *The Wellspring*, Olds breaks up the collection into four unnamed sections and includes poems describing sex in sections two and four, flanking section three, devoted to tender memories of her children and the realization they are growing and will soon be leaving home. Sections two and four include the poems "Early Images of Heaven" (section 2) and "True Love" (section 4), both detailing a woman's thoughts on sexual activities with a man. In "Early Images of Heaven," the woman considers the design of penises, suggesting she has handled several, and her satisfaction with penises leads her to see her own godlike power:

> It amazed me that the shape of penises,
> their sizes, and angles, everything about them
> was the way I would have designed them if I had
> invented them.
> . . . .
> —I could not get over all this,
> the passion for it as intense in me
> as if it were made to my order, or my
> desire made to its order—as if I had
> known it before I was born, as if
> I remembered coming through it, like God
> the Father all around me. (ll. 1–4, 8–14)

The woman gives herself a tremendous amount of agency here, arguing early in the poem that penises were designed by her for her benefit. Importantly, she discusses not vaginal sex, but fellatio, in positive terms. She likes the way penises horizontally and vertically fill her mouth, and this description begins her connection with the Christian God.

Taking the penis, in this context, is akin to taking communion, of feeling oneness with God, and the poet extends this experience throughout the poem. Of course, the act of fellatio does not fit within most Christian guidelines of sex for the primary purpose of procreation. For the female speaker and, although absent, male, oral sex occurs for the purpose of sexual pleasure, not the kind of activity narratives of intensive mothering deem useful. The woman in the poem clearly finds that contemplating and handling penises have spiritual ramifications. As Vicki Feaver has suggested of other Olds poems, "through the body and its sexual acts, Olds seems to be saying, we can reach not only a transcendence that is equivalent to the transcendence claimed for religious experience but also the 'goodness' that is more usually attributed to religious than sexual practices" (151). The speaker of "Early Glimpses of Heaven" certainly experiences transcendence when contemplating penises, and she also understands the importance of seeking further meaning when she considers whether her desire and satisfaction with the shape of a penis has more to do with cultural constructions or biology, "as if it were made to order, or my / desire made to its order." Even as she shares her clear admiration of penises because they provide her with sexual pleasure, she notes how some microscopic element of her genetic memory came through her father's penis, thus potentially preprogramming her to acknowledge supremacy of the penis. This supremacy, then, may extend to larger patriarchal projects that privilege men over women. As a result, the poem takes readers on a circuitous journey of how social institutions converge with biology to construct gender roles, such as mothering, or sexual activities.

Olds's poems more fully interrogate and reject culturally prescribed roles in section four of *The Wellspring* with "True Love," which ends the collection and offers a sentimental and touching description of two heterosexual lovers after sex. The poem further complicates reserving sex for procreation and eliminating sex as an activity worthy of women who are mothers. The poem begins with the two lovers walking down the hallway to the bathroom "after making love" and "in / complete friendship" (ll. 2–3). These two, then, are not simply love-struck individuals giddy with post-sex passion. The friendship occurs because

> we are bound to each other
> with huge invisible threads, our sexes
> muted, exhausted, crushed, the whole
> body a sex—surely this
> is the most blessed time of my life,
> our children asleep in their beds, each fate
> like a vein of abiding mineral
> not discovered yet. (ll. 10–17)

As she sits on the toilet, she sees snow piled upon the window pane, and "I quietly call to you / and you come and hold my hand and I say / I cannot see beyond it. I cannot see beyond it" (ll. 23–25).

"True Love" exemplifies Olds's ability to question tenets of sexual propriety and the new momism by turning them upon one another. As the lovers accompany one another to the bathroom, for, perhaps, cleaning up and, certainly, urinating, the woman uses these base acts to level the potentially transcendent experience of sex. In this context, sex appears no more uncommon than urinating; they are both biological needs of the human body. The woman, however, complicates the comparison as she immediately returns to spiritual imagery, describing her life as "blessed," when she fondly remembers sex and thinks of her "children asleep in their beds." Just as quickly as sex becomes a basic and common element of her life, she moves sex into a powerful religious experience, considering the yet unexplored potential her children will make of their lives. Once again, Olds depicts the stereotypical heterosexual mother, comforted by the thought of her sleeping children and the hand of her male lover, who can face the unknown future, but this representation is only a component of the larger picture of a woman who has contented herself with sex so thoroughly that her "whole / body [is] a sex." The Western binary distinctions of man and woman have merged for the poem's speaker because she and her lover have satiated and spent themselves with sexual pleasure. We see a woman who easily and successfully shifts among various discourses of her life. She experiences no dissonance when she shifts among sex for pleasure, spiritual peace, and mothering. These elements, then, clearly exist as basic, everyday, and necessary yet simultaneously transcendent components of a woman's life, and she refuses to permit the rhetoric of intensive mothering to restrict her movement among these roles.

The woman's ability to navigate among these roles stems, in part, from being a healthy and holistic individual, and in part from understanding that the requirements of intensive mothering or the new momism—selfless devotion and sacrifice to the child—do nothing but create empty women who are left with no sense of self when their children leave home. "True Love" and the poem discussed earlier, "Early Glimpses of Heaven," flank section three in The Wellspring. Olds begins section three with "First Birth," in which the woman remembers her daughter, her first child, in terms of delivery and how "I felt as if / I was nothing, no one, I was everything to her, I was hers" (ll. 18–19). While these closing lines suggest intensive mothering—a woman who did not exist before she became a mother and exhibits selfless devotion to the child—the poems that follow in section three demonstrate that while the woman-as-mother is dedicated, she must also consider herself separate from the children. The poems in this section chronologically follow birth, youth, and young adulthood of the woman's daughter and son, with the early poems recounting such emotions as the woman's fears of her son's fevers and physical wounds. Near the end, she begins to encounter her children's young adulthood, and must confront, like all mothers, the impact of children leaving home.

In "Physics," for example, the daughter's physical and intellectual development remind the mother she must not allow herself to live only for and through her daughter. The poem shows the woman coming to terms with her identity formation throughout her life, and her discontent with the structure offers her the opportunity to reconstruct her notion of mothering. She reworks generations of mothering and separates herself from her mother's and her daughter's identities. After her daughter explains how, according to basic principles of physics, a 50-foot ladder, when thrown at the speed of light through a 20-foot barn, would remain, for a split second, completely inside the barn, the woman reflects

> I have thought her life was inside my life
> like that. When she reads the college catalogues, I
> look away and hum. I have not grown up
> yet, I have lived as my daughter's mother
> the way I had lived as my mother's daughter,
> inside her life. I have not been born yet. (ll. 22–27)

The act of reading college catalogues becomes the impetus for the woman-as-mother to reconsider how she has created or fallen into her life, and she discovers she has for too long lived as someone else's construction. She needs to define herself on her own terms because she soon will no longer be needed, indeed, be extant, if she continues to live as the individual defined by her daughter. Because "Physics" appears in section three and "True Love" closes the collection, the woman suggests she is finding new ways to define herself on her own terms through physical experiences with her lover, even as she maintains successful and sentimental connections to her children. She can succeed as a woman only by understanding the multiplicities of her desires as a mother and a sexual being.

This redefining of self and rejection of intensive mothering extends into *Blood, Tin, Straw* and appears vividly in the fifth and final section of the collection, "Light," when the poems "Sometimes" and "First Thanksgiving" appear on facing pages. By constructing the collection in this way, Olds offers her most forceful criticism of the danger inherent in separating sexual pleasure and mothering. While "First Thanksgiving" reflects on a woman's feelings as she expects her daughter's first return home from college, "Sometimes" engages in a treatise on a woman's feelings during what seem to be endless and repeated orgasms. The poem begins, "And then, sometimes, you have come many times / and you feel you can't stop, and he doesn't want you to stop," and it ends explaining,

if you were not sealed in bliss, feeling
complete, you could be exhausted, lost,
as if nothing would point you home as if
this were your home,
purposeless, as if each net
of undoing throbs were one pulse of what had
no beginning or end. (ll. 17–23)

Certainly, "Sometimes" exists as a powerful and active description of a female's sexual pleasure at the hands of a male whose purpose is to pleasure her endlessly. We see images of clitoral stimulation with lines ending in "grow" (l. 9) and "longer" (ll. 11, 13), and we see orgasms taking place with lines ending "you have come many times" (l. 1) and "you come again" (l. 12). After an orgasm, the woman finds herself merging with the man and the orgasm—"the center of pleasure" (l. 11)—as if she permits her identity to become pure, sexual fulfillment. She realizes, however, the danger in this kind of absorption, and because she is temporarily "sealed in bliss," she will not be "lost" in pleasure. She will be neither "directionless" nor "purposeless" in her formation of identity. As with "Making Love," the poem stops short of the woman identifying herself solely with sexual gratification, and, in the case of "Sometimes," relying only on gratification at the hands of a man. Finally, the throbs of the orgasm, described as having "no beginning or end," remind us again of Christian imagery, the doxology verses of glorifying the Father, Son, and Holy Ghost, "As it was in the beginning, is now and ever shall be, world without end. Amen. Amen." While the apparent endlessness of the orgasms encourages her to follow into what is similar to the purported safety of male-dominated Christian imagery, she separates the spiritual state of "bliss" from the physical happiness of "bliss," and, in doing so, the woman asserts her ability and decision to define herself and her experiences.

Her resolution to construct herself appears in the facing poem, "First Thanksgiving." This woman will neither be woman-as-sexual-pleasure nor woman-as-mother, but, rather, she will revel in her multiplicities. In "First Thanksgiving," she is looking forward to her daughter's return home from college and imagining what will take place. Thoughts of hugging her daughter lead the woman to remember late-night nursing and walking when her daughter was an infant. The woman understands her daughter no longer "need[s] love like that, she has / had it" (ll. 14–15), but the woman also knows "we will talk, / and then, when she's fast asleep, I'll exult to have her in that room again, / behind that door!" (ll. 15–18). Obviously, women who have mothered a child for almost two decades do not simply brush off those experiences and wipe away the satisfaction and relief of the child sleeping soundly in the same home, but the woman understands her gratitude and comfort will be private during her daughter's homecoming. This woman-as-mother is actively redefining the role of "mother" because she understands mothering, like mothers and children, must change over time. We see a significant development in the woman's sense of self from "Physics" to "First Thanksgiving," and primarily this change occurs because her daughter has gone from reading college catalogues to attending college. "First Thanksgiving" ends with the woman reflecting upon the parallel between mothering and watching bees she had caught as a child. As the bees left her hands, they "entered / the corrected curve of their departure" (ll. 23–24). Just like the bees, her daughter—the "vein of abiding mineral / not discovered yet" from "True Love"—determined her life's arc separate from her mother's life and hands.

In a similar fashion, we see the woman-as-woman separating herself from woman-as-mother through the course of the poems presented in Sharon Olds's collections. This woman determines her own sense of proper womanhood and mothering, but, importantly, she does not do so in some kind of isolation. Instead, she responds to and sometimes imitates contemporary notions of intensive mothering and the new momism. Certainly she cannot possibly attempt to live her life "off the grid" of mothering. Like the bees, she, too, tries different arcs of narratives of womanhood and mothering, and we see how tempting she finds the narrative of intensive mothering as she alternates between subsuming her identity beneath that of her children's and remaking her identity on her own terms. When considering her own desires, she typically does so by asserting her sexual side, discovering pleasure through activity with a male lover. The woman in Sharon Olds's poetry finds pleasure in her roles as both mother and lover, and she experiences no conflicts in performing both roles. In fact, it is ultimately the lover role that permits her to shift from a woman whose children live at home and compose a significant portion of her daily life to a woman whose children live elsewhere and return only for temporary visits. Olds's poetry offers readers an important response to intensive mothering and the new momism and, in doing so, urges women to consider their own paths to successful womanhood.

Notes to Chapter 15

1 For discussions about Olds as a sexually explicit poet, see, for example, Alicia Ostriker's "I Am (Not) This: Erotic Discourse in Bishop, Olds, and Stevens," *The Wallace Stevens Journal* 19.2 (1995): 234–54; Calvin Bedient's review of *The Father*, "Sentencing Eros," *Salmagundi* 97 (1993): 169–81; and Terri Brown-Davidson, "The Belabored Scene, the Subtlest Detail: How Craft Affects Heat in the Poetry of Sharon Olds and Sandra McPherson," *The Hollins Critic* 29.1 (1992): 1–10. For discussions about Olds as a poet who is a daughter, see, for example, Brian Dillon, "'Never Having Had You, I Cannot Let You Go': Sharon Olds's Poems of a Father–Daughter Relationship," *Literary Review* 37.1 (1993): 108–19; and Kristin Lindgren, "Birthing Death: Sharon Olds's *The Father* and the Poetics of the Body," *Teaching Literature and Medicine*, ed. Anne Hunsaker Hawkins and Marilyn Chandler McEntyre (New York: MLA, 2000) 260–66; and as a mother, Elizabeth M. Johnson, "Mothering in the Poems of Sharon Olds: The Choice Not to Abuse," *Journal of the Association for Research on Mothering* 4.2 (2002): 156–72.

2 Ostriker identifies this culture as one "in which sexual pleasure is divided from procreation, and motherhood is sentimentally honored but institutionally disempowered and without status" (245).

Works Cited

Brown-Davidson, Terri. "The Belabored Scene, the Subtlest Detail: How Craft Affects Heat in the Poetry of Sharon Olds and Sandra McPherson." *The Hollins Critic* 29.1 (1992): 1–9.

Douglas, Susan J., and Meredith W. Michaels. *The Mommy Myth: The Idealization of Motherhood and How It Has Undermined Women*. New York: Free Press, 2004.

Feaver, Vicki. "Body and Soul: The Power of Sharon Olds." *Contemporary Women's Poetry: Reading/Writing/Practice*. Ed. Alison Mark and Deryn Rees-Jones. Hampshire, UK: Palgrave, 2000. 140–56.

Hays, Sharon. *The Cultural Contradictions of Motherhood*. New Haven: Yale University Press, 1996.

Olds, Sharon. *Blood, Tin, Straw*. 1999. New York: Knopf, 2005.

——. *The Dead and the Living*. 1983. New York: Knopf, 2005.

——. *The Wellspring*. 1995. New York: Knopf, 2004.

Ostriker, Alicia. "I Am (Not) This: Erotic Discourse in Bishop, Olds, and Stevens." *The Wallace Stevens Journal* 19.2 (1995): 234–54.

Traina, Cristina L. H. "Maternal Experience and the Boundaries of Christian Sexual Ethics." *Signs: Journal of Women in Culture and Society* 25.2 (2000): 369–405.

16

(Grand)mothering "Children of the Apocalypse": A Post-postmodern Ecopoetic Reading of Margaret Laurence's *The Diviners* | BY DI BRANDT

What does the prospect of imminent cultural collapse in an ecologically stressed environment have to do with mothers and mothering? Well, everything, according to Margaret Laurence's brilliant 1974 novel, *The Diviners*, arguably the most important, most unusual, most prescient Canadian novel of the twentieth century. Unlike the first few novels in the Manawaka series, which scrutinized mothers and mothering in the domestic cauldron of the modern nuclear family and mid-century small-town Canadiana, *The Diviners* blows the subject of mothering wide open. Gone is the family kitchen, the family living room, the hearth; gone is the sustaining local community, such as it was; gone is the family as such, even in its nuclear configuration. The mother here is a single, isolated figure, living a quiet, modest professional and contemplative life in a rural setting not far from Toronto; her closest companions are the river that flows by her cottage, the weeds in her neglected but beloved garden, the birds that scratch her roof every morning, a few scattered neighbours, and one long-time, long-distance pen pal friend, Ella. Morag Gunn, descendant of Scots-Presbyterian immigrants to the Prairies turned novelist, earns her living by her wits, intuition, hard work, frugality, and vision. She conceived her daughter, Pique, disreputably, by mainstream Canadian social mores of the 1970s, in a temporary though passionate transracial affair with a Métis man, Jules Tonnerre, an itinerant musician, after walking out on a secure and "respectable," that is, white and white-collar, and upwardly mobile, marriage. Morag is in the throes of menopause, that heightened moment when women of all races say goodbye to their reproductive powers, and if they are mothers, also to their children leaving home, or at least, their care. In this heightened moment of "the change," Morag experiences profoundly mixed emotions. Some of these emotions are the predictable ones of grief at the loss of a significant life phase with its particular challenges and powers, and a combined fear for the child's safety in the big world, along with pride and admiration for her precocious, energetic youthfulness. But there is something more here in Morag's understanding, something unprecedented and terrible in our culture, a sense of dread about the future she is launching her daughter into. "Children of the apocalypse" is how the children now see themselves, she thinks with that same mixture of guilt, fear, and anxiety many of us feel now, facing our uncertain and increasingly ecocidal future (12): "My grand-children will say *What means Fish?* Peering through the goggle-eyes of their gasmasks. Who will tell old tales to children then? Pique used to say *What is a Buffalo?* How many words and lives will be gone when they say *What means Leaf?*" (187). But the novel is after all not as grim as this. It can also be read as an uplifting story of feminist liberation from the stultifying post-war social roles of the 1950s and 1960s into a successful, empowered erotic, maternal, artistic, and visionary life; as the recuperation of a sense of indigenous cultural and land practices, and in the process making reparative gestures in the ongoing unjust relations between settler and Indigenous communities in postcolonial Canada; and as an ecofeminist manifesto of what needs to be done to mitigate (or even simply face) the negative consequences of the environmental crisis. Recuperating (grand)maternal agency and power in a culture where mothers and grandmothers have been typically disregarded, dishonoured, and frequently silenced is, according to Laurence, central to meeting these momentous cultural challenges of our time—it is a message environmentalists and lawmakers of our time might heed more thoughtfully! Here I want to list some of the multiple themes of this large, sprawling novel which address these urgent environmental concerns, and highlight the centrality of maternal thinking, agency, and influence to each of them.

Recovering (Grand)Maternal Agency

Reclaiming feminist and maternal agencies in a masculinist culture comes at a high cost, according to *The Diviners*. In the early 1970s, such reclamation, where even possible, involved high-risk social rebellion, usually leading to separation or divorce and loss of financial security and social community for women and their children. Or it meant losing their children to their ex-husbands, who usually had more financial means to defend their paternal interests, if they so chose. Whether things have gotten easier or harder for young women 30 and 40 years later, after several decades of feminist progress and the anti-feminist backlash and the globalization of hyper-capitalism of the 1990s, and in the face of increased environmental anxieties of our present decade, is moot, and one of the themes of this essay. Feminist liberation in the 1970s and 1980s also involved extensive self-scrutiny and politicized analyses of maternal subjectivity and relations from many angles, as was well theorized by Adrienne Rich (*Of Woman Born*), Marianne Hirsch (*The Mother/Daughter Plot*) and Mary O'Brien (*The Politics of Reproduction*), to name but a few of the key texts of the era. This is the kind of work Laurence performed in the earlier Manawaka novels in the intense examination of several different kinds of families and several versions of self-empowerment, involving in each case the strengthening of maternal ties and valorization of maternal consciousness and nurturing behaviours in women (whether biologically mothers or not), while at the same time prying women gently loose from (often maternally inflected) subservient subjectivities and situations. One thinks of Hagar Shipley's gradual easing into joy and appreciation (reciprocally, both of and by others) after her life of hardship, first as an exploited daughter, then as an oppressed wife, and later as an exhausted, and increasingly bitter, overworked single mother in *The Stone Angel*, anxiously cared for by her loyal if plodding son, Marvin, and daughter-in-law, Doris. We remember Rachel Cameron, the sexually frustrated single woman schoolteacher protagonist in *A Jest of God*, who learns sexual pleasure and psychic independence while continuing to care for her demanding aging mother. And there's Stacey Cameron, who learns how to be a better mother to her growing children and even, paradoxically, a better wife to her unimaginative husband through the pursuit of erotic and spiritual fulfillment outside the strictures of her 1960s housewife role and marriage, in *The Fire Dwellers*.

Having laid out multiple dynamics of primary empowerment for women through self-scrutiny, imaginative exploration, and spiritual/erotic liberation in her previous Manawaka novels, Laurence is interested now, in *The Diviners*, in exploring the powerful potentiality of mothering in the public sense, tracing motherhood on the symbolic level of artist, prophet, and visionary, and transgenerationally and archetypally, as elder, grandmother, wise woman to the culture—though she does not gloss over the ongoing hardships of single mothers who give up spiritually stultifying marital security and social respectability for professional and imaginative empowerment,

nor the hardships of a previous generation of women, like the hapless, ineffectual, obese Prin, tragically ruined Piquette, and her own dead mother,
trapped in other versions of restricted womanhood, none of whom made it
to grandmotherly status. She is also interested in the lives of women who
choose not to have children, like Fan Brady, the eccentric exotic dancer, and
Eva Winkler, who can't have children of her own due to a botched abortion
after a teenage pregnancy in an abusive, incestuous relationship with her
father. She does not explore lesbian or bisexual relationships in the novel
as such, though there are several intimate friendships between women that
would clearly rate along the "lesbian continuum" of erotic intimacies between women, in Adrienne Rich's influential phrase (1994). The road to
elderhood involves all the stages of sexual liberation and self-definition
explored in the previous novels, but again, blown wide open—perhaps not
as wide as today's libertarian options would suggest, but very experimen-
tal compared to her previous novels and the mores of the time. For Morag,
sexual discovery ranges from marriage (with Brooke, happy at first but stultifying as she becomes more independent and sure of her career aspirations), an adulterous affair (with Dan McRaith), casual sex with a stranger
(Chas), and a lifelong erotic friendship and shared child (with Jules). In all
of these configurations, erotic fulfillment and satisfying companionship far
outweigh questions of stability or permanence or even exclusivity. Morag
eventually develops a code of ethical sexual behaviour which balances the
interests of freedom and social responsibility around the question of maternity: after a frightening episode with the psychotic (or at least seriously
misogynist) Chas and brief pregnancy scare, she decides she will never again
sleep with any man whose child she "couldn't bear to bear" (352). There was
a brief time in the 1970s and 1980s when improved birth control methods
and easy access to abortion appeared to "free" women from the risk of unwanted pregnancy, thus putting them on more "equal" footing with men socially and professionally. Since then, the health risks of these new methods
of birth control have proved to be high, as well as overreaching: in a few
short decades we have gone, through widespread chemical proliferation,
from fear of pregnancy to fear of infertility and ovarian cancer and other
health problems for women, not to mention the water systems and animals
and fish. Meanwhile, the reproductive technologies that have sprung up to
deal with the new problem of infertility seem likewise more interested in
corporate-based profit and power than in enhancing the quality of women's
lives and reproductive experiences (see Maria Mies's overview in her essay
"New Reproductive Technologies: Sexist and Racist Implications" 1993).
Laurence was never among those cheering for the absolute divorce of eroti-

cism from maternity that has been promoted in certain feminist circles as much as in the techno-scientific realm. Nor was she ever in favour of taming or controlling the wild aspect of sexuality and reproduction for the purposes of power over them. In *The Diviners*, as in every book she ever wrote, Laurence is clear in her defence of women's self-determination in every aspect of their lives; but she is equally clear in her respect for the larger life processes we are part of, and sexuality in both its erotic and reproductive aspects is something to be surrendered to with awe and in ecstasy, on the one hand, while at the same time carefully, lovingly, cautiously, respectfully managed (as opposed to absolutely controlled), on the other. Abortion, also, is not to be taken lightly; it has a major impact on women's lives, as well as men's and of course the children's, and in Laurence's view is best avoided, if possible. (However, she is among the first to acknowledge the numerous kinds of situations where abortion might be necessary and unavoidable, most notably, where pregnancy was the tragic result of sexual violence, as in the case of poor Eva Winkler.)

Having taken us through quite a wild range of sexualities in Morag's younger life in The Diviners, Laurence is able to bring a sense of wide experience and burgeoning wisdom to bear upon the present moment of the novel, in Morag's middle age, at 47 years. The novel is more concerned, here, with the dynamics of professional success, public life, and menopause than with domestic relations as such (though Laurence never uses the word "menopause"; it was not yet fashionable when she wrote the novel, nor would she want to have evoked the more medical and even pathological associations the term is often associated with nowadays). This is the grand liminal moment in a woman's life when she loses her reproductive sexual power in exchange for experience and hopefully wisdom, and if she's lucky enough to be situated in a socially supportive community, elevated elder status. For Morag, the moment is a difficult one, as it tends to be for women in this culture, even if they have achieved a high level of success in their personal and professional lives. This is because women frequently experience social isolation and even denigration as they move from primary reproductive and caretaking situations into symbolic mothering and aging, bereft of the acknowledgments and consolations of traditional womanly elderhood such as a lively community of nearby children and grandchildren, and acknowledgment of advisory status in managing the public good. For Morag, who is at the height of her powers as a novelist and visionary, having learned how to "divine" stories the way her old friend Royland, "Old Man of the River," divines for water, sensitively, perceptively, intuitively, and enjoying considerable success and fame, it is a moment of shock, at the

loneliness and emptiness of a transition that should have come with high
social honour and gratitude and affection. She is often struck with black
moods, the rising up of Morag Dhu, the "Black Celt," in her. The surprise
turn in the novel—and this is what makes it so prescient for our time—is
Laurence's interpretation of this blackness not so much as a personal short-
coming, or repressed memory, or other kind of correctable or diagnosable
personal problem, as in previous novels, but rather, as an accurate, perceptive, emotional response to the present moment, gazing at the world around
her with her visionary, motherly, and grandmotherly writer's eyes, contemplating its spiritual impoverishment and the spectre of hard times ahead for
her daughter and the generations to come (if indeed there will be a world for
them at all). This is how the novel becomes a portrait of our time, a
post-humanist, post-psychological eco-grandmaternal-feminist-spiritual-
socialist-environmentalist manifesto, a precursor to the post-postmodern
era we are now so rapidly entering, a warning about the formidable existen-
tial challenges we now face in the environmentally burdened world, and
sage advice about where to go and what to do next.

Connecting Morag's black mood, her visionary sense of dread, with her
Celtic ancestry through the nickname Morag Dhu (given her by her Scot-
tish lover, Dan McRaith) adds an interesting historical resonance to this
moment, evoking as it does the eclipsed history of two other troubled (and
doomed) civilizations in her ancestry, the Highland Scots and the Celts before them, visionary cultures that honoured the feminine as divine power
and cosmic principle as *The Diviners* also, implicitly, exhorts us to do. In
this way, Laurence is able to elevate Morag's social and subject position to
mythical status without having to gloss over the harsh realism of a palpable
lack of community and respect for aging women and its depressing effect on
them. She is also able to allude to the possibility of cultural apocalypse with
a certain tragic grandeur, without simply caving in to despair or dread.

How is apocalyptic gloom a (grand)maternal and visionary act? Because, filtered through the detailed consciousness of (grand)maternity—the
extensive, creative, humble, even sacrificial commitment to caring, nurturing, growing, and giving away that mothering and grandmothering is—the
environmental crisis seems profoundly misguided, foolish, and avoidable.
"The end of the world" (as we know it now) will not be a fire-and-brimstone
punitive act from Nobodaddy God, or capricious uncaring Nature; nor will
it be an act of betrayal or limitation of a faltering planet's. It will be, merely,
tragically, the consequences of human wrongdoing against one another,
and against the earth, that has given us so much rich abundance and which
we have exploited with such carelessness, callousness, and greed in return,

"in a world now largely dedicated to Death" (379). This is the insight gleaned by Morag in her long hours of "river watching," worrying over the safety of the birds on her roof, and the fish in the river, delighting perversely (and prophetically) in her overgrown weed (and potentially wild herb) garden, "of amazing splendours, in which God did all the work" (186); worrying and fussing over the safety and destiny of her young daughter, Pique. Meanwhile, she is heroically engaged in rewriting the Western literary heritage in her novels and short fiction, including in the "memoir" that becomes in a self-reflexive closing gesture the present novel, *The Diviners*, so as to challenge most of the basic assumptions of modernity and to pave the way for radically revising our approach to survival and pleasure, to life on earth, in the present and future.

Recovering "Indigenosity"

I am borrowing the term "indigenosity" from American Mayan writer and shaman Martín Prechtel, who argues, in a series of extraordinary books about his life with the Mayans of Guatemala, that what we have lost, in modernity, is a deep, intimate connection to the earth that all ancient cultures intuitively understood and celebrated, both ritually and in their land practices (*The Secrets of the Talking Jaguar*; *The Disobedient Daughter of the Sun*; *Long Life, Honey in the Heart*, etc.). His aim is to teach us, the citizens of the modern "Land of the Dead," the traditional, indigenous "ways of the Living," still profoundly understood and practised by contemporary Mayans, so that we may mend our culturally and environmentally suicidal and murderous ways before it is too late (*Secrets* 281). What Prechtel means by "indigenous" is an intimate erotic, physical, and spiritual connection to the earth as a living, breathing, sentient, spirit-filled body, our Mother, who deserves and requires our frugal and grateful respect and homage, as do human and animal mothers who enact her creativity and life-giving generosity in the species realm (*Disobedient* 109–25). This was once the spiritual practice of cultures across the globe. We have vestigial memories of a maternally imaged, intimate relation to nature even in contemporary industrialized monoculture, in the figure of "Mother Nature" who still regularly makes appearances in our public lexicon, most often nowadays in relation to the weather, though with very little evidence of the kind of homage traditionally accorded her and her species avatars. The exploitation and enslavement of Indigenous peoples and destruction of their ancestral mother- and earth-honouring, spiritually based land practices was not accidental to the rise of modernity, as is abundantly clear to anyone who cares to look at its origins;

it was—and, horrifically, continues to be, around the world—both its fuel and foundation. As Carolyn Merchant and others have insightfully documented, the invention of modern "science," which accompanied the rise of modernity and is closely allied with the development of technology and expansionist globalizing capitalism, was based on the suppression of traditional indigenous ways, most infamously in its adoption of Inquisition-style interrogation methods to "extract Nature's secrets from her," in Francis Bacon's influential investigative formula, the way the Church extracted confessions from women under torture (Merchant ch. 7). Correcting the imbalances and excesses of modernity therefore has to include a long, hard look at the history of colonialism and the place of Indigenous peoples in it. We must consider ways to make restitution to their descendants, and allow their deep traditional knowledge of ecological land practices to inform and transform our present age in the direction of sustainability. Here is biologist Vandana Shiva's similar description of traditionalist, women-centred land practices in India, now being similarly radically eroded under the banner of "progress," and her call to return to indigenous, and maternally informed, knowledges and ways:

> As a source of life, nature was venerated as sacred, and human evolution was measured in terms of the human capacity to interact in harmony with her rhythms and patterns, intellectually and emotionally. In the final analysis, the ecological crisis is rooted in the mistaken belief that human beings are not part of the democracy of nature's life, that they stand *apart* from and *above* nature. ("Decolonizing" 265)

Shiva, significantly for our context here, cites colonialist seventeenth-century English scientist and governor of the New England Company Robert Boyle's observation that "the veneration, wherewith men are imbued for what they call nature [as a kind of goddess], has been a discouraging impediment to the empire of man over the inferior creatures of God" (266). Breaking up the ritual earth- (and mother- and animal- and plant-) honouring practices of First Nations people was therefore a central strategy in the colonization of First Nations people and wildlife and land. Lakota cultural historian Paula Gunn Allen adds to this point the insight that it was women's influential social position in traditional First Nations cultures that especially offended the European explorers and led them to become their particular target. According to Allen, "the physical and cultural genocide of American Indian tribes is and was mostly about patriarchal fear of gynocracy" (3).

In *The Diviners*, it is the troubled Tonnerre family that represents the inheritance of colonial exploitation upon First Nations and Métis people in Canada. But in the midst of its ravages, which include the tragic life and death of Piquette and her children in a house fire, the Tonnerres demonstrate remarkable gifts. Jules is both a great lover to Morag (though only sporadic father to their child Pique), and talented, visionary itinerant singer-songwriter. Pique eventually chooses to return to the land of her Métis ancestors, to Galloping Mountain, blessed by Jules and his song to Pique's deceased aunt, and the "land that holds her name," as the song goes. It is not Morag's land; she is after all a child of the settler-pioneers who drove Canada's First Nations peoples onto reservations and road allowances. She is not invited along on this trip "home." Neil ten Kortenaar and Frank Davey have criticized *The Diviners* for proposing a dishonest atonement for Morag's (and Laurence's) colonial settler guilt by having a child with a Métis man, thereby acquiring Canadian indigenosity for her lineage by inauthentic means (ten Kortenaar 28; Davey 41). I disagree with this argument. Besides the questionable implication that sexual union and marriage are false or devious or dishonest means of social location—after all, it was practically the only avenue of affiliation and advancement allowed to women for many centuries—ten Kortenaar and Davey imply that Morag and Laurence conflate racial identification and ethical cultural and land practices in simplistic and essentialist ways, which is certainly not the case. Nor is her "union" with Jules an easy or comfortable one. It is erotically and spiritually satisfying, but only because both are relentlessly honest about their limitations and needs, their mutual love for nature and the body, and their relative roles in the bigger historical stories they are part of, including its analogous heroisms and resonant affiliations, as well as its oppositional hostilities and politically problematic, separate yet entwined legacies; it is a friendship negotiable only in a few brief and sporadic, if transcendent, moments. Nor is her relationship with Pique, their daughter, an easy one. It is fraught with intense intergenerational and cross-racial tensions and anxieties, and leads to a fairly wide separation between them at the end of the novel, precisely on the question of cultural heritage and family affiliation and sense of place, and "home." "Why did you have me?" is their daughter Pique's anguished cry, experiencing her first violent encounter with racism in early adolescence. Canadian Innu critic Kristina Fagan hears her question as a protest against the problems of mixed-race children in this culture, which Morag has so blithely brought her daughter into (253)—though, after all, not without her Métis father Jules' assent or without first-hand knowledge of and detailed attention to these problems. Her question resonates perhaps even more with Brooke's cynical question to Morag earlier, when she was asking him for a child: "Does it seem like the kind of world, to you," Brooke asks coldly, over a martini, "to bring children into?" To which Morag's silent reply is this:

> To that, there is no answer. None. No, it does not seem like the kind of world, etcetera. But she wants children all the same. Why? Something too primitive to be analyzed? Something which needs to proclaim itself, against all odds? Or only the selfishness of wanting someone born of your flesh, someone related to you? (266)

It would be a misreading of the novel to take Pique's side in the conversation, as many readers are tempted to do, believing, with Pique, that Morag's wish for a child is wrong or selfish or misguided, in these (and many other) circumstances. Laurence is highly sensitive to Pique's dilemma as a mixed-race child in a postcolonial country with lingering racist attitudes and practices. She is also deeply sensitive to the dilemma of parents trying to invest in the future in dire circumstances. But to suggest that Pique's moment of rage and despair here is definitive for the novel would be to take Brooke's side in his argument with Morag earlier, and to promote his kind of self-hating, coldly despairing, and ultimately selfish view of history, where it's better to party and quit than to keep investing in the future, despite the odds, and to work as hard as possible to improve things in the present and for the generations to come. (It is also to buy too quickly into mother blame as an answer to social ills that are not of mothers' making, but indeed, stem from the suppression of maternal interests and power.)

Morag's writerly preoccupations as an adult woman are, after all, about nothing if not the recovery a more spiritually—and maternally—based appreciation for the natural world in the context of modernity gone wrong, and the healing of her own colonial (but also displaced, exilic) settler heritage, and in the process thinking about sustainable ways of living that honour the wild freedom of all living beings, including especially the dignity of First Nations people, history, and ways of being. Like A-Okay and Maudie, her young "back-to-the-land" urban hippie neighbours, Morag has left the city to live closer to nature; like them, she worries about sustainability. She is less optimistic about the future than they are, but maybe more far-sighted. While they seem to believe in the large-scale practicability of their local gardening experiment, she darkly foresees a time when we may have to go back to wild herb gathering, after our overreaching "progress" has, perhaps catastrophically, failed us (432). She is also less invested in rationalist approaches to the environmental crisis than they are (or to childrearing, for that matter, that other dear investment in the future): she is more aware of the larger historical and biological forces that shape us, whose powers we must either obey or confront heroically. "One of the disconcerting aspects of middle age was the realization that most of the crises which happened to other people also ultimately happened to you" (63). Morag's repeated reflection on "the terrible vulnerability of parents" (386) undercuts the conventional hierarchical sense of the parent's power over the child with a reminder of the deep responsibility to the future inherent in the privilege of raising children (but at the same time, stops short of the kind of parental and especially mother blame for problems not of their making and far beyond their capacity to fix that is fashionable in some circles). As a result, her consciousness takes a much deeper, darker, profounder spiritual turn than we have seen with characters in Laurence's previous novels. Learning to "divine" for stories not only means trusting in the intuitive creative process, it means casting into the past and future, into earth and sky, into self and other, for help in confronting the monstrous aspects of the ecocrisis now looming before us, that is of our own human making and yet seems too big and hopeless to turn around. It means trusting, along with Lear, in another time—at the other end of the secular and often cynical experiment called modernity—that beyond the long reach of human folly and self-destructiveness and error, "there's a divinity that shapes our ends, rough-hew them how we will." Morag's glimpse of a great blue heron above the river at McConnell's Landing represents such a divining moment:

> A low unhurried takeoff, the vast wings spreading, the slender elongated legs gracefully folding up under the creature's body. Like a pterodactyl, like an angel, like something out of the world's dawn. The soaring and measured certainty of its flight. Ancient-seeming, unaware of the planet's rocketing changes. The sweeping serene wings of the thing, unknowing that it was speeding not only towards individual death but probably towards the death of its kind. (380)

The moment inspires awe in Morag, and also mobilizes her to get back to work, to take more of the kind of visionary action that is her writerly gift: to continue to resist, heroically, her impulse to hide (to find an "island") from the great spectre of our times, the looming possibility of mass extinction under the burden of our technological and chemical violations of natural processes, to invest imaginatively and practically in the continued evolution of our species and the world toward greater spiritual wisdom and caring, for and with the earth that is our home.

Rewriting the Terms of Modernity

Growing up on the wrong side of the tracks as an orphaned descendant of ousted refugee Highland Scots, and identifying considerably with the simi-larly denigrated subject position of her Métis schoolmate and neighbour Jules Tonnerre, Morag began questioning her formal education, that is, her induction into the terms of modernity, at a young age. Writing a Christmas rhyme in a grade-six Sunday school class, she creatively transplants the story of Christ's birth into the familiar Canadian prairie climate: "Despite the cold and wintry blast, / To Bethlehem they came at last," etc. (89). Her teacher, Mrs. McKee, admonishes her for geographical incorrectness: "it was a Far Eastern desert country, dear, so they wouldn't have a wintry blast, would they?" (90). Her face aflame with shame, Morag quickly rewrites the poem, but her belief in honouring local landscapes in our storytelling, even when we're telling stories that may have originated in another place and time, and indeed, honouring local landscapes as one of the main functions of storytelling, remains with her into adulthood and throughout her writ-ing career. The American philosopher David Abram has proposed that the tragic divorce of story from place, which is characteristic of modernity, had its origin in the invention of the alphabet: alphabetic writing made it pos-sible for language and story to become portable and abstracted from bush and tree and stone, from the earth as local geography, as "home." The pos-sibility of invading other landscapes and imposing a foreign story on them (and simultaneously fostering a perpetual sense of exile) arose out of this same divorce of story from place, from a local, embodied relation to place (197). *The Diviners* is a beautiful example of reconnecting language to place, in the way that Abram calls for, in order to resist imperialist actions, and to "reinhabit place," in ways that could lead us back to a joyful, sustainable relationship to the earth, its Indigenous peoples, its animals and habitat. A related incident is the humorous childish misinterpretation of the French words of the Canadian national anthem in Morag's elementary schoolroom as "Teara da nose ah you" (76), a bawdy subversion of nationalist earnest-ness by reducing its military aspirations to the rough and tumble of school-yard politics: perhaps if we did this more often, laugh at the pugnacious and childish nature of most territorial disputes, we could avoid some of the large-scale horrors of modern war. Many years later, the adult writer Morag re-asks the question of home and nation in a trip to the land of her ancestors, the Sutherlanders, and en route realizes that it's not necessary to go there after all. "Adoption ... is possible," she reflects (458), both in the personal and geopolitical sense: she has not been as fatherless as she supposed, having been so lovingly if eccentrically cared for by Christie Logan, the Manawaka Nuisance Grounds keeper (240); and she has found a home in the New World despite difficult beginnings. In grade nine, another teacher, Miss Melrose, tries to explain the term "pathetic fallacy," or why we should never ascribe human or spiritual traits to our nonhuman fellow beings in the natural world. "What if Miss Melrose is wrong, though, just in that one way?" Morag wonders. "Not that clouds or that would have human feelings, but that the trees and river and even this bridge might have their own spirits? Why shouldn't they?" (140). She also questions the 1960s women's fashion rule against mixing blue and green. "What about sky and grass," she muses (125), again choosing to value nature as exemplary rather than something to be corrected or overcome, in the tradition of the English Romantics but even more so in the rich tradition of Indigenous peoples, the venerable First Nations of her adopted homeland.

At the same time, Morag is developing her own narrative poetics under the compelling influence of Christie's mythical storytelling and inspired rants, which draw on the ancient Gaelic epic tradition, interwoven with contemporary local realisms with a decidedly ecopoetic slant. Morag retreats to her room after Christie's late-night performances to write down her own female-centred version of the myths, and to practise epic and ecopoetic narrative techniques of her own. In particular, she is inspired by Christie's sense of the grandeur of the human spirit, and the heroism (and often ignominy) of human events and actions. "Oh what a piece of work is man oh what a bloody awful piece of work is man," intones Christie, grandiosely echoing Hamlet, "enough to scare the pants off you when you come to think of it the opposite is also true hm hm" (99). Morag is inspired by his sense of generosity and gratitude in telling the stories—though she doesn't find out until many years later, from Prin on her deathbed, just how generous his stories of her own deceased father were: how he transformed the young, frightened Colin Gunn into a courageous hero as a gift to her, to inspire her (224). In Christie's eyes the Nuisance Grounds become happy hunting grounds for reusable items and the sacred burial place for the unwanted detritus of the townspeople, sometimes with shameful and even tragic aspects, such as the discarded foetus wrapped in newspaper he once found. "By their christly bloody garbage shall ye know them in their glory, is what I'm saying to you, every saintly mother's son," he intones, high on spirits of both the alcoholic and inspirational kind (85). *The Diviners* is our first Canadian novel about menopause; it is also our first novel about garbage, a timely topic that will only get more urgent as we move into the twenty-first century, as we come to face the inevitable troublesome consequences of our profligate and

careless use of natural resources and increasing levels of chemical toxins and plastic junk littering our beautiful earth: the coincidence of these
themes is significant. Christie's point is that garbage is not just garbage:
that we ought to value what we discard because it is, from an ecopoetic point
of view, just as important as what we consume—more so, even, because it
becomes the compost and legacy for future generations. His project is akin
to Morag's later writerly project of gathering in the unseemly aspects of our
cultural heritage, such as modernity's denigration of mothering and grandmothering and Canada's colonialist actions against First Nations and Métis peoples, and devaluing of indigenous knowledges and practices, such
as a more intimate, loving, humble land practice, and transforming them
through remorse, rectification, and adoption. How long will it take to gather
and clean up the detritus of chemical and electromagnetic toxins we are
proliferating upon the earth and our own bodies and psyches now? It is a
question that must fill us with grief, for there seems to be no end to it. How
much time do we have to make these radical changes to our cultural and land
practices before it's too late?

Laurence's intertextual dialogue with *The Tempest* and the ongoing postcolonial debate, initiated by Martinician poet and playwright Aimé Césaire's
negritude adapation *Une Tempête* in Paris in the 1960s, about the implied
racial slur in Shakespeare's depiction of Caliban and his mother, Sycorax,
as half animal, half human, reaches its culmination in Morag's novel, *The
Diviners*, which she finishes writing, in a neat self-reflexive gesture on Laurence's part, as we finish reading it. But this question is explored in multiple ways in Morag's other fictions as well, most explicitly in *Prospero's Child*.
Here we see a beautiful feminist as well as postcolonial inversion of *The
Tempest*'s imperialist hierarchies: the authoritarian and aggrieved deposed
duke has been deposed even further to the station of Nuisance Grounds
keeper—or we might say, promoted, in the ecologically oriented vision of
The Diviners, wherein Christie becomes Christ, sacrificial hero and sin-
eater. Miranda, the pure innocent daughter, has been liberated to become
the not-so-innocent, self-possessed, lusty Morag. And Caliban is Jules:
shaman artist and, ironically, surprisingly, given his frequent absences
from the novel, its most faithful, though decidedly unpatriarchal, father.
And Sycorax, the witch-mother, has vanished from the story altogether—
unless it is Morag herself who takes her place, as grandmother-elder of the
runaway 16-year-old Pique, the middle-aged, grieving Morag Dhu who has
let her hair down, literally, by letting it grow long, and spends much of her
day in deep communion with nature, half wild, smoking cigarettes, "river
watching." If Caliban is half animal, half human, so are we all, *The Divin-*

ers suggests.[1] Honouring our animalness is not regressive; it is the recognition that may save us from ecological ruin. Mastery of nature is not, after all, a virtue, given our complete dependence upon nature's bounty. Humility and gratitude could take us much further. People think you can't change the past, Morag reflects, but it's not true, people go back and change the past all the time, by revisiting and rewriting our histories, the stories we make of them (70). It's what we have to do in order to keep an ethical relation with our less than pristine human history, in order to not have to repeat past and present atrocities and errors, but rather release them into grief and creative transformation. The river, as Morag poetically observes, "flows both ways."[2] Like Christie, and like Jules too, Morag believes in mythical elevation of the ordinary, not in order to deny the worth of the daily, the historical, but to maximize its creative and even heroic potential in us, so that we can be psychically mobilized to rise to the formidable challenges of our time. Morag's friend Royland, "Old Man of the River," assumes grandeur in her eyes as a diviner, finder of water, companion, and bearer of news. Jules becomes the singer of songs that can help restore right relation to the land and to her Métis heritage, for their daughter, Pique, and for future generations, if not for Morag, who must struggle for her own right relation to her small piece of earth and water at McConnell's Landing. We are, we must all become, artists, singers, visionaries, scavengers, Nuisance Grounds keepers, diviners now, the novel suggests, each in our small corner of the world, drawing spiritual strength from the bountiful, struggling earth, and the powerful "feminine life principle," in Vandana Shiva's resonant phrase (*Staying Alive* 14), that brings forth such rich and variant life forms and is now so overburdened by our technologies. I am obviously disagreeing with Christian Bök's negative assessment of the "oracular" and "sybilline" aspects of Morag's vision in his 1992 essay on *The Diviners*, but then I don't share his optimistic faith in rationalist modernity and the possibility of a reasonable future coming out of it, at least not without major renovation. In any case, I don't know if he would make the argument differently now—the Homeric voyage in his tour de force pataphysical poetry collection, *Eunoia* (2002), ends after all, with the ship going down and we in it. It does seem we have passed the time when global catastrophe could have been averted and must develop extravagant and ecstatic measures now, in precisely the ways Laurence taught us. (Indeed, I am astonished, looking back over the oeuvre of Laurence criticism of the past few decades, how invisible her theme of environmental apocalypse has been altogether in our various readings of *The Diviners*, given its prominence throughout the novel.) With enough intuition, enough faith in the mysterious processes that bring forth planetary life, Laurence teaches us, embracing a grand(maternal) vision of this cosmic experiment we find ourselves in, we can enlarge our capacity for love and remorse, heroic right action, and creative invention—for the sake of humanity, for the animals and birds and fish, and trees and rivers and air, for biodiversity, for our children, for our continued survival. And if that is not possible, then we must prepare for our spiritual salvation in the face of annihilation, an impossible thought we must consider thinking now, in these "apocalyptic," environmentally critical, times.

Notes to Chapter 16

1 See Barbara Godard's 1990 essay, "*The Diviners* as Supplement: (M)othering the Text," for a previous maternally inflected but less ecopoetic, more postmodern reading of Morag's novels and gloss on Laurence's fictions, 26–73.

2 My students at the University of Windsor in the late 1990s were tempted to metaphorize Morag's river out of existence. Even though I explicitly instructed them not to, they insisted on reading the river exclusively as a metaphor for Morag's intellectual life—until the day a member of the Windsor-Detroit River Keepers, an environmental watchdog organization, came to class and described the pollution problems plaguing the Detroit River near their homes. Suddenly "river watching" became a real activity to them. If Margaret Laurence were writing the novel now, she might be more inclined to focus on "air watching," air quality having become an urgent problem in industrialized countries now.

Works Cited

Abram, David. *The Spell of the Sensuous: Perceptions and Language in a More-Than-Human World*. New York: Pantheon, 1996.

Allen, Paula Gunn. *The Sacred Hoop: Recovering the Feminine in American Indian Traditions*. Boston: Beacon Press, 1986.

Bök, Christian. "Sibyls: Echoes of French Feminism in *The Diviners* and *Lady Oracle*." *Canadian Literature* 135 (Winter 1992): 80–93.

———. *Eunoia*. Toronto: Coach House, 2002.

Césaire, Aimé. *Une Tempête: D'après "la Tempête" de Shakespeare—Adaptation pour un théâtre nègre*. Paris: Seuil, 1969.

Davey, Frank. *Post-National Arguments: The Politics of the Anglophone-Canadian Novel since 1967*. Toronto: University of Toronto Press, 1993.

Fagan, Kristina. "Adoption as National Fantasy in Barbara Kingsolver's *Pigs in Heaven* and Margaret Laurence's *The Diviners*." *Imagining Adoption: Essays on Literature and Culture*. Ed. Marianne Novy. Ann Arbor: University of Michigan Press, 2001. 251–66.

Godard, Barbara. "*The Diviners* as Supplement: (M)othering the Text." *Open Letter* 7.7 (Spring 1990): 26–73.

Hirsch, Marianne. *The Mother/Daughter Plot: Narrative, Psychoanalysis, Feminism.* Bloomington: Indiana University Press, 1989.

Laurence, Margaret. *The Diviners.* 1974. Toronto: McClelland & Stewart, 1988.

———. *The Fire Dwellers.* 1969. Toronto: McClelland & Stewart, 1988.

———*A Jest of God.* 1966. Toronto: McClelland & Stewart, 1974.

———. *The Stone Angel.* 1964. Toronto: McClelland & Stewart, 1988.

Merchant, Carolyn. *The Death of Nature: Women, Ecology, and the Scientific Revolution.* New York: HarperCollins, 1980.

Mies, Maria. "New Reproductive Technologies: Sexist and Racist Implications." *Ecofeminism.* By Maria Mies and Vandana Shiva. Halifax: Fernwood; London: Zed Books, 1993. 174–97.

O'Brien, Mary. *The Politics of Reproduction.* London; New York: Routledge & Kegan Paul, 1986.

Prechtel, Martín. *The Disobedient Daughter of the Sun: Ecstasy and Time.* Cambridge, MA: Yellow Moon Press, 2001.

———. *Long Life, Honey in the Heart: A Story of Initiation and Eloquence from the Shores of a Mayan Lake.* New York: North Atlantic Books, 2004.

———. *The Secrets of the Talking Jaguar: Memoirs from the Living Heart of a Mayan Village.* New York: Putnam, 1999.

Rich, Adrienne. *Of Woman Born: Motherhood as Experience and Institution.* 10th anniversary ed. New York: W. W. Norton, 1986.

———. "Compulsory Heterosexuality and Lesbian Existence." *Blood, Bread, and Poetry.* New York: Norton 1994. 23–75.

Shiva, Vandana. "Decolonizing the North." *Ecofeminism.* By Maria Mies and Vandana Shiva. Halifax: Fernwood; London: Zed Books, 1993. 264–76.

———. *Staying Alive: Women, Ecology and Development.* London: Zed Books, 1989.

ten Kortenaar, Neil. "The Trick of Divining a Postcolonial Canadian Identity: Margaret Laurence Between Race and Nation." *Canadian Literature 149: Postcolonial Identities* (Summer 1996): 11–35.

Part 4: Maternal Communication

17

Colonialism's Impact on Mothering: Jamaica Kincaid's Rendering of the Mother– Daughter Split in *Annie John* | BY NICOLE WILLEY

Jamaica Kincaid's *Annie John* speaks directly to the problems facing women, particularly Third World women of colour in their relationship to the state or the colonizer, and how that relationship affects their roles as mothers and daughters. The central conflict of this novel is the tension of the mother–daughter relationship. Annie John and her mother's relationship is fraught with (largely rhetorical) violence because it cannot be separated from colonial discourse and violence. In *Rhetoric of Motives*, Kenneth Burke's rhetorical theory concerning identification, particularly his ideas on "killing," opens up the dynamics of their relationship and shows that, to use his terms, the novel is one with which readers all over the world are able to "identify" due to the mother–daughter relationship, but we are also "persuaded" by the colonial discourse taking place throughout. This reading will provide more than just a rhetorical study; this novel will be read through the various lenses of feminist and African feminist theories, specifically those related to motherhood and voice. This reading of *Annie John* will show that when women are kept from self-definition due to the oppressions of race and class, it can become difficult or even impossible to pass on positive definitions of womanhood and motherhood to their daughters. However, when women (in this case, a daughter and grandmother) follow African feminist principles, it becomes clear that self-identification, naming, and "othermothering" are ways to break the cycle of colonization.

The 1998 printing by the Noonday Press of *Annie John* has a cover that boasts a review from *The New York Times Book Review* that reads, "So touching and familiar it could be happening to any of us ... and that's exactly the book's strength, its wisdom, its truth." I do not deny that the book is a product of certain wisdom, but I do question the notion of one "truth," as do most feminist and postcolonial critics. Why would a book written by a Caribbean author have such universal appeal? And why do Antigua and the political circumstances surrounding the novel become secondary to the "universally familiar and wrenchingly real" (book jacket) relationship between the daughter and mother? Diane Simmons makes note of commentaries that do not mention colonialism, the legacy of slavery, or institutionalized racism while discussing the book as having a "universal" theme (40).

Annie John (1985) is the story of a young Antiguan girl's coming of age, and the violent rupture and abrupt break from her mother and her colonial-subject status that must happen if she is ever going to be able to define herself. Jamaica Kincaid was born in Antigua in 1949. She is a colonial subject herself, so colonial themes make their presence known throughout the work. Richard Patteson names Kincaid a member of the "third wave" of Caribbean writers to reach an international audience (3). Rather than moving to England, as Annie does at the end of the novel, Kincaid moved to America at the age of 16, where she became an *au pair*; 14 years later she was hired on to the staff of *The New Yorker*. It wasn't until 1983, though, with the publication of *At the Bottom of the River*, that Kincaid became a recognized voice in American letters, and she has widely been acknowledged to be "one of the most important and provocative new voices in the current generation of Caribbean-born women authors" (Bouson 517). She is a prolific writer, who is still publishing works on Caribbean and other themes—family life and gardening, for instance—from her home in Vermont.[1]

Due to her origins and the concerns that are prevalent in *Annie John*, the mother–daughter relationship cannot simply be a universal one in this book—it is also a relationship that mirrors the relationship of the colonized subject to the colonizer. The mother represents not simply a generic authority from which Annie is trying to break free; in this case, the mother represents the authority of the Empire: "Mother and daughter are acknowledged enemies in a power struggle over Annie's future and even her soul ... for Annie's relationship with her mother mirrors the relationship between colonized and colonizer" (Simmons 112). It seems that a truly complete reading will not occur until an African feminist lens is used to understand the novel. Gerise Herndon partially does this in her article "Anti-Colonialist and Womanist Discourse in the Works of Jamaica Kincaid and Simone Schwarz-Bart." She does an excellent job of using knowledge of African epistemology, but she does not deal directly with the absence of the mother's voice in her article. Needed is an African feminist lens combined with Adrienne Rich's and Marianne Hirsch's theories of motherhood, because as Kincaid reminds us, Annie sees the world through the eyes of her mother (Cudjoe 227).

Further, because the mother–daughter relationship is central, but the daughterly voice is the only access we have to the mother's story, and because the daughterly voice seems primarily concerned with identifying[2] or un-identifying with the mother throughout the text, I am also going to employ Kenneth Burke's theory of identification in this analysis. A rhetorical reading that uses Kenneth Burke's definition of identification (which will be described below) offers this text yet another layer, a layer that could possibly explain much of the tension of ambivalence that can be found in the novel. The daughter wants to identify with her mother at times, but at other times repels her. The mother often identifies with the Empire and British values, yet the daughter consistently refuses to identify with both. These issues of identification are the thrust of the plot, the tension that causes the action. In fact, these identification issues are so powerful that they cause readers to identify closely to the characters and to the power struggle that is happening between the mother and daughter. Combining the African feminist theory with rhetorical theory may be unusual, but it is one more way to ensure a balanced reading.

The story itself, with all of its tension and ambivalence, almost seems a story of un-identification, but the hype around the novel stresses the audience's ability to identify with the "traditional story of a young girl's passage into adolescence" (book cover). This is why understanding Burke's identification becomes a useful way into the novel. Identification in his terms is a person's attempt to negotiate the dialectic between unity and individuation (19). In order to feel real, a person must find ways to be like and unlike other people with whom she or he comes into contact. Burke expands his definition with the concept of "consubstantiality," which he describes as the state of one who can be "both joined and separate, at once a distinct substance and consubstantial with another" (21). The tension of *Annie John* lies in the fact that Annie and her mother cannot reach a point of identification that will lead them to consubstantiality. They identify strongly when Annie is a child, but when she reaches adolescence, this changes.

Rich states in *Of Woman Born*, "The loss of the daughter to the mother, the mother to the daughter, is the essential female tragedy" (237). She goes on to note various works of art that acknowledge the split between father and daughter, mother and son, but bemoans the mother–daughter split as one not recognized in literature, lost to ancient myths. But *Annie John* is this story, the recognition of the tragedy. As the novel begins, the narrator paints a loving portrait of her mother. We learn that the preadolescent Annie loves her holidays from school, a time when she can shadow her mother in everything: "I spent the day following my mother around and observing the way she did everything" (15). Annie details her mother's beauty for the reader:

> Her head looked as if it should be on a sixpence. What a beautiful long neck, and long plaited hair, which she pinned up around the crown of her head because when her hair hung down it made her too hot. Her nose was the shape of a flower on the brink of opening. Her mouth, moving up and down as she ate and talked at the same time, was such a beautiful mouth I could have looked at it forever if I had to and not mind. (18–19)

At this point, Annie did not understand that this "paradise" (25) with her mother would eventually end, by her mother's choice.

The summer Annie turns 12, she begins to notice her physical maturation, and soon after, during a shopping trip for cloth, during which her mother usually buys enough cloth to make identical dresses for each of them, the break between mother and daughter becomes apparent. Annie's mother tells her she's "too old" for looking like a smaller version of herself. When she asks her mother to go through her trunk, commenting on the pieces of Annie's childhood and telling her story, the break becomes a fact:

> A person I did not recognize answered in a voice I did not recognize, "Absolutely not! You and I don't have time for that anymore." Again, did the ground wash out from under me? Again, the answer would have to be yes, and I wouldn't be going too far. (27)

The next few chapters chronicle Annie's various rebellion tactics against her mother. She is a hurt child; she was not prepared for the change in herself to cause changes in her mother, and to protest she begins to act to spite her mother. She has two intense relationships with other girls, one she knows her mother would not approve of, and she begins playing with marbles against her mother's wishes. These rebellious acts help Annie begin to self-identify, to mark herself as separate from her mother.

The final break comes when Annie's mother sees her in a verbal exchange with four boys on the street. One is an old playmate of Annie's. Even though Annie is the innocent victim of the boys' degradation of her ("I knew instantly that it was malicious and that I had done nothing to deserve it other than standing there all alone" [95]), Annie's mother sees her and accuses her of being a "slut" in patois when Annie gets home. Annie is hurt and confused, and still not sure how to fit in a space somewhere between girlhood and womanhood.[3] Her mother betrays her by blaming her for the indiscretion of being seen with a group of boys. Simmons notes, "The mother not only betrays the girl, but betrays herself in seeing maturity as a crime" (115). Simmons goes on to explain that the mother's strong reaction to Annie's nonexistent offence is due to the fact that she sees herself in her daughter. Unfortunately, this is not the right kind of identification, and it definitely does not lead to consubstantiality. Annie wants to "rest my whole body on [hers] the way I used to" (103). She couldn't move toward her mother, and "when [she] looked down, it was as if the ground had opened up between [them], making a deep and wide split. On one side of the split stood [her] mother ... on the other side stood [she] ... inside carrying the thimble that weighed worlds" (103). Consubstantiality is no longer a possibility for these two women. The fragmentation is evident, and it comes from her mother's ability to identify with her daughter only through the parts of herself of which she is ashamed. Rich points out that a mother "identifies intensely with her daughter, but through weakness, not through strength" (244).

Kincaid now says that her own mother was the "victim of a colonial and racist system," similar to the mother in *Annie John*,[4] and that her mother's act of calling her a "slut" was a product of seeing her African heritage as one that brought on "rampant sexuality" (Simmons 24). Of course, her mother identified with (Western/British) values that denigrated her African heritage and which made it seem barbaric and overly sexual. The effects of colonialism on the mother, and the conflict between the cultures, cannot be underestimated in their effect on the relationship between the mother and the daughter.

Rich, writing about the tragedy of the loss of the mother to the daughter, is writing about a primarily Western construct and experience. An African worldview makes such a split less likely, in that women (even mothers and daughters) are more likely to bond through the necessities of their roles and jobs. Clearly, colonialism and the history of slavery have distorted the African relationship of mother to daughter. Burke's definition of identification depends upon the ability to find both union and individuation in a relationship. A woman who is only able to identify in weakness with her daughter (in part due to the effects of colonialism) will not be strong enough to allow for individuation, and this is much of the tension, which leads to violence, in Annie and her mother's relationship.[5]

Burke's identification theory in *Rhetoric of Motives* also entails images of killing in literature: "The imagery of slaying is a special case of transformation, and transformation involves the ideas and imagery of *identification*. That is: the *killing* of something is the *changing* of it, and the statement of the thing's nature before and after the change is an *identifying* of it" (20). Annie is concerned with death throughout the novel. Chapter 1, "Figures in the Distance," opens with Annie watching for funeral processions on a daily basis. Many mentions are made of her interest in death, particularly the death of children. She also relates her mother to death because her mother was present at death or helped prepare dead bodies on several occasions during her young life. Annie says that she "began to look at [her] mother's hands differently" after Nalda, a child in her community, died and her mother prepared her body (6).

Annie's preoccupation with death as a young child leads into death imagery later in the novel, and it accompanies homicidal urges that Annie has at points toward her mother. A sort of mantra that Annie repeats to herself in a dream follows: "My mother would kill me if she got the chance. I would kill my mother if I had the courage" (89). Annie says that she chanted these words with a "happy note" in order to never give her mother the "chance." It is clear that Annie does not really believe the words she is saying literally, but that she is frustrated about her relationship with her mother, one that is increasingly marked by the ambivalence of love and hate:

> I had never loved anyone so or hated anyone so. But to say hate—what did I mean by that? Before, if I hated someone, I simply wished the person dead. But I couldn't wish my mother dead. If my mother died, what would become of me? I couldn't imagine my life without her. Worse than that, if my mother died I would have to die, too. (88)

Burke notes that "fantasies of killing may at times be no more than a dramatic way of saying, 'I wish I were, at the moment, free of this particular person'" (262). Annie knows that she cannot survive at this point without her mother, and death actually terrifies her. But the feelings she has toward her mother are so frightening that killing becomes a fantasy of transforming the relationship.

The ambivalence of her feelings carries over into the fight she has with her mother over her behaviour with the four boys. After their fight, Annie feels alone, and says, "At that moment, I missed my mother more than I had ever imagined possible and wanted only to live somewhere quiet and beautiful with her alone, but also at that moment I wanted only to see her lying dead, all withered and in a coffin at my feet" (106). These ambivalent thoughts demonstrate the final break between Annie and her mother. After Annie insinuates that her mother must also be a slut, her mother says, "Until this moment, in my whole life I knew without a doubt that, without any exception, I loved you best," and then she turns her back on her daughter (103). Her mother's manipulation of her daughter at this point makes Annie's killing fantasies understandable. We can only speculate about the mother's reasons for overreacting at this point, since we see her only through Annie's eyes. It seems, though, that these moments are born out of love and/or fear for her daughter; she just wants what is best for her. Unfortunately, in identifying out of her own weakness rather than in the strength they could have together, the break becomes final. These instances are points at which Annie is most alienated, and the moments in which she has the most need to transform their relationship. Annie "kills" her mother the only way she knows how, by rebelling against her, in hopes that this will lead to a transformation. Eventually, this rebellion leads to Annie's purposeful separation from her mother, another way of killing and transforming their relationship.

While critics are eager to find the universals in a novel that many read as a "coming of age" story about a daughter's *necessary* break from her mother,[6] it is clear that much more is going on in their relationship than the usual Western trials and tribulations of the mother–daughter relationship. Colonialism and the extent to which Annie's mother identifies with the Empire are certain and serious impediments in their relationship. Because Annie's mother identifies with the British Empire, and because Annie refuses to identify with the Empire, a relationship that is often fraught with tension becomes almost violent in the force of the opposing wills. Mother and daughter become enemies.

Annie's mother thinks that she is doing right by her daughter in forcing her to be a good citizen of the Empire. Simmons notes that at puberty, Annie is no longer allowed in her mother's world, but is instead sent off to lessons that will make her a "young lady" (107): "Because of this young-lady business, instead of days spent in perfect harmony with my mother ... I was now sent off to learn one thing and another. I was sent to someone who knew all about manners" (27). Annie's mother has a stake in Annie rising from the lower to the middle class, and she feels that Annie must do this by going to a school with an English teacher and by becoming more "civilized" or "ladylike." Her mother even takes Annie to an English doctor when she becomes very ill after their final break: "Dr. Stephens and my mother were one in their feeling against germs, parasites, and disease in general" (110).[7]

Burke notes that identification for an ill purpose can sometimes occur:

> The fact that an activity is capable of reduction to intrinsic, autonomous principles does not argue that it is free from identification with other orders of motivation extrinsic to it.... The shepherd ... acts for the good of the sheep.... But he may be "identified" with a project that is raising the sheep for market. (27)

It is clear that while Annie's mother feels she is doing the right thing in trying to raise her daughter as a lady, she is actually identifying with imperial powers that do not have the best interests of Annie or her mother in mind. While the mother herself cannot be blamed for this identification due to the pervasiveness of colonial influence in her culture, it is nonetheless a rift between the two women.

Annie also has more opportunities and insights than her mother as a result of her education. The very thing Annie despises most about her mother—her "giving over" of her own life to that of her husband and children (and thereby providing an education for her daughter)—is precisely the thing that gives Annie an intellectual edge.[8] Annie and her friends "were sure that the much-talked-about future that everybody was preparing us for would never come, for we had such a powerful feeling against it, and why shouldn't our will prevail this time?" (50). Annie, almost unconsciously, refuses to identify with the Empire whenever she has that option. Annie says about the queen and her school materials, "so glad was I to get rid of my old notebooks, which had on their covers a picture of a wrinkled-up woman wearing a crown on her head and a neckful and armfuls of diamonds and pearls" (40). She enjoyed a picture in her textbook entitled "Columbus in Chains," depicting the outcome of his argument with Bobadilla, because she "did not like Columbus" (77). Under the picture she wrote "The Great Man Can No Longer Just Get Up and Go" (78). She is, of course, punished by her teacher as well as her parents for this indiscretion, an indiscretion that is a product of her ability to make a truthful but disrespectful observation about not only Columbus, but the state of colonialism as well. The irony is that she wrote this in Old English lettering, "a script I had recently mastered" (78). Later, she discusses *Jane Eyre* as her favourite book.[9] Clearly, Annie is still a colonial subject, even with her instinctively rebellious mind. It is not the enjoyment of British texts that is the problem, but her inability (at this age) to recognize and analyze the incongruities of her beliefs and enjoyments.

As Carole Davies (116) and others note, including Kincaid herself, this novel is concerned with colonial issues. Kincaid believes that she had a colonial awareness as early as nine years of age (Cudjoe 217), and it is no stretch to see this mirrored in Annie John's rebellions against her mother and the headmistress, the two major colonial figures in Annie's life (Ferguson 50). Ironically, Annie's most rebellious act, her separation from her family and her island, is also her most colonial act. The morning Annie is leaving, she narrates for herself her own autobiography (an act of decolonization that allows her to take the power away from the oppressor in order to name and define herself). She never plans to marry or have to take care of a man the way her mother does. She realizes that her parents made her what she is, but once she grew, it was no longer comfortable for her to be with them: "I don't love them now the way I used to" (133). They clearly provided her with the opportunities she needed in order to grow and desire more, but those same desires necessitate more space for her. We also see her still nursing the hurt of the loss of her mother:

> Why, I wonder, didn't I see the hypocrite in my mother when, over the years, she said that she loved me and could hardly live without me, while at the same time proposing and arranging separation after separation, including this one, which, unbeknownst to her, *I* have arranged to be permanent?... I have made a vow never to be fooled again. (133)

The great irony, of course, is that she is leaving for England. She is going "away from [her] home, away from [her] mother, away from [her] father, away from the everlasting blue sky, away from the everlasting hot sun" (134). The most important freedom is freedom from her mother, but the secondary notion that she will be free of her island and her people is also present in her thoughts. Fleeing to England, the "motherland," is akin to demonstrating her own hatred for her heritage and, consequently, herself. This is not a surprising choice, however. Countless people make the choice to flee their homeland for more and better opportunities in the "motherland." This is her final act of rebellion, and in a sense, another attempt to "kill" her relationship with her mother. This separation will, finally, transform the relationship. While the transformation does not in this novel lead to consubstantiality, it does show the marked improvement, at least in Annie's opinion, of an undesirable situation.

But while Annie seems to be forsaking her own heritage for that of the colonizer, there is much evidence to suggest that *Annie John* still demonstrates the healing possibilities of an African feminist tradition. This tradition, and the benefits of it, can mainly be seen through Annie's grandmother, Ma Chess. Many critics see her as central to the novel and central to Annie's African/Caribbean heritage. Ferguson notes that Ma Chess is both

Amerindian and African, and that her central role in the novel is that of healer (69). Donna Perry notes the matrilineal bond as the strongest force in the novel, and that line includes Ma Chess, Annie's mother, and Annie (251).[10] Timothy also makes the important point that the grandmother is a central part of Annie's process of looking for her own identity/cosmology during her sickness (241). Finally, Simmons says that Ma Chess symbolizes rebirth (28).

Annie's sickness, while the topic of only one chapter, is clearly the turning point for Annie, and Ma Chess is the reason Annie is able to become stronger through the sickness, rather than weaker. Ma Chess arrives mysteriously and leaves mysteriously, sensing intuitively when she is needed and when she should leave. While she is there, she is Annie's main comfort, an othermother who gives Annie her own healing strength—through her body and through obeah:

> Ma Chess settled in on the floor at the foot of my bed, eating and sleeping there, and soon I grew to count on her smells and the sound her breath made as it went in and out of her body. Sometimes at night, when I would feel that I was all locked up in the warm falling soot and could not find my way out, Ma Chess would come into my bed with me and stay until I was myself. (125–26)

Annie visualizes her grandmother as her healer, while her mother goes on with her own life, taking meals with her father to keep him company. Ma Chess performs "all the other things that my mother used to do" (126). The distance between Annie and her mother grows, but the model of Ma Chess shows that tradition (even a choice like obeah over Western medicine) is what gives a colonized female subject strength.

Ma Chess chooses the strength that women hold in her traditional cultures—she is both Amerindian and African (Ferguson 69)—and she consciously refuses patriarchy (Covi 352), at least the Western brand of patriarchy. Her refusal can be seen in her unwillingness to forgive (or even to ever speak to) her husband when her son died after treatments with Western medicine. Symbolically, she tells Annie's father, a carpenter who is leaving for his job of building houses, that she would rather live in a "nice hole in the ground, so [she could] come and go as [she] please[d]" (126). We can read the hole as one more sign of her inability to fit into Western constructions and of her preference for nature. Ma Chess, in choosing her African heritage, proves to be a pillar of strength and healing to Annie. Kincaid's work suggests that valorizing tradition, even within a colonial context, is absolutely necessary to healthy development. Kincaid upholds womanist or

African feminist principles, such as the importance of the matrilineal line, the value of women, the necessity of networking (with her female friends), and the ability not to just survive, but to thrive, regardless of the situation in which one finds oneself.

It is important to make note of the way in which the mother is represented as a character in this novel. Marianne Hirsch notes that while much writing by African American women since the 1960s has been concerned with the mother–daughter relationship, "nearly all of those perspectives have belonged to daughters" (415). Hirsch recognizes that while Black women writers have developed more literature in which the mother is central, they still write from a "daughterly" perspective. It is still true, however, that while maternal discourse may actually mark a "gap" in the language, daughters' stories are informed by their mothers' stories (418). Deborah Kleopfer, also interested in the representation of the mother in literature, is trying to "find a way to talk about the relationship of the mother and the writing daughter" in such a manner as to make clear why the mother figure is central but absent (3). Rich notes that the mother is central in her own writing, but that if her mother were to write her own story, "other landscapes would be revealed" (221).

It is precisely because the daughterly voice rules the text that consubstantiality can never be reached. The mother never speaks for herself in this novel, obviously. The closest we get to hearing the mother's voice is in certain pieces of dialogue where she is quoted (and they are few compared to the narration), but the narrator is unreliable because of her anger for her mother.

Giovanna Covi argues that the novel contains a "fully multiple voice" and that the mother is present throughout the entire book (351, 353). But, while her mother is certainly present, she is the agent *against* which Annie is acting. Ferguson notes that because Annie cannot compete with her mother (the mother is more powerful than she), she lives in opposition to her (46–47). In fact, that explains clearly the difference between Annie and her mother. Her mother does not live in opposition to the powerful colonizer; rather, she tries to take what power she can within the system. Simmons explains this phenomenon by noting that the mother internalizes both worldviews (30). Furthermore, just as Annie is colonized by her mother (but fights back), all colonized people are basically seen as children by the colonizers, and are never permitted to mature (Simmons 102). Annie lives in constant opposition to the authority figures in her life because she refuses to give in to their perspectives about who she should be. The mother is constantly present in the dialogue with Annie, but we do not see a complete integration of the mother's voice because we really see the mother only from Annie's point of view. Since Annie feels that she must have complete separation from her mother in order to grow, we obviously have a one-sided picture of the relationship. Annie wants to identify (and even merge) with her mother at various points in the novel (Ferguson 44); she wants to return to the pre-Oedipal unity she had as a child, seen in chapters 1 and 2 (Covi 351). But because consubstantiality can never be reached,[11] Annie needs to find her own identity.

Annie's acts of self-definition are rebellions, and they are the same forces that make this novel a *Bildungsroman* and eventually lead Annie to herself. It is of the utmost importance that the last chapter begins with Annie naming herself: "My name is Annie John" (131). While leaving her mother and her island may hold many contradictions, it cannot be denied that by the end of the novel, Annie is finally taking control of her life.

Annie John's overall effect matches Burke's purpose in *Rhetoric of Motives*: they both seek to move the focus from persuasion to identification. Readers identify with the central relationship in the novel; they see themselves in Annie, and they read the book as a "universal" or a "coming of age" story. However, interspersed throughout Annie's coming of age are African feminist principles that allow her to move beyond identification with the colonizer, who is also her mother. Annie carves out her own identity through her rebellions and self-naming, and also through the strength fostered in the matrilineal line with her grandmother. Even as Annie seems to defy tradition in breaking with her mother's values, she actually reifies important African feminist traditions that allow her to transform her own life.

Notes to Chapter 17

1 Biographical information in this section is easily found in a variety of sources, but I used J. Brooks Bouson's entry on Kincaid from the collection *Writing African American Women: An Encyclopedia of Literature by and about Women of Color.*

2 Davies also sees *Annie John* as a novel in which separation from the mother is Annie's main goal, but at the same time, she is striving to retain the identification she once held with her mother (124).

3 After the incident with the boys, Annie wants to return home to safety as soon as possible. She feels "alternately too big and too small" (101).

4 Birbalsingh posed the question, "[The mother figure] was no doubt based on your own mother?" to which Kincaid began a long discussion of her own mother and some scenes that mirrored scenes in the novel, such as when her mother found all the books she had hidden under the house and burned them (143).

5   Rich's model for a nurturing mother is one who "has respect and affection for her own body, who does not view it as unclean or as a sex-object.... A woman who feels pride in being female will not visit her self-deprecation up her female child" (245).

6   Rich has shown that this break, or at least the violence found in this break, is not necessary but is forced on women by the institution of motherhood, an institution that sets all women up as failures (223).

7   It is interesting to note that when Annie's condition worsens, she uses British medicine and also calls on her mother to practice obeah in order to make her well (117).

8   As will be discussed, this same education is colonial in nature and causes some conflicts for Annie herself.

9   This is especially ironic (or not so surprising) considering Rochester's fortune and Jean Rhys's rewriting of the book in *Wide Sargasso Sea*.

10 I do take issue with the use of "strongest," because she does not properly account for the break between the mother and daughter, and says only that the mother forces Annie out for her own good (251–52).

11 Simmons cites the narcissistic mother as the cause of the boundary confusion, which later leads to her need to self-identify (25–26).

Works Cited

Birsbalsingh, F. M., ed. "Jamaica Kincaid: From Antigua to America." In *Frontiers of Caribbean Literature in English*. New York: St. Martin's Press, 1996. 138–51.

Bouson, J. Brooks. "Kincaid, Jamaica (1949–)." *Writing African American Women: An Encyclopedia of Literature by and about Women of Color*. Vol. 2. Ed. Elizabeth Ann Beaulieu. Westport, CT: Greenwood Press, 2006. 517–23.

Burke, Kenneth. *A Rhetoric of Motives*. Berkeley: University of California Press, 1969.

Covi, Giovanna. "Jamaica Kincaid and the Resistance to Canons." *Out of the Kumbla: Caribbean Women and Literature*. Ed. Carol Boyce Davies and Elaine Savory Fido. Trenton, NJ: Africa World Press1990. 345–54.

Cudjoe, Selwyn R. "Jamaica Kincaid and the Modernist Project: An Interview." *Caribbean Women Writers: Essays from the First International Conference*. Ed. Cudjoe. Wellesley, MA: Calaloux, 1990. 215–32.

Davies, Carole Boyce. *Black Women, Writing and Identity: Migrations of the Subject*. London: Routledge, 1994.

Ferguson, Moira. *Jamaica Kincaid: Where the Land Meets the Body*. Charlottesville: University of Virginia Press, 1994.

Herndon, Gerise. "Anti-Colonialist and Womanist Discourse in the Works of Jamaica Kincaid and Simone Schwarz-Bart." *Womanbeing and African Literature*. Ed. Phanuel Akubueze Egejuru. Trenton, NJ: Africa World Press, 1997. 159–68.

Hirsch, Marianne. "Maternal Narratives: Cruel Enough to Stop the Blood." *Reading Black, Reading Feminist: A Critical Anthology*. Ed. Henry Louis Gates, Jr. New York: Merdian, 1990. 415–30.

Kincaid, Jamaica. *Annie John*. 1985. New York: Noonday Press, 1988.

Kleopfer, Deborah Kelly. *The Unspeakable Mother: Forbidden Discourse in Jean Rhys and H. D.* Ithaca: Cornell University Press, 1989.

Patteson, Richard F. *Caribbean Passages: A Critical Perspective on New Fiction from the West Indies*. Boulder: Lynne Rienner, 1998.

Perry, Donna. "Initiation in Jamaica Kincaid's *Annie John*." *Caribbean Women Writers: Essays from the First International Conference*. Ed. Selwyn R. Cudjoe. Wellesley, MA: Calaloux, 1990. 245–53.

Rich, Adrienne. *Of Woman Born: Motherhood as Experience and Institution*. New York: Norton, 1976.

Simmons, Diane. *Jamaica Kincaid*. New York: Twayne, 1994.

Timothy, Helen Pyne. "Adolescent Rebellion and Gender Relations in *At the Bottom of the River* and *Annie John*." *Caribbean Women Writers: Essays from the First International Conference*. Ed. Selwyn R. Cudjoe. Wellesley, MA: Calaloux, 1990. 233–44.

18

Mother to Daughter: Muted Maternal Feminism in the Fiction of Sandra Cisneros | BY RITA BODE

The biographical note in some Vintage editions of Sandra Cisneros's work rejects for the author two traditional social signifiers for women when it unequivocally proclaims her to be "nobody's mother, nobody's wife."[1] The roles of mother and wife for female identity are perhaps especially true for the Latino community, with its simultaneous privileging of both men and family, the latter of which is a significant subject in Cisneros's fiction. The biographical statement's refusals raise the question of how this Mexican American woman/writer arrived at the point of being confidently positioned outside the traditional roles for women. In her fiction, especially in her two novels, *The House on Mango Street* (1984) and the more recent *Caramelo* (2002), Cisneros suggests a possible answer, for in both works, she links the feminist orientation of Latina daughters to an inclusive maternal presence and influence composed of mothers as well as othermothers, such as grandmothers and aunts. These maternal figures do not themselves live feminist lives, but in their various, sometimes odd awareness of their own unrealized potential, they display a muted feminism that leads them to recognize and nurture, consciously as well as instinctively, the possibilities for independence and self-fulfillment in their daughters. In examining the complex nature of the mother–daughter relationship as Cisneros presents it, my paper proposes that the interactions of Cisneros's daughter/narrators with their maternal figures give both Esperanza, in *Mango*, and Celaya, or

Lala as she is usually called, in *Caramelo*, a feminist perspective, and guide them toward autonomous female selfhood.

Born in 1954 in Chicago to a Mexican father and a Mexican American mother, Cisneros has become one of the best-known authors among Latino writers who have emerged in the United States since the 1980s. Like other Chicana writers, Cisneros privileges the Chicana subject, placing the lives of Mexican American girls and women at the very centre of her stories. Cisneros recounts that during her attendance at the University of Iowa's famed Writers Workshop, her sense of alienation from a communal knowledge in which her fellow students all seemed so confidently to share led her to consider that her different knowledge and experience offered a rich source for the creation of her own art. Seeing her classmates as "fine hothouse flowers," she began to write from her own perspective, as the "yellow weed among the city's cracks" (qtd. in Ganz 24), and to draw on her deep involvement with Chicana/o culture.

"Las tres madres," Gloria E. Anzaldúa calls the three most significant female presences in Chicana/o myth and history (192), who together suggest the centrality of mother figures in Chicana/o culture. They are La Llorona, the mythical weeping woman whose drowning of her own children has made her into a figure of both maternal betrayal and maternal resistance; La Malinche, the Aztec mistress of the Spanish conqueror Cortez, seen as a traitor to the Aztec people as well as the mother of the Mestizo nation; and la Virgen de Guadalupe, the holy Mother, who appeared to a poor boy in 1531 on the Tepeyac hillside outside Mexico City, leaving her lasting image imprinted on his cloak and on the nation. As the brief descriptions suggest, there is an ambivalence surrounding the interpretations of La Llorona and La Malinche. Both being suspect, they sometimes collapse into one, and Cisneros herself identifies only two of these figures when commenting on Mexican influences on her writing: "black-white ... good-bad," Cisneros states, "it's very prevalent in my work and in other Latinas. We're raised with a Mexican culture that has two role models: La Malinche y la Virgen de Guadalupe. And you know that's a hard route to go, one or the other, there's no in-betweens" (qtd. in Petty 119).[2]

Her dual focus pinpoints all the more forcefully the binary oppositions at the heart of these archetypal representations of maternal womanhood. Sinner and saint, whore and virgin subsume any separate identity for the maternal into two restrictive types. But despite her emphasis on "one or the other" in her commentary, Cisneros, like some feminist theorists, posits in her fiction a separate category for the mother. When French psychoanalyst Luce Irigaray was asked to name "the basic representations in the symbolic

masculine world by which the oppression of women is articulated," she initially supplied three categories rather than two: "virgin, mother, whore"
(Todd 239).[3] Like Irigaray, Cisneros remains well aware of the oppression
that married life posits for women, and in her fiction, motherhood, with or
without marriage, is often an overwhelming prospect. But Cisneros's pre-
sentation of motherhood is not limited to oppression; nor are her wives and
mothers entirely powerless. She allows for a distinct maternal space that
involves moving outside of stereotypical, dualistic thinking. Her fiction
acknowledges the social advantage of men and the significant influence of
fathers, both nurturing and threatening, on daughters, but, more importantly, it foregrounds the strengths of her fictional girls and women, especially through maternal interactions with daughters.

In her pioneering study on matrilineal identification in *The Mother/
Daughter Plot*, Marianne Hirsch shifts the focus from a concept of traditional
inheritance between fathers and legitimate sons, which excludes females,
to the transmission of a maternal heritage among mothers and daughters.[4]
In Cisneros's fiction, this transmission of maternal inheritance becomes
the legacy of maternal knowledge making the mother–daughter relationship for her narrators central to their social and creative liberation as Chicana daughters. Cisneros's maternal figures refuse to become what Phillipa Kafka, in her study of contemporary Chicana writers, calls "cultural
collaborationists" in Chicano culture; they refuse the role of "custodians
or gatekeepers" of the traditional patriarchal rules and expectations that
rigidly determine and limit the lives of Chicana daughters (Kafka 10). Cisneros seems intent on carving out a separate social space for the mother
which transcends cultural dualities, and from which the maternal presence
promises to transcend the oppression, if not for herself then at least for
her daughter. While their own freedom and autonomy may be limited, Cisneros's mothers convey to their daughters feminist insights and attitudes
through their close relational connection.

As Andrea O'Reilly and Sharon Abbey's introduction to *Mothers and
Daughters* suggests, the paradigm for female maturation as entailing a necessary separation from the mother has been superceded by the recognition
that the mother–daughter connection facilitates rather than impedes the
daughter's movement toward autonomous selfhood (1–18). Suzanna Danuta
Walters's contention that the mother–daughter relationship, "as one constructed in conflict," may be "a phenomenon limited to white, bourgeois
society" (173) is borne out in much of the literature of African American
women writers and seems equally true for Chicana writing.[5] In her poem
"Mothers and Daughters," acclaimed Chicana poet Pat Mora invokes the

intimacy of the relationship in her image of "the arm-in-arm-mother-daughter-stroll;" she recognizes that this very intimacy makes the relationship susceptible to tensions, to the "tug-/of-war that started in the womb / the fight for space / the sharp jab deep inside," but in continually circling back to the "arm-in-arm / around the world" stroll (152), she privileges the pervasive binding link of the mother–daughter relationship. Similarly, it is not so much that conflict between mothers and daughters is absent in Cisneros's work, but rather, that her work foregrounds their connection. Continuities and links with maternal figures inform the daughter/narrators's maturation. Cisneros's focus is on issues of transmission that connect a daughter's future with a mother's past, through communication and understanding rather than rejection. In her fiction, the transmission of female experience and knowledge engages both mothers and daughters as equal participants, for while reaching back, the transmission also looks forward toward the potential for transformations in the daughters' lives.

Consisting of brief narrative vignettes, *The House on Mango Street* tells the story of young Esperanza through the clear, bright, insightful eyes that she directs at her family, friends, her Latino culture, and the ethnic urban neighbourhood in which she is growing up. In a novel about childhood and female adolescent maturation, told from the child's point of view, the pervasive parental presence of "Mama" and "Papa" comes as no surprise. Cisneros never names Esperanza's parents. This omission seems to emphasize rather than diminish the importance for Esperanza of the child–parent relationship, and, especially, the mother–daughter one, as Cisneros gives the maternal presence particular authority.[6] Esperanza's refrain of "Mama says" (71, 73) and "My mother says" (82, 88) indicates the child's strong faith in the maternal words and knowledge, which Esperanza's mother fully justifies. The mother's wise advice to the daughter falls into a feminist tradition going back to Mary Wollstonecraft (1759–97) of how women can better their lives.[7] "Esperanza, you go to school. Study hard" (91), her mother tells her.

Significantly, more than advising, her mother reveals to Esperanza her own story of past choices, making available to her daughter what O'Reilly and Abbey identify as the "strategies of struggle" required to construct "an alternative script of coming into womanhood" (5). She re-creates for Esperanza the girl she once was, the academically able "smart cookie" who quit school because she lacked "nice clothes." Her mother's statement that "shame is a bad thing.... It keeps you down" seems to come "out of nowhere" for Esperanza, but for her mother, it comes out of the observance of her daughter through several vignettes that record Esperanza's sense of shame over rice sandwiches, over shoes, over their house (91). The mother's telling of her own story and her refusal to meet her daughter's shame with maternal blame make the knowledge of what "shame" can do accessible to Esperanza. Opera, the mother's great enjoyment, becomes the paradigm for creative maternal behaviour, quiet listening followed by active expressing "with velvety lungs powerful as morning glories" (90). The maternal communication is smooth, powerful, and hopeful, offering the bridge to carry her daughter's pending choices away from her own past mistakes.

In the "Chanclas" vignette, Cisneros focuses on shoes to suggest the importance of the mother in helping Esperanza situate herself with confidence as a young Chicana in the public sphere. The vignette's title does double duty: Cisneros not only plays with the old adage of being able to truly know others (in this case the self) only by walking in their shoes, but by using Spanish—*chanclas* are flip-flops—she reminds us that cultural differences continually pose additional complications for self-realization. The vignette begins with the mother's arrival home bringing "new clothes" for Esperanza to wear to her cousin's baptism party (*Mango* 46), but, more significantly, having forgotten to buy her daughter new shoes. Sonia Saldívar-Hull sees the mother's omission as "thoughtless" (97), but probably the money runs out before she gets to the shoes. Regardless of the reason, the mother's forgetting the shoes forces her daughter into her everyday shoes, into "the old saddle shoes I wear to school.... My feet scuffed and round, and the heels all crooked that look dumb with this dress" (*Mango* 47). These everyday shoes reflect her everyday self, suggesting authenticity for her social appearance at the baptism party.

Shoes are powerful female signifiers in *The House on Mango Street*.[8] In an earlier vignette, donning colourful "magic high heels" turns Esperanza and her friends, Lucy and Rachel, into sexual objects of male desire as they strut and teeter to the corner, "where the men can't take their eyes off us" (40). This context makes Esperanza's dancing with her uncle at the baptism celebration in her "ordinary shoes" a triumph of individual assertion. Here, too, everyone watches her—"who are those two who dance like in the movies" (47)—and everyone claps in admiration. There is a sexual tension here as well, for "all night the boy who is a man watches me dance" (48), but the adulation does not come exclusively from an objectifying male gaze, and its source is her active talent in dancing. Cisneros emphasizes further the mother's role by reiterating her involvement at the moment of Esperanza's triumph. The shoes in which she performs the dance are "the kind my mother buys each year for school" (47), and the uncle "walks me back in my thick shoes to my mother who is proud to be my mother" (48). In the earlier vignette, after the three girls lose interest in dressing up, Lucy hides the sexually charged "magic high heels" on her back porch, where her mother, while cleaning, finds them and throws them out. Lucy's mother, as Esperanza tells us, is "very clean," but her act of discarding the shoes is entirely fitting in other ways, for symbolically it speaks to a maternal intervention in and resistance to society's detrimental views of young females (42).

Through Esperanza's engagement with othermothers, the strength and pervasiveness of familial female connections among generations becomes further apparent. "My great-grandmother, I would have liked to have known her," Esperanza thinks, about the deceased "wild horse of a woman" whose name she shares (10–11). She knows the great-grandmother's story of how she "wouldn't marry. Until my great-grandfather threw a sack over her head and carried her off.... And the story goes she never forgave him. She looked out the window her whole life, the way so many women sit their sadness on an elbow." Esperanza hears the story's silences: "I wonder if she ... was sorry because she couldn't be all the things she wanted to be." Esperanza's listening to her great-grandmother's story helps her to define her own unfulfilled desires and hopes for the future. "I have inherited her name, but I don't want to inherit her place by the window," she concludes (11). In turn, her Aunt Lupe's listening to Esperanza prods the young girl toward the fulfillment of her emergent longings, especially her artistic ones.

Aunt Lupe, though bedridden and blind, communicates effectively with her niece: "She listened to every book, every poem, I read her." Esperanza recounts how "one day I read her one of my own.... That's nice. That's very good, she said in her tired voice. You just remember to keep writing, Esperanza. You must keep writing. It will keep you free" (60–61). Esperanza and her friends feel great guilt for playing at imitating Aunt Lupe in her illness on the very day that she dies, but Cisneros associates a far more beneficial cause–effect pattern with Aunt Lupe when at the vignette's end, Esperanza reveals, "And then she died, my aunt who listened to my poems. And then we began to dream the dreams" (61), the dreams that carry them forward. A few sections later, the poetic "Four Skinny Trees" vignette reminds us that Esperanza is writing the poetry that Aunt Lupe had encouraged. "Keep, keep, keep, trees say when I sleep" (75), Esperanza interprets for the four skinny trees outside her window, echoing the three "keeps" that Aunt Lupe repeats to her: "keep writing ... keep writing. It will keep you free" (61).

Geoffrey Sanborn sees in Esperanza's description of the "four skinny trees" an evocation of Emily Dickinson's "Four Trees—upon a solitary Acre—" (1340).[9] Cisneros is aware of the vast differences between herself and Dickinson in many areas: social, cultural, racial/ethnic, and more. In a piece first delivered to students in Santa Barbara, she muses that Dickinson "even had a maid, an Irish housekeeper.... Maybe Emily Dickinson's Irish housekeeper had to sacrifice her life so that Emily could live hers locked upstairs in the corner bedroom writing her 1,775 poems" (qtd. in Sanborn 1341).[10] Dickinson, however, remains one of her favourite poets, a source of inspiration to embrace but also one from which to diverge. The interweaving of Esperanza's trees with Dickinson's affirms the young girl's emerging, maturing poetic self whom Aunt Lupe's influence continues to nurture into existence. In sharing their reading, Aunt Lupe affirms for Esperanza the enjoyment and importance of other literary traditions—they both love Charles Kingsley's *The Waterbabies*, for instance—while encouraging Esperanza to find and "keep" her own poetic voice.

Near the novel's end, the three fateful sisters who confront Esperanza embrace perhaps all the novel's female characters, young and old, who have influenced her, but as "aunts," they speak especially for the generations of women who have come before her—her mother, her great-grandmother, her Aunt Lupe; furthermore, as "three who did not seem related to anything but the moon" (103), Cisneros specifically links the sisters, as she does Esperanza's other maternal figures, to female destiny. "When you leave you must remember always to come back" (105), one of them admonishes her. In Esperanza's projected return is the promise of a return to the self on multiple levels. Her mother figures, too, are among "the ones I left behind" (110). In the context of the mother–daughter connection, her return acknowledges her maternal legacy and affirms the strength of the female continuity into which the novel's maternal figures consistently draw her. Her going away to "come back" freely (110) fulfills the promise that she sensed in her wild great-grandmother, the same promise that her mother and aunt recognized and nurtured in her to enable "an alternative script" to theirs (O'Reilly and Abbey 5).

The deceptive simplicity of *The House on Mango Street* turns into the complex family narrative of *Caramelo*, where the presence of an older narrator, alongside her younger self, becomes more pronounced. Through *Caramelo's* daughter/narrator, Celaya, or Lala, as she is most often called, Cisneros continues the exploration of the narrator/daughter's relationship to a range of maternal figures, including her own mother. Cristina Herrera's discussion of the mother–daughter relationship in *Caramelo* positions the mother as representing traditional Mexican patriarchal family values, which form a significant source of conflict between mother and daughter. Though as a Mexican American, Lala's mother, Zoila, is outside mainstream society, like many women in the years following the Second World War, she does not work outside the home. She occupies the private domestic sphere, the space traditionally associated with women since industrialization and a site frequently signifying their subordination to the public male realm. But Cisneros seems intent on emphasizing in Zoila a steadfast resistance to patriarchal ideology which is perhaps most evident in her resistance to the Church: "In our house votive candles never flicker from bedroom bureaus night and day" begins Lala's anti-litany of what religious observances her "godless ... mother" disallows (311). The conflict between mother and daughter is more pronounced here than in *Mango* since Lala is older than Esperanza for much of the story, but her mother, like Aunt Lupe, is nonetheless a significant influence on her developing artistry: "Mother's mopping, and I'm sweeping. Every once in a while, out of nowhere, Mother will ask, — And then what happened? Even though I haven't been telling a story. It's kind of a game between us. I have to come up with something out of the blue, the more outrageous the better. It helps pass the time" (308). The question that Lala's mother poses is one, moreover, that Lala sometimes puts to others (246); Zoila thus affirms her daughter's interest in stories. But while Lala's relationship with her mother is very important, and, like Esperanza, she also connects with aunts, the maternal figure who is her most challenging and intimate companion is her grandmother, her father's mother, the "Awful Grandmother."

Both Tey Diana Rebolledo and, more recently, Erlinda Gonzales-Berry see the representations of the abuelita, the grandmother, in Chicana literature positively, Rebolledo as the Chicana writer's "mythic mirror image of integration in the journey into herself" ("Abuelitas" 148), and Gonzales-Berry as the "mediator between Chicana mothers and daughters" (124, n. 7). Phillipa Kafka, however, positions the abuelita less favourably, among the "cultural collaborationists" in patriarchy mentioned earlier (10). While at least some of these aspects, both good and bad, are present in *Caramelo*'s abuelita, Cisneros again refuses to sanctify or vilify, but she complicates the process of maternal transmission through a range of significant obstacles: Mexican from Mexico, Soledad, the Awful Grandmother, hears the English language of her American grandchildren as the chatter of monkeys (*Caramelo* 28); the maternal line between Lala and the Awful Grandmother zigzags around the father, for *Caramelo*'s abuelita is the father's mother and her greatest attachment is to her first-born son; perhaps most significantly, she dies, leaving her most influential talks with her granddaughter to occur posthumously.

In the relationship of Lala and her grandmother, *Caramelo* shifts the focus from an older generation's endeavours to communicate self-valuing attitudes, to a younger generation's ability to understand the maternal past. To achieve the liberating transformation that maternal transmission offers, Lala, both literally and metaphorically, must not only hear and listen but also translate the grandmother's story, across obstacles and borders, for herself and for the grandmother. "For your good understanding and my poor telling," she seems to be explaining to the reader in the first chapter of part 2 as she begins narrating her life "history" (91), but perhaps she is also speaking to her grandmother.

From the very first in *Caramelo*, Cisneros places storytelling itself in a female tradition of handiwork when, in the novel's "Disclaimer," she talks about the truth of her stories as "bits of string, odds and ends found here and there, embroidered together to make something new." Elaine Hedges's important discussion of texts and textiles, "The Needle or the Pen: The Literary Re-Discovery of Women's Textile Work," finds in female handiwork "a major source for understanding women of the past, and, as well, a source of subject matter and of images and metaphors for new creative work" (338). *Caramelo*'s symbol of the *rebozo*, the intricate, handwoven Mestizo shawl, fulfills Hedges's observations on all counts. Cisneros describes both *rebozos* and stories in terms of strands and loops (93, 115). The *rebozo*'s entanglements of braids and knots reflect not only the layered, complicated narrative, specifically situating it in Latin culture, but also the important mother–daughter legacies that a female tradition of handiwork and storytelling fulfills. The *rebozo* keeps reappearing throughout *Caramelo*. It connects the Awful Grandmother and the granddaughter/narrator who inherits it. For both, it functions as a defence (26) and a solace (263, 388) at different times. And as the older narrator, Lala, comes to realize, it is central to the understanding of the Awful Grandmother's story, to the time before she "became awful" (91).

The parents of Soledad, the Awful Grandmother, were "famed *robeceros*," but it was the mother's skilled "fingers that gave the shawls their high value because of the fringe knotted into elaborate designs. The art of *las empuntadoras*" (92) was a legacy bequeathed from mothers to daughters:

> Guillermina's mother had taught her the *empuntadora*'s art of counting and dividing the silk strands, of braiding and knotting them into fastidious rosettes, arcs, stars, diamonds, names, dates, and even dedications, and before her, her mother taught her, her mother taught her as her own mother had learned it, so it was as if all the mothers and daughters were at work, all one thread interlocking and double-looping, each woman learning from the woman before, but adding a flourish that became her signature, then passing it on. (93)

For Soledad, the Awful Grandmother, the thread breaks, and in this sever-
ance of the mother–daughter connection, she loses access not only to the
skill with threads but also to a maternal language: "When Soledad was still
too little to braid her own hair, her mother died and left her without the
language of knots and rosettes.... There was no mother to take her hands
and pass them over a dry snakeskin so her fingers would remember the patterns of diamonds" (94). The language of the *rebozo* becomes lost to her.
When she sees her future husband, Narciso, for the first time, "because she
didn't know what else to do, Soledad chewed on the fringe of her *rebozo*. Oh,
if only her mother were alive. She could have told her how to speak with her
rebozo.... But who was there to interpret the language of the *rebozo* to Soledad?" (105).

Cut off from her mother, Soledad becomes similarly cut off, too, from
her daughter and her daughter's generation. She alienates both her own
daughter and her daughter-in-law, Lala's mother. The "unfinished *rebozo*"
her mother, Guillermina, left behind at her death, with its "design so complex no other woman was able to finish it without undoing the threads and
starting over," remains for her great-granddaughter, Lala, our narrator, to
continue (94). Significantly, at the same time that Guillermina was learning
the *empuntadora*'s art from her mother, she was also "weaving stories" (93).
Lala, by telling her grandmother's story, picks up the broken thread, weaving the Awful Grandmother, and herself, back into the female strands from
which they have been severed.

Ignorance of the Awful Grandmother's story leaves Lala vulnerable to
repeating it. Continually confronted by the Awful Grandmother from beyond the grave, Lala finally cries, "Grandmother, why do you keep haunting
me?" to which the Awful Grandmother proffers a counter-accusation: "Me?
Haunting you? It's *you*, Celaya, who's haunting *me*. I can't bear it. Why do
you insist on repeating my life? Is that what you want? To live as I lived?
There's no sin in falling in love with your heart and with your body, but wait
till you're old enough to love yourself first" (406). In the mother/daughter
plot, as Hirsch points out, repetition, "the daughter repeating a maternal
story that is unspeakable" (118), limits women writers and their fictional
heroines alike. But when they know their maternal stories intimately,
daughters have choice. They can "repeat and not repeat" (116), achieving
self-realization without sacrificing connection. The grandmother's presence in her life urges Lala to take up the *empuntadora*'s art in another form.
Instead of tying "knots" in her own "tangled life," as her grandmother had
done, Lala begins untying the knots of others's lives (408). "You'll tell my
story, won't you, Celaya?" the grandmother begs. "So that I'll be under-

stood? So that I'll be forgiven?" (408). Though not yet the mature narrator/ writer who comes forward at different times in the story, Lala is a young woman by the novel's end coming into the realization and acknowledgment of her legacy as the Awful Grandmother's granddaughter, the future writer. "Maybe it's my job to separate the strands and knot the words together for everyone who can't say them, and make it all right in the end. This is what I'm thinking," she states (428).

Telling her abuelita's story moves Lala closer to the truth of her own, but a daughter's attempt to speak the lives of her maternal predecessors carries danger. In her discussion of daughters' memoirs of their mothers' lives, Walters questions if "in narrating the elusive experience of past events," a daughter can "do justice to the felt realities of her mother's existence?... Who can speak another's life with ... surety?" But Walters goes on to distinguish between two kinds of daughter voices: one that assumes it is "a repository" for the mother's life, and thinks, "your history ends here with me: I am the result of your life, and I can speak the truth of it," and another that lays claim only to interested chronicling. Cisneros's narrative method fits Walters's definition of the "dialogic chronicler" who "realizes ... that the sifting through the complex meanings of generations of women is about dialogue, a multitude of voices, a dialectic of mothers and daughters.... To be a chronicler is to be ... wary of any claims to truth, aware that there are many chroniclers, many ways of telling a story" (167–68). In Lala's account of the Awful Grandmother's life, Cisneros blatantly engages in just such a chronicling dialectic. *Caramelo*'s part 2, "When I Was Dirt," has not only Lala telling the Awful Grandmother's story, but also the Awful Grandmother intervening directly in her account, attempting to balance Lala's "lies" with her own truths (188). The double-voiced narrative includes Lala's resistance but also the grandmother's withdrawal—"From here on, you're on your own," she tells Lala, speaking out of annoyance over what she perceives as a one-sided misreading of facts (205). But in granting autonomy to her granddaughter over the storytelling of which her own life is the subject, Soledad also enacts faith, however begrudging, in her female successor.

Cisneros's multivoiced storytelling rejects the possibility of a master narrative for mothers and daughters. Her paradigm is fluid; its vision, inclusive. It acknowledges not only the untold— "unspeakable"—stories of maternal lives (Hirsch 118), but also the unspeakable acts of paternal begettings and abandonings that have an impact on mothers and children. *Caramelo* begins with the family portrait that is "incomplete" because Lala is missing. "It's as if I didn't exist," she thinks, initially, but her second thought, "it's as if I'm the photographer," proves more true, and the novel ends with her own *recuerdo* of another missing daughter (4). The title's *caramelo* refers to the design of the unfinished *rebozo*—"a beautiful blend of toffee, licorice, and vanilla stripes flecked with black and white" (94)—but also to the daughter of her grandmother's washerwoman, to "the girl Candelaria," who has "skin the color of a caramelo ... smooth as peanut butter, deep as burnt-milk candy" (34). The double reference to the prized *rebozo* and Candelaria is the visible expression of bonds that run deep, for Candelaria is the unacknowledged daughter of Lala's father, the daughter he had with Ampara, the old washerwoman.

Perhaps Lala's embrace of feminism is most evident in her attempt to retrieve the illegitimate Candelaria, the missing daughter, the lost sister, from obscurity, and establish her connection to the maternal figures of her father's family. Lala attempts to give Candelaria her place in the grandmother's story—she is surely among the reasons for the Awful Grandmother's seeking forgiveness—but also to recognize Candelaria's life as a subject in its own right. At first, Candelaria is the secret passed on from mother-in-law to daughter-in-law to cause pain; then, she becomes the secret that Lala's mother reveals to her when her father is ill in the hospital and does not want her "to find out from somebody mean and be surprised" as she was (404). Lala's mother says, "I can't think of her name" (404), but Lala names her, recalling their family vacation in which she was included as the "*criada* [housemaid] who went with us"—"I think about Candelaria'" she affirms, "bobbing in the sea at Acapulco. The sun sparkling in little gold flecks all around her. Her face squinting that squint that I make, that Father makes. Her face suddenly Father's face" (405) which "is the same as the Grandmother's, the same face as mine" (430). She remembers Candelaria's weaving of the palm frond for her—"My hands taught me," Candelaria says of her skill—that places her as Guillermina's direct descendant (77).

At the novel's end, Candalaria is still missing. The washerwoman and the washerwoman's daughter disappeared "as if the earth swallowed them up" (69). The novel's title only half names the lost sister, and she remains still the lost daughter. Nonetheless, the focus on the lost sister reaffirms the importance of female experience, and the value of female continuity. Lala's telling is only partial, but the recovery has begun. "The girl Candelaria, my sister, the oldest, and me, the youngest," Lala thinks, placing them together in a continuum (428). In acknowledging their shared father, Lala forces too the recognition of multiple mothers. *Caramelo*'s narrative is a site of resistance to the erasure of mothers and daughters who can lay no claim to paternal recognition and acknowledgment. The daughter/narrator bears witness to their existence, defies their elision and disappearance.

The maternal figures surrounding Cisneros's narrators tend to be strong. They talk back at the patriarchy in a variety of ways, most times gently, sometimes more lustily. Perhaps their daughter/narrators' feminist progression is most evident in both Esperanza's and Lala's talking eventually for other women rather than back at men. The daughter/narrators move from listening to their own telling, ensuring a path from the past to a different kind of future. They follow a model for moving forward that encompasses and embraces, rather than rejects their maternal legacies, one that encourages their awareness of women's situations and advances their individuality even as they continue to stroll "arm-in-arm" (Mora 152). The daughter/narrators' stories become a kind of maternal begetting, for in daring to notice and express the multitude of details, they end up recording the fullness of female lives.

Notes to Chapter 18

1 The autobiographical note in the Vintage Contemporaries edition of *The House on Mango Street* (following p. 110), in copies printed before the publication of *Caramelo* in 2002, and in the *Vintage Cisneros* of 2004 (inside the front cover) contains these descriptions of Cisneros.

2 For an overview of female archetypes in Chicana literature, see, for example, Leal, and Rebolledo, *Women Singing*, ch. 3.

3 Irigaray adds a further suggestion: "One might also add the mask of femininity that one sees in mythology beginning with Athena" (Todd 239).

4 While Hirsch's discussions are limited to white, mainstream literature, mostly from the nineteenth and early twentieth centuries, her ideas remain suggestive starting points for interpreting literary mother–daughter relationships generally; see, for instance, Yi-Lin Yu's use of Hirsch in her recent work on mother–daughter relationships in women writers of the diaspora.

5 See Gutierrez (57–61), who suggests how the cultural context complicates the mother–daughter relationship for Chicanas. For discussions of mother and daughter relationships in literature by women of colour, see Bell-Scott et al. and Brown-Guillory.

6 See, for instance, de Valdes, Doyle, and Ganz, for discussions of the influence that both Cisneros's and Esperanza's mothers have on the developing daughter/artist. In her interview with Martha Satz, Cisneros comments on the similarity between her own mother and Esperanza's. For a reading of *Mango* in the *Bildung/Künstlerroman* tradition, see Eysturoy 89–112.

7 Wollstonecraft's *A Vindication of the Rights of Woman* (1792) is an early contribution to the tradition of liberal feminism that seeks equal rights for women through

legal and social reforms without revolutionary change. For a concise definition,
and summary of its implications, see "liberal feminism" in *Encyclopedia of Feminist Theories*, edited by Lorraine Code.

8 See Sugiyama for a discussion of feet and shoes in *Mango Street*.

9 Sanborn uses the Johnson edition of Dickinson's poems in which this is poem 742.

10 Sanborn quotes from Sandra Cisneros, "Notes to a Young(er) Writer."

Works Cited

Anzaldúa, Gloria E. "Quincentennial: From Victimhood to Active Resistance:" Ines-Hernandez Avila y Gloria E. Anzaldua (1991). *Interviews Entrevistas*. Ed. AnaLouise Keating. New York: Routledge, 2000. 177–94.

Bell-Scott, Patricia, et al., eds. *Double Stitch: Black Women Write about Mothers and Daughters*. 1991. New York: HarperPerennial 1993.

Brown-Guillory, Elizabeth, ed. *Women of Color: Mother-Daughter Relationships in 20th-Century Literature*. Austin: University of Texas Press, 1996.

Cisneros, Sandra. *Caramelo*. 2002. New York: Vintage, 2003.

——. *The House on Mango Street*. 1984. New York: Vintage, 1991.

——. "Notes to a Younger(er) Writer." *Americas Review* 15.1 (1987): 74–76.

——. *Vintage Cisneros*. New York: Vintage, 2004.

Code, Lorraine, ed. *Encyclopedia of Feminist Theories*. London: Routledge, 2000.

Dickinson, Emily. *The Complete Poems*. Ed. Thomas H. Johnson. Boston: Little, Brown & Co., 1960.

Doyle, Jacqueline. "More Room of Her Own: Sandra Cisneros's *The House on Mango Street*." *MELUS* 19.4 (1994): 5–35.

Eysturoy, Annie O. *Daughters of Self-Creation: The Contemporary Chicana Novel*. Albuquerque: University of New Mexico Press, 1996.

Ganz, Robin. "Sandra Cisneros: Border Crossings and Beyond." *MELUS* 19.1 (Spring 1994): 19–29.

Gonzales-Berry, Erlinda. "The [Subversive] Mixquiahuala Letters: An Antidote for Self-Hate." *Chicana (W)rites on Word and Film*. Ed. María Herrera-Sobek and Helena María Viramontes. Berkeley, CA: Third Woman Press, 1995. 115–24.

Gutierrez, Ramon. "Community, Patriarchy and Individualism: The Politics of Chicano History and the Dream of Equality." *American Quarterly* 45.1 (1993): 44–72.

Hedges, Elaine. "The Needle or the Pen: The Literary Re-Discovery of Women's Textile Work." *Tradition and the Talents of Women*. Ed. Florence Howe. Urbana: University of Illinois Press, 1991. 338–64.

Herrera, Cristina. "The Rejected and Reclaimed Mother in Sandra Cisneros's *Caramelo*." *Journal of the Association of Research on Mothering* 10.2 (Fall/Winter 2008): 184–95.

Hirsch, Marianne. *The Mother/Daughter Plot: Narrative, Psychoanalysis, Feminism.* Bloomington: Indiana University Press, 1989.

Kafka, Phillipa. *(Out)Classed Women: Contemporary Chicana Writers on Inequitable Gendered Power Relations.* Westport, CT: Greenwood Press, 2000.

Leal, Luis. "Female Archetypes in Mexican Literature." *Women in Hispanic Literature: Icons and Fallen Idols.* Ed. Beth Miller. Berkeley: University of California Press, 1983. 227–42.

Mora, Pat. "Mothers and Daughters." *In Other Words: Literature by Latinas of the United States.* Ed. Roberta Fernandez. Houston: Arte Publico Press, 1994. 152.

O'Reilly, Andrea, and Sharon Abbey, eds. *Mothers and Daughters: Connection, Empowerment, and Transformation.* Lanham, MD: Rowman & Littlefield, 2000.

Petty, Leslie. "The 'Dual'-ing Images of la Malinche and la Virgen de Guadalupe in Cisneros's *The House on Mango Street.*" *MELUS* 25.2 (2000): 119–32.

Rebolledo, Tey Diana. "Abuelitas: Mythology and Integration in Chicana Literature." *Woman of Her Word: Hispanic Women Write.* Ed. Evangelina Vigil. Houston: Arte Publico Press, 1983. 148–58.

——. *Women Singing in the Snow: A Cultural Analysis of Chicana Literature.* Tucson: University of Arizona Press, 1995.

Saldívar-Hull, Sonia. *Feminism on the Border: Chicana Gender Politics and Literature.* Berkeley: University of California Press, 2000.

Sanborn, Geoffrey. "Keeping Her Distance: Cisneros, Dickinson, and the Politics of Private Enjoyment." *PMLA* 116.5 (2001): 1334–48.

Satz, Martha. "Returning to One's House: An Interview with Sandra Cisneros." *Southwest Review* 82.2 (Spring 1997): 166–85.

Sugiyama, Michelle Scalise. "Of Woman Bondage: The Eroticism of Feet in *The House on Mango Street.*" *The Midwest Quarterly* 41.1 (1999): 1334–48.

Todd, Janet, ed. "Luce Irigaray Interviewed by Lucienne Serrano and Elaine Hoffman Baruch." *Women Writers Talking.* New York: Holmes & Meier, 1983. 231–45.

Valdes, Maria Elena de. "In Search of Identity in Cisneros's *The House on Mango Street.*" *Canadian Review of American Studies* 23.1 (1992): 55–71.

Walters, Suzanna Danuta. *Lives Together/Worlds Apart: Mothers and Daughters in Popular Culture.* Berkeley: University of California Press, 1992.

Yu, Yi-Lin. *Mother, She Wrote: Matrilineal Narratives in Contemporary Women's Writing.* New York: Peter Lang, 2005.

19

Cracking (Mother) *India* | BY TANJA STAMPFL

In her 1991 novel *Cracking India* Bapsi Sidhwa narrates the terror of Indian Partition from the point of view of eight-year-old Lenny.[1] Many critics have paid special attention to Sidhwa's (and Lenny's) privileged position as a Parsi, a member of a minority community that remained neutral in the national struggle. Feroza Jussawalla, for example, has explained how "Parsis have kept themselves apart. In *Cracking India*, this is a strength because the Parsis are then not implicated in the Hindu-Muslim struggles" (261). This advantage is not only rooted in religion, however, but pertains very much to class, since Lenny belongs to a well-to-do family. And it this distinction that Ambreen Hai has criticized most strongly, accusing Sidhwa of silencing the poorer (and darker) Ayah while privileging the voices of the more wealthy family members. While both critics' arguments are valid, this essay will take these interpretations a step further and offer a reading of *Cracking India* that emphasizes the multiple narrative planes of the text and its place in Indian culture. I argue that Bapsi Sidhwa's novel is a critique of traditional female allegories as Sidhwa revises acts of nation building through her exploration of textual mothers.

I therefore read *Cracking India* as a critique of the concept of Mother India (*Bharat Mata*) and an investigation of female nation building. The strength of Sidhwa's novel lies in its many textual and metaphorical layers concerning the figure of the mother, namely, mothers, mothering, and

Mother India. While biological mother-daughter bonds are mostly dysfunctional in the novel, women on a communal level take up the pieces and begin to unify and heal broken bodies and a cracked country, creating a new motherland that transcends the concept of *Bharat Mata*. Thus, the figure of the mother in *Cracking India* is central to the main discourse since it functions on historical, mythological, sociological, and literary levels.

Starting with its title,[2] *Cracking India* immediately draws attention to the role of the allegory. In his seminal article "Third-World Literature in the Era of Multinational Capitalism," Fredric Jameson has argued that all Third World texts are to be read as national allegories: "The story of the private individual destiny is always an allegory of the embattled situation of the public third-world culture and society" (69). While this assertion constitutes a "sweeping hypothesis," as Jameson himself has acknowledged, figures such as that of the Ayah in Sidhwa's novel do invite such allegorical interpretations. Firstly, Ayah is an occupation (nanny) and not a personal name, which reduces the character to a type. Secondly, as the 18-year-old Ayah attracts British, Hindu, and Muslim suitors, so do Great Britain, Nehru, and the Muslim League vie for a young India that is full of promises. Lastly, the Ayah becomes the most central victim of Partition violence in the novel, thereby symbolizing the suffering of the nation as it is divided.

The question arises, however, whether a purely allegorical reading as Jameson proposes it limits the interpretation of the text. In fact, a direct parallel between Ayah and the new nation of India[3] ignores the many other voices in the national discourse and the role of women more generally. On a more textual level, therefore, Ayah's role as a surrogate mother for Lenny suggests a link between the allegory of India and the figure of the mother. Interestingly, the mothers in this narrative have a rather distant and complicated relationship with their daughters, while the mother figures,[4] women who perform acts of mothering, develop a strong bond that overcomes religious and ethnic enmities, thus rebuilding and creating a new nation.

The mothering figures in Lenny's life inspire love and trust, while Lenny's biological mother leaves her daughter unsure and confused. In order to foreground the central role of the mothering figures in her life, Lenny describes Ayah and her godmother in detail right at the beginning of the novel. Of Ayah, Lenny says that "the covetous glances Ayah draws educate me," (12) hinting at a duty that has been traditionally associated with the mother.[5] It is Ayah who introduces Lenny to the outside world by pushing the little girl in her pram, and through Ayah Lenny experiences most personally the violence and hatred of Partition. As Ayah performs the role of the motherly educator, Godmother offers the motherly love and affection that Lenny needs: "The bond that ties [Godmother's] strength to my weakness, my fierce demand to her nurturing, my trust to her capacity to contain that trust—and my loneliness to her compassion—is stronger than the bond of motherhood. More satisfying than the ties between men and women" (13). The connection between Lenny and Godmother is stronger than any other conceivable relationship, even stronger than motherhood.

In contrast, Lenny introduces her relationship to her biological mother as one fraught with insecurities and unfulfilled longing. When her cast is being removed, Lenny cries out for help to her mother, who does not respond. Lenny concludes that "she too is aligned with them" (15). A few days later, Lenny realizes that she has been tricked into silence and "my mother collaborated in the betrayal" (17). While these may seem childish complaints, Lenny hints at a deeper instability in her poignant description of her mother's unreliable love:

> Her motherliness. How can I describe it? While it is there it is all-encompassing, voluptuous. Hurt, heartache and fear vanish. I swim, rise, tumble, float, and bloat with bliss. The world is wonderful, wondrous—and I a perfect fit in it. But it switches off, this motherliness. I open my heart to it. I welcome it. Again. And again. I begin to understand its on-off pattern. It is treacherous. (50–51)

Rather than offering security and constancy as Godmother's or Ayah's love does, Lenny's relationship with her mother is characterized by doubts, questions, and feelings of inferiority.

Lenny and her mother, however, are still the mildest example of dysfunctional mother–daughter relationships in the novel.[6] While Lenny feels she cannot rely on her mother's love, Papoo cannot trust her mother, Muccho, at all. Muccho hates Papoo and habitually abuses her. Lenny is outraged by the brutality that pervades this relationship: "Submissive in all other respects, Muccho's murderous hatred of [her] daughter makes her irrational" (55). Not only does she insult Papoo and beat her almost into unconsciousness regularly, but Muccho takes her ultimate revenge when she drugs Papoo and marries her to "an elderly and cynical dwarf" (199). After the ceremony, Muccho feels vindicated, and Papoo disappears from the narrative without a trace, like so many abused women during Partition. In fact, as we lose Papoo, Hamida enters the narrative. She was abused by Sikhs and her husband will not take her back, even though she is the mother of two children. Although she loves her children, she will remain absent in their lives. So, all three women, Lenny's mother, Muc-cho, and Hamida, are distanced from their daughters, either emotionally or physically, and thus indicate a serious rupture between mothers and daughters.

While the alienation between mothers and daughters does not consti-tute a major theme in Indian literature,[7] it is quite prominent in the works of women writers from the West Indies.[8] On the one hand, the distancing can be understood as what Laura Niesen de Abruna calls "the effects of the loss of maternal matrix. The alienation from the mother becomes a meta-phor for the white Creole girl's alienation from the mother culture, Eng-land" (14). Prominent writers like Jamaica Kincaid and Michelle Cliff, for example, have elaborated on this complex mixture of estrangement and longing in their novels. Since *Cracking India* is set during the time of In-dependence and Partition, an alienation from the British seems to be only logical. The British are still quite visible in the beginning of the text, but they are preparing their departure, predicting a bloodbath as the various religious and ethnic groups will fight for power among themselves. This comparison, however, does not do justice to the gendered quality of the metaphor without an additional qualification.

Once the British have departed, Mother India does not present herself as a nurturing nation, but rather continues some of the oppression initi-ated during Imperialism, especially toward her daughters. Indian women are oppressed by the British nationally, but they are also subjugated by their own men locally. Radha Kumar has demonstrated this double standard through the trope of rape:

> By the end of the nineteenth century, therefore, the issues of rape and racism were interlinked.... Yet if nationalists were beginning to use rape as example of impe-rialist barbarism, it was clearly seen as a violation of community—or national—honour, rather than an act of violence against women. Rape, it seems, was a taboo subject, nameable only when committed by outsiders. (37)

The imperialist rape metaphor emerges in *Cracking India* not through the British but through Indian men.[9] It seems that the only change Indepen-dence brought to the women of India was the skin colour of their rapists. The British have left and now the Sikh neighbour, Muslim butcher, or Hindu friend becomes the outsider who will rape and murder. The promise of a new nation as a nurturing and safe home has turned into a patriarchal power game of violence.

As India loses its common enemy and differences emerge more strongly than ever among Indians, women are the main victims of the ensuing violence. *Cracking India* demonstrates this alienation succinctly:

> One day everybody is themselves—and the next day they are Hindu, Muslim, Sikh, Christian. People shrink, dwindle into symbols. Ayah is no longer just my all-encompassing Ayah—she is also a token. A Hindu.... Imam Din and Yousaf, turning into religious zealots, warn Mother they will take Friday afternoons off for the Jhuma prayers.... Hari and Moti-the-sweeper and his wife Muccho, and their untouchable daughter Papoo, become ever more untouchable as they are entrenched into their low Hindu caste.... Godmother, Slavesister, Electric-aunt and my nuclear family are reduced to irrelevant nomenclatures—we are Parsee. What is God? (101–02)

While the new religious awareness, and ensuing division, encompasses everybody, the novel seems to emphasize that it is mainly men who act on these differences. Ayah's admirers turn against one another, and the Sikh male neighbours invade Ranna's village and rape and kill all Muslim women and children they can get their hands on. It is a group of Muslim *men* who come to Lenny's house to take away all Hindus. And it is a group of Hindu men who stop trains and cut off the breasts of Muslim women. No religious group is better than the other, but the perpetrators are almost always men, and the majority of the victims are women.

While the mother nation does not look out for them, women perform their motherly duties toward one another. Women are not only victims in this novel; they reach out to help one another and, in contrast to the men, ignore religious and ethnic differences. Lenny's female family members, such as her mother and her aunt, first bring gasoline to areas that are in need and then establish the camp for fallen women in the back of Lenny's house. They provide for these women and take care of them regardless of their religious beliefs. Godmother, on the other hand, searches actively for Ayah and is not afraid to confront Ice-Candy-Man. Indeed, female loyalty even extends across species when Lenny's mother interferes with Imam Din's chastisement of a cat that has been stealing food from the kitchen. "'Let her go at once!' screams Mother, slamming shut the door of the car. She cannot see the cat's gender—it is secreted behind the door—but the rest of us seem to know it's a *him*. Mother grabs hold of Imam Din's shirt.... She strikes his legs, arms, shoulders and even his shaven head" (237). While Lenny might feel insecure of her mother's love, the bond between women in general is undoubtedly very strong. Sangeeta Ray has claimed that *"Cracking*

India brilliantly represents the manner in which the referent home is un-moored from a localized space and translated into a metaphor—the moth-erland—in masculine, nationalist vocabularies" (134). While Sidhwa indicts this masculine image of the nation by depicting its brutality and irrational-ity, she balances the male representation of the motherland with a female version of nation making as the women pick up the pieces and begin to unify and mend broken bodies and a cracked country.

The women in this novel thus transcend the role of the other—which the British inhabited and the Indians projected on to one another after Inde-pendence—by building a community. Sandria Freitag has linked this con-cept specifically to the act of nation making: "If we take communalism ... to mean a politicized community activism focused on any group smaller than the emerging postimperial nation, we see two broad new ideologies developing in this period: communalism and nationalism" (291). Lenny's mother and Electric-aunt's actions in particular can certainly be seen as ac-tivist since they have to act secretly and put themselves in danger. Moreover, actions like the recovery of missing women are not purely imaginary, but constitute a fictional representation of real activism conducted by women in India and Pakistan during Partition, as Urvashi Butalia among others has shown.[10] They become the new mothers of the nation by actively creating connections and building bridges between religions and classes in their own communities.

The more traditional and passive role of the woman in the nation thus only precedes an active engagement with history; women in the commu-nity hold together when the nation is breaking apart. Sangeeta Ray in par-ticular has explained the more traditional influential role of feminism in India: "After 1857 the figure of the Hindu woman begins to function as a crucial semiotic site in and around which the discourses of imperialism, nationalism, an Indian postcolonialism, and feminism are complexly in-scribed" (8). Ayah especially symbolizes this figure when she entertains her suitors of all religious backgrounds and participates in the plans of the fu-ture nation. When she becomes a victim of the ensuing battle for land and nationhood, Ayah allegorizes the traditional public female side of Partition: victimization and self-sacrifice. And yet, Godmother and Lenny's mother recognize the danger and consequences of the political changes for women and recover Ayah, as well as many other fallen women. With *Cracking India*, Sidhwa thus reinserts the female voice and agency into the official version of Indian history.

This act of healing and communalism is not only political in a national sense, but is also linked to the national allegory of *Bharat Mata*, a conservative and oppressive trope that valorizes women's suffering for the national cause. Kumari Jayawardena claims that even Nehru was very much aware of women's plight in the postcolonial nation: "He was quite conscious that women had to engage in a double struggle, against imperialism and against oppression by men and that these struggles were intimately linked" (98). Elsewhere, Jayawardena further explains that "the movement towards women's emancipation ... was acted out against a background of national struggles, aimed at political independence, asserting a national identity, and modernizing society" (3). While the nationalist struggle is intimately linked to the feminist movement, *Cracking India* does not completely deconstruct the traditional role of the mother. Rather, Sidhwa sets up Mother India as a dangerous and yet realistic trope that the characters grapple with. Even though some characters seem to overcome conservative ties and transcend traditional gender roles, Mother India always lurks in the shadows of the text.

A good example of the conflict between the principles of Mother India and the role of a new activist mother presents itself in Lenny's mother. She is an activist for women but remains very dependent on her husband. In fact, Lenny explicitly comments on the difference in her mother's behaviour between the intimate family circle and in public when she and her brother Adi hide underneath the dinner table and are discovered by the adults. "She beamed at us in that way I have begun to notice and resent: her 'other people-are-around' way.... Half asleep I can still hear them laugh.... And that hooting and rollicking woman my remote and solemn mother?" (74). In line with the performance in front of dinner guests, Lenny's parents are entrenched in a ritual where the father constantly either ignores or scolds the mother, and she is his obedient servant. Some passages even hint at physical abuse and leave Lenny's mother completely dependent on her husband's favours and money.[11] It is indeed difficult to link the activist and courageous woman with the suppliant and yielding mother.

And yet, this seemingly jarring depiction becomes quite coherent when viewed through the lens of metaphorical nationalist language. Sumathi Ramaswami, for instance, has clarified the gendered notion of the nation:

> Bourgeois nationalisms in many parts of the world renegotiated and reaffirmed a new sexual division of labor in which man reigned over the public realm of politics and power, while woman was placed on a pedestal as the hallowed essence of the nation, even as she was firmly put in her place, in the home, as the mother of its future citizens. (2)

This conservative and idealized notion also matches Sandhia Shetty's definition of Mother India, where she describes the mother as "divine goddess or spiritual, domestic, non-working asexual bourgeois mother—exemplary of ideal bourgeois-nationalist femininity" (70). Interestingly, Lenny attributes godlike qualities to both Ayah and her mother. Ayah displays the "unconcern of the Hindu goddess" (12), and Lenny's mother exhibits a remote and godlike beauty: "The hint of coldness, common to such chiseled beauty, is overwhelmed by the exuberance of her innocence. I feel she is beautiful beyond bearing" (50).

Even more to the point, the idea of Mother India parallels Gandhi's idea of women. Kumari Jayawardena explains that Gandhi recognized women's struggle and supported gender equality, but in a limited way:

> Gandhi's view on women was located within a religious sense of the word and within the patriarchal system, projecting a concept of women's role as being complementary to that of men and embodying virtues of sacrifice and suffering. In 1921 he stated: "To me the female sex is not the weaker sex; it is the nobler of the two: for it is even today the embodiment of sacrifice, silent suffering, humility, faith, and knowledge." (95)

Gandhi's view of women is significant because he is also one of the front fighters of Indian Independence, and thus his views have communal and national implications. And while he does not specifically name the concept of Mother India, Gandhi's description of the woman's role and the trope of Mother India are too similar to be overlooked if we consider Vijay Mishra's definition of the term as a translation of "*bharata mata* behind which stands the Sanskrit compound *matrbhumi*, Motherland" (125). So while *Bharat Mata* signifies a national ideal, especially so shortly after Independence, Partition exposes the inherent patriarchal matrix within this ideal as two nations wage war on the bodies of their women.

Moreover, Mother India and the idealization of a victimized and broken woman does not stop at the political level, but extends to cultural, religious, and artistic traditions. On the one hand, Mother India is a common artistic trope, as Katherine Mayo's 1927 book and Mehboob's 1956 eponymous film demonstrate. The first depicts a woman who coheres exactly to Gandhi's ideal, and the second criticizes the concept by treating the subject ironically.[12] What is more, in his book *Mother Worship* (1982) James Preston has shown that this patriarchal (and imperial) depiction of the mother and the nation also emerges in religion: "These female deities were associated with the founding of the raja's kingdom in legends portraying his successful conquest and right of sovereignty over local tribal peoples. Thus, the raja's tutelary goddess was a composite of numerous tribal goddesses who became amalgamated and absorbed into the protective service of the royal household" (213). The cult of motherhood and the veneration of Mother India is thus a problematic national and religious symbol that aims at uniting all Indians but in fact aids in suppressing women's status and equality.[13]

Cracking India comments on traditional Indian literature and religion by engaging, challenging, and deconstructing the concept of Mother India. Lenny's mother fits Gandhi's ideal since she is both devout and humble; she fights for her nation in a nonviolent way without neglecting her duties toward her children and husband. She is both innovator and conservator. Even more significantly, Gandhi appears in the text, and Lenny and her mother react quite differently to the great spiritual leader. Lenny's mother listens to him devoutly, follows his instructions obediently, and gains his blessing:

> Beneath her blue-tinted and rimless glasses Mother's eyes are downcast, her head bowed, her bobbed hair—and what I assume is her consternation—concealed beneath her sari. But when Gandhijee pauses, she gives him a sidelong look of rapt and reverent interest. And two minutes later, not the least bit alarmed, she earnestly furnishes him with the odor, consistency, time and frequency of her bowel movements. When she finishes she bows her head again, and Gandhijee passes his hand over her head: and then, absently, as if it were a tiresome afterthought, over mine. (95)

This passage demonstrates both Lenny's mother's absolute devotion, which she will continue to exhibit throughout the rest of the novel by adhering to his womanly ideal in her private home, and Lenny's more complicated and doubtful attitude toward Gandhi. And while he is the first man in front of whom Lenny lowers her eyes, she also hints at a reversal of that humility and explicitly links Gandhi to Partition violence. "It wasn't until some years later—when I realized the full scope and dimension of the massacres—that I comprehended the concealed nature of the ice lurking deep beneath the hypnotic and dynamic femininity of Gandhi's non-violent exterior" (96). Lenny seems to detect a certain level of deceptiveness in Gandhi, who on the one hand propagates (female) nonthreatening nonviolence, and yet idealizes the suffering of women in the national struggle. Only by becoming the literal violated body of the nation or by upholding traditional patriarchal structures can Indian women aspire to the ideal of Mother India.

This difference in the perception of Gandhi's beliefs between Lenny and her mother offers a cultural reading of the alienation between the two. In addition to a displacement from the imperial culture in India, Lenny feels alienated from her mother culture: a tradition that sanctions the op-pression of women and tolerates the sexual harassment, assault, and abuse of its own mothers, daughters, and sisters, a tradition venerated in the form of Mother India. For while the public mass violence surges only during one time period, the general and more local harassment exists before, during, and after Partition. Every man who ever lays his eyes on Ayah tries to seduce her, regardless of the historical or political circumstances. Lenny's mother has to obey her husband at all times, and Lenny is subject to the voyeurism of her brother and the sexual advances of her cousin even after the official violence is over.[14] In fact, Lenny's cousin promises to show her what rape is one day, extending and continuing the public violence and humiliation of Partition into the private home.

The strength of Sidhwa's novel thus lies in its many textual and meta-phorical layers. *Cracking India* depicts national allegories that link her text to traditional "Third World literature" and to Indian and Hindu culture and religion, and at the same time critiques and transcends them. This text re-writes Indian Partition history from a female point of view, thus revealing the double oppression of imperial and patriarchal powers, offering a vari-ety of approaches and reactions to these oppressions. Sidhwa engages in creating what Timothy Brennan has called "the myth of the nation," which "supplies a retrospective pattern of moral values, sociological order, and magical belief, the function of which is to strengthen tradition and endow it with a greater value and prestige" (45). In this sense, *Cracking India* aims at a more inclusive image of India while at the same time acknowledging that any metaphor or allegory for the whole nation has to deconstruct itself. The novel lends a voice to the otherwise silent protagonists of Partition, and articulates their issues on a national and international level. Sidhwa is not afraid to criticize patriarchal traditions nationally and to expose those who follow them blindly, and she also contributes to an image of Southeast Asia on an international level by balancing famous national allegories like Sal-man Rushdie's *Midnight's Children* (1982), which presents a primarily male version of nation building, with a more female version.[15] *Cracking India* is not only a reaction to patriarchal and traditional texts, but a subtle narration of individual and national destinies that are engaged in creating a sense of community that each of them can call home.

Most importantly, the novel sheds new light on the role of the mother in the Third World on a private, national, cultural, and literary plane. The postcolonial landscape in countries like India and Pakistan has created new responsibilities for women. The traditional mother culture, revered and idealized under imperial and foreign rule, might be treacherous and finally be revealed as propagating oppressive patriarchal values. The communication and education between mothers and daughters, therefore, might be tainted by imperialistic and paternalistic discourse that is of no help to the young generation of nation builders. Rather, *Cracking India* seems to propose a fresh way of mothering, one that transcends religious and national borders; these acts of mothering do not operate on difference, but recognize sameness without blindly equalizing experience. The trope of the national allegory can never be sufficient because the solidarity and nation building the women in this novel engage in is not limited to India or Pakistan. The danger of simplistic unification lies in neglecting the variety of communities and individuals engaged in postcolonial history. Rather, *Cracking India* aims to do justice to a variety of experiences and is careful not to generalize the experience of Partition. Instead of erecting borders between people, as Partition did, the women dismantle barriers by embracing one another's differences and reaching out regardless of class, religion, and nationality. This transformation proves complex and difficult because it involves a conscious effort to question and reject traditional roles. Women have to consciously engage in mothering acts to birth new nations that are free of boundaries, discrimination, and violence.

Notes to Chapter 19

1 One day before India gained its independence from Great Britain in August 1947, the country was partitioned into the secular state of India and the Islamic state of Pakistan. This division led to much violence on both sides of the border, prompted by religious hatred between Hindus, Muslims, and Sikhs. Fear of oppression and discrimination led to mass migrations of Pakistani Hindus to India and of Indian Muslims to Pakistan.

2 I am using the American title of the novel, even though the British title, *Ice-Candy Man*, invites an allegorical reading as well that makes the male body, in this case the Ice-Candy-Man, a national allegory.

3 Even though *Cracking India* is a Pakistani novel, the story centres around Partition and thus the breaking up of the Indian nation primarily. While I do not want to generalize Indian and Pakistani experience, I do aim to emphasize that Sidhwa's national critique is not limited to one nation in particular. Rather, she makes a statement about nation building in a postcolonial context in general by using the example of India.

4 I distinguish the biological mothers from the mother figures as women who perform a mothering or nurturing function in the text.

5 Speaking from a German context, but nevertheless relevant for this discussion, Friedrich Kittler has pointed out the inherent connection between the mother and education: "The maternal gift is language in a nascent state, pure breath as a limit value from which the articulated speech of other begins.... Maternal instruction, in its positivity, was the input component of elementary acculturation techniques" (27).

6 I will mention here three mother figures primarily: Lenny's mother, Muccho, and Hamida. The figures of Electric-aunt and Ranna's mother do not offer much commentary on their role as biological mothers and in many ways serve as double images to Lenny's mother and Hamida respectively. Also, it seems that especially the mother–daughter relationship proves problematic, which I will explain in a feminist context.

7 This statement is based on findings of research on the figure of the mother in Indian literature, which is quite sparse and hardly mentioned.

8 Caribbean literature quite frequently elaborates on and details complex and complicated mother–daughter relationships. Jamaica Kincaid's novel *The Autobiography of My Mother* (1996), for example, narrates a daughter's search for her roots and ancestry, which are symbolized by the missing mother. Similarly, in her novel *Lucy* (1990) Kincaid describes a very intense and difficult bond between the protagonist, Lucy, who goes to the United States, and her mother in the Caribbean. Jean Rhys's *Wide Sargasso Sea* (1966), a Caribbean postcolonial response to *Jane Eyre* (1847), moreover, centralizes the image of the mother that has been projected onto the daughter, which leads to the daughter's decline into madness.

9 Kumar also explains that with the British prostitution increased and the red light districts developed where Ice-Candy-Man will hold Ayah (34–35). Prostitution, like rape, is a colonial act perpetrated by Indian (or Pakistani) men once the British have left.

10 In her book *The Other Side of Silence* Urvashi Butalia interviews women who were actively involved in rescue operations and thus lends a voice to the women who helped and those who were abused. She also points out quite shockingly how women were encouraged to kill themselves in order to maintain their honour. In some cases, men would kill their own wives and daughters before the mob reached them. Because the honor of the whole family is tightly connected to the women, men direct their violence always against women.

11 The scene where Lenny's mother has to coax and beg for a meagre sum of money and in the process has to take abuse and insult in the form of a game shows this dependence most clearly (77).

12 Sandhya Shetty describes Mayo's controversial book as a "sweeping diatribe against Hindu culture" and sees the work's primary importance in reinscribing "the figure [of Mother India] as a copulative and reproductive body. Pathologized,

this body was then refigured in the text as a sign of India's public health problem, in turn a symptom of a diseased body politic that justified its continued political subjection to imperial England" (61).

13 David Kinsley explains the concept of Mother India in his book *Hindu Goddesses* also as a religious concept that calls especially on the sons of India, who in this novel neglect their role and leave it up to the daughters of India to mend the pieces. Kinsley explains: "The fundamental conviction that the earth itself, of the Indian subcontinent itself, as a goddess, indeed, that she is one's mother, pervades the modern cult of Bharat Mata (Mother India), in which all Indians are called sons or children of India and are expected to protect their mother without regard for personal hardship and sacrifice" (181).

14 The relationship between Lenny and her cousin mirrors and demonstrates most clearly the inequality between women and men because they enact the same power games and rituals as Lenny's parents do. Moreover, many of Cousin's ideas and approaches are laden with sexuality and hint at violence.

15 Even though the scope of this essay does not allow for an in-depth comparison between Saleem and Lenny, *Cracking India* can be read as a female response to Rushdie's *Midnight's Children* as both protagonists are children and their lives are directly linked to the fate of the nation. Saleem's birth coincides exactly with India's official independence, and Lenny celebrates her birthday on the day of the partition between India and Pakistan. Both Rushdie and Sidhwa, however, invite a simple allegorical reading only in order to deconstruct it later in the text. As I have shown above, one of the greatest strengths of *Cracking India* lies in the questioning and critiquing of national allegories, a concept we have already seen when Saleem in *Midnight's Children* explodes because he cannot hold the multitude that India presents.

Works Cited

Abruna, Laura Niesen de. "Family Connections: Mother and Mother Country in the Fiction of Jean Rhys and Jamaica Kincaid." *Modern Critical Views: Jamaica Kincaid*. Ed. Harold Bloom. Philadelphia: Chelsea House, 1998. 13–35.

Brennan, Timothy. "The National Longing for Form." *Nation and Narration*. Ed. Homi Bhaba. London and New York: Routledge, 1990. 44–70.

Butalia, Urvashi. *The Other Side of Silence: Voices from the Partition of India*. New York: Penguin Books, 1995.

Freitag, Sandria B. *Collective Action and Community: Public Arenas and the Emergence of Communalism in North India*. Berkeley: University of California Press, 1989.

Hai, Ambreen. "Border Work, Border Trouble: Postcolonial Feminism and the Ayah in Bapsi Sidhwa's *Cracking India*." *Modern Fiction Studies* 46.2 (Summer 2000): 379–426.

Jameson, Fredric. "Third-World Literature in the Era of Multinational Capitalism." *Social Text* 15 (Fall 1986): 65–88.

Jayawardena, Kumari. *Feminism and Nationalism in the Third World*. 5th ed. London: Zed Books, 1994.

Jussawalla, Feroza. "Bapsi Sidhwa (1938–)." *South Asian Novelists in English: An A to Z Guide*. Ed. Jana C. Sanga. Westport, CT: Greenwood Press, 2003. 260–64.

Kincaid, Jamaica. *The Autobiography of My Mother*. New York: Farrar, Straus and Giroux, 1996.

——. *Lucy*. New York: Farrar, Straus and Giroux, 1990.

Kinsley, David. *Hindu Goddesses: Visions of the Divine Feminine in the Hindu Religious Tradition*. Berkeley: University of California Press, 1986.

Kittler, Friedrich A. *Discourse Networks 1800/1900*. Stanford, CA: Stanford University Press, 1990.

Kumar, Radha. *The History of Doing: An Illustrated Account of Movements for Women's Rights and Feminism in India 1800–1990*. New Delhi: Kali for Women, 1993.

Mishra, Vijay. "The Texts of *Mother India*." *Kunapipi* 11.1 (1989): 119–37.

Preston, James J., ed. *Mother Worship: Theme and Variations*. Chapel Hill: University of North Carolina Press, 1982.

Ramaswami, Sumathi. "The Demoness, the Maid, the Whore, and the Good Mother: Contesting the National Language in India." *International Journal of the Sociology of Language* 140 (1999): 1–28.

Ray, Sangeeta. *En-Gendering India: Woman and Nation in Colonial and Postcolonial Narratives*. Durham, NC: Duke University Press, 2000.

Rhys, Jean. *Wide Sargasso Sea*. New York: Norton, 1992.

Rushdie, Salman. *Midnight's Children*. New York: Penguin Books, 1982.

Shetty, Sandhya. "(Dis)figuring the Nation: Mother, Metaphor, Metonymy." *Differences* 7.3 (1995): 50–79.

Sidhwa, Bapsi. *Cracking India*. Minneapolis: Milkweed Editions, 1991.

20

Asian American Mothering in the Absence of Talk Story: *Obasan* and *Chorus of Mushrooms*

BY ANNE-MARIE LEE-LOY

> Whenever she had to warn us about life, my mother told stories ... a story to grow up on.
>
> —Hong Kingston 5
>
> Talk-story becomes a courageous act that leads to transformation and discovery, to the inscriptions of self.
>
> —Ho 135

Feminist debates surrounding mothering have been particularly interested in how the construction and maintenance of the institution of motherhood might be complicit with the oppressive strategies of patriarchal societies. Despite their various takes on the subject, however, these debates basically begin from the premise that mothering is fundamentally an act of caregiving or caretaking; that is, "maternal practice is governed by ... demands for [children's] preservation, growth and acceptability" (Ruddick 348). In this regard, the relationship between mothers and daughters is significant as mothering in North America inherently involves preparing daughters to live in a patriarchal society. Here, an important difference of experience has been identified between mothering among WASP families in North America and those of different racial and ethnic backgrounds. Specifically, WASP mothers have been accused of training their daughters to be silent and submissive, thereby perpetuating patriarchal culture. That a different priority underlies maternal practice in other racialized ethnic groups is memorably articulated by African American feminist bell hooks when she writes that "this emphasis on woman's silence may be an accurate remembering of what has taken place in the households of women from WASP backgrounds in the United States, but in black communities (and diverse ethnic communities), women have not been silent" (6).

hooks posits a very different model of motherhood when she asserts that mother–daughter mothering for African Americans and "diverse ethnic communities" takes place within a "world of woman speech, loud talk, angry words, women with tongues quick and sharp, tender sweet tongues, touching our world with their words" (6). For hooks, such speech is neither trivial nor trite; instead, it is an "act of resistance, a political gesture that challenges politics of domination" (8). When she also explains that her pseudonym was chosen to honour and ally herself with a female ancestor known for her boldness of speech (essentially identifying this relative as a mother figure), hooks shifts both the central goals and means of mothering in a significant fashion. Instead of perpetrating the institutions of the dominant culture, mothering is defined as an act that prepares daughters to "survive in systems that would oppress them" and "to challenge the systems of racial oppression" primarily by means of "woman speech" (Collins 68, 69).

The connection between mothering that aims to produce resistance and survival and the "world of speech" that hooks privileges finds particular resonance in Wendy Ho's analysis of Asian American writing. In *Her Mother's House: The Politics of Asian American Mother–Daughter Writing*, Ho argues that "talk stories"[1] in Chinese American fiction must be understood as a "heroic and subversive form of verbal expression—passed on from one woman to another across dislocations and relocations, generations, cultures and continents" (135). Embedded in such stories are the skills and knowledge that mothers believe their daughters will need to survive and contest North American discourses and practices of domination; thus, talk story must be understood to be an act of mothering through "woman speech." The actual content of such stories is also significant, for as hooks recognizes, "it is important that we speak. What we speak about is more important" (18). Fictional depictions of Asian American talk story are heavily invested in ethnic and cultural reproduction. They affirm and record ethnically specific legends and myths, as well as personal, communal, and national histories. Reading talk story as maternal practice rather than simply "textual tropes for the diaspora situation" or "a symbolic search for cultural roots" (Grice, *Negotiating Identities* 45) reveals that for ethnic mothers, fostering a "meaningful racial identity in children within a society that denigrates people of color" is a seminal component of mothering (Collins 68). Indeed, the development of an identity that incorporates a confident sense of ethnicity becomes both the hallmark of survival and the grounds upon which daughters can resist North American racism.

The Japanese Canadian novels *Obasan* and *Chorus of Mushrooms* are striking in that they lack traditional depictions of talk story as found in much Asian American fiction. Unlike Maxine Hong Kingston's *The Woman Warrior* or Amy Tan's *The Joy Luck Club*, for example, mothers, grandmothers, and aunts do not sit down with their daughters, granddaughters, and nieces to regale them with legends from Japan or to relate their personal struggles. Nevertheless, the mothers of *Obasan* and *Chorus of Mushrooms* are no less interested in the survival of their daughters. They choose, however, silence as their primary method of mothering. Although this choice apparently supports the daughters' physical survival, the novels reveal that it ultimately fails to bridge their daughters' sense of disconnection from both their ethnic heritage and their Canadian culture. Without such grounding, the daughters lack the "defiance that heals, that makes new life and new growth possible" in Canada (hooks 9). Thus, the absence of talk story in *Obasan* and *Chorus of Mushrooms* and the subsequent failure of the daughters to thrive emotionally and socially reifies the significance of talk story to Asian American mothering.

Of the two novels, Joy Kogawa's *Obasan* is undoubtedly the better known. Published in 1981, the novel garnered immediate critical and popular attention as the first Canadian fiction to address the history of Japanese Canadian internment and relocation during the Second World War. The story, told from the point of view of Naomi, who was a child during the war, is dominated by Naomi's quest to understand the disappearance of her mother. The unravelling of this mystery is intertwined with the telling of the larger story of Japanese Canadian Second World War experiences and an exploration of their devastating, long-term impacts on Japanese Canadian communities. Hiromi Goto's *Chorus of Mushrooms*, published over a decade after *Obasan*, focuses on a family of Japanese Canadians living on an isolated mushroom farm in the small town of Nanton, Alberta. Three generations of women share the house: Naoe; her daughter, Keiko; and Keiko's daughter, Muriel. Blurring the lines between voices, characters, and individual experiences, the novel explores the various ways in which each woman seeks to overcome her sense of dislocation and displacement.

The silence that Naomi encounters as she tries to discover what happened to her mother is arguably the overriding trope of *Obasan*, and it is this feature of the novel that has garnered significant critical comment.[2] It is not the intention of this essay to repeat such arguments here; rather, I would draw attention to the type and purpose of silence in the novel. It is true that Obasan speaks little throughout the novel, and, due to her absence and determination not to tell her story, Naomi's mother's voice is basically silenced. What is also significant, however, is what is lost with the refusal to speak: stories. The silence of the novel is the absence of talk story. The novel emphasizes this loss by marking a clear distinction between Naomi's life with her mother before the war and her life afterwards. Naomi remembers her early childhood as a period that was steeped in "stories, the voices of my mother ... or Obasan or Grandma Kato, soft through the filter of my sleepiness, carrying me away to a shadowy ancestry" (58). In particular, Naomi recalls that her mother often told her the Japanese folk story of Momotaro, the boy found in the peach. All stories apparently vanish, however, after the disappearance of her mother and Obasan's subsequent decision to push her language "deeply underground" (33).

Unlike *Obasan*'s, the household of *Chorus of Mushrooms* is filled with sound throughout Muriel's childhood. Every day, Naoe sits in the centre of the home releasing a "torrent of words, this tumble of sounds such roaring, sweeping, chanting, sighing" (21). What Naoe recounts is the traditional subject matter of talk story: her own personal history and Japanese legends and folk tales. Despite this riot of sound, however, talk story cannot be said to truly exist: Naoe will speak only Japanese, a language Muriel does not know. Since they are spoken but not communicated, Naoe's talk stories are effectively silenced. Further, Keiko refuses to tell stories of her own, leaving Muriel to describe her childhood with the caustic remark, "My Mom didn't tell tales at all. And the only make-believe she knew was thinking that she was as white as her neighbour" (29). Language barriers and the determined willfulness of Keiko to "put Japan behind" them leaves Muriel to grow up in an environment that is as barren of talk story as is Naomi's (207).

That the mothers' silence is to be read as maternal practice is revealed in its motivation. Specifically, this silence is meant to safeguard the children from Canadian politics of domination. Both novels reveal deeply embedded racism within cultural constructions of Canadian identity through the children's growing understanding that because of their ethnic heritage they are not seen as truly Canadian. For Naomi and her brother, Stephen (and, indeed, the Japanese Canadian community as a whole), the awareness that they are seen as outsiders occurs most overtly during the war with the recognition that they had been "named ... defined and identified by the way [they] were seen" (126). Similarly, Muriel describes a gradual childhood realization "that the shape of my face, my eyes, the colour of my hair affected how people treated me" (175). Furthermore, the children all discover that to be "seen" is also to have imposed upon them a set of limited and negative stereotypes, whether it be as an "enemy alien" in the case of Naomi and Stephen, or as an "exotic Oriental" in the case of Muriel.

The mothers in both novels are highly aware of the devastating impact of such racism for the children on both material and emotional levels, and their silence is meant to moderate some of its potential damage. Aunt Emily's journals of the time around the family's relocation, for example, specifically note that Obasan was behaving "very calm" and had made it clear that regarding their relocation, there should not be "any discussion in front of the kids. All she's told them is that they're going for a train ride" (117). Clearly, through her silence, Obasan tries to lessen the fear and pain of their forced dispersal. Naomi herself later identifies Obasan's behaviour as a "protective silence.... 'Kodomo no tame. For the sake of the children....' Calmness was maintained" (22). Similarly, Naomi's mother's injunction against the telling of her horrific experience in Nagasaki, along with her refusal to return to Canada, is motivated by a "wish to protect" her children (265). Keiko's choice to silence talk story, along with her change of diet and religion, is also a protective gesture. Muriel's father makes this clear when he explains their choices to Muriel:

> When we moved to Canada, your Mom and I, we decided it would be best for our children if we let them slip in with everybody else. Sure, we couldn't change the colour of their hair, or the shape of their face, but we could make sure they didn't stand out. That they could be as Canadian as everyone around them. (206–07)

Keiko is much more blunt when she tersely states, "If you want a child to have a normal and accepted lifestyle, you have to live like everyone else" (189).

As mother to Keiko and grandmother to Muriel, Naoe's decision to speak only in Japanese must also be read as an act of mothering; however, while Obasan's and Keiko's silence seems to spring from a desire to ensure the survival of their daughters on very practical levels—that is, ensuring that they do not "stand out"—Naoe's refusal to speak anything but Japanese has other motivations. Naoe seeks to protect and fortify Muriel's ethnic identity, and in doing so, to provide Muriel with the confidence needed to define and claim space for herself as a Japanese Canadian; or, as Naoe might put it, to "scrape [her] heel into the black ice on the highway and inscribe [her] name across this country" (108). The novel's opening images of Naoe as a disruptive force in the household ("People have to pass me to get inside this house. Don't try to sneak by, I might stick out my foot…. No one moves in this house without meeting my eyes. Hearing my voice" [4]) and as being specifically in conflict with the Canadian prairie winds ("Someone, something must stand against this wind and I will. I am" [5]) become central tropes of the novel. Through her voice, Naoe stakes a claim for a self-articulated Japanese presence on Canadian soil. Keiko's compulsive cleaning cannot erase Naoe, and the Canadian winds can neither blow Naoe away nor drown her out. Her Japanese voice is here to stay. Thus, although it is true that her stories are not literally understood by Muriel, Naoe's insistence on telling her stories becomes a powerful way to assert the validity of her ethnic experience and identity in the face of denigrating cultural forces. As such, her "silenced stories" provide Muriel with an important wall of defence in safeguarding her sense of self and, in the long run, gain Naoe acknowledgment as the family's "sentinel" and "protectress" (175).

In the short term, silencing talk story is somewhat effective in providing the daughters with some level of emotional and material protection. Naomi remembers that she found it comforting to hear the adults talking calmly while she went through the trauma of forcible relocation, while Muriel admits that her mother's decision to assimilate made her life easy in Nanton. A more long-term understanding of survival based on the daughters' ability to "carve out new territory in alien lands" does not, however, occur (Ho 137). Indeed, one of the first images in *Obasan* is that of Naomi in the coulee with her fingers tunnelled in the dirt. Naomi claims that her "fingers are roots," but quickly adds that she is marked by a "persistent thirst" (3). Such imagery suggests that Naomi's roots in Canada are shallow at best, a condition re-emphasized by the fact that Naomi is constantly identified by others as a foreigner. Combined with the powerful symbol of childlessness in Naomi's immediate family, these images vividly convey a picture of a people whose silence provides no substantial protection from Canadian discourses that define Japanese as "other" to "Canadian." Instead of ensuring that the next generation successfully survives by defining a place for itself in Canada, silence as maternal practice contributes to their "[disappearance] from the earth without a whimper" (21).

Muriel's memories of childhood reveal a similar sense of alienation despite her mother's assimilation to Nanton's norms: Muriel annually receives Valentine's Day cards with pictures of stereotypical Oriental women; she avoids other Asian children because she knows that while "Oriental people in single doses were well enough,… any hint of a group" was dangerous to her social survival (123); and her first boyfriend asks her to engage in "Oriental Sex." Muriel sums up these experiences in the simple yet evocative sentence, "It was hard growing up in a small prairie town, the only Japanese-Canadian for miles around" (121). As with *Obasan*, *Chorus of Mushrooms* extends the imagery of Muriel's alienation to the family as a whole by expressing the trauma of their displacement in terms of the body. The images of infertility, abortion, and physical damage (such as tonguelessness) in *Obasan* find parallels in the depictions of Muriel and her family as malnourished and suffering from aphasia. Indeed, the extent of Muriel's displacement is memorably captured when she barely musters the pathetically tentative, "I think I'm Canadian," when asked to identify herself (122).

The failure of silence as maternal practice to enable a deep level of survival for the daughters reveals both a particular collusion between issues of survival and identity that shape motherhood in ways peculiar to racialized ethnic women and the importance of talk story to Asian American mothering specifically. Because WASP, middle-class mothers and their children are automatically accorded access to societal structures of power and privilege on the basis of their race, the relationship between mothering, survival, and identity is primarily focused on "producing a child acceptable to the next generation" (Ruddick 354). In other words, the child's survival is based on his or her ability to take the place defined for her or him within such systems. The child's survival is not, therefore, entangled with the survival of a racial or ethnic identity. This is not the case for racialized ethnic mothers. Their attempts to ensure both the physical survival of their children and to help them find a place for themselves in society are inextricably commingled with issues of race and, oftentimes, class:

> Although white children can be prepared to fight racial oppression, their survival does not depend on gaining these skills. Their racial identity is validated by their schools, the media and other social institutions. White children are socialized into their rightful place in systems of racial privilege.... [Children of racialized ethnicities] must first be taught to survive in systems that would oppress them. Moreover, this survival must not come at the expense of self-esteem. Thus, a dialectical relation exists between systems of racial oppression designed to strip subordinated groups of a sense of personal identity and a sense of collective peoplehood, and the cultures of resistance to that oppression extant in various racial ethnic groups. For women of color, motherwork for identity occurs at this critical juncture. (Collins 68)

Caught in this "critical juncture," Obasan and Keiko silence talk story to focus on ensuring their daughters' physical and immediate safety. In the process, they are unable to foster that "culture of resistance" that grows out of a strong sense of ethnic validity. Without language, it is difficult, if not impossible, to counter and construct alternative representations of ethnicity to those produced in discourses of domination. Indeed, by depicting the failure of other cultural practices to foster the ethnic validation so necessary for the emotional survival of racialized ethnics, the novels affirm the importance of talk story as a maternal practice. For example, traditional Japanese culture places a strong emphasis on personal hygiene and grooming, including ear cleaning. Loved ones, particularly mothers and daughters, according to Naoe, will often clean each other's ears with specially constructed devices called *mimikaki*. Such ear cleaning occurs in *Chorus of Mushrooms*, but it is an activity that takes place in silence. Language barriers prevent Keiko and Naoe from speaking, and Keiko admonishes Muriel with the words "no more talking" as she cleans her ears (156). Practised in silence, this cultural activity clearly does not provide the groundwork for a constructive sense of ethnicity. In fact, despite having their ears cleaned by their mothers, Keiko continues her relentless pursuit of assimilation, and Muriel is described as being "so lonely I almost can't stand it" (161).

The failure of public bathing, another common practice in traditional Japanese culture, to engender a positive ethnic identity also reveals the weaknesses inherent in mothering without talk story. Public baths and bathing have particular cultural resonance to the Japanese, not only as a matter of hygiene, but because bathhouses are understood to be sites in which cultural values and socialization can be practised and a more culturally specific "group-think" mentality expressed (Murphy 78). Public bathing exists in *Obasan*, and if one considers the ritual of washing Naoe's hair as a type of bath, in *Chorus of Mushrooms* as well. But, as with the ear cleaning in *Chorus of Mushrooms*, it is an ethnic practice that is depicted as being largely conducted in the absence of talk story. Indeed, the most memorable depiction of bathing is the silent bathhouse in Slocan when Naomi and Obasan are rejected by the other women in the community. Significantly, in this episode, silence actually converges with cultural practice to fragment rather than fortify an ethnic identity.

The depiction of food in both novels provides yet another opportunity to explore how the loss of talk story negatively affects the ability to develop a spirit of resistance based on a confident articulation of ethnicity. It is perhaps unsurprising that attention would turn to the depiction of food in an analysis of mothering. After all, food is a basic necessity in ensuring survival, and food preparation is an "area of work and cultural activity traditionally … viewed as a 'natural role' for women" (Beoku-Betts 535). For ethnically marginalized groups, however, food can have additional significance as a symbol of cultural retention and the transmission of an ethnic identity. It has been argued, for example, that in *Obasan*, "expressions of resistance to racism and its internalization center on enjoyment or plea- sures specific to Japanese culture" and, even more specifically, to the enjoy- ment of Japanese food (Xu 60). In this regard, the traditional Japanese meal that Obasan cooks upon Uncle's reunion with the family in Slocan is read as a particularly radical rejection of the Canadian government's attempts to denigrate and dehumanize the family. It is important to note, however, that the scenes in which food is depicted as being a source of comfort and beauty are continually juxtaposed against the much more unappealing de- pictions of food throughout the rest of the novel: the tea dirtied with twigs and bits of rice puffs; the dried-up jam on Obasan's plastic tablecloth; her fridge containing "indescribable items ... too old for mould and past pu- trefaction" (48); and, of course, the food image that dominates the novel, namely Uncle's bread, described consistently as "stone." To understand this discrepancy in depiction, one need only consider the relationship be- tween Naomi's brother, Stephen, and food.

Stephen is often depicted as rejecting traditional Japanese food. On the train to Slocan, for example, he curtly tells Obasan "not that kind of food" (123) when she offers him a sticky rice ball. In Slocan, Stephen's lunches consist of "peanut-butter sandwiches, an apple, and a thermos of soup" in- stead of the more traditional Japanese food that Naomi eats (166). Stephen's rejection of Japanese food is not simply a matter of taste; rather, it must be contextualized in light of his exposure to the popular discourses of Japa- nese identity of the period: "All the Jap kids are ... bad and you're a Jap," his classmates inform him (76); "all the Japs have mustard-coloured faces and buck teeth" in the comic books he reads (109); in his board game (sig- nificantly called "Yellow Peril") "to be yellow ... is to be weak and small ... to be chicken" (165). The provision of ethnic food does not in and of itself address or challenge the negative stereotypes that Stephen faces. A sticky rice ball cannot re-envision the image of a weak, buck-toothed, mustard- yellow "Jap" in the way that alternative images and discourses, like those that might be created in talk story, can. Lacking the ability to challenge and contest discourse, ethnic food has no more power to nurture an assertive and confident sense of ethnicity than the spoiled, dirty, and rock-hard un- eaten bread of the novel has to provide nutrition.

In *Chorus of Mushrooms*, the connection between food and an ethnic identity is much more explicit. Keiko's assimilation and suppression of her ethnic identity is, for example, always described by alluding to her refusal to cook anything other than stereotypically Canadian fare. As Naoe puts it,

Keiko has "forsaken identity ... [c]onverted from rice and *daikon* to weiners and beans" (13). Keiko is also described as malnourished, imagery that finds parallel in the depictions of Muriel's constant hunger and craving, the result of her own "malnourished culture" (99). Naoe's resistance to assimilation is also expressed through her diet. She refuses to eat the food that Keiko prepares, preferring the salted squid, rice crackers dipped in soya sauce, and bottles of *sake* that her brother sends her. Even Muriel's father's fragile connection to his ethnic heritage is expressed in food, namely, the salted seaweed paste he continues to eat and his decision to make the family name Tonkatsu.[3] The logical extension of such imagery is that the characters' reconnection to their Japanese ethnic heritage is also expressed in terms of food. The two most memorable depictions of such reconnection are when Muriel describes herself as being "replete" (91) after eating a whole box of "Jap oranges" and when Muriel begins the process of healing in her family by replacing a meal of toast, eggs, and ketchup with that of miso soup, rice, pickled *takuwan*, and *taonkatsu* served on cabbage.

Significantly, in the novel, the relationship between ethnic Japanese food and the development of a strong sense of ethnic self is not based on the consumption of food alone. Instead, it is the opportunity for talk story to occur over the course of a meal that is important. In other words, the food itself does not transmit identity; the conversation that surrounds eating does. Thus, when Naoe shares her secret hoard of Japanese food with Muriel, the importance of that moment lies not only in the shared food, but in the fact that "Muriel places her head in [Naoe's] bony lap and [Naoe begins] to speak [her] words" (15). Similarly, after Muriel begins to cook from the Japanese cookbook, Keiko's words are said to be "slowly coming back" (153). One of the most important discussions of the relationship between food and talk story occurs in the last few pages of the novel, when eating ethnic food is described as a

> point of departure. A place where growth begins. You eat, you drink and you laugh out loud.... You tell a story, maybe two, with words of pain and desire. Your companion listens and listens, then offers a different telling. The waiter comes back with the main course and stays to tell his version. Your companion offers three more stories and the people seated at the next table lean over to listen. You push all the tables together and the room resounds with voices. (201)

In this passage, eating ethnic food is identified as a means by which to access talk story, and storytelling is when real emotional growth occurs. Thus, it is such growth that is stunted in the absence of talk story.

Although the exchange of stories between mother and daughter does not occur regularly in either *Obasan* or *Chorus of Mushrooms*, the novels are not entirely void of storytelling. After all, Naomi does remember her mother telling her the story of Momotaro, and as readers, we have access to all the stories that Naoe and Muriel tell. In many ways, the novels are themselves forms of talk story, particularly in the manner in which they validate and give voice to Japanese Canadian experiences. The representations of storytelling that do occur in the novels reveal the powerful potentialities of talk story as a maternal practice. In particular, by drawing attention to three storytelling attributes, the novels are able to demonstrate clearly why it is that silence fails to mount the "active resistance to ... erasure and invisibility" that has been deemed seminal to the emotional survival of ethnic children (hooks 3).

First, as mentioned above, talk story provides a unique space for the construction of alternative images that challenge those found in dominant discourses. The legend of Momotaro related in *Obasan*, for example, explicitly celebrates the discovery of the boy in the peach: "The delight of it. And the wonder. Simply by existing a child is delight" (59). The language of desire for and celebration of a Japanese child, and by extension of "Japaneseness," stands in direct contrast to the negative depictions of the Japanese that fill Naomi's childhood. Similarly, the stories of Muriel's growing up experiences challenge the stock images of immigrants, such as those found in the story of Kenji, the immigrant boy who brings a skunk to school (written by the significantly named "Janet Duncan"),[4] which reduce their lives to marginal and amusing anecdotes in the greater story of Canadian experiences.

Second, talk story is able to challenge the assumptions on which discriminatory and racist discourses are based in powerful and subtle ways. In the legend of Momotoro, for example, the binary division between Japan and Canada that must be maintained to support the "Us/Them" dichotomy inherent in Canadian narratives of identity is destablized when Naomi speaks of being transported "to the gray-green woods" as her mother tells the story (58). The fact that it is unclear whether the woods she is imagining are located in Japan or in Vancouver, combined with the association made between the Japanese peach of the story and the peaches outside Naomi's Vancouver bedroom window, effectively blurs the boundaries between Japan and Canada. A similar blurring of spaces is evident in *Chorus of Mushrooms* when a *tengu* appears driving a truck down a Canadian highway, complete with western hat and North American accent.[5] More importantly, questions over the relationship between truth and narrative that are so often raised in the conversation between Muriel and her lover that frames the novel's narrative, provide a particularly powerful way to undermine the authority of national and socio-political discourses by revealing the constructed nature of both truth and reality, and by extension, the constructed nature of any discourse. In this regard, the last line of the novel—"You know you can change the story"—is particularly radical since it denies even the authority of the novel to impose a certain degree of closure on the story (220).

Third, both novels emphasize the intimate and mutual act of creation by both listener and storyteller that must occur for a story to take shape. As such, storytelling becomes an important symbol of the potential that the exchange of stories has to create new concepts of Canadian identity and new relationships within the country. This is particularly important since both novels are self-conscious disruptions to various narratives underpinning cultural constructions of Canadian identity. Most obviously, *Obasan* challenges national histories and multicultural myths by exposing the story of Japanese Canadian experience during the Second World War, while the self-articulated desire of *Chorus of Mushrooms* to be "an immigrant story with a happy ending" signifies its intentions to intervene into Canadian discourses surrounding immigrants and immigration (212). Inherent in such discoursive disruptions is the aim of creating new ways of interaction between members of minority ethnic groups and those of the dominant Canadian culture, particularly in relation to the exercise of power. The ability of stories to help foster the development of new power relationships in the gaps caused by these disruptions is symbolized in *Chorus of Mushrooms* in the manner in which the creation and sharing of stories always creates new levels of intimacy between listener and speaker, as demonstrated in the relationships between Muriel and her grandmother, Muriel and her lover, and Naoe and Tengu. In each relationship, true intimacy and close connections are always preceded by and interwoven with storytelling. Even more importantly, in both novels, stories are given the power to transform the narratives that create the Canadian cultural landscape so that it becomes "home space" for "Japaneseness."

That stories have the power to create new worlds is powerfully suggested by the focus on creation myths in Naoe's storytelling. In the legend of Izanami and Izanagi, for example, worlds are created simply at the words of the gods, while the *yamanba* who descends from the mountain to find a destroyed earth begins the process of re-creation by stating, "I will speak my words aloud and shape the earth again ... I will tell you stories" (116). In a larger socio-political context, the stories in *Chorus of Mushrooms* create new cultural landscapes for Canada in vivid ways. The *tengu* with whom

Naoe hitches a ride, for example, clearly fits into his Alberta environment with his Stetson and accent. Even more importantly, the novel ends with the literal inclusion of Naoe into Canadian mythic space in the creation of the Purple Rider legend that becomes part of the Calgary Stampede experience. Both incidents reveal the ability of a Japanese presence to be deemed "Canadian" by embedding itself in new Canadian myths; or, as Naoe might put it, "my home [is found] ... in the small hollows of my mouth," that is, in stories (203).Telling the story of Momotoro has a similar impact as revealed in Aunt Emily's response to Naomi's query as to whether or not the story represented some type of culture clash. Aunt Emily refutes this idea by stating, "Momotaro is a Canadian story" (61). In this simple affirmation, Aunt Emily suggests that in the transportation of the story to Canadian soil, Naomi's mother has effectively radically rewritten cultural constructions of Canadian identity to allow space for both "milk and Momotaro" (61).

Faced with Aunt Emily's anger over the treatment of Japanese Canadian citizens during the Second World War, Uncle defends Canada by stating, "This country is best. There is food. There is medicine. There is pension money" (44). His language is echoed in Naoe's own memories of the war when she states, "During the war, there are no thoughts forever. Three things only: Is there water? Is there food? Who is alive?" (50). Both statements speak to a limited understanding of survival in its most basic form—a survival of the body. Ensuring such physical survival, the simple preservation of life, is central to motherhood. For racialized ethnic mothers, however, such survival is not enough. Their children's long-term emotional, social, and political survival—their ability to thrive instead of being oppressed and marginalized—involves becoming engaged with and contesting institutions, practices, and discourses of domination so that they can challenge their marginalization in North American spaces. In other words, racialized ethnic mothers must move beyond ensuring "preservation, growth and acceptability" to fostering "survival, power and identity" (Collins 61). In *Obasan* and *Chorus of Mushrooms*, the use of silence as maternal practice, including the silencing of talk story, is revealed to have only limited power in terms of ensuring this level of survival. Rather than securing the daughters' well-being, such silence is depicted as contributing to their continuing marginalization and displacement, for, unlike talk story, it has no means to construct or contest articulations of identity. This is not to say that the novels depict a naively romantic celebration of the power of storytelling. Indeed, both novels are highly aware of the limitations of language, the instability of meaning, and the possibilities of "misreading" that are inherent in the act of storytelling. Nevertheless, by revealing the inability of silence as a maternal practice to protect daughters from developing a sense of isolation and alienation or to help them combat their displacement, *Obasan* and *Chorus of Mushrooms* suggest that the content and practice of talk story remain one of the best tools for mothers who "face the complicated task of shepherding their children through the racism of the dominant society" (Collins 71).

Notes to Chapter 20

1 "Talk story" is a Hawaiian expression describing casual, everyday storytelling, particularly concerned with the sharing of life stories. Subsequent to Maxine Hong Kingston's use of the term in *The Woman Warrior*, talk story has become a popular means of describing mother/daughter storytelling in Asian American literature.

2 See, for example, Gayle Fujita's "To Attend the Sound of Stone": The Sensibility of Silence in *Obasan*"; Shirley Geok-Lin Lim's "Japanese American Women's Life Stories: Maternality in Monica Sone's *Nisei Daughter* and Joy Kogawa's *Obasan*"; and Helena Grice's "Reading the Nonverbal: The Indices of Space, Time, Tactility and Taciturnity in Joy Kogawa's *Obasan*."

3 On a visit to an Asian grocery story, Muriel learns that her last name, Tonkatsu, is the same word for a deep-fried breaded pork cutlet (137). Her father explains that *tonkatsu* was one of the few Japanese words that he could articulate after he and Keiko made the decision to assimilate (208).

4 Sara Jeannette Duncan was the author of the turn-of-the-century Canadian novel *The Imperialist*. Duncan's literary representation of Canada helped to establish the nation's WASP identity.

5 A *tengu* is a spirit or supernatural creature of Japanese myth and folk legends.

Works Cited

Beoku-Betts, Josephine A. "We Got Our Way of Cooking Things: Women, Food, and Preservation of Cultural Identity Among the Gullah." *Gender and Society* 9.5 (October 1995): 535–55.

Collins, Patricia Hill. "Shifting the Center: Race, Class and Feminist Theorizing about Motherhood." *Representations of Motherhood*. Ed. Donna Bassin, Margaret Honey, and Meryle Mahrer Kaplan. New Haven and London: Yale University Press, 1994. 56–74.

Fujita, Gayle K. "To Attend the Sound of Stone": The Sensibility of Silence in *Obasan*." *MELUS* 12.3 (Autumn 1985): 33–42.

Geok-Lin Lim, Shirley. "Japanese American Women's Life Stories: Maternality in Monica Sone's *Nisei Daughter* and Joy Kogawa's *Obasan*." *Feminist Studies* 16.2 (Summer 1990): 289–312.

Goto, Hiromi. *Chorus of Mushrooms*. Edmonton: NeWest Press. 1994.

Grice, Helena. *Negotiating Identities: An Introduction to Asian American Women's Writing*. Manchester and New York: Manchester UP, 2002.

———. "Reading the Nonverbal: The Indices of Space, Time, Tactility and Taciturnity in Joy Kogawa's *Obasan*." *MELUS* 24.4 (Winter 1999): 93–105.

Ho, Wendy. *In Her Mother's House: The Politics of Asian American Mother–Daughter Writing*. Oxford: AltaMira Press, 1999.

Hong Kingston, Maxine. *The Woman Warrior: Memoirs of a Girlhood among Ghosts*. New York: Vintage Books, 1989.

hooks, bell. *Talking Back: Thinking Feminist, Thinking Black*. Toronto: Between the Lines, 1989.

Kogawa, Joy. *Obasan*. Toronto: Penguin Canada, 1983.

Murphy, Colum. "On the Trail of the Ultimate Onsen." *Far Eastern Economic Review, Hong Kong* 170.3 (April 2007): 78–79.

Ruddick, Sara. "Maternal Thinking." *Feminist Studies* 6.2 (Summer 1980): 342–67.

Xu, Wenying. "Sticky Rice Balls or Lemon Pie: Enjoyment and Ethnic Identities in *No-No Boy* and *Obasan*." *Literature Interpretation Theory* 13 (2002): 51–68.

21

Baby, Boo-Boo, and Bobs: The Matrilineal Auto/biographies of Zelda Sayre Fitzgerald, Frances Scott Fitzgerald, and Eleanor Lanahan

BY ELIZABETH PODNIEKS

The life of Zelda Sayre Fitzgerald is, according to biographer Sally Cline, "the stuff of myth." During Zelda's lifetime, from 1900 to 1948, "myth-makers invented and reinvented Zelda Fitzgerald as American Dream Girl, Romantic Cultural Icon, Golden Girl of the Roaring Twenties and most often as a Southern Belle, relabelled the First American Flapper by her husband Scott Fitzgerald, the quintessential novelist of the Jazz Age, which he named" (1). Zelda also "invented and reinvented" herself as a mother, as well as a writer, dancer, and artist.[1] She spent her adulthood mediating her maternal and creative desires, ambitions, and frustrations through a variety of forms, such as her autobiographical novel *Save Me the Waltz* (1932), her paintings, and her series of paper dolls. These works reflect some of the ways in which she perpetuated, challenged, and negotiated stereotypes and assumptions that divide and threaten women's domestic and professional identities. Zelda and Scott's only child, Frances Scott Fitzgerald Smith (who went by the name "Scottie"), explored similar themes in her writing. Five months before her death from esophageal cancer in 1986, Scottie began a memoir about her life as the daughter of the famous but tragic couple: Scott, an alcoholic, died of a heart attack in 1940; Zelda, a frequent patient of psychiatric hospitals, died in an asylum fire in 1948. Scottie's daughter Eleanor Lanahan used the unfinished manuscript as the foundation for a biography of *her* mother, published as *Scottie, the Daughter of ...: The Life of Frances Scott*

Fitzgerald Lanahan Smith (1995), a text that also inscribes the autobiography of Eleanor.

Beyond the obvious genealogical ties between Zelda (called "Baby" by her parents even as an adult), Scottie (called "Boo-Boo" by Zelda), and Eleanor (called "Bobs" by Scottie), the life writings produced by and about them can be viewed as a tapestry of maternal and matrilineal design, for their narratives are threaded with the themes of mothering and being mothered. Taking my cue from Virginia Woolf, who suggested in *A Room of One's Own* that "we think back through our mothers if we are women" (83), I want to explore how Zelda, Scottie, and Eleanor think back through their respective selves and subjects who were, or are, mothered and mothers, looking at how they document, interrogate, and mediate the importance of mothering as a defining feature in the formations of female selfhood and self-expression in the twentieth century.

My research is further inspired by two of Zelda's most recent biographers, who contend that Zelda's relationship with her daughter has not been given adequate scholarly attention.[2] Sally Cline tells us that she was moved by the paintings made by Zelda circa 1932–34:

> When I saw her vivid, unpredictable paintings they stirred my imagination, but gave rise to a strange anxiety. I looked at a nursing mother with a red blanket, an agonized portrait which flies in the face of acceptable motherhood. The mother has half her head severed while the baby sucks at what looks like the mother's entrails. Powerful but hardly comforting, it set me off on an untrodden trail to discover Zelda's overlooked relationship to her daughter Scottie. (2)

Zelda's art had a similar impact on Linda Wagner-Martin:

> Some of the most haunting paintings [that Zelda made] are two gouaches of a mother and child, the mother nursing the baby. Figures are disproportionate. Done largely in shades of blue, each painting features a slash of what might be seen as either a blanket or a stream of breast milk—one done in red ("Nursing Mother with Red Blanket"), the other in a different shade of blue. ("Nursing Mother with Blue Blanket")

These paintings help to shape the direction of the biography: "Given the evident passion—even if ambivalent—inscribed in these paintings, Zelda's relationship with her child is clearly much more important than most biographical accounts make it" (61). Exploring this important relationship, my chapter will show that motherhood informs not only Zelda's life texts but also those of Scottie and Eleanor.

Wagner-Martin identifies a number of themes that motivate, and problematize, the telling of women's lives not only in biography but in all forms of literature:

> The problem of being recognized as someone's daughter, someone's wife, or someone's mother rather than as oneself, is a recurrent motif; another is society's reaction to a woman's ambition—whether she is denigrated or applauded for it. A third is a woman's struggle to both fit into her family and her community and to avoid the restrictions that those entities might create for her. Still another is a woman's attempt to balance the demands of loved ones against her individual needs. (*Telling* x–xi)

These themes all potentially speak to the ways in which being a mother have an impact on both the life and life narratives of a woman; more specifically, they constitute the maternal issues addressed and negotiated by Zelda, Scottie, and Eleanor. Their stories dichotomize the mother figure as being either "good" or "bad" while also blurring those facile distinctions with an awareness of how complex and often ambivalent the mother–child relationship is. Their texts pull at the tensions a woman experiences between fulfilling both her own and society's expectations that she mother, with wanting to develop an autonomous identity for herself. The personal and public successes and failures registered in their narratives, which span over 70 years, underscore the ongoing difficulty women face in negotiating and reconciling these tensions.

Perhaps it is not surprising that Carolyn G. Heilbrun contends that mothers "are the single greatest problem in the stories, whether called fiction or memoirs, that women write and have written" (61), for every woman who writes is a daughter who must on some textual level confront the legacy of her mother. More specific to life writing, Jo Malin identifies "a hybrid form of autobiographical narrative containing an embedded narrative of the mother" (11), that is, "a biography of the writer/daughter's mother." She explains that it is "impossible to separate the autobiography of the daughter from the biography of the mother" in certain texts, which "become conversations or dialogues between a mother and a daughter" (1–2). In the same spirit, Audre Lorde and Yi-Lin Yu, as explained in the introduction to this collection, describe and theorize, respectively, a matrilineal narrative predicated on the grandmother–mother–daughter triad. These generic features serve us well in understanding Zelda's autobiographical novel, which speaks about and to Scottie as well as to Zelda's mother, Minnie Machen, and to Scottie and Eleanor's auto/biography, which not only is a composite of both women's voices but also draws Zelda into the multigenerational conversation.

A brief examination of these texts reveals the extent to which the authors have, in the spirit of Woolf, thought back through generations of mothers in remarkably similar terms. Twentieth-century notions of mothering can be traced to the late eighteenth century in both Europe and North America where, as E. Ann Kaplan summarizes, "The Cult of True Womanhood" was firmly established in its promotion of the four basic qualities every woman should espouse: "piety, purity, domesticity and submissiveness" (24). These qualities stem from Rousseau's inauguration of what Kaplan calls "the 1st phase of modern motherhood discourse" (21), which puts the mother at the centre of her children's lives (20). Elisabeth Badinter further explains that women, "told to be mothers first and foremost" (117), had two choices: "Either they could stick to the prescribed model as closely as possible, or they could try to stand apart from it, in which case there was hell to pay" (206–07). From the nineteenth century on, "anathemas were hurled at bad mothers" (237), who included the selfish, the working, and the intellectual mother (242–45). Molly Ladd-Taylor and Lauri Umansky show, in their research into how American culture has become particularly eager to brand mothers as "bad" over the last few decades, that this label is often applied simply, and systemically, to "those who did not live in a 'traditional' nuclear family" (2).

Connected to the "bad" mother is the ambivalent one. Acknowledging that "None of us find it easy to truly accept that we both love and hate our children," Rozsika Parker explains that "maternal ambivalence constitutes not an anodyne condition of mixed feelings, but a complex and contradictory state of mind, shared variously by all mothers, in which loving and hating feelings for children exist side by side." These conflicts are personal as well as societal, for she argues, "much of the ubiquitous guilt mothers endure stems from difficulties in weathering the painful feelings evoked by experiencing maternal ambivalence in a culture that shies away from the very existence of something it has helped produce"; indeed, cultural assumptions about idealized mothering "render ambivalence a source of shame or object of disbelief" (17).

Women have not, of course, always embraced or heeded the edicts for prescribed maternal conduct. Shari L. Thurer emphasizes that throughout history, most women who mother have also had jobs outside the home, and or relied on childcare (xix). Donna Bassin, Margaret Honey, and Meryle Mahrer Kaplan show that "the predominant image of the mother in white Western society is of the ever-bountiful, ever-giving, self-sacrificing mother" but has long been argued against—especially since the 1970s—by feminists who expose the patriarchal underpinnings of the ideology of motherhood (2–3). However, as Adrienne Rich concedes through personal example, stereotypes are so ingrained that even being aware of them does not prevent her from feeling guilty or even monstrous for not adhering to them.[3]

Born in Montgomery, Alabama, on 24 July 1900, Zelda was perfectly poised on the cusp of change. She emerged as a debutante or "belle" from within the turn-of-the-century culture of the American Deep South, where, as Wagner-Martin stresses, "ultimately, belles were to take on the roles of wives and, particularly, of mothers" (*Zelda* 2).[4] Yet her identity was also shaped during the transition from Victorian expectations that women be "angels in the house" to Anglo-American modernist imperatives for both men and women to "make it new"; as an active participant in modernism (roughly 1900 to 1945), Zelda renounced convention and tradition in both life and art. But like so many women of her day, she remained precariously perched between a life of conformity and rebellion, a positioning that had a significant impact on her role as a mother.

Her own mother, Minnie Machen, was one of the "angels"—though she earned her wings begrudgingly—and biographers of Zelda draw attention to how Zelda, intensely close with Minnie, defined herself through various acceptances and rejections of this maternal model. Though Minnie had aspired to a stage career, her father refused to allow her to act in public, an edict she never forgot (Cline 18–19; Wagner-Martin 3). And though Minnie had been asked by a publisher in Kentucky to write a novel, she had to turn down the offer because she was too busy running a household, being a society hostess, and raising the five children she had with her husband, Anthony Sayre, a prominent judge (Cline 19). Minnie's domestic performance is critiqued by Wagner-Martin, who represents Minnie as paying lip service to patriarchy: "During these twenty-five years of Anthony's involvement in his law career, Minnie was devoting twenty-five years to playing the role of competent wife and mother" (7). The fact that Minnie became known throughout her community of Montgomery, Alabama, as "Mama Sayre" (Milford 9) underscores the extent to which her identity had become submerged in maternity.

Perhaps hoping to avoid her mother's fate—and moniker—Zelda married aspiring novelist Scott Fitzgerald on 3 April 1920. Though she professed to love him, she also saw him as a ticket out of Alabama to more exciting places like New York and Europe, where she could develop her own artistic career. However, she quickly found herself playing Scott's wife rather than the meatier role of literary partner, and it is not surprising that Zelda turned to motherhood at this point in her life.[5] Wagner-Martin suggests Zelda became pregnant in part because she felt her mother was disappointed in her for not having a baby; Zelda believed her mother showed preference for Zelda's sister Clotilde, who did (54). Minnie's disappointment may have stemmed from the fact that Zelda and Scott had become notorious chain-smoking partiers and drunken pranksters (their marriage would deteriorate under increasingly acrimonious terms over the next 20 years), and Zelda wanted to get back into her mother's good books—a baby would offer the ultimate proof that she was doing her duty, performing like a "good girl" and thus fulfilling the same patriarchal imperatives that guided her own mother's life (54).[6] Indeed, when Minnie's fictional counterpart in Save Me the Waltz is informed that her daughter has given birth, she sends a telegram stating, "My blue-eyed baby has grown up. We are so proud" (57).

Patricia Frances Fitzgerald, nicknamed Scottie, was born on 26 October 1921. In January and February 1932, Zelda would pen Save Me the Waltz in part, arguably, to document a decade's worth of mothering. Significantly, the novel was completed at the Phipps Clinic of Johns Hopkins Hospital: Zelda suffered a number of breakdowns that landed her in a series of clinics and psychiatric institutions in Europe and the United States for much of her adult life. Her poor mental health, coupled with the stigma of being (wrongly) diagnosed as schizophrenic, rendered her more often than not physically and emotionally incapable of mothering, certainly in any traditional sense of the term.[7] The complex reasons for her breakdowns are beyond the scope of my inquiry here, but it is important to note that women in Zelda's time who rebelled against the dictates that they serve husband and child, and who sought a life for themselves beyond their patriarchal parameters, were too quickly labelled—and dismissed as—crazy.[8] Such an acknowledgment not only helps to recuperate for Zelda a position of "sanity" but it also contextualizes her work as a writer, dancer, and artist. Wagner-Martin notes that when Zelda turned her attention to her own creative drives (as opposed to merely supporting those of her husband) "she became an object of criticism" by her friends who "seemed to unite in a chorus of 'How dare Zelda become a dancer?'" (107). Eleanor Lanahan describes a Zelda who had become "mentally unbalanced" due to the "feverish pitch" of her passion for dance so that she was twice hospitalized in April and May 1930.[9] One of her doctors observed that "family life and her duties towards her daughter were not enough to satisfy her ambition and her artistic leanings," and when he questioned eight-year-old Scottie's place in her life she replied, "That is done now, I want to do something else'" (Scottie 41–42). This rather stunning dismissal of motherhood evokes Parker's comment that maternal ambivalence "is curiously hard to believe in" (17), and yet, certainly during Zelda's time in the 1930s, mental hospitals often sought to cure patients through "psychological 'reeducation' towards femininity, good mothering and the revaluing of marriage and domesticity" (Cline 265). No wonder that Zelda felt both thwarted and confused.

It was during another period of hospitalization, in 1932, that Zelda wrote *Save Me the Waltz*, a text that articulates these competing and debilitating tensions through the protagonist Alabama Beggs—note that the mother and child paintings described earlier are dated circa 1932–34, in which the themes of ambivalence are equally, though more graphically, depicted. The basic facts of the novel correspond, almost entirely, to Zelda's actual life, in its treatment of her childhood in Montgomery, her courtship and marriage to Scott Fitzgerald (renamed David Knight, famous painter), the birth of their only child, Scottie (fictionalized as Bonnie), their expatriate adventures in France, their failing marriage, and her increasing obsession with training for a ballet career. Eleanor confirms that the novel "comprises an almost transparent self-portrait" of Zelda (*Zelda: An Illustrated* 6), and though we should recognize that life-writing scholars now generally accept that textual selfhoods are to some degree products of imagination and (re)construction, we can nonetheless speculate that Zelda, described by Cline as a "merciless self-historian" (1), used this space to offer one possible interpretation of her life and self.[10] Of particular relevance is the way that Alabama's ambitions to dance are pitted against her responsibilities to her daughter.

Throughout the first half of the narrative Alabama is restless. When she tells a friend, "it is exceedingly difficult to direct a life which has no direction," he replies, "You've a child, haven't you?" implying that motherhood should be direction enough. Her response of "Yes ... there's the baby—life goes on" (109) signals that she remains unfulfilled. She takes up dance hoping that "in proving herself, she would achieve that peace which she imagined went only in surety of one's self" (118). Her commitment to her craft, however, serves to weaken an already troubled relationship with her daughter. Bonnie reports, for instance, that her mother was "nicer before" she became "too sérieuse" about ballet (138), and when Alabama discovers a picture Bonnie made with the caption, "My mother is the most beautiful lady in the world," Alabama realizes, "She had almost forgotten about Bonnie's mind going on and on, growing," and "Alabama reproached herself bitterly" (151).

When Alabama is offered her first job as a dancer, in Italy, she initially turns it down because it means leaving Bonnie and David in Switzerland, where they have been living, but "When she thought of giving up her work she grew sick and middle-aged" and she accepts the position (151–52).

Alone in Naples she thrives on her career but misses her daughter so much that she literally has to dull the pain with drugs—"Alabama took the yellow sedative at night to forget Bonnie's letters" (158). Bonnie comes with her nanny for a two-week visit, but the reunion is disastrous. As soon as her daughter leaves, though, Alabama realizes "how much fuller life was with Bonnie there. She was sorry she hadn't sat more with her child when she was sick in bed. Maybe she could have missed rehearsals." Alabama's anxiety is evidence that women too often have to choose between their children or a career. Further, Alabama "had wanted her child to see her dance the ballet. In one more week of rehearsal she would have her debut as a ballerina!" (167). Alabama hoped her child could value her as someone other than a mother, as an accomplished artist. Though the narrative tells us that "Bonnie was proud of her father" (168), a successful painter, we never hear that she is proud of her mother. The final rub comes when Bonnie writes her mother, "I was glad when you were home" (175) and tells her father, "It is better here [home] than with Mummy's success in Italy" (176). At this point in the narrative, Alabama gets such severe blood poisoning from the glue in her dance shoe that she can never dance again, a fact celebrated by her husband, who exclaims that now they can be "together again" (181). Now, too, she can begin what Cline refers to as her "psychological 'reeducation' towards femininity, good mothering and the revaluing of marriage and domesticity" (265).

The one glaring fiction in *Save Me the Waltz* is the plot line in Naples: Zelda was really offered such a dance contract but turned it down. While her biographers struggle to make sense of this decision, Cline posits that Zelda in part did not want to leave her daughter (236).[11] *Save Me the Waltz* could stand as Zelda's imaginative projection of what may have happened had she taken the job. Her protagonist's fate is symbolic in that the mother is punished for wanting a life outside of the home. Toward the end of the novel, Zelda paints what is likely a portrait of her own mother, Minnie (renamed Millie): Alabama refers to Millie as "the good mother" (185), and "saw her mother as she was, part of a masculine tradition" that honours husband and nurtures children (186). To be sure, "Her mother's white hair was done in a crown around her head like a Florentine saint" (187), an image suggesting the cultural stereotypes of the Victorian angel in the house. What's more, this "good mother" serves as a standard against which Alabama measures herself and is found wanting—that is, found to be a "bad mother" who must be indicted, in this case, poisoned. The opening line of *Save Me the Waltz* is also its ironic message: "'Those girls,' people said, 'think they can do anything and get away with it'" (9), but as the story proves, girls like Alabama and her sisters cannot "get away" with anti-conventional maternal behaviour; Alabama is forced off the stage, just as "the good mother" Millie/Minnie was before her.[12]

If the Naples episodes are imaginative projections, they also reflect some of the realities of maternal ambivalence experienced and practised by Zelda, and hence her desire to confront them in both cathartic and empowering ways on the page. Zelda's narrative written from within the asylum delivers a lucid analysis of her personal and cultural condition. The text assigns guilt and blame to the absent and career-driven mother, a culturally prescribed castigation according to Kaplan, Badinter, and Rich, but the text also critiques a society that forces women into limiting roles in which they have no room to accommodate their disparate selves, an awareness suggested by the work of Thurer and Bassin et al. *Save Me the Waltz* is a kind of embedded maternal autobiography identified by Malin in that it offers a life narrative of Zelda dialogically engaged with the stories of her mother and daughter, and through it, Zelda strategically bridges the gap between her need to work and her longing to mother by composing a text about both.

More than 50 years later, Zelda's daughter wrote her own maternal story that echoes with the themes and tensions of the mother's. This second narrative is offered to us by Scottie's daughter Eleanor, who has incorporated it into her biography of Scottie. As Eleanor explains of their joint production, "My mother, Frances Scott Fitzgerald Lanahan Smith, started this book in 1986, five months before she died," when "she began to dictate a diary for us children. She included a brief memoir of her childhood, schooling, and marriage and halted abruptly in 1951, with the birth of my sister, Cecilia" (1). Scottie gave the 74 typed pages, as well as her massive personal archive (filling 64 boxes), to Cecilia and Eleanor. Eleanor tells us that "After she died I decided to put together the book that she never wrote, telling her life as she would have liked it told, and using her words as much as possible" (3). The biography runs to just under 600 pages of text: in addition to Scottie's slim memoir, the biography draws on diary fragments, letters, stories, and articles written, and interviews given, by Scottie, and on Eleanor's own recollections and research, which are delivered in the first (rather than the typical biographical, "objective" third) person. We can thus approach it as an embedded auto/biography as well as a matrilineal multigenerational triad. The text depicts the interconnected relationships among Zelda, Scottie, and Eleanor in their varied roles of mother, daughter, and grandmother, and how those roles continued to be played within and against the competing demands by the women for independent and artistic self-realization.

Scottie's narrative was composed at the end of her life when she was able to reflect on more than 30 years of mothering her four children, the result of which is a voice that sounds at once bitter and resentful, and apologetic and sympathetic, as much toward Zelda and Eleanor as toward herself. Zelda's relationship with Scottie was almost always a strained one, due in part to Zelda's desire to forgo traditional female roles in order to dedicate herself to creative work, and to her increasingly weakening mental health, both of which meant that Scottie was largely raised by her alcoholic father and a series of nannies until she was sent to boarding schools, her care during holidays often further relegated to other family members and friends. By the time she enrolled at Vassar College in 1938, Scottie had developed a long-term resentment and seeming embarrassment of her mother. Though Scottie made the requisite visits to her mother both in and out of hospital, and engaged in an extensive epistolary correspondence with her, these filial acts were often performed with a sense of duty and resistance.[13] In a 1944 letter, Zelda's sister Marjorie accused Scottie of being thoughtless toward Zelda: "I think your chief trouble is a lack of sympathy and not much ability to put yourself in another person's place.... I hope someday you will have children of your own and know what it is to love a child—unless you are abnormal that way and have no natural instincts" (*Scottie* 154).

Marjorie's query was prophetic, for Scottie would later come to question whether in fact she *had* such instincts. After marrying the future lawyer Jack Lanahan and having four children—Eleanor, the second, was born on 25 January 1948—Scottie discovered that the very tensions that had threatened her mother were now haunting her, and Scottie's life began to follow an eerily similar path as her mother's to both maternal and professional failure and disappointment.

Having inherited her parents' literary sensibilities, Scottie, while at college, began her career as a journalist, one that would see her writing society articles, columns, and short stories for publications such as the *Vassar Miscellany News*, *The New Yorker*, and the *Washington Post*. Two months after the birth of her first son, Tim, on 26 April 1946, Scottie eagerly returned to work at *The New Yorker*, as she recorded at the time: "Bébé squeals when he laughs and wiggles all over—always roars in early morning—so cute but I wish it weren't at 6 o'clock.... This work-or-not issue drives me crazy—I know Jack would rather I'd take care of Bébé but I have no patience & calm to do it—he is so cute but Miss. M. [Muirhead, the nurse] is better for him" (174). This description underscores two of the recurring, related themes in Scottie's and Eleanor's narrative: personal and familial frustrations with the ways in which Scottie's professional aspirations and maternal responsibilities collide, and Scottie's professed lack of interest in, and talent for, mothering.

Scottie went on to have three more children. At one point in her story, Eleanor notes, "My parents continued to follow the 1950s blueprint for a large, happy, family—a dream diametrically at odds with my mother's desire to accomplish something besides the raising of children" (211). Scottie did "accomplish" other things: she continued to write, and as a public figure she was a founding member of the Multiple Sclerosis Society of Washington, D.C., and spent her life campaigning for the Democratic Party in Washington. Yet accomplishments such as these came at a cost, as Eleanor admits; "As a teenager I entirely blamed my mother for so determinedly pursuing her own interests, for being headstrong and independent" (215); and Eleanor "harbored a submerged resentment that I wasn't more important to her" (256)—feelings that echo with Bonnie's criticism that Alabama was "nicer before" she became "too sérieuse" about ballet (138), and Zelda's cutting remark about mothering, "That is done now." Recalling Adrienne Rich's admission that even while she resisted the stereotypes of the selfless mother, she was haunted by them, we can understand how Scottie came to blame herself for being what she considered a bad mother. In a 1981 diary entry, Scottie examined her maternal ambivalence. Affirming, "I was not a good mother," she explains:

> The only reason I survived as a mother at all was that I tried so hard, with my immense limitations, but it was swimming upstream always; it never came naturally. I loved my children dearly, but I had no patience, no *aptitude*—I probably would have committed child abuse if I hadn't been able to afford to hire people to give me the freedom I needed to breathe. I found children essentially boring—even my own—boring isn't the work, *suffocating*, because of their constant demands and needs. (491)

These feelings of suffocation may be similar to those reflected in the images of the baby devouring the mother in Zelda's paintings, described earlier.

Eleanor believes that Scottie "died with a sense of disappointment in her own accomplishments" (3), and in addition to—and connected with—disappointments in mothering, Eleanor's biography charts Scottie's two unsuccessful marriages, her elder son's suicide, and her increasingly debilitating alcoholism, issues dramatically similar to those faced by her parents. Moreover, one of Scottie's greatest disappointments was her longed for but unrealized dreams of literary success; she had always wanted, but was unable, to write a novel—though Zelda had managed one, *Save Me the Waltz* received mixed reviews and sold poorly.[14]

It is possible that her disappointments, in many ways so similar to Zelda's, provided Scottie with the means to reflect on her mother's life with greater insight into and understanding of Zelda's conflicted roles of mother and aspiring artist. These conflicts give rise to Scottie's own ambivalent narrative. She is at pains to emphasize how happy her childhood was, responding defensively, for example, to a reporter: "The fact that I spent a lot of time with nurses instead of with my parents does not strike me as being the deprivation it seems to appear to certain people, particularly young people of the Dr. Spock generation. When I go to high schools to talk, they always ask me about my miserable childhood.... But in fact, in Europe in the '20s, children were pretty much raised by nurses" (36)—as was Zelda herself. Eleanor records Scottie's preoccupation with reiterating, when asked, that her childhood was "golden" (2) and "wonderful" (486). The fact that Scottie never introduced the subject of her childhood to her own family leads Eleanor to believe that Scottie was protecting herself from painful memories. Indeed, later in her life, Scottie writes to her daughter Cecilia about the difficulties in raising children, explaining how she never had a break: "you really cannot go off to Europe for 2 weeks leaving your children in the charge of a 21 year old French girl who may or may not rush off with her boyfriend in the middle of the night" (465). However, given that this practice is close to what Scott and Zelda did throughout her childhood, perhaps Scottie is voicing (however unconsciously) her sense that she was not well tended to by her parents, and that in calling her childhood golden she was protesting too much. She has an emotional stake in telling this version, for it confers upon her a narrative happiness that helps to sustain her when she becomes an adolescent and sees her family as tarnished—her father an alcoholic and her mother a "madwoman"—and who concedes, "There was no glamour during the time that I was old enough to know what was happening" (51), and "it is true that life then wasn't much fun for me" (62).[15]

Scottie's ambivalence to Zelda is especially manifested when she erases Zelda from her life story, telling Eleanor that "never having had a mother" she has no "guide-lines as to how to properly behave" as a mother herself (468–69). But at other times Scottie celebrates Zelda, affirming, "Mama was such an extraordinary person" (182) who, creatively speaking, "could do anything with her hands" (24). As executor of her parents' estates, Scottie controlled access to and influenced public perceptions about her parents. Of particular interest here is that Scottie—and later Eleanor—dedicated much time and effort to recovering, archiving, and showcasing Zelda's talents.

For instance, in addition to dancing, Zelda was a prolific painter, and Scottie seemed proud to display her work in her own home. Eleanor recalls, "Throughout my childhood Zelda's watercolors of the streets and cafés of Paris and New York hung with ancestral permanence on the walls of our sunporch and library," and her "paintings of fairy tales decorated our bedrooms" (11–12). Eleanor also describes playing with the enormous collection of paper dolls that Zelda had made for Scottie, who now stored them in "wondrous portfolios." Scottie reminisces that some of the dolls

> represented the three of us [Scottie, Zelda, Scott]. Once upon a time the dolls
> had wardrobes of which Rumpelstiltskin could be proud. My mother and I had
> dresses of pleated wallpaper, and one party frock of mine had ruffles of real lace
> cut from a Belgian handkerchief. More durable were the ball dresses of Mesdames
> de Maintenon and Pompadour and the coats-of-mail of Galahad and Launcelot,
> for these were lavishly painted in the most minute detail in water color so thick
> that it has scarcely faded.

Scottie concludes, "It was characteristic of my mother that these exquisite dolls, each one requiring hours of artistry, should have been created for the delectation of a six-year-old; at the time she died, she was working on a series of Bible illustrations for her oldest grandchild, then eighteen months" (11–12).

In addition to these historical and religious themes, Zelda also created a line of fairy-tale dolls and built lavish houses for the dolls (*Scottie* 30, 33). Cline convincingly posits that the dolls were "a special way to communicate with Scottie, from whom she felt increasingly distanced" (207). Beyond the obvious fun Zelda had in making the dolls—and Scottie in receiving them—may lie Zelda's subversive approach to mothering and art: by making dolls (babies), Zelda was doing what was expected of her as a mother, but in putting such effort into them, and inscribing carefully researched historical, religious, and literary themes, she was conscious of working within a tradition, detailed by Cline, of nineteenth- and twentieth-century French illustrational art (206). Zelda may have been signalling her challenge to the fact that women as artists are too often relegated to the feminine sidelines, their work dismissed or not preserved, for she made her ephemeral paper playthings "in water color so thick that it has scarcely faded," as attested to by Eleanor (12).

According to Cline, "This children's art, begun in 1927, became a lifelong preoccupation. Over the years she made several hundred paper dolls, which, together with the fairy-tale scenes, formed a quarter of her 1974 retrospective exhibition at the Montgomery Museum of Fine Arts" (206). Scottie's heavy involvement with this exhibition—which included the paintings of mother and child—may have given Zelda some posthumous satisfaction, for recall that Alabama desperately wanted Bonnie to witness her accomplishment as a dancer. When Jake Wagnon, a member of the board of the Montgomery Museum of Modern Art, had proposed the show, Scottie not only contributed her collection of over 100 dolls and paintings, but also wrote an essay for the catalogue, which Eleanor reproduces in her biography. Scottie, however, is cautious in her assessment of Zelda's art. She refers to Zelda's "unusual talents and ebullient imagination" but suggests that Zelda failed to amount to little more than an amateur: "It was my mother's misfortune to be born with the ability to write, to dance and to paint, and then never to have acquired the discipline to make her talent work for, rather than against, her" (434–35). Scottie specifically debunks the notion that Zelda was "the classic 'put down' wife"—and I would add here, "mother"—and assigns the blame to Zelda herself, though Scottie does not seem to consider that cultural, patriarchal forces may have had something to do with Zelda's inability to channel the necessary egotistic "discipline" required for art. Several years later, in a 1979 interview, Scottie allows for a more contextualized reading of her mother, affirming that women today "have more freedom" than they had in the 1920s. And, as Eleanor tells us, "When asked why Zelda had become a 'cult figure' among feminists, [Scottie] answered, 'There's a terrible shortage of women who've been able to break out of traditional bounds. Zelda's attempt and failure make her a tragic figure'" (479).

If Zelda's failures speak to the first half of the century, Scottie's own speak to the second. Eleanor begins her biography on this note: "I realized that she [Scottie] had encountered almost all of the problems and frustrations of American women of her generation," emphasizing that she "tried to balance work and family, self-expression and femininity, independence and the need for companionship, and tried to reconcile her extreme generosity with self-preservation" (3–4). Like Zelda, Scottie could be regarded as unsuccessful, as Eleanor states: "She insisted that her life wasn't worth writing about, that her goals weren't met, that the sum total of her life wasn't much" (532). It is especially ironic, then, that although both Zelda and Scottie were seemingly "bad mothers," it is their daughters who ensure that their mothers are remembered, for better or for worse, proving that they are indeed "worth writing about."

Eleanor establishes her connection to the women when she writes,

> I was two months old when my grandmother died in a fire at Highland Hospital in Asheville, North Carolina. Zelda's last letter to my mother in 1948 said that she longed to meet the baby. For me, that letter has been an important thread to the past, an almost accidental link between the generations; it's a comfort that my grandmother knew of my existence. ("Introduction" to *Dear* xxiv)

In writing the biography, Eleanor finds comfort in knowing her own mother, a move likely facilitated by Scottie turning back to her now-adult children and "repairing, as best she could, whatever damage had been done by what she considered her inadequate mothering" (417) . To some extent she was certainly successful, as Eleanor reveals that she "drew strength from [Scottie] again" (417) and that, during a difficult period in Eleanor's life, Scottie "was a ministering angel and exerted all her skills at spiritual resuscitation" due to "a shift in her mothering" (490), which included lavishing attention on her grandchildren. Zelda, we should note, at the end of her life also devoted herself to her grandson, Tim, finding added renewal in her relationship with Scottie while living out her last few years with *her* mother, Minnie.[16] Eleanor finds catharsis in textually confronting her mother, for as she discovers in the process of writing, "Much as I had resisted my mother, I had never diluted her influence or loosened her invisible grip" (7). She begins her book by affirming "my everlasting debt is to my mother for caring so much and for leaving so much behind" (xiii). Eleanor carries on the matrilineal tradition, begun by Zelda, and leaves this auto/biography behind.

As Scottie lay dying, Eleanor "told her mother, probably for first time, that she loved her" to which Scottie replied, "I love you deeply. You know that" (533). Faced with the loss of Scottie, Eleanor laments, "It is incredible to me that someone so completely extraordinary had simply ceased to be—No phone number. No forwarding address. She wouldn't be back" (536). Scottie has, of course, reached *us*, through Eleanor's thinking "back through her mother," just as Scottie and Zelda thought back through theirs. Toward the end of Scottie's life, Eleanor had again complained to a friend about feeling shut out of Scottie's life, to which the friend replied, "Scottie was doing it *her* way. Mothers can never meet all the expectations of their daughters" (527). True enough, but the trajectory of life texts produced by Zelda, Scottie, and Eleanor suggest some of the narrative ways in which they try.

Notes to Chapter 21

1   Throughout this chapter I refer to my subjects by their first names. As a scholar I am reluctant to do so, especially in light of Scottie Fitzgerald's 1959 introduction to *Six Tales of the Jazz Age*, in which she highlights this passage from the *Fitzgerald Newsletter* (dedicated to her father's work): "The FN ... has long regarded with distaste the liberties taken with the author's wife. It is clearly impudent for writers who never knew her to refer to Mrs. Fitzgerald as 'Zelda'—just plain 'Zelda.' It does not seem to us that this is a mark of affection. Rather it appears to carry a sanctimonious snicker ... the same familiarities have long been taken with

Fitzgerald, of course, but we were startled when he turned up as 'Scott' in a Ph.D. dissertation which presumably had been approved by a board of scholars" (*Scottie* 233). I ask the Fitzgerald estates for their indulgence: I am writing about a number of family members who share last names—Minnie Machen Sayre, Zelda Sayre Fitzgerald, Scott Fitzgerald, Frances Scott Fitzgerald Lanahan, Eleanor Lanahan—and to use last names would make identifying them, and keeping their identities clear, difficult; to refer to them each time by their full names would be cumbersome to the reader.

2 I would like to thank my two research assistants, Carolyn Winters and Christopher Richardson, who while students at Ryerson University created for me invaluable summaries of the Zelda and Scottie biographies. Though Nancy Milford published the first biography on Zelda (1970), my chapter draws largely on the more recent studies by Cline and Wagner-Martin.

3 Bassin et al. make this observation (3) based on their reading of Rich's *Of Woman Born*.

4 Note that from this point, all quotations from Wagner-Martin are from *Zelda*.

5 For Zelda as a trophy wife, see Wagner-Martin (43, 44, 49); for examples of how Scott borrowed—even stole—ideas and whole stories written by Zelda and published them under his own name, and how he violently fought to prevent Zelda from producing and publishing under her own name, see Wagner-Martin (51, 52, 80, 123, 166).

6 Despite years of estrangement, Scott and Zelda remained in on-again, off-again epistolary contact, and never formally divorced.

7 From Cline: "Zelda's hospital label in the Thirties was schizophrenia; by the Fifties her last psychiatrist suggested (too late) that it might have been manic depression." Cline also contends that Zelda "suffered as much from the treatment as from the illness itself" (9).

8 See Cline, for example (9). Of special note is Cline's discovery that "we see that emotions engendered in all absentee mothers and artists inside closed institutions were remarkably similar.... Bewilderment, guilt and powerlessness clung to the role of absentee motherhood. The evidence from Zelda's writings and comments from people close to her show such feelings led to incompetence over practical matters and swings from extreme harshness to wild indulgence towards her daughter Scottie" (9).

9 *Scottie*, 41. All quotations by Scottie and Eleanor are from this text, unless otherwise noted. Cline states that Zelda's dancing "has been consistently viewed as obsession rather than as artistic commitment," beginning with her husband and doctors, who forced her to end her career out of seeming concern for her health (3).

10 See, for example, the scholarship by Dow Adams, Eakin, and Olney for how fact and fiction, or memory and imagination, fuse in life writings.

11 See Wagner-Martin (125) and Cline (236–38) for discussion of why Zelda did not take the job.

12 Zelda was the youngest child in her family of three sisters and one brother. It is important to note that Minnie, though the dutiful wife and mother, never fully renounced her own wild, creative spirit. Scottie recalls, "Both the Judge and my grandmother apparently took the position that their girls could do no wrong, for they fended off all criticism of their iconoclastic ways" (*Scottie* 435). Such a position likely contributed to Zelda's own ambivalences toward accepting and or rejecting conventional norms.

13 Scottie, for example, did not want Zelda to attend her college graduation (though she did), and sent the invitation to her wedding so late that Zelda was unable to attend (*Scottie* 89, 150).

14 As the daughter of one of the most famous authors of the century, Scottie acknowledged that she was paralyzed by anxieties of influence (*Scottie* 473–74).

15 Scottie's relationship with her father was, of course, equally complex and ambivalent, and is treated at length in the texts by Eleanor Lanahan, Cline, and Wagner-Martin, among others.

16 From April 1940, until her death in 1948, Zelda lived alone as an outpatient with her widowed mother in her hometown of Montgomery, returning periodically to the Highland Hospital in Asheville, North Carolina, where she died.

Works Cited

Badinter, Elisabeth. *The Myth of Motherhood: An Historical View of the Maternal Instinct*. London: Souvenir Press, 1981.

Bassin, Donna, Margaret Honey, and Meryle Mahrer Kaplan. Introduction. *Representations of Motherhood*. Ed. Donna Bassin, Margaret Honey, and Meryle Mahrer Kaplan . New Haven: Yale University Press, 1994. 1–25.

Cline, Sally. *Zelda Fitzgerald: Her Voice in Paradise*. London: John Murray, 2002.

Dow Adams, Timothy. *Telling Lies in Modern American Autobiography*. Chapel Hill: University of North Carolina Press, 1990.

Eakin, Paul John. *Fictions in Autobiography: Studies in the Art of Self-Invention*. Princeton: Princeton University Press, 1985.

Fitzgerald, Zelda Sayre. *Save Me the Waltz: The Collected Writings of Zelda Fitzgerald*. Ed. Matthew J. Bruccoli. Tuscaloosa: University of Alabama Press, 1991. 1–196.

Heilbrun, Carolyn G. *Women's Lives: The View from the Threshold*. Toronto: University of Toronto Press, 1999.

Kaplan, E. Ann. *Motherhood and Representation: The Mother in Popular Culture and Melodrama*. London: Routledge, 1992.

Ladd-Taylor, Molly, and Lauri Umansky. *"Bad" Mothers: The Politics of Blame in Twentieth-Century America*. New York: New York University Press, 1998.

Lanahan, Eleanor. Introduction. *Dearest Zelda: The Love Letters of F. Scott and Zelda Fitzgerald*. Ed. Jackson R. Bryer and Cathy W. Barks. New York: St. Martin's Press, 2002. xxiii–xxxi.

———. *Scottie, the Daughter of ...: The Life of Frances Scott Fitzgerald Lanahan Smith*. New York: HarperCollins, 1995.

———, ed. *Zelda: An Illustrated Life: The Private World of Zelda Fitzgerald*. New York: Harry N. Abrams, 1996.

Lorde, Audre. *Zami: A New Spelling of My Name*. London: Sheba, 1982.

Malin, Jo. *The Voice of the Mother: Embedded Maternal Narratives in Twentieth-Century Women's Autobiographies*. Carbondale: Southern Illinois University Press, 2000.

Milford, Nancy. *Zelda: A Biography*. New York: Harper & Row, 1970.

Parker, Rozsika. "The Production and Purposes of Maternal Ambivalence." *Mothering and Ambivalence*. Ed. Wendy Hollway and Brid Featherstone. London: Routledge, 1997. 17–36.

Olney, James. *Metaphors of Self: The Meaning of Autobiography*. Princeton: Princeton University Press, 1981.

Rich, Adrienne. *Of Woman Born: Motherhood as Experience and Institution*. New York: W. W. Norton & Co., 1986.

Thurer, Shari L. *The Myths of Motherhood: How Culture Reinvents the Good Mother*. New York: Penguin, 1994.

Wagner-Martin, Linda. *Telling Women's Lives: The New Biography*. New Brunswick, NJ: Rutgers University Press, 1994.

———. *Zelda Sayre Fitzgerald: An American Woman's Life*. New York: Palgrave Macmillan, 2004.

Woolf, Virginia. *A Room of One's Own*. London: HarperCollins, 1977.

Yu, Yi-Lin. *Mother, She Wrote: Matrilineal Narratives in Contemporary Women's Writing*. New York: Peter Lang, 2005.

22

Revelations and Representations:
Birth Stories and Motherhood on the Internet

BY KIM HENSLEY OWENS

> I don't depend on doctors, Nestle bottles, or the goodness of the establishment....
> The woman who has homebirth and breastfeeds a long time, is using the power
> that Nature gave her. She is free and powerful.
>
> —Gabriela, unassistedchildbirth.com

> Joseph was born on Oct 6, 1995 and at that time I didn't know there was such
> a web-site devoted to this type of issue; it would have been a great help.... The
> hospital and doctors dealt with my physical problems quite effectively but there
> was no emotional support in my hospital and no information about what I had
> gone through.
>
> —Joseph's mother, childbirth.org

As the Internet becomes host to websites devoted to parenting and child-birth, sites that invite readers to share their birth stories, thousands of women are posting their stories about childbirth, their initiation into motherhood. Some, like Gabriela, offer sweeping pronouncements and po-litical statements. Others, like Joseph's mother, announce their gratitude for the space and freedom to write, their need for birth stories and online communities. Although authors and scholars as diverse as Cherríe Moraga, Isabel Allende, Suzanne Arms, and Robbie Davis-Floyd have published about their personal experiences with childbirth and motherhood, until recently contemporary women who are not "writers," those whose vocations range from stay-at-home mother to lawyer to bus driver, have not generally written their experiences for the public. But the Internet has changed that, bringing everyday women's birth experiences into other women's ken. These online accounts of childbirth entertain and educate; they also reveal aspects of women's experiences and attitudes toward childbirth, motherhood, and their roles in society.

Childbirth narratives, of course, have long been shared by everyday women. They have tended to circulate orally in maternity wards, in childbirth classes, and among female friends and relatives, and they have appeared in letters and diaries. Such birth stories, however, have traditionally been limited in their intended and reached audiences. Written childbirth stories have begun to reach academic audiences through the work of scholars such as Cynthia Huff, a rhetorician who studies women's quotidian writing, and Judith Leavitt, a historian whose comprehensive childbirth history relies in part on her analysis of women's diaries and letters. In this newly digital age, as birth stories have begun to be shared online, they are spreading to far wider and more disparate audiences than ever before. Women now can and do write emails, keep blogs, and post their personal stories on childbirth and parenting websites. Women who write online birth stories depend upon previous incarnations of the birth story—often "horror stories" told to pregnant women—even as they alter that genre in this new medium of the Internet. Because mothers of varied backgrounds are now embracing the Internet as a space to share birth stories, scholars and the public alike now have access to these self-representations. In this essay I extend Adrienne Rich's claim that women's childbirth choices and limitations always have political ramifications. Through an analysis of online childbirth narratives alongside responses to a childbirth writing survey, I argue that women's rhetorical choices in representing their childbirth experiences online are also political, and can have material effects on those who write and read them.

I draw birth narratives from five websites—childbirth.org, thelaborof love.com, plomp.com, unassistedchildbirth.com, and birthstories.com. While these five are not the only sites devoted to birth stories and information, I chose them because they demonstrate the breadth of options readily available on the Internet. In addition to hundreds of birth stories, child birth.org, birthstories.com, and thelaboroflove.com offer extensive general information and external links to further information and products. These three sites are clearly sponsored by advertising funds; their birth stories draw readers—potential consumers—to the sites. By contrast, the other two sites, plomp.com and unassistedchildbirth.com, each run by one woman, have no apparent corporate tie-ins or external advertising. Unas sistedchildbirth.com and plomp.com provide less generalized information than the other three sites, and both cater at least somewhat to particular audiences. Unassisted childbirth.com explicitly targets women who are intrigued about giving birth alone. Plomp.com attracts mothers with large numbers of children: the site owner herself has seven children, and various websites devoted to large family issues or values link to this site.

In 2005, after obtaining approval for my online and survey research from the Institutional Review Board at the University of Illinois, I wrote to 120 mothers who had posted their birth stories on the above sites, asking them to complete a childbirth writing survey. Thirty-four women (32 American and two Canadian) completed the survey. Although the respondents' occupations range from historian to homemaker, bus driver to pastor, the majority surveyed identify themselves as white, middle class, and Christian, which aligns with general American Internet usage demographics (Lenhart et al. 5). While women of other races and nationalities do post stories on these sites, as we see for example with Gabriela above, who mentions she is Argentinian, most women do not include demographic information. Email addresses, however, suggest most live in North America. While similar demographically, survey respondents' birth expectations and experiences were markedly varied, representing the wide spectrum of birth experiences: from homebirth to hospital birth, C-section to medication-free.

Sociologist Ann Oakley describes women as falling into one of two categories after childbirth: victims and victors. Her classifications are "interpreted in terms of three sets of factors: the mother's social context, the medicalization of the birth, and the *mediation of maternal feelings* about this" (176; emphasis added). I build on Oakley's understanding of mediation to examine how writing about childbirth online helps women reconcile their childbirth expectations with their experiences. I demonstrate that writing and reading these public stories empowers women to avoid "victim" status, regardless of their childbirth experiences. A few women explicitly advocate an avoidance or transcendence of victimhood: one, for example, writes, "Women giving birth are not powerless victims of nature. We were **made/evolved** to give birth, with or without external help. **WE CAN DO IT!**" (Laura Joy; her emphasis). In writing their stories, women mediate their experiences, enabling an intercession between memory and expression. Beyond mediation on the emotional level, however, these stories also qualify as remediations in that they are reformulations of birth itself and of birth stories told in other forms, through other media.

In suggesting that online birth stories are remediations, I am invoking Jay David Bolter and Richard Grusin's landmark essay, "Remediation" (and subsequent book of the same title). Bolter and Grusin argue that "all current media function as remediators and that remediation offers us a means of interpreting the work of earlier media as well" (345). While it is not my intent to interpret the work accomplished by earlier birth stories told in letters and diaries, an awareness of the generic components of these documents informs my research into their online descendants. Bolter and Grusin explicate three instances of what they call the "double logic" of remediation: (1) remediation is the mediation of mediation, (2) remediation is the inseparability of mediation and reality, and (3) remediation is reform (346). In each of these senses, online birth stories qualify as remediated, although not always in the same ways Bolter and Grusin might identify. That is, I see women's appropriation of this new medium to share these stories as enacting a move toward reform of childbirth itself, not as an effort "to refashion or rehabilitate other media" (346). Birth stories as remediation constitute a type of reform, a reform that includes but is far more extensive than that of the medium itself.

Bolter and Grusin allow that "remediation can also imply reform in a social or political sense" (351), and it is in this sense that I apply the term here. The digitized birth story, because of its accessibility, accomplishes far more than traditional forms of birth stories with their more limited audiences. The online birth story represents the remediation of a genre; the medium of the Internet invites shared stories and offers a promise of potential connection to the stories' authors. While this promise is sometimes unfulfilled because of the ephemeral nature of contact information like email addresses, the promise of connection affects the style and content of the birth stories in this medium, enabling and encouraging the formation of rhetorical and political stances. My aim is to explore what women are doing, how they are reacting, and what they are enacting through their childbirth writing. My analysis shows that the empowerment made possible by these public stories frees women to embrace motherhood with a heightened sense of their own agency.

Women write online birth stories out of a desire to share and work through their own personal experiences, but also to encourage, educate, and empower other women. Birth story authors want to help others learn both from their mistakes and their successes. They also tend to advocate particular understandings of and beliefs about birth. These narratives are part of an ongoing conversation about what it means to be a birthing woman—and ultimately a mother—in North America. They simultaneously react against and reinscribe norms. These online stories, an inchoate but significant genre, offer insight into myriad meanings of childbirth and motherhood, as composed and understood by the mothers themselves. Online birth narratives signify in multiple ways: as cathartic writing experiences, as social and political commentaries, and as consumer testimonials. Below I explore these multiple significations, beginning with catharsis.

The women surveyed, most of whom are not quotidian writers and are not accustomed to writing for emotional reasons, claim repeatedly, forcefully, and without prompting that writing online stories was cathartic for them. Psychologist James Pennebaker, who studies the connections between writing about the self and health, defines catharsis as the "linking of thoughts and feelings" (39). The online *Oxford English Dictionary* provides three distinct definitions of catharsis:

   a. Purgation of the excrements of the body; *esp.* evacuation of the bowels.

   b. The purification of the emotions by vicarious experience, esp. through the drama (in reference to Aristotle's *Poetics* 6). Also more widely.

   c. *Psychotherapy*. The process of relieving an abnormal excitement by re-establishing the association of the emotion with the memory or idea of the event which was the first cause of it, and of eliminating it by abreaction. ("Catharsis")

Childbirth itself can certainly be viewed as a bodily purge of sorts, although one which results in much more than bodily waste. Childbirth as an event has also, however, long been considered cathartic in the sense of psychological release, aligning with *The New Oxford American Dictionary*'s definition of the term: "the process of releasing, and thereby providing relief from, strong or repressed emotions" ("Catharsis"). Robbie Davis-Floyd's examination of childbirth as a rite of passage firmly formulates childbirth as a profoundly significant, transformative event—not only physically but psychologically and socially as well; childbirth is frequently viewed as cathartic in all these senses. Although it might be somewhat surprising to suggest that merely writing about one's childbirth experience can also be cathartic, psychologists and writing scholars alike have found that writing can provide or encourage catharsis (see, for example, Pennebaker; Harris). Composing childbirth narratives allows women the opportunity to relive the bodily experience of birth emotionally and psychologically. The writing thus mimics, to a certain extent, the event itself, but in this reproduction, this remediation, the woman herself—rather than her body, birth attendants, or technology—controls every aspect of the story. This retroactive assertion of control may be one reason women find writing birth narratives to be cathartic.

Online birthing narratives often demonstrate catharsis both implicitly and explicitly. During labour, women can sometimes be perceived as (and/or feel) unstable, or rhetorically *disabled*. Writing birth narratives may restore women's voices, enabling them to impose rhetorical agency after the fact, as mothers and mindful, healthy people; we might call them "rhetorically enabled subjects," to borrow Catherine Prendergast's phrase (200). While oral narratives may also serve this purpose to a certain extent, writing "permits the careful construction of a cohesive narrative in a way that simply talking about experiences does not," argues Judith Harris, author of *Signifying Pain* (56). While Harris distinguishes between writing and therapy, she asserts that writing does permit catharsis and self-analysis. As this chapter demonstrates, writing online childbirth narratives not only results in catharsis and self-analysis, but also allows women to assert themselves socio-politically.

The idea that the personal is political resonates, significantly, as a credo of second-wave feminism. For mothers writing birth narratives, while the personal may often be implicitly political, much of their personal writing is also overtly political, in the sense that they advocate particular stances and childbirth choices that have real social and political ramifications for women. This writing follows a significant but somewhat hidden history of women's writing; as Kathryn Flannery has shown for 1968–75, women's writing, albeit essential in obtaining feminist advances, has often been discounted or ignored in histories (2). Gail Hawisher and Patricia Sullivan claim that even though women may not always know how to "harness e-spaces as sites for feminist power ... women's participation in e-space will necessitate a rethinking of public and private space" (195). Aligning themselves with Carol Stabile, they "agree that feminists must harness the new technologies to serve their own just political and social goals" (195). While women writing birth stories, like other women in the general public, may not identify themselves as "feminists," their actions demonstrate their ability to harness e-spaces; they use this form of public writing to advance political and social goals even as they may, on the surface, seem to simply be sharing personal stories. An analysis of online birth narratives not only demonstrates the integration of the personal and the political so common in this genre, but also complicates the ways in which we categorize writing.

Women's birth narratives, although intensely personal and personally valuable, are not simply useful for the women who write them (although they are certainly that). They are also consistently produced and read as educational tools for other women, some with an eye toward explicitly challenging dominant beliefs about childbirth. These narratives can function not only as personal writing, then, but also as political writing. The catharsis enabled by such writing is a personal catharsis in the usual emotional sense, and a bodily catharsis as well, an emotional release of a bodily experience. These dual catharses work to help women themselves, but the writing, both covertly through personal stories—where personal experience serves as warrant for a larger political claim—and overtly through particular recommendations and advice, also works to help and educate other women.

I asked survey respondents to complete the following sentence: "Writing/posting this story was _____ for me." Responses seemed to coalesce into three emotional categories: transformative, positive, and complex. I call "transformative" any term that denotes a change from one emotional state to another, such as "healing," "therapeutic," or "cathartic." Words like "exciting" and "enjoyable" did not seem to connote a perceptive shift, and were placed into the more static "positive" category. Ambiguous emotional responses that were neither clearly positive nor transformative, such as "sentimental" and "scary," were labelled "complex." More than half fell into the transformative category.

Asked what effect their stories were intended to have—whether on themselves or on others—survey respondents wrote of emotional transformations and other benefits they experienced through writing. Slimgirl156 responds, "It was like therapy to write it [my online birth story]." Echoing this response, Michele writes, "When I write something down I am more easily able to let it go, and I don't sit and dwell on it as much." Anna, too, finds catharsis the goal of her story: "It was just something that affected me deeply and needed to be written down to stop bothering me so much." While Slimgirl156, Michele, and Anna explicitly describe personal transformation, Katrina states more generally, "It was good for me to write it down when I did," but offers no further comment about why it was "good." One woman, Autumn, says she wrote her birth story "to empower [her]self," while another, Beth, focuses on how she can benefit from the belief that her story could help others: "I thought that writing down my experience to help others would make me feel better about the things I did not like in my birth experience." While a few women had more simple, casual expectations— Julie writes, "It was fun," and Anna explains she wanted "to satisfy [other pregnant women's] curiosity"—the majority of survey responses extend the idea that writing the birth story provided an emotional release. Responses here further establish the cathartic value of posting birth stories for many of these women.

For these women, writing birth stories served a powerful transformative purpose. Most set out to write their stories with an eye toward helping themselves emotionally. They used writing to (re)mediate their experiences, and overcame what Oakley calls "victim" status in doing so. Recall that Oakley's determination of victim versus victor status relies upon a woman's social network, the level of medical intervention in the birth, and how the mother deals with her emotions about the medicalization. Oakley's categorization of postpartum women, then, relies on their interpretations of the birth as much as it does on the facts or experience of the birth. As readers might expect, traumatic births seem to provide fodder for cathartic writing experiences: seven of the 16 women who experienced catharsis through writing had births that did not go as planned, births where interventions and/or complications deviated drastically from their expectations. Traumatic births did not account for all cathartic writing, however. Even some of those women who had childbirth experiences very close to their expected ideals, who do not feel they lost their communicative power during childbirth, also wrote of experiencing catharsis through writing about it. Five of the women for whom birth writing was transformative described births that went extremely well—by both medical and their own emotional standards. Evidence from the survey suggests that writing provides an emotional release for women who report traumatic childbirth experiences; it also suggests that writing correlates with the broader range of emotional work women can benefit from following any childbirth experience.

Beyond experiencing catharsis through the individual process of writing and posting their stories, some women seem to seek personal benefit along with social or political change by reaching out to others. Some women encourage readers to contact them, seeking to forge connections that might help both themselves and others. Of course, as suggested above, because email addresses and providers change quickly, the connective promise of the web is often unfulfilled; what is significant here is the rhetorical choice to permit or invite that connection. Women surveyed often express their hope that others will respond to their stories. Carolyn offers a poignant example: "My birth did not go as planned and I wanted to be reassured that it was not my fault." Carolyn's statement suggests that she hopes her writing, and the responses she might receive from it, will free her to mother without residual guilt from childbirth. Online narratives like Carolyn's reveal women's beliefs in the connective power of the Internet. Two other women whose stories include invitations to write them, along with explicit advice, are Jenny and Beth, who both post at thelaboroflove.com. Jenny concludes her narrative by writing, "Well, there's my story. I would be happy to share more information on hospital birth, c-section, homebirth, postpartum depression with anyone interested. Jenny [link to her email address]." Beth, too, shifts in her conclusion from storytelling to networking: "Here is my advice for all expecting mothers—(1) read all the birth stories you can, and (2) make a birth plan so others will know what you want when you can't speak for yourself. If you have any questions or have had a similar experience and would like to contact me please feel free to do so. My [email] address is ..." Jenny and Beth both offer readers the opportunity to connect with them. They explicitly see the birth story as a valuable source of information for women. Because such stories are more readily accessible online than anywhere else, they implicitly advocate women's use of the Internet. Beth encourages women to inform themselves and almost to arm themselves. Their advice suggests that women need to protect themselves from standard hospital birth practices, a political position aimed at helping other women.

Women I surveyed acknowledge hopes that their writing will help other women. Many responses reflect an abiding belief in childbirth as something other than a medical event. Shannon wants women to read her story and come to see "the practice of natural and unmedicated childbirth" positively. Jessica, while less explicit, suggests a similar take: "I hoped my stories would encourage women to look at all options in childbirth." Sherry and Karen, like Gabriela above, take this notion a step further, explicitly advocating homebirth over hospital birth. Sherry writes that she wanted "to share positive homebirth stories to encourage women to look at safe options for childbirth." Karen also stresses the safety of homebirth; she hoped that her story would "make them [other pregnant women] realize that it is possible to give birth out of the hospital, and be ok." Jennifer's goals are more ambiguous; rather than advocating a particular stance toward childbirth options, she writes that she wanted "to share, to teach." And others wanted to reassure women with medical problems, women who would without question be birthing in hospitals. Melissa, for example, "wanted other pregnant women to know that even with a complicated pregnancy, the outcome can still be a positive one."

Each of these women offers her story, then, not simply out of a desire for personal benefit, but to persuade, teach, or otherwise inspire her audience. Birth narratives function not only as personal records and socio-political commentaries, but also as product or service testimonials. Women testify in their stories that particular services are worthwhile, particular types of attendants helpful, particular locations better than others. In providing these service recommendations, women display themselves as satisfied (or dissatisfied) customers. This consumer element provides another layer of the competing interests and influences at play in this genre. As we see with Karen's comment above, who wants readers to "realize that it is possible to give birth out of the hospital, and be ok," some women write out of an explicit desire to affect other women's opinions and increase their knowledge.

In the survey, women were asked to provide this kind of metadata about their narratives. Their responses are reflections on already completed writing. The narratives themselves, though, also reveal these impulses without prompting. Online birth stories share all things personal—intimate details about everything from sex in labour to gory surgeries—but many reveal an explicit dual purpose by the end of the narrative. The birth finished, the baby born, reactions registered, the stories become part advice column, part consciousness-raising tract. Sherry provides one example of this rhetorical move: she begins by explaining the day, date, how far along she is, and continues to describe her labouring hours with an inward focus, following the expected conventions of the genre. In her final paragraph, however, she shifts attention to the reader:

> For more information on natural childbirth, I recommend reading the following books: *Birth Reborn* by Michel Odent, M.D., *Childbirth Without Fear* by Dr. Grantly Dick-Read, *Husband-Coached Childbirth* by Dr. Robert Bradley and *Birthrights* by Sally Inch. I read more than twenty pregnancy-related books during this pregnancy, but these are some of my favorites *having information that you may not be able to find anywhere else.* (Sherry; emphasis added)

The significance of Sherry's rhetorical move away from describing her experience and toward offering advice extends beyond her awareness of her audience as women seeking knowledge about the birthing process—it speaks to her belief that even the wealth of information about childbirth offered by doctors, in childbirth classes, and in countless books combined is not always complete. Sherry is "convinced that home birth with [only] intermittent fetal monitoring and someone trained to deal with complications is the safest way to have a baby," a view that resists dominant understandings and institutions in North American society. She uses her writing to document her own resistance and to encourage other women to question widespread assumptions, to educate themselves against the common grain.

Recommendations do not always work against the traditional North American hospital birth experience; some women suggest epidurals, particular painkillers, even C-sections. What the recommendations all have in common, however, is their function as consumer testimonials. These testimonials are sometimes overtly aimed at an audience, but can also be couched in terms of personal preference, with the preferences shared such that they operate as recommendations.

Some women simply and explicitly offer their recommendations, writing, for example, "I would suggest to anyone having a c-section to write a birth plan" (Melissa) and "My advice to pregnant women is this: epidural! and breathe"(Krystle). Summer and Autumn, on the other hand, both connect their advice to their own experiences. One advocates a particular pain-management strategy: "If you're trying to figure out which birthing method to try, check out birth hypnosis! It works!" (Summer) while the other argues for homebirth: "I would never have a baby any other place than at home, and I would never suggest anything else for anyone"(Autumn). Readers are left to believe that because hypnosis worked for Summer, it could, and even should, work for them. Autumn's preference for a homebirth may be a hard sell in the United States, where 99 percent of births take place in hospitals (Rooks 345), but her rhetorical impulse is the same as Summer's: the personal is the political, one story could be everywoman's story.

Some women, however, complicate this notion of relying on others' experiences to guide their own. One writes, "Good luck to all the mothers-to-be who read this. And do not let others tell you that what you are doing during pregnancy is wrong. Just because those who are going through it or have been through it weren't able to, doesn't mean that it does apply to you" (Jess). She says other women's [bad] experiences should never be a reason not to do or try something. Women often tell tales of their own thwarted expectations and in doing so imply to other women that their hopes—for a drug-free labour, or for any particular or positive birth experience—are unreachable. Jess seems to be writing against this typical "horror story." In doing so she hints at an understanding that all women's experiences are different, at least in terms of ignoring negative stories.

Amy, too, writes to offer a narrative that may counter negative stories women encounter elsewhere. She writes to offer, simply, "hope," using her experience as the proof that such hope is warranted: "In response to the recent concerns surrounding VBAC (Vaginal Birth After Cesarean) I wanted to write my birth story and give hope to those wanting to experience a vaginal delivery after a cesarean.... Take Care and God Bless"(Amy). Another writer, Cynthia, also affirms others' potential through her own experience as a consumer of particular birth services. She felt capable of natural birth because she employed a doula: "I am also glad we hired the doula, she was great and I wouldn't have been able to go natural without her I know it.... I'm also glad that I did a lot of research and knew my rights and my desires for my birth" (Cynthia). Her declaration serves as a powerful suggestion to other women that they, too, can benefit from hiring a doula. Although Cynthia does not offer advice overtly, by asserting her own experience she makes the implicit claim that if other women make the same choices and do their homework (which she calls "a lot of research") they, too, can get the birth they want. Each of these women writes to support and influence other women's choices as consumers.

Online birth narratives are not the first instance in history of women advocating particular consumer choices, nor do they provide the first instance of women doing so through writing. As historian Judith Leavitt has ably demonstrated, American women invited physicians to their birthing rooms, and eventually, in an early feminist bid, argued for their rights to hospital births and anesthetized birth (see Leavitt, particularly on twilight sleep, 128–40). It is important to bear in mind this history of women's roles *as consumers* of childbirth services. Of particular interest is the relative ease with which American women fought for the right to obstetric interventions and hospital admission versus the efforts of some to avoid obstetric interventions in an era where hospital admission for childbirth is nearly universal. Women's expectations as consumers have shaped their political goals, but political accomplishments have also shaped women's expectations as consumers.

The significance of women's roles as consumers of childbirth services is layered with the emotional and socio-political significance of both childbirth itself and of childbirth writing. While women's identities as consumers don't replace their other crucial identities, their childbirth narratives offer a palimpsest of these various identities. The consumer testimonial and the traditional birth narrative merge, particularly in this online environment, to form a new genre. This new genre reflects pregnant/birthing North American women's response to being treated and constructed by others as consumers first, and anything else second.

Women's expectations as consumers are reflected in the narratives in constructions such as "my epidural," suggestive of a certain sense of entitlement. This phrasing is particularly poignant when women write about the epidural in the possessive before they have one, and even when they never get one. Women's epidural expectations are often thwarted by anything from the particulars of birth experiences to hospital staffing to medication simply not "taking." Any deviation from expectations can produce a dissatisfied customer. Online narratives offer a range of consumer responses.

One, for example, describes her epidural experience: "Not too long after I was admitted, I was given my epidural. What a life saver! I was able to relax and call people to tell them I was in labor" (Kim). Kim's description of her epidural follows a standard rhetorical pattern for testimonials: she specifies the intervention received and describes its benefits. Melissa's narrative, too, reflects this pattern. She writes, "I was really happy when they came to get me because I knew I'd get my epidural in a matter of minutes. I was having a c-section, I wasn't supposed to feel any pain until afterwards! I was taken to the OR and got my epidural" (Melissa). Beyond the pattern of intervention and benefits, however, Melissa includes the expectation that she feel *no* pain. Her phrasing notes the potential for dissatisfaction ("I wasn't supposed to feel any pain") and suggests that as a customer, she was satisfied, but only barely. Another woman shares a similar story: "I got my epidural, but barely. If they hadn't checked me, it would've been too late" (Krystle). Krystle hints that the nameless "they" almost made an egregious error of timing. Thomas's mother offers perhaps the most interesting use of the possessive because the epidural she repeatedly refers to as hers is one she never receives, despite her hopes and the nurse's willing collusion to permit her one after the time deemed appropriate by hospital protocols.

> We arrived at the hospital at 14:50 and I promptly and politely started requesting my epidural.... I was told the anaesthetist was elsewhere and would be with us as soon as he could. What! I wanted my epidural and I wanted it now! She said she had better put down that I was 5cm dilated because any more and I wouldn't get my epidural (I was actually 6cm).... At 15:30 I was told the anaesthetist would be half an hour. Panic set in because things were going so fast ... and I hadn't had my epidural. (Thomas's mother)

By writing of particular services in the possessive, these women construct themselves as consumers and medical services as commodities. These narratives represent a common thread in online birth narratives of women writing as consumers; these remediations of childbirth reflect the multiple lenses through which women review their births: personal experience, socio-political significance, and consumer influence.

Childbirth and parenting websites offer public spaces for women to share their private birth stories, enabling women and scholars unprecedented access to women's self-representations of themselves as birthing women and new mothers. These birth stories—part memoir, part political tract, part testimonial—form a new genre, a remediation that deserves scholarly attention alongside more familiar forms of literature. These stories are rich rhetorical documents that accomplish multiple and even conflicting goals simultaneously. Women compose their birth stories with myriad goals in mind, from the intensely personal to the imploringly political. As John Duffy reminds us, "individuals have the capacity to call upon ... multiple influences to fashion rhetorics of their own, creating personal and collective narratives of history and experiences that can disrupt the interests of dominant institutions" (43). Women write online birth narratives to heal and celebrate themselves, to help others, and to promote change. These mothers use writing to change and challenge how childbirth—an important rite of passage linking mothers around the world and across the ages—is represented, interpreted, and even experienced.

Works Cited

Allende, Isabel. *Paula*. New York: HarperCollins, 1995.

Amy. "My Vbac Homebirth." 5 December 2005, http://www.thelaboroflove.com/birthstories/397.html.

Arms, Suzanne. *Immaculate Deception: A New Look at Women and Childbirth in America*. Boston: Houghton Mifflin, 1975.

Autumn. "Five Hours of Pushing = Perfect Princess." 26 January 2006, http://www.birthstories.com/stories/2566.php?wcat=5.

Beth. "Birth Story of Brendan David Hoover." 5 December 2005, http://www.thelaboroflove.com/birthstories/bren.html.

Bolter, Jay David, and Richard Grusin. "Remediation." *Configurations* 4.3 (1996): 311–58.

"Catharsis." *The New Oxford American Dictionary*. Ed. Elizabeth J. Jewell and Frank Abate. New York: Oxford University Press, 2001.

"Catharsis." *Oxford English Dictionary Online*. Great Basin College Lib., Elko, NV, 1989, http://dictionary.oed.com.

Cynthia. "Birth Story of Bridges." 26 January 2006, http://www.plomp.com/Bridgescmd102.htm.

Davis-Floyd, Robbie. "From Technobirth to Cyborg Babies." *Cyborg Babies: From Techno-Sex to Techno-Tots*. Ed. Robbie Davis-Floyd and Joseph Dumit. New York and London: Routledge, 1998. 255–84.

Duffy, John. "Other Gods and Countries: The Rhetorics of Literacy." *Towards a Rhetoric of Everyday Life: New Directions in Research on Writing, Text, and Discourse*. Ed. Martin Nystrand and John Duffy. Madison: University of Wisconsin Press, 2003.

Flannery, Kathryn Thomas. *Feminist Literacies, 1968–75*. Urbana: University of Illinois Press, 2005.

Harris, Judith. *Signifying Pain: Constructing and Healing the Self through Writing.* Albany: State University of New York Press, 2003.

Hawisher, Gail, and Patricia Sullivan. "Women on the Networks: Searching for E-Spaces of Their Own." *Feminism and Composition Studies: In Other Words.* Ed. Susan C. Jarratt and Lynn Worsham. New York: Modern Language Association, 1998. 172–97.

Huff, Cynthia A. "Textual Boundaries: Space in Nineteenth-Century Women's Manuscript Diaries." *Inscribing the Daily: Critical Essays on Women's Diaries.* Ed. Suzanne L. Bunkers and Cynthia A. Huff. Amherst: University of Massachusetts Press, 1996.

Jenny. "Zachary's Birth Story." 30 November 2005. http://www.thelaboroflove.com/birthstories/jenny.html.

Jess. "A Baby and Promotion All in One Day." 5 December 2005, http://www.birthstories.com/stories/1775.php?wcat=5.

Kim. "Birth Story of Joshua Bradley Doering." 26 January 2006, http://www.plomp.com/joshuacmd5.htm.

Krystle. "First Baby, Epidural, Easy." 27 January 2006, http://www.birthstories.com/stories/1714.php?wcat=35.

Laura Joy. "Zachary—Having a Baby 'On the Way!'" 30 November 2005, http://www.unassistedchildbirth.com/ucstories/zach.html.

Leavitt, Judith Walzer. *Brought to Bed: Childbearing in America, 1750 to 1950.* New York: Oxford University Press, 1986.

Lenhart, Amanda, et al. "The Evershifting Internet Population: A New Look at Internet Access and the Digital Divide." *Pew Internet and American Life Project.* 2003, http://www.pewinternet.org/~/media//Files/Reports/2003/PIP_Shifting_Net_Pop_Report.pdf.pdf.

Melissa. "Laurel's Birth Story." 26 January 2006, http://www.thelaboroflove.com/birthstories/271.html.

Moraga, Cherríe. *Waiting in the Wings: Portrait of a Queer Motherhood.* Ithaca: Firebrand Books, 1997.

Oakley, Ann. *Women Confined: Toward a Sociology of Childbirth.* New York: Schocken Books, 1980.

Pennebaker, James W. *Opening Up: The Healing Power of Confiding in Others.* New York: Avon Books, 1990.

Prendergast, Catherine. "On the Rhetorics of Mental Disability." *Towards a Rhetoric of Everyday Life: New Directions in Research on Writing, Text, and Discourse.* Ed. Martin Nystrand and John Duffy. Madison: University of Wisconsin Press, 2003.

Rich, Adrienne Cecile. *Of Woman Born: Motherhood as Experience and Institution.* New York: Norton, 1976.

Rooks, Judith Pence. *Midwifery and Childbirth in America*. Philadelphia: Temple University Press, 1997.

Sherry. "Mariah Elizabeth Kennedy's Birth." 30 November 2005, http://www.child birth.org/articles/stories/1999/99MEK.html.

Summer. "An Amazing Drug-Free Hypnobirth." 5 December 2005, http://www .birthstories.com/stories/2789.php?wcat=2.

Thomas's mother. "Thomas Hall's Birth." 6 February 2006, http://www.childbirth .org/articles/stories/1998/98TWH.html.

Coda

"Stories to Live By": Maternal Literatures and Motherhood Studies | BY ANDREA O'REILLY

We opened the introduction to this collection with Ruddick's oft-cited quotation referencing the absence of language in which to articulate the "ordinary and extraordinary pleasures and pains of maternal work." "Maternal voices," as Ruddick explains further, "have been drowned by professional theory, ideologies of motherhood, sexist arrogance, and childhood fantasy. Voices that have been distorted and censored can only be *developing* voices. Alternatively silenced and edging toward speech, mothers' voices are not voices of mothers as they are, but as they are becoming" (40; emphasis in original). Our aim in developing this collection was to create a space for the articulation of maternal voices, "to edge toward speech" the discursive and literary narratives of textual mothers and maternal texts as represented in contemporary women's literature and literary criticism. In this, the collection engages in and extends the excavational work of maternal scholarship, to unearth women's meanings and experiences of motherhood. The aim of this conclusion to *Textual Mothers / Maternal Texts* is to locate the volume in the larger context of motherhood studies and its task of what O'Reilly has termed an archaeology of maternity (2004).

Di Brandt opens the prologue to her 1993 book *Wild Mother Dancing* by recalling how the birth of her first child in 1976 called into question all that she had learned—or thought she had learned—in her master's English literature program completed the same year. She writes: "It was like falling into a vacuum, narratively speaking. I realized suddenly with shock, that none of the texts that I had so carefully read, none of the literary skills I had acquired so diligently as a student of literature had anything remotely to do with the experience of becoming a mother" (3). Similarly, Sharon Abbey and Andrea O'Reilly open their 1998 book, *Redefining Motherhood: Changing Identities and Patterns*, by citing Adrienne Rich's 1976 oft-cited quote, "We know more about the air we breathe, the seas we travel, than about the nature and meaning of motherhood" (11). Significantly, in the 20 years between the publication of Rich's landmark *Of Woman Born* and *Redefining Motherhood*, we witnessed a proliferation of scholarly texts on motherhood. The years 1988–92 in particular saw the publication of numerous, now-classic motherhood texts, including Kathryn Allen Rabuzzi's *Motherself: A Mythic Analysis of Motherhood*, Sara Ruddick's *Maternal Thinking*, Paula Caplan's *Don't Blame Mother*, Marianne Hirsch's *Mother/Daughter Plot*, Barbara Katz Rothman's *Recreating Motherhood*, Miriam Johnson's *Strong Mothers, Weak Wives*, Patricia Hill Collins's *Black Feminist Thought*, and Patricia Bell-Scott et al.'s *Double Stitch: Black Women Write about Mothers and Daughters*. Indeed, by 1998, most academic disciplines, from anthropology to women's studies, were engaged in some form of motherhood research. And while scholarship on motherhood in some disciplines still struggled for legitimacy and centrality, there was the recognition that motherhood studies was emerging as a distinct field within the larger disciplines of feminist scholarship and women's studies.

However, despite the exponential growth of scholarship on motherhood in the 1990s, there did not exist a scholarly association, journal, or press to acknowledge the profundity of this topic and uphold its continued inquiry. Scholars from a multitude of fields named motherhood as their central research area, yet these many scholars did not have a scholarly association or journal they could "call their own," one that specifically focused on their research interests. In response to this need, the Association for Research on Mothering (ARM) was established in 1998, its journal in 1999, and its press in 2006 to promote, showcase, and make visible maternal scholarship, to accord legitimacy to this academic field, and to provide a community for like-minded scholars who research and work in the area of motherhood.[1]

Over the last decade the topic of motherhood, as a result in part of the research activities of ARM, has emerged as a distinct field of scholarly inquiry. Indeed, today it would be unthinkable to cite Rich's quote on the dearth of maternal scholarship, as *Redefining Motherhood* did a mere ten years ago. A cursory review of motherhood research reveals that hundreds of scholarly articles have been published on almost every motherhood theme imaginable. *The Journal of the Association for Research on Mothering (JARM)* alone has examined motherhood topics as diverse as sexuality, peace, religion, public policy, literature, work, popular culture, healthcare work, young mothers, motherhood and feminism, feminist mothering, mothers and sons, mothers and daughters, lesbian mothering, adoption, the motherhood movement, and mothering, race, and ethnicity to name a few. In 2006 Andrea O'Reilly coined the term "motherhood studies" to acknowledge and demarcate this new scholarship as a legitimate and distinctive discipline, one grounded in the tradition of maternal theory developed by scholars such as Patricia Hill Collins, Adrienne Rich, Sharon Hays, Paula Caplan, Susan Maushart, Andrea O'Reilly, Fiona Green, Miriam Johnson, bell hooks, Patrice DiQuinzio, Susan Douglas/ Meredith Michaels, Alice Walker, Marianne Hirsh, and Sara Ruddick. Similar to the development of women's studies as an academic field in the 1970s, motherhood studies, while explicitly interdisciplinary, cross-disciplinary, and multidisciplinary, has emerged as an autonomous and independent scholarly discipline in the last decade, a fact underscored by the forthcoming publication of the first ever (three-volume, 750-entry) encyclopedia on the topic of motherhood (O'Reilly, 2010a).

What is significant and seldom observed in discussions on the rise of motherhood studies is the central and pivotal role women's literature and feminist literary studies have played in its development. Such was made most apparent when *JARM* published its issue on mothering and literature in 2002: of the 20-plus issues the journal has published since 1999, this issue received the most submissions, far more than the number submitted for any other journal issue on topics as diverse as work, public policy, health, law, sexuality, religion, and feminism. The exponential growth of motherhood scholarship over the last 20 years is paralleled, if not surpassed, by the same in women's literature on and about motherhood. In this collection, most of the creative works studied have been published in last 20 years, with many coming out in the last decade. Literary mothers today may be found in a multitude of texts across a wide range of perspectives and locations.

In the 30-plus years since the publication of Rich's *Of Woman Born*, motherhood research has focused upon the oppressive and empowering dimensions of mothering and the complex relationship between the two. Almost all contemporary scholarship on motherhood draws upon Rich's distinction "between two meanings of motherhood, one superimposed on the other: the *potential relationship* of any woman to her powers of reproduction and to children; and the *institution*, which aims at ensuring that that potential—and all women—shall remain under male control" (13; emphasis in original). Within motherhood studies the term "motherhood" is used to signify the patriarchal institution of motherhood, while "mothering" refers to women's lived experiences of mothering as they seek to resist the patriarchal institution of motherhood and its oppressive ideology. An empowered practice/theory of mothering, therefore, functions as a counter-narrative of motherhood: it seeks to interrupt the master narrative of motherhood to imagine and implement a view of mothering that is empowering to women. "Empowered mothering" may refer to any practice of mothering that seeks to challenge and change various aspects of patriarchal motherhood that cause mothering to be limiting or oppressive to women. Or, to use Rich's terminology, an "empowered maternal practice" marks a movement from motherhood to mothering, and makes possible a mothering against motherhood.

Building upon this distinction between motherhood and mothering, motherhood studies may be divided into four interconnected themes or categories of inquiry: motherhood as institution, motherhood as experience, motherhood as identity or subjectivity, and motherhood as agency. While scholars who are concerned with the ideology or institution investigate policies, laws, ideologies, and images of patriarchal motherhood, researchers who are interested in experience examine the work women do as mothers, an area of study paved with insights from Sara Ruddick's concept of maternal practice. The third category, identity or subjectivity, looks at the effect that becoming a mother has on a woman's sense of self, in particular, how her sense of self is shaped by the institution of motherhood and the experience of mothering respectively. Since the turn of the millennium, a new theme in motherhood has emerged, which Andrea O'Reilly among others has termed "agency" (O'Reilly, 2010b). Scholars concerned with this theme of agency focus upon feminist childrearing and maternal activism and consider mothering as a social and political act through which social change is made possible. Patriarchal motherhood characterizes childrearing as a private, nonpolitical undertaking; in contrast, mothers of agency foreground the political-social dimension of motherwork. More specifically, they challenge traditional practices of gender socialization and perform anti-sexist childrearing practices so as to raise empowered daughters and empathetic sons. Their commitment to both feminism and to children becomes expressed as maternal activism. Whether it is in the home or in the world at large, expressed as anti-sexist childrearing and maternal activism, empowered mothers use their position as mothers to lobby for social and political change.

In the introduction we suggested that the twentieth century's much needed critical investigation into the institution of motherhood was launched by a pen. Indeed, it is in literature that we find these four organizing themes of motherhood studies most fully considered and scrutinized. In *Writing a Woman's Life*, Carolyn Heilbrun observes: "Lives do not serve as models, only stories do that. And it is a hard thing to make up stories to live by. We can only retell and live by stories we have heard. Stories have formed us all: they are what we must use to make new fictions and new stories" (32). However, there are few maternal stories "to live by." "Motherhood," as Marni Jackson noted in her 1992 memoir *The Mother Zone: Love, Sex and Laundry in the Modern Family*, "is an unexplored frontier of thought and emotion that we've tried to tame with rules, myth and knowledge. But the geography remains unmapped" (9). "Motherhood may have become an issue," Jackson continues, "but it's not yet a narrative" (3). Today, as evidenced by this collection, maternal authors, while acknowledging this difficulty in speaking that which has been censored, distorted, and silenced, struggle to make the maternal story narratable in literature. In rendering audible the censored and silenced maternal voice, maternal texts, such as those examined in this collection, have aided, if not made possible, motherhood studies and its critique of patriarchal motherhood as well as its endeavour to imagine and achieve an empowered experience of mothering.

Editors Jean O'Barr, Deborah Pope, and Mary Wyer in the introduction to their 1990 collection *Ties That Bind: Essays on Mothering and Patriarchy* write, "The geography of mothering is a complex, shifting terrain. On the one hand, there are routes assiduously travelled and surveyed, well marked by popular sentiment and signposted by professional opinion, on the other, there are territories that remain obscured in turns and thickets, unarticulated in their reaches and vistas" (1). Marni Jackson in her 1992 memoir cited above describes motherhood as an "unexplored frontier" and "like Albania—you can't trust the descriptions in the books, you have to go there" (9). Likewise, Andrea Buchanan, in her 2003 memoir *Mother Shock: Loving Every (Other) Minute of It*, explains that when we become mothers, "we enter into a strange new world with a language, culture, time zone and set of customs all its own. Until we become acclimated to this new, seemingly unfathomable territory, we exist in a state of culture shock. We are in mother shock" (ix–x). The repeated use of geographical and expedition metaphors in the above texts, and in particular the positioning of motherhood as a foreign and unexplored country, reveal how motherhood literature functions as a discursive "travel guide" of motherhood as both experience and institution. Matrifocal narratives, written as they are in the voice of the mother and from her perspective, serve to map the lived and real contours and configurations of maternal experience, those masked and distorted by patriarchal cartographies of motherhood.

Over the last few years, "the motherhood as country" metaphor has held particular significance as motherhood studies scholarship has sought to explore motherhood in a global context, to map and chart this experience beyond the usual North American parameters. And again we find that it has been women's literature and feminist literary criticism that have pioneered and navigated this investigation. As evidenced by this collection, in chapters from and about North American, European, Caribbean, Asian, and Australian perspectives, motherhood in literature and literary studies points to the global direction that has eluded motherhood studies until very recently.[2] *Textual Mothers / Maternal Texts* seeks to enact, facilitate, and propel this needed and long overdue repositioning of motherhood studies as a truly expansive discipline. It is for this reason that we conclude the volume with the section "Maternal Communication" to situate maternal voices in dialogue with one another across regions, generations, and academic disciplines. Our intent—and hope—in locating motherhood across such differences is to map that unexplored frontier of motherhood so as render known the "language, culture, time zone and set of customs" of motherhood. To discover, in other words, "stories to live by."

Notes to Coda

1 Established in 1998 by Andrea O'Reilly at York University, Toronto, ARM is the first and still the only scholarly association on the topic of mothering and motherhood. Please visit ARM's website for information on the association, its journal, and its press, Demeter Press: www.yorku.ca/arm.

2 Motherhood studies scholarship has been largely North American in perspective and content. However, over the last few years there has been some movement toward a more global understanding of motherhood in both research and theory. The Feminist Mothers and their Allies Caucus of the National Women's Studies Association, for example, has chosen for the first time "motherhood in a global context" as its topic for the 2009 annual conference.

Works Cited

Abbey, Sharon, and Andrea O'Reilly. *Redefining Motherhood: Changing Identities and Patterns*. Toronto: Second Story Press, 1998.

Bell-Scott, Patricia, et al. *Double Stitch: Black Women Write about Mothers and Daughters*. Boston, MA: Beacon Press, 1991.

Brandt, Di. *Wild Mother Dancing: Maternal Narrative in Canadian Literature*. Winnipeg: University of Manitoba Press, 1993.

Buchanan, Andrea. *Mother Shock: Loving Every (Other) Minute of It*. New York: Seal Press, 2003.

Caplan. Paula. *Don't Blame Mother: Mending the Mother–Daughter Relationship*. New York: Harper & Row, 1989.

Collins, Patricia Hill. *Black Feminist Thought: Knowledge, Consciousness and the Politics of Empowerment*. New York: Routlege, 2000.

Heilbrun, Carolyn. *Writing a Woman's Life*. New York: Ballantine Books, 1989.

Hirsch, Marianne. *The Mother/Daughter Plot: Narrative, Psychoanalysis, Feminism*. Bloomington: Indiana University Press, 1989.

Jackson, Marni. *The Mother Zone: Love, Sex, and Laundry in the Modern Family*. New York: H. Holt, 1992.

Johnson, Miriam. *Strong Mothers, Weak Wives: The Search for Gender Equality*. Berkeley: University of California Press, 1990.

O'Barr, Jean, Deborah Pope, and Mary Wyer. *Ties That Bind: Essays on Mothering and Patriarchy*. Chicago: University of Chicago Press, 1990.

O'Reilly, Andrea. *Motherhood at the 21st Century: Experience, Identity, Policy, Agency*. New York: Columbia University Press, 2010a.

———. *Encyclopedia of Motherhood*. Los Angeles: Sage Press, 2010b.

———, ed. *Mother Matters: Motherhood as Discourse and Practice*. Albany: ARM Press, 2004.

Rabuzzi, Kathryn Allen. *Motherself: A Mythic Analysis of Motherhood*. Bloomington: Indiana University Press, 1988.

Rich, Adrienne. *Of Woman Born: Motherhood as Experience and Institution*. New York: W. W. Norton & Co., 1986.

Rothman, Barbara Katz. *Recreating Motherhood: Ideology and Technology in a Patriarchal Culture*. New York: W. W. Norton, 1989.

Ruddick, Sara. *Maternal Thinking: Toward a Politics of Peace*. 1989. Boston: Beacon Press, 2002.

Notes on the Contributors

ELIZABETH BEAULIEU (PHD) is dean of the Core Division at Champlain College in Burlington, Vermont, where she oversees the design and implementation of a new interdisciplinary curriculum. She is the author or editor of *Black Women Writers and the American Neo-Slave Narrative: Femininity Unfettered* (1999), *The Toni Morrison Encyclopedia* (2003), and *Writing African American Women: An Encyclopedia of Literature by and about Women of Color* (2006).

RITA BODE is associate professor of English literature at Trent University in Oshawa, where she is currently serving as associate dean. Her main area of research is nineteenth- and early-twentieth-century American and British literature. She has published on the maternal presence/absence in Melville's *Moby-Dick* and in the writings of L. M. Montgomery.

DI BRANDT holds a Canada Research Chair in Canadian Literature and Creative Writing at Brandon University, Manitoba. She is the author of numerous award-winning books of poetry, essays, an opera, and a novel. Her books on mothers and mothering include: *questions I asked my mother* (1987), *mother, not mother* (1992), *Wild Mother Dancing: Maternal Narrative in Canadian Literature* (1993), and *So This Is the World & Here I Am in It* (1997). Her website address is www.dibrandt.ca.

MYRL COULTER (BA, MA, PHD UNIVERSITY OF ALBERTA) specializes in Canadian literature and writing practices. Her writing and research interests are feminism, maternal theory, literary nonfiction, and popular culture. Her work explores writing as a highly complex process influenced by social, cultural, political, and environmental forces.

KATE DOUGLAS is a senior lecturer in the Department of English, Creative Writing and Australian Studies at Flinders University (South Australia). She is the author of *Trauma Texts* (with Professor Gillian Whitlock) and *Contesting Childhood: Autobiography, Trauma and Memory*.

SUSAN DRIVER is an associate professor in communication studies at York University. She has written *Queer Girls and Popular Culture* and edited the collection *Queer Youth Cultures*.

NATHALIE FOY teaches Canadian literature at the University of Toronto. Her most recent project is an examination of motherhood in contemporary Canadian fiction.

JOANNE S. FRYE is professor emerita of English and women's studies at the College of Wooster in Ohio. Author of *Living Stories, Telling Lives* and *Tillie Olsen: A Study of the Short Fiction*, she has recently completed a memoir about her experiences as a single mother, tentatively titled *Biting the Moon*.

SHEILA HASSELL HUGHES is associate professor and Chair of English at the University of Dayton, Ohio. Born and raised in British Columbia, she earned her MA (English) from the University of Toronto and PhD (women's studies) from Emory University. Her research focuses on gender and religion in Louise Erdrich's work.

EMILY JEREMIAH is a lecturer in German at Royal Holloway, University of London. She is the author of *Troubling Maternity: Mothering, Agency, and Ethics in Women's Writing in German of the 1970s and 1980s*. Her research interests include mothering, migration, gender, and sexuality.

RITA JONES (PHD, WASHINGTON STATE UNIVERSITY) is the director of the women's centre and affiliate faculty in women's studies at Lehigh University. She was formerly the director of women's studies at the University of Northern Colorado. Her research interests include motherhood in America and connections between feminist movement and literature.

KATHLEEN KELLETT-BETSOS is associate professor in the Department of French and Spanish Languages and Literatures at Ryerson University, specializing in Franco-Canadian literature. She has published articles on authors such as Louise Maheux-Forcier, Anne Hébert, and Daniel Poliquin in various journals including *Québec Studies* and *Studies in Canadian Literature*.

DENYS LANDRY is a PHD candidate at the University of Montreal, where he also teaches English composition. His dissertation focuses on prostitution in the work of Tennessee Williams. His fields of interest include drama, American literature, gender studies, and popular culture (with special emphasis on Madonna).

ANNE-MARIE LEE-LOY is assistant professor in the English Department at Ryerson University. Currently she is exploring how Asian Caribbean and Asian American experiences intersect. Her articles and essays have appeared in *Asian Studies Review, Anthurium, The Arts Journal,* and the collection *The Chinese in the Caribbean.* Her book *Searching for Mr. Chin: Constructions of Nation and the Chinese in West Indian Literature* is forthcoming with Temple University Press.

ANDREA O'REILLY is associate professor in the School of Women's Studies at York University. She is editor of more than 12 books, including *Feminist Mothering.* O'Reilly is author of *Toni Morrison and Motherhood: A Politics of the Heart* and *Rocking the Cradle: Thoughts on Motherhood, Feminism, and the Possibility of Empowered Mothering.* O'Reilly is director of the Association for Research on Mothering, the *Journal of the Association for Research on Mothering,* and Demeter Press. She is editor of the first encyclopedia on motherhood, forthcoming 2010.

KIM HENSLEY OWENS is assistant professor of writing and rhetoric at the University of Rhode Island. She recently developed and taught a graduate seminar entitled Rhetorics of/and Reproduction. Her writing appears in such journals as *Written Communication* and *Pedagogy.* Kim is currently at work on a book project focusing on the rhetorics of childbirth.

RUTH PANOFSKY is professor of English at Ryerson University, where she specializes in Canadian literature and culture. She is the author of *The Force of Vocation: The Literary Career of Adele Wiseman* and *At Odds in the World: Essays on Jewish Canadian Women Writers.* Her volume of poetry, *Laike and Nahum: A Poem in Two Voices,* received the 2008 Helen and Stan Vine Canadian Jewish Book Award for Poetry.

NANCY PELED, PHD, teaches literature at Haifa University and coordinates the academic English program at Oranim Academic College in northern Israel. Her research interests include modern female authors and stereotypic paradigms of expression in contemporary narratives. Originally from Canada, she now lives on a kibbutz, where she raised her four children.

ELIZABETH PODNIEKS is an associate professor in the Department of English at Ryerson University. Her teaching and research interests include mothering, life writing, modernism, and popular/celebrity culture. She is the author of *Daily Modernism: The Literary Diaries of Virginia Woolf, Antonia White, Elizabeth Smart, and Anaïs Nin* and the co-editor of *Hayford Hall: Hangovers, Erotics, and Modernist Aesthetics*.

GILL RYE (PHD, UNIVERSITY COLLEGE, LONDON) is Reader at the Institute of Germanic & Romance Studies, University of London, and director of the Centre for the Study of Contemporary Women's Writing. Publications include *Reading for Change, Women's Writing in Contemporary France* (co-edited), and *Narratives of Mothering: Women's Writing in Contemporary France*.

TANJA STAMPFL, a native of Italy, is assistant professor in the English Department at the University of the Incarnate Word. Her research and teaching centre on the convergence of race, gender, and identity in twentieth-century postcolonial and world literature.

NICOLE WILLEY is an associate professor of English at Kent State University Tuscarawas, where she teaches African American and other literatures. Her research interests include mothering, memoir, nineteenth-century American literature, and slave narratives. She wrote *Creating a New Ideal of Masculinity for American Men: The Achievement of Sentimental Women Writers in the Mid-Nineteenth Century* and is currently working on a collection about motherhood memoirs.

Index